SEVEN SEAS ENTERTAINMENT PRESENTS

PANDORA IN THE CRIMSON

story by SHIROW MAS

TRANSLATION
Jocelyne Allen

ADAPTATION
Ysabet Reinhardt MacFarlane

LETTERING
Roland Amago

LAYOUT
Bambi Eloriaga-Amago

COVER DESIGN
Nicky Lim

PROOFREADER
Janet Houck
Danielle King

ASSISTANT EDITOR
Jenn Grunigen

PRODUCTION ASSISTANT
CK Russell

PRODUCTION MANAGER
Lissa Pattillo

EDITOR-IN-CHIEF
Adam Arnold

PUBLISHER
Jason DeAngelis

KOUKAKU NO PANDORA volume 7
© Koushi RIKUDOU 2015
© Shirow Masamune 2015
First published in Japan in 2015 by KADOKAWA CORPORATION, Tokyo.
English translation rights arranged with KADOKAWA CORPORATION, Tokyo,
through TOHAN CORPORATION, Tokyo.

No portion of this book may be reproduced or transmitted in any form without
written permission from the copyright holders. This is a work of fiction. Names,
characters, places, and incidents are the products of the author's imagination
or are used fictitiously. Any resemblance to actual events, locales, or persons,
living or dead, is entirely coincidental.

Seven Seas books may be purchased in bulk for educational, business, or
promotional use. For information on bulk purchases, please contact Macmillan
Corporate & Premium Sales Department at 1-800-221-7945 (ext 5442)
or write specialmarkets@macmillan.com.

Seven Seas and the Seven Seas logo are trademarks of
Seven Seas Entertainment, LLC. All rights reserved.

ISBN: 978-1-626924-57-4

Printed in Canada

First Printing: April 2017

10 9 8 7 6 5 4 3 2 1

FOLLOW US ONLINE: www.gomanga.com

READING DIRECTIONS

This book reads from *right to left*, Japanese style.
If this is your first time reading manga, you start
reading from the top right panel on each page and
take it from there. If you get lost, just follow the
numbered diagram here. It may seem backwards at
first, but you'll get the hang of it! Have fun!!

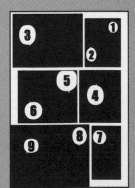

 **STAFF**

Original story	Shirow Masamune (in cooperation with Crossroad)
Production	Rikudou Koushi
Composition/ Art	Hitotose Rin Rikudou Koushi
Art assistance	Takepon G Kibayashida Unamu
Editing	Ochiai Koichiro (Kadokawa)
Design	Jinguji Noriyuki (Zin Studio)
Special Thanks	Seishinsha Co., Ltd. Prhythm Vision, Inc.

GHOST URN

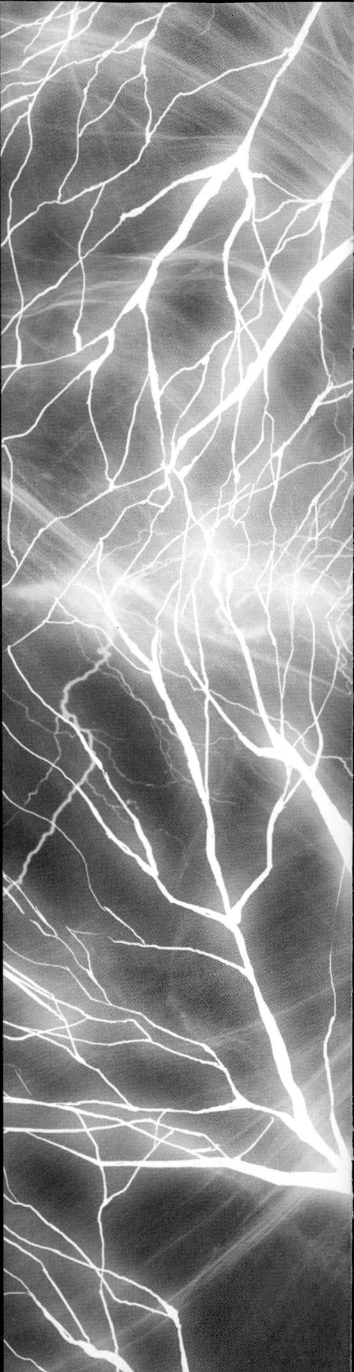

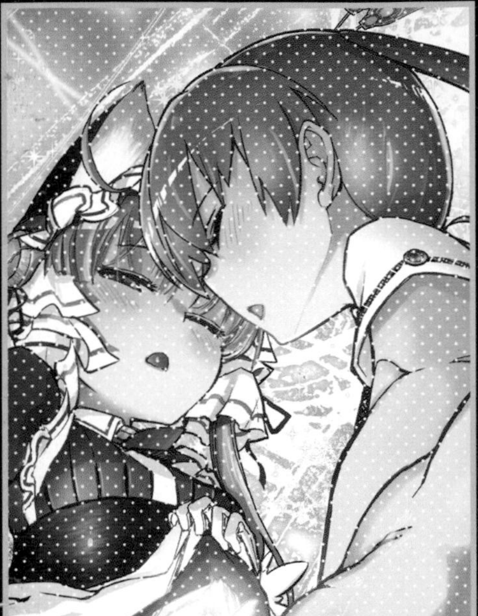

GHOST URN 07

PANDORA IN THE CRIMSON SHELL

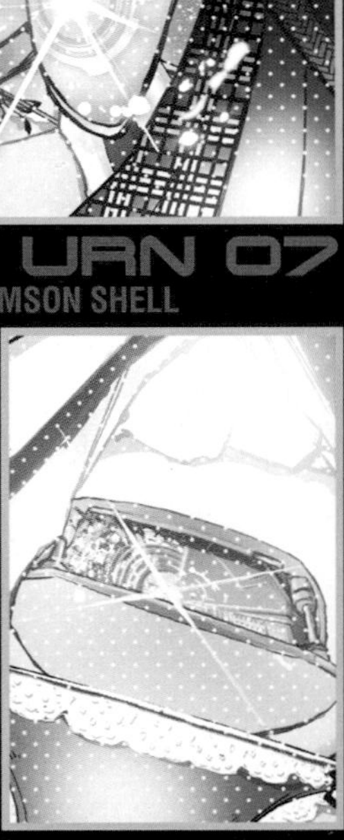

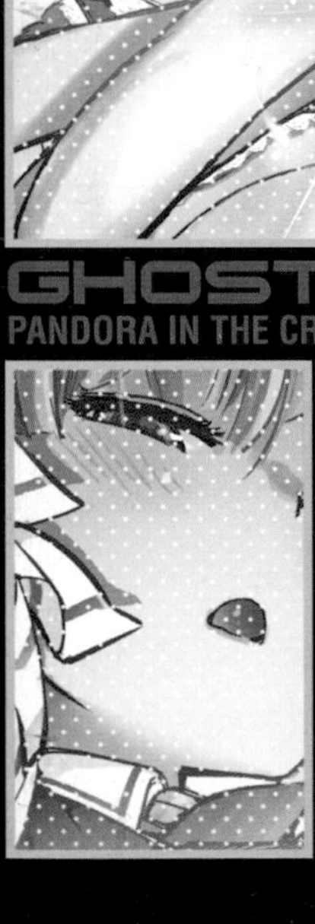

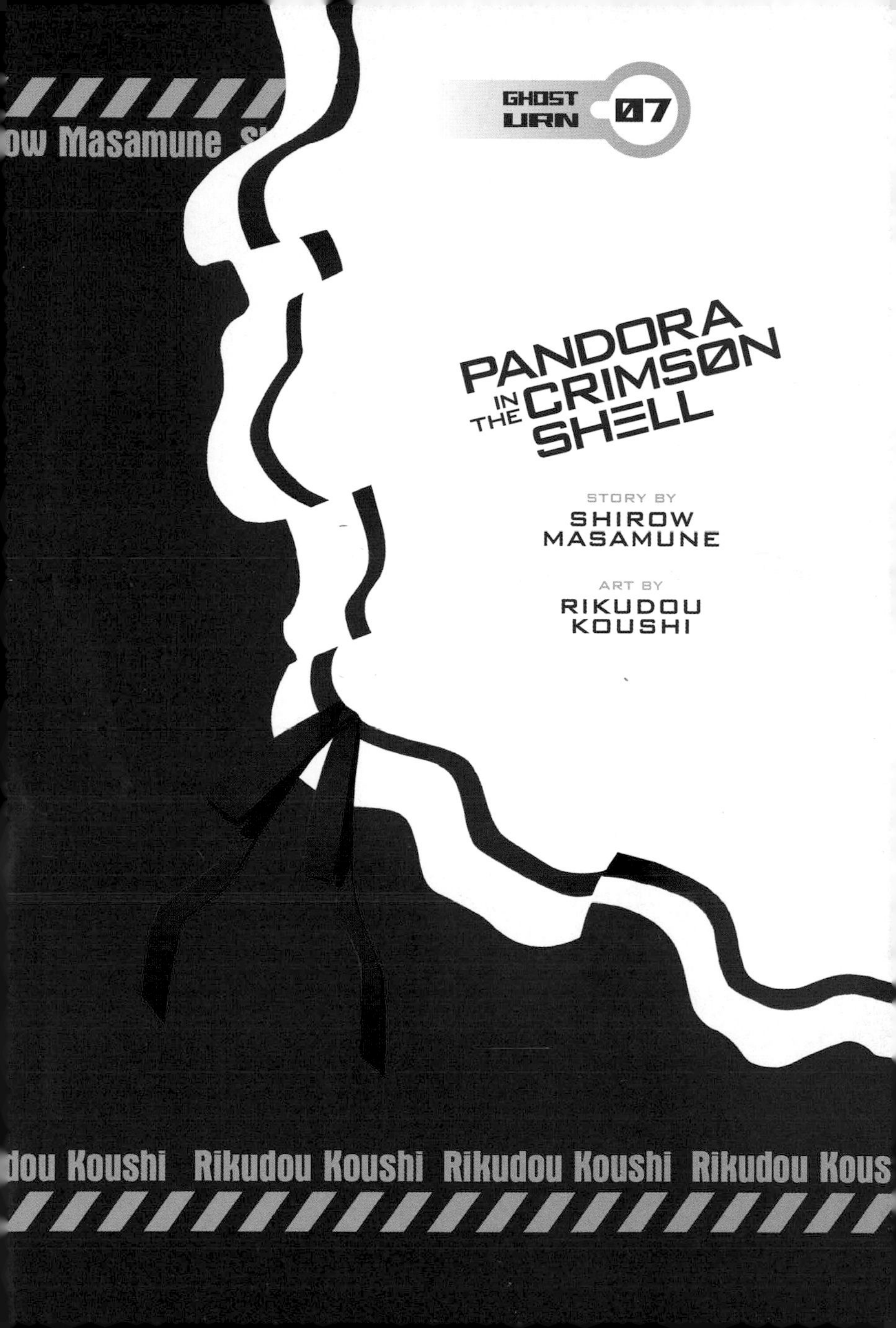

ow Masamune Sh
GHOST URN 07
PANDORA IN THE CRIMSON SHELL
STORY BY
SHIROW MASAMUNE
ART BY
RIKUDOU KOUSHI
dou Koushi Rikudou Koushi Rikudou Koushi Rikudou Kous

Shirow Masamune Shirow Masamune Shirow Masamune Shirow Masa

GHOST URN-EPISODE.log — The story so far!

Nene and Clarion have been safely reunited, but now they have to face off against a combat android called Fear, unleashed by Colonel Kurtz! And to make matters worse, Kurtz has also broken through the barriers between him and Buer's main body, and is ready to release and take control of the massive boring machine. Nene and Clarion are up against what look like impossible odds...!

Rikudou Koushi Rikudou Koushi Rikudou Koushi Rikudou Koushi Rikud

GHOST URN-CHARACTERS — Main Characters

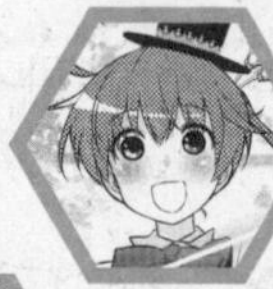

■ Nanakorobi Nene

A girl whose brain was implanted into an entirely artificial body after an accident when she was young. Nene has one of the few full-body prosthetics in the world!

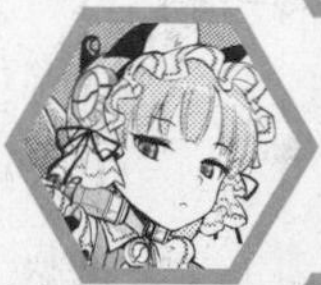

■ Clarion

A combat android owned by Uzal. Clarion has many top-secret, illegal programs tucked away inside her.

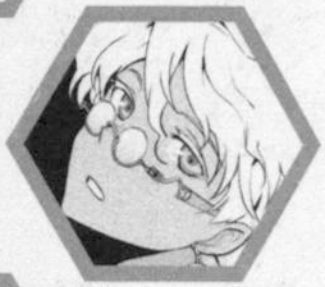

■ Uzal Delilah

The mysterious Uzal (real name: Sahar Schehera) is a well-known international businesswoman, but she has plenty of secrets. She vanished during the chaos when Buer ran wild.

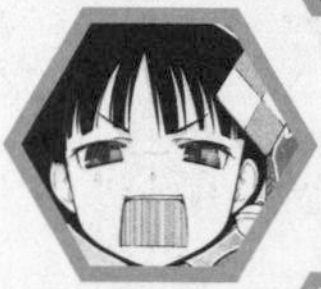

■ Korobase Takumi

Age unknown. She heads up the Korobase Foundation, which controls cybrain marketing, but has a pathological fear of people.

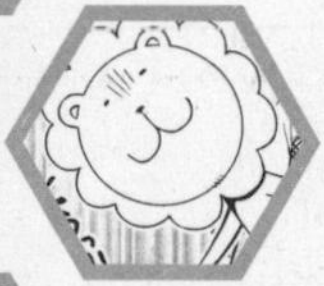

■ Massive boring machine Buer: Central Nervous Unit

The central control unit for the large multi-legged boring machine Buer. As Buer's actual body is currently dormant underground, the central nervous unit is accompanying Nene. This pompous-sounding entity provides a constant stream of perverted, leering commentary.

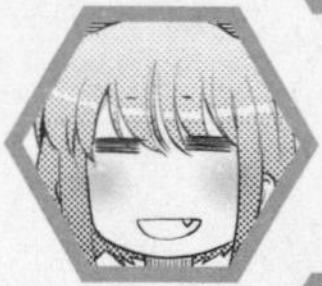

■ VlindXX XXXX

A perky, enthusiastic freelance reporter who dreams of taking her place among the top idols *and* the top reporters in the world! Dragging her two staffers in her wake, she's working hard to conquer mass media.

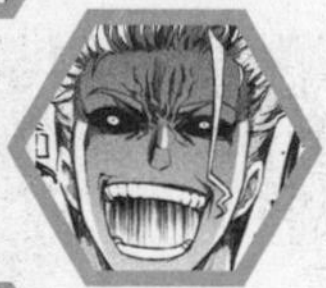

■ Colonel Ian Kurtz

A member of the American Imperial army. Since encountering a mysterious organization called Poseidon, he's been carrying out his plans on their behalf.

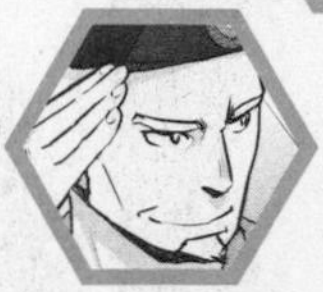

■ Captain Robert Altman

A captain with the Cenancle Defense Forces, currently under the command of Special Military Advisor Kurtz. A passionate tough guy who loves justice and peace.

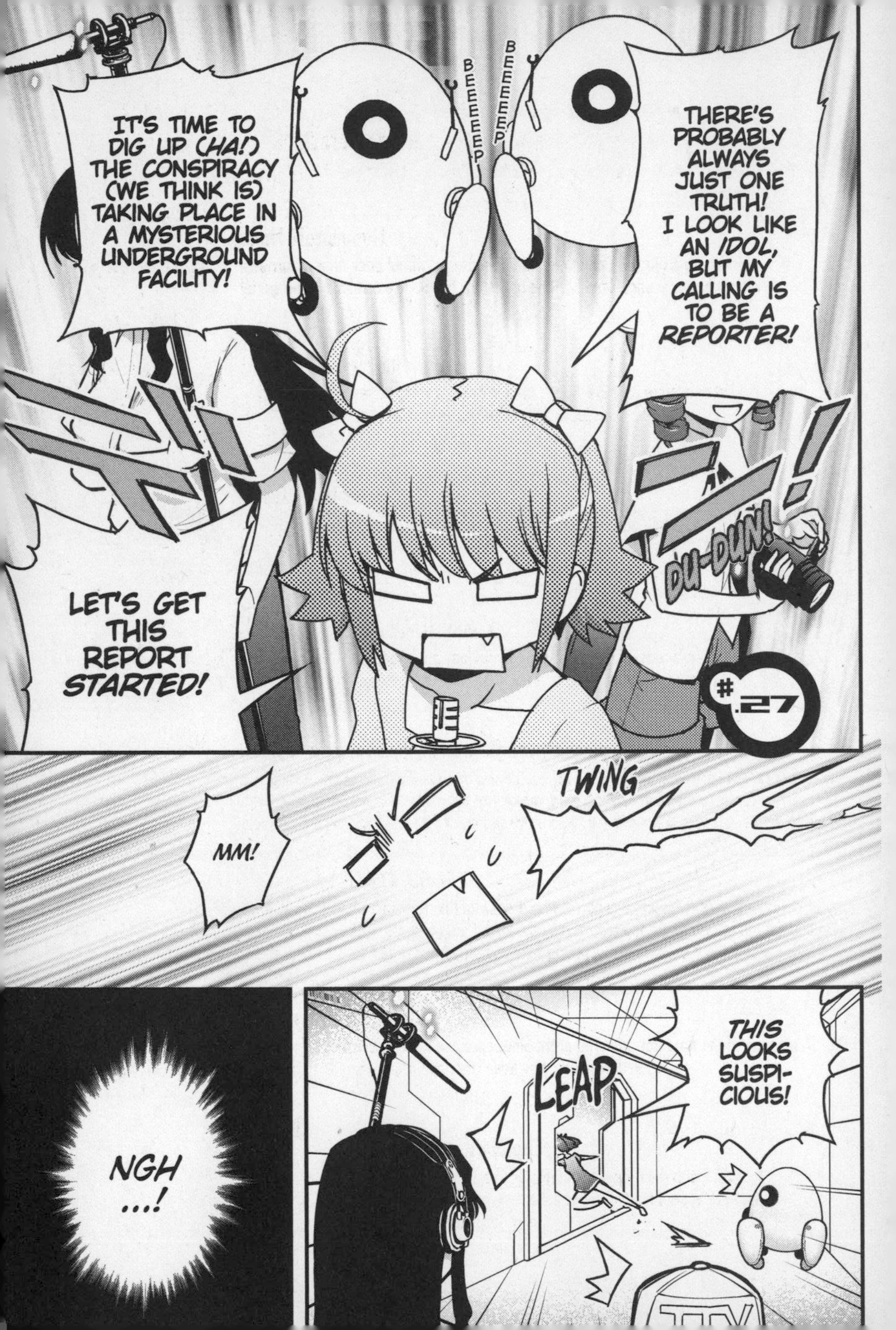
THERE'S PROBABLY ALWAYS JUST ONE TRUTH! I LOOK LIKE AN *IDOL,* BUT MY CALLING IS TO BE A *REPORTER!*
BEEEEEEP
BEEEEEEP
IT'S TIME TO DIG UP (*HA!*) THE CONSPIRACY (WE THINK IS) TAKING PLACE IN A MYSTERIOUS UNDERGROUND FACILITY!
DU-DUN!
#.27
LET'S GET THIS REPORT *STARTED!*
TWING
MM!
THIS LOOKS SUSPI-CIOUS!
LEAP
NGH ...!

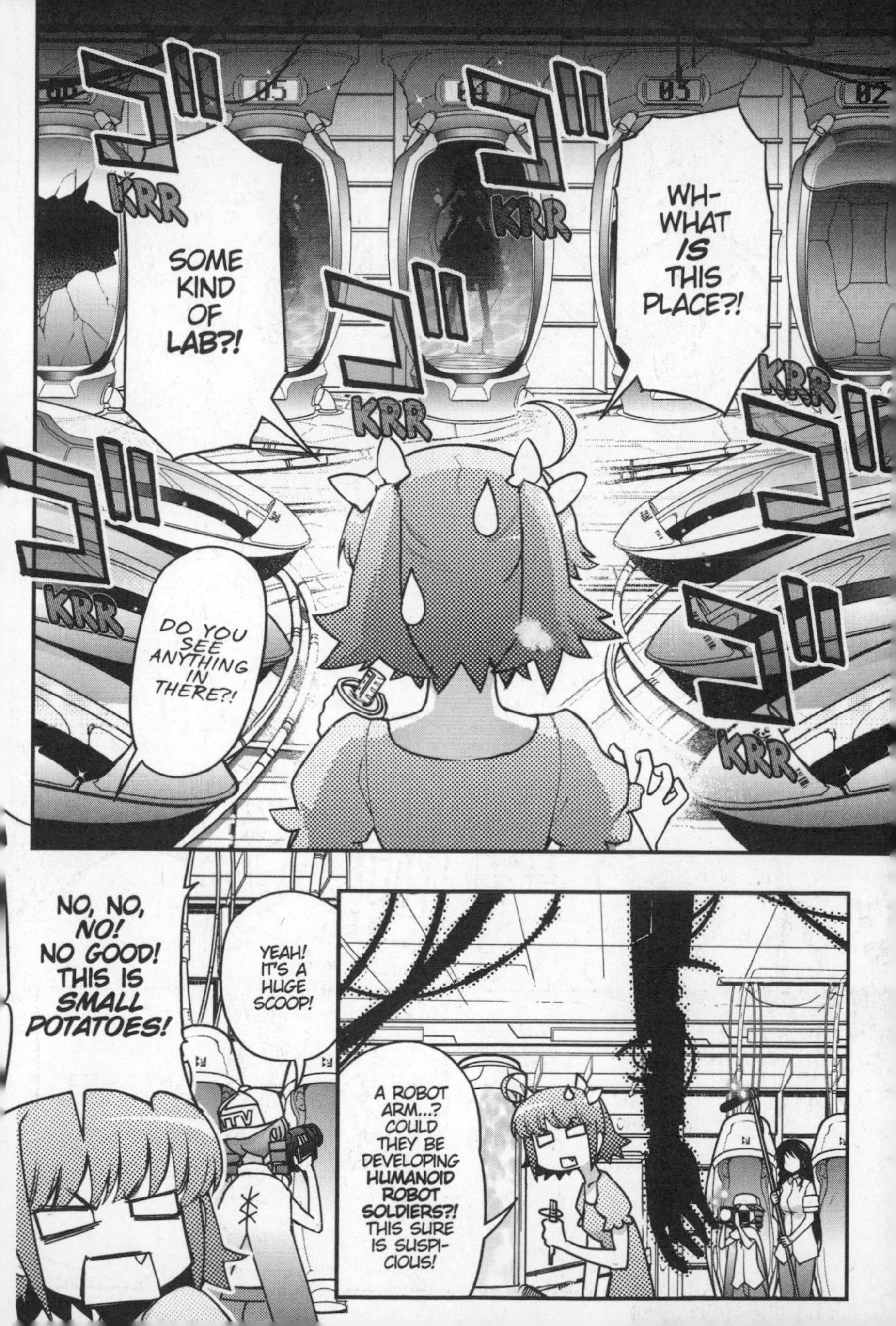

KRR
KRR
WH-WHAT IS THIS PLACE?!
SOME KIND OF LAB?!
KRR
KRR
KRR
KRR
DO YOU SEE ANYTHING IN THERE?!
A ROBOT ARM...? COULD THEY BE DEVELOPING HUMANOID ROBOT SOLDIERS?! THIS SURE IS SUSPICIOUS!
YEAH! IT'S A HUGE SCOOP!
NO, NO, NO! NO GOOD! THIS IS SMALL POTATOES!

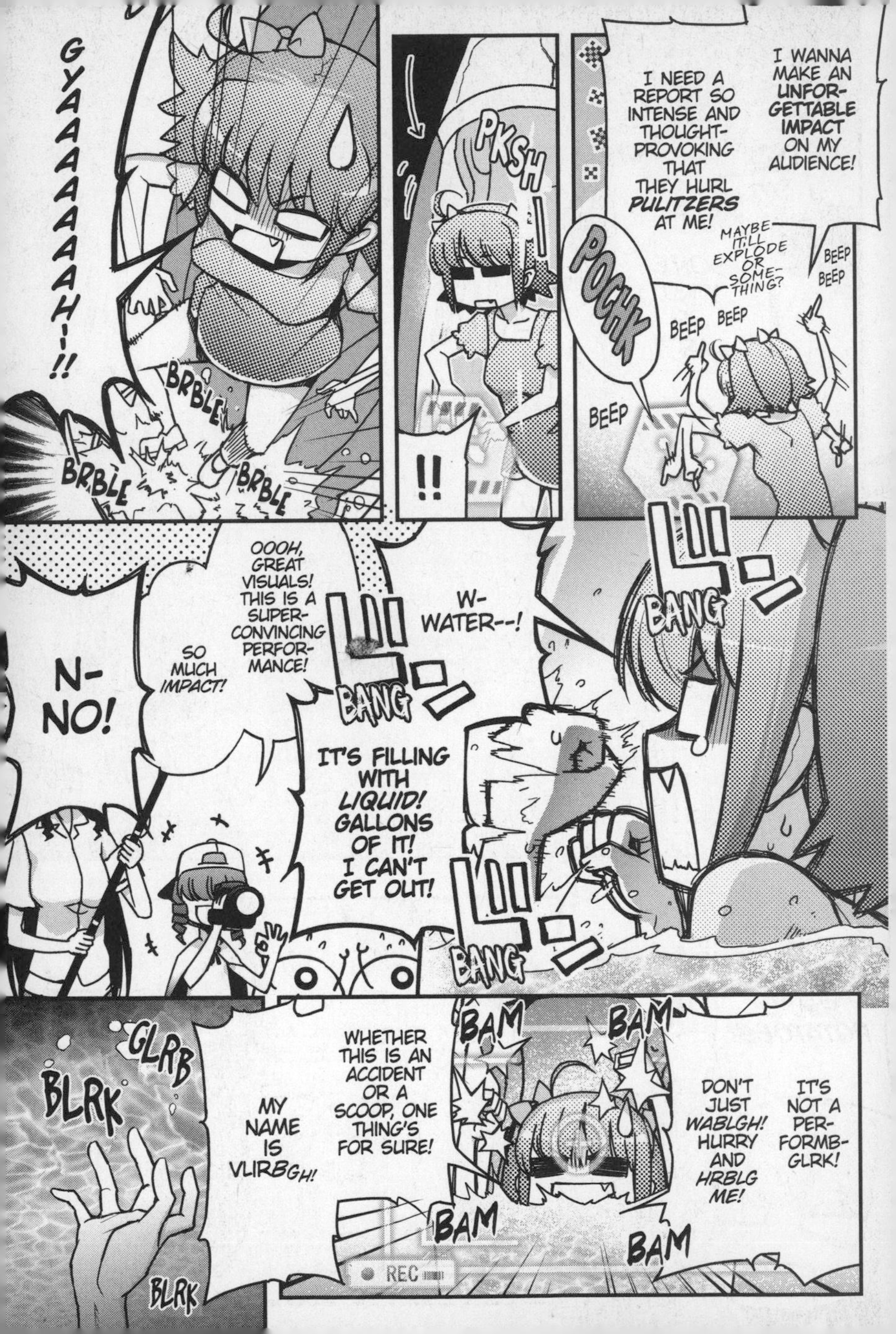
I WANNA MAKE AN UNFORGETTABLE IMPACT ON MY AUDIENCE!
I NEED A REPORT SO INTENSE AND THOUGHT-PROVOKING THAT THEY HURL PULITZERS AT ME!
BEEP BEEP
MAYBE IT'LL EXPLODE OR SOMETHING?
BEEP BEEP
POCHK
BEEP
PKSH
!!
GYAAAAAAAAAAH!!
BRBLE
BRBLE
BRBLE
BANG
W-WATER--!
OOOH, GREAT VISUALS! THIS IS A SUPER-CONVINCING PERFORMANCE!
SO MUCH IMPACT!
N-NO!
BANG
IT'S FILLING WITH LIQUID! GALLONS OF IT! I CAN'T GET OUT!
BANG
IT'S NOT A PERFORMB-GLRK!
DON'T JUST WABLGH! HURRY AND HRBLG ME!
BAM
BAM
WHETHER THIS IS AN ACCIDENT OR A SCOOP, ONE THING'S FOR SURE!
MY NAME IS VLIRBGH!
BAM
BAM
REC
GLRB
BLRK
BLRK

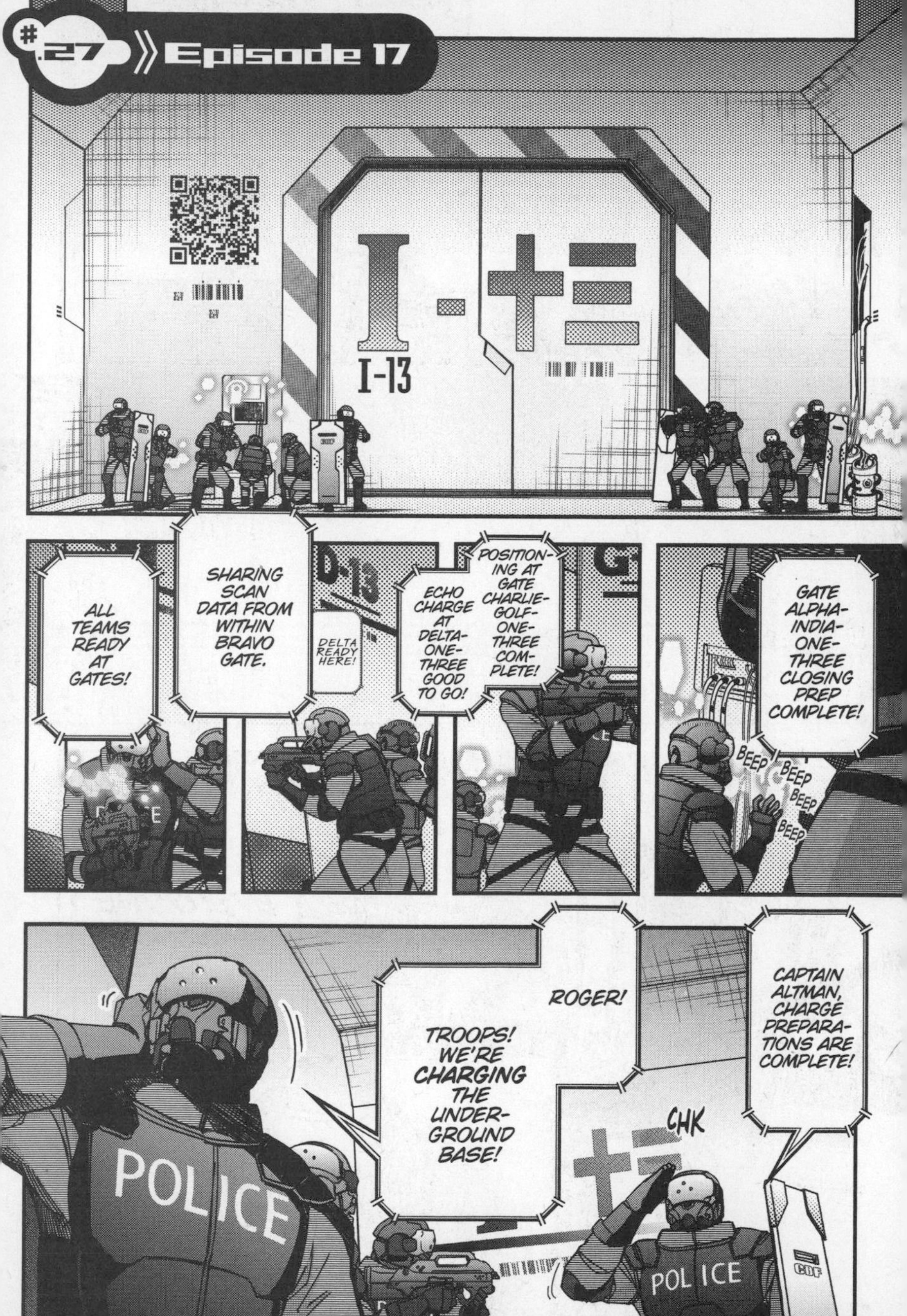
#.27 Episode 17
I-13
GATE ALPHA-INDIA-ONE-THREE CLOSING PREP COMPLETE!
BEEP BEEP BEEP BEEP
POSITIONING AT GATE CHARLIE-GOLF-ONE-THREE COMPLETE!
D-13
ECHO CHARGE AT DELTA-ONE-THREE GOOD TO GO!
DELTA READY HERE!
SHARING SCAN DATA FROM WITHIN BRAVO GATE.
ALL TEAMS READY AT GATES!
CAPTAIN ALTMAN, CHARGE PREPARATIONS ARE COMPLETE!
CHK
CDF
POLICE
ROGER!
TROOPS! WE'RE CHARGING THE UNDERGROUND BASE!
POLICE

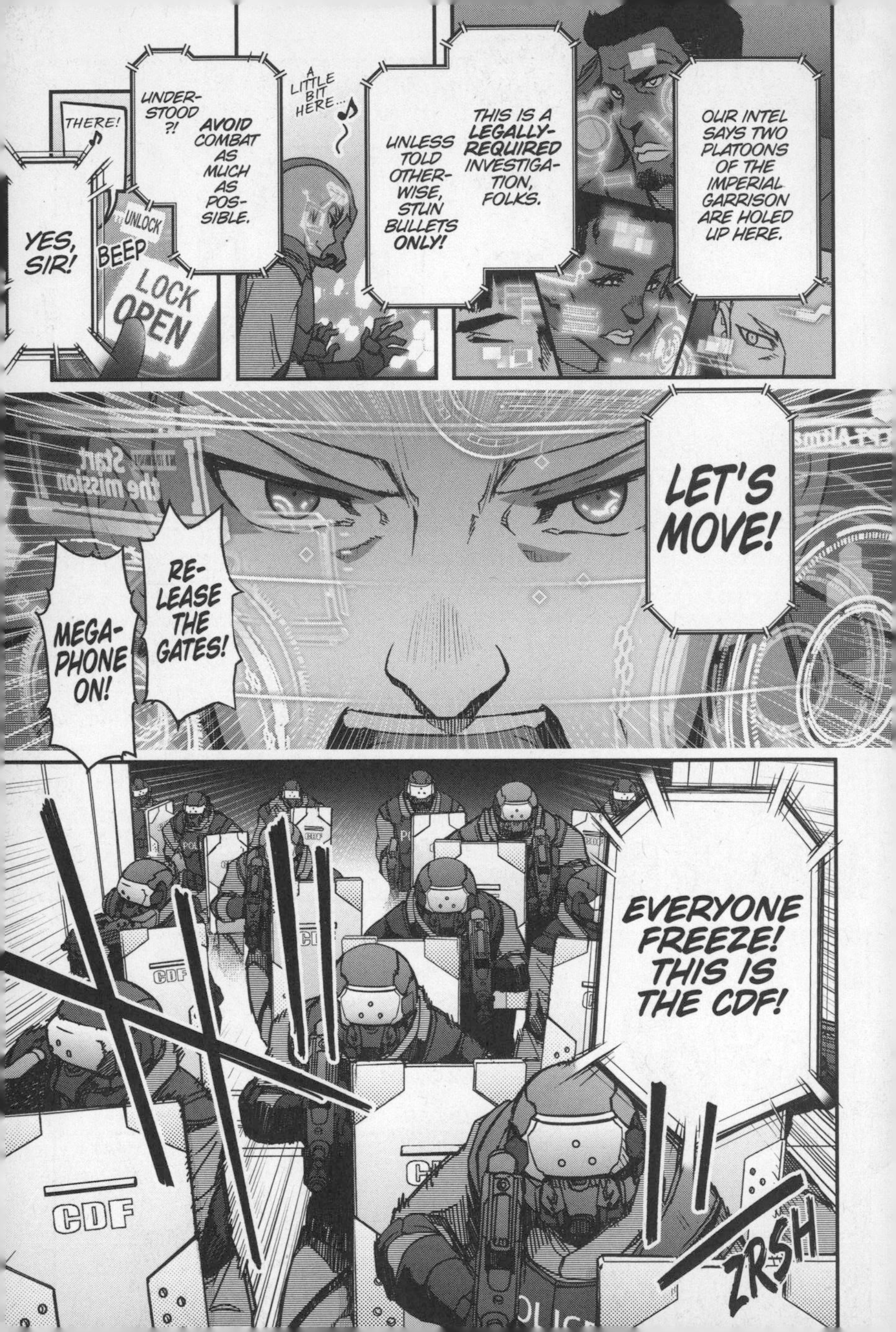
OUR INTEL SAYS TWO PLATOONS OF THE IMPERIAL GARRISON ARE HOLED UP HERE.
THIS IS A LEGALLY-REQUIRED INVESTIGATION, FOLKS.
UNLESS TOLD OTHERWISE, STUN BULLETS ONLY!
A LITTLE BIT HERE...
AVOID COMBAT AS MUCH AS POSSIBLE.
UNDERSTOOD?!
THERE!
UNLOCK
BEEP
LOCK OPEN
YES, SIR!
LET'S MOVE!
RELEASE THE GATES!
MEGAPHONE ON!
EVERYONE FREEZE! THIS IS THE CDF!
CDF
CDF
ZRSH

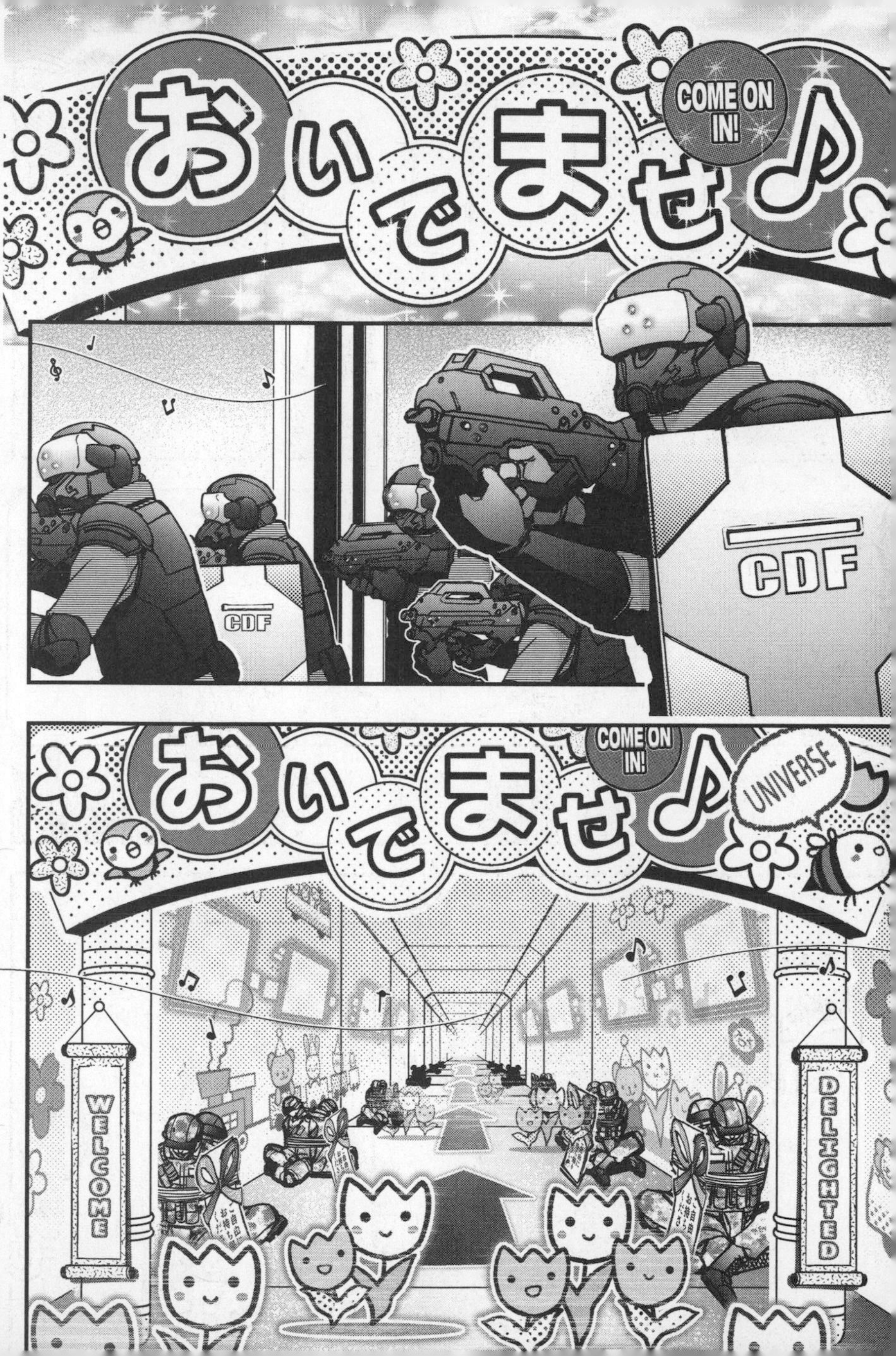
COME ON IN!
おいでませ♪
CDF
CDF
COME ON IN!
UNIVERSE
おいでませ♪
DELIGHTED
WELCOME

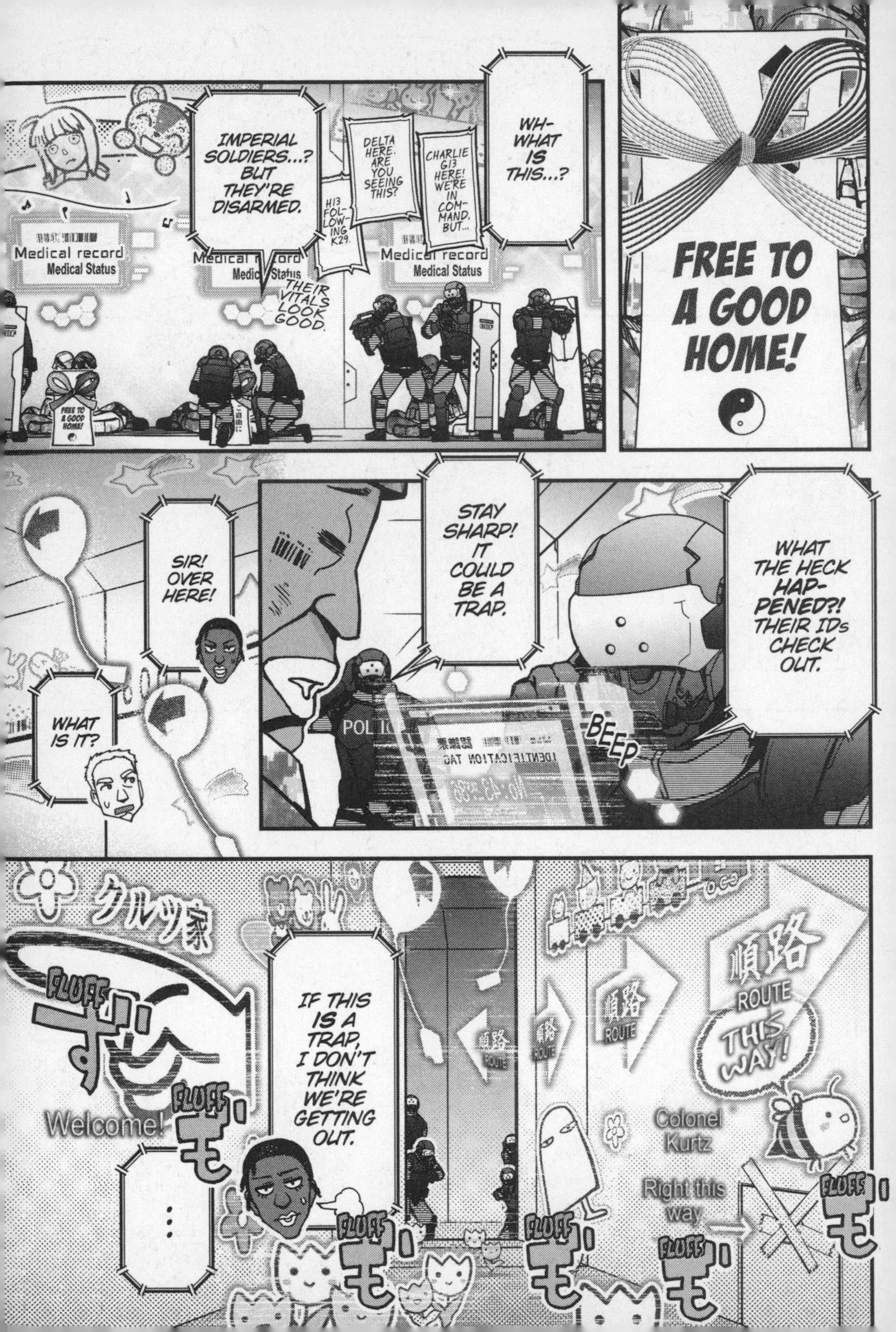

FREE TO A GOOD HOME!
WH-WHAT IS THIS...?
CHARLIE G13 HERE! WE'RE IN COMMAND, BUT...
DELTA HERE. ARE YOU SEEING THIS?
H13 FOLLOWING K29.
IMPERIAL SOLDIERS...? BUT THEY'RE DISARMED.
Medical record
Medical Status
THEIR VITALS LOOK GOOD.
FREE TO A GOOD HOME!
WHAT THE HECK HAPPENED?! THEIR IDs CHECK OUT.
BEEP
IDENTIFICATION TAG
STAY SHARP! IT COULD BE A TRAP.
POLICE
SIR! OVER HERE!
WHAT IS IT?
順路
ROUTE
THIS WAY!
Colonel Kurtz
Right this way
FLUFF
IF THIS IS A TRAP, I DON'T THINK WE'RE GETTING OUT.
クルツ家
Welcome!
FLUFF
...

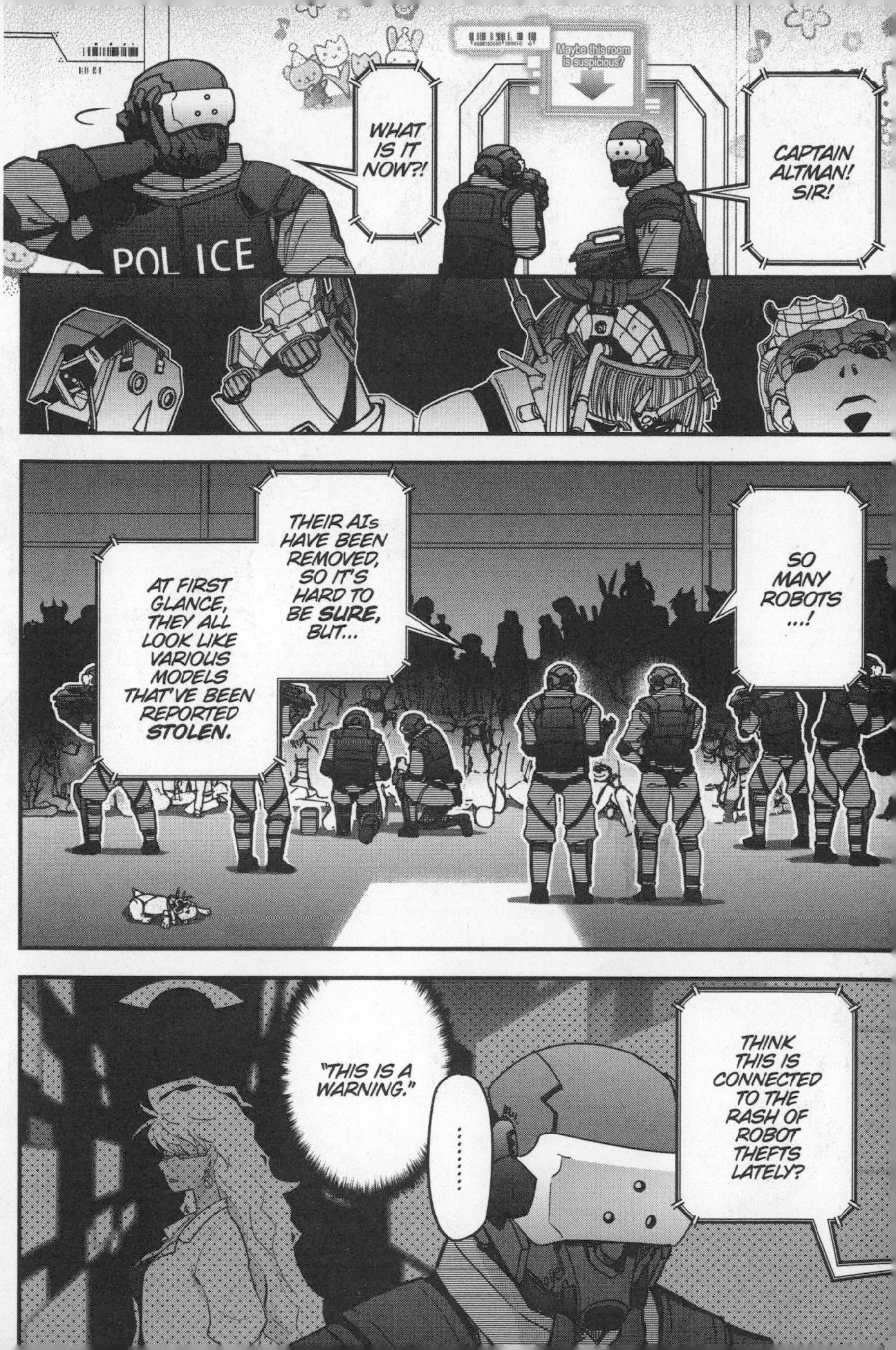
CAPTAIN ALTMAN! SIR!
Maybe this room is suspicious?
WHAT IS IT NOW?!
POLICE
SO MANY ROBOTS ...!
THEIR AIs HAVE BEEN REMOVED, SO IT'S HARD TO BE SURE, BUT...
AT FIRST GLANCE, THEY ALL LOOK LIKE VARIOUS MODELS THAT'VE BEEN REPORTED STOLEN.
THINK THIS IS CONNECTED TO THE RASH OF ROBOT THEFTS LATELY?
....
"THIS IS A WARNING."

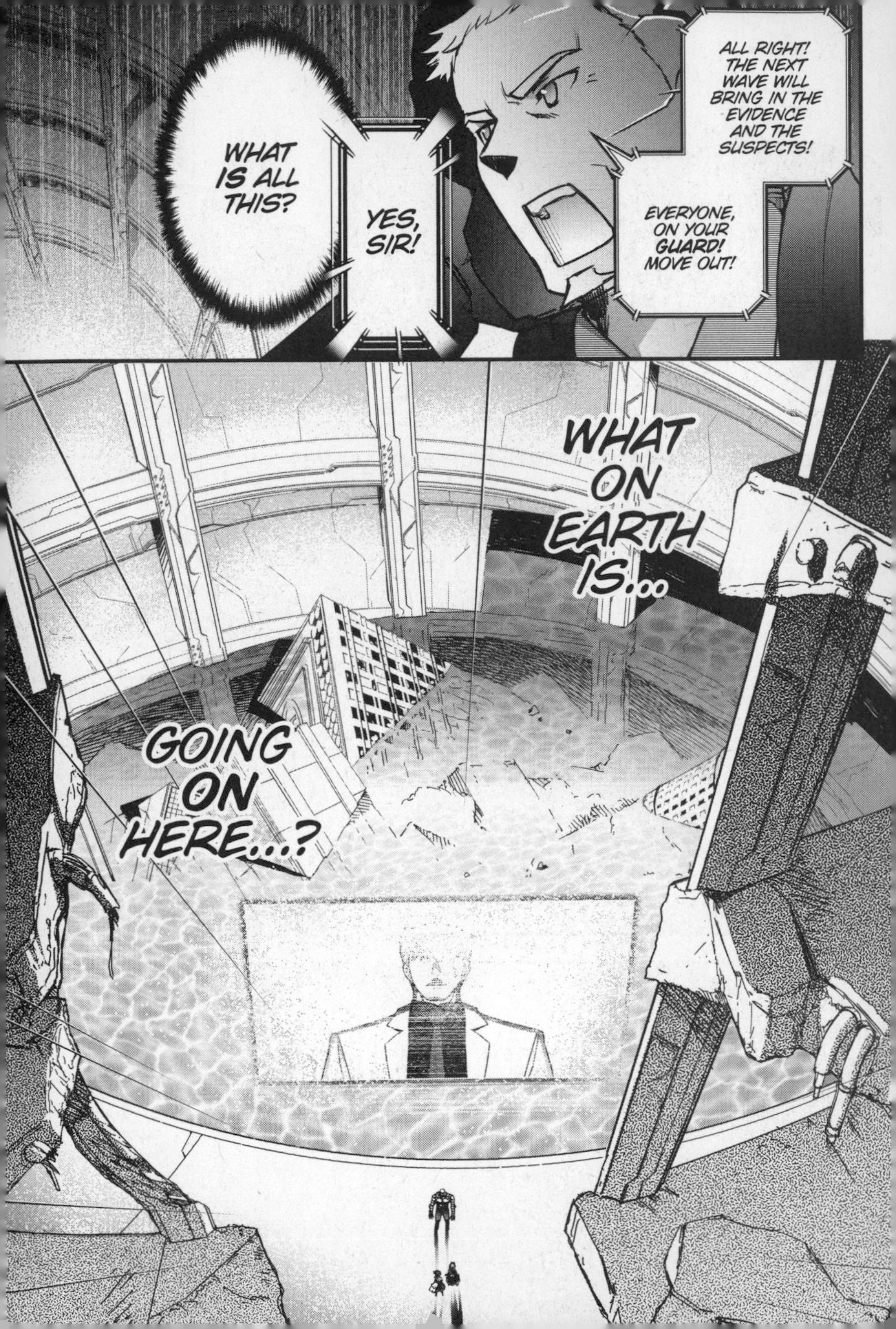
ALL RIGHT! THE NEXT WAVE WILL BRING IN THE EVIDENCE AND THE SUSPECTS!
EVERYONE, ON YOUR GUARD! MOVE OUT!
YES, SIR!
WHAT IS ALL THIS?
WHAT ON EARTH IS...
GOING ON HERE...?

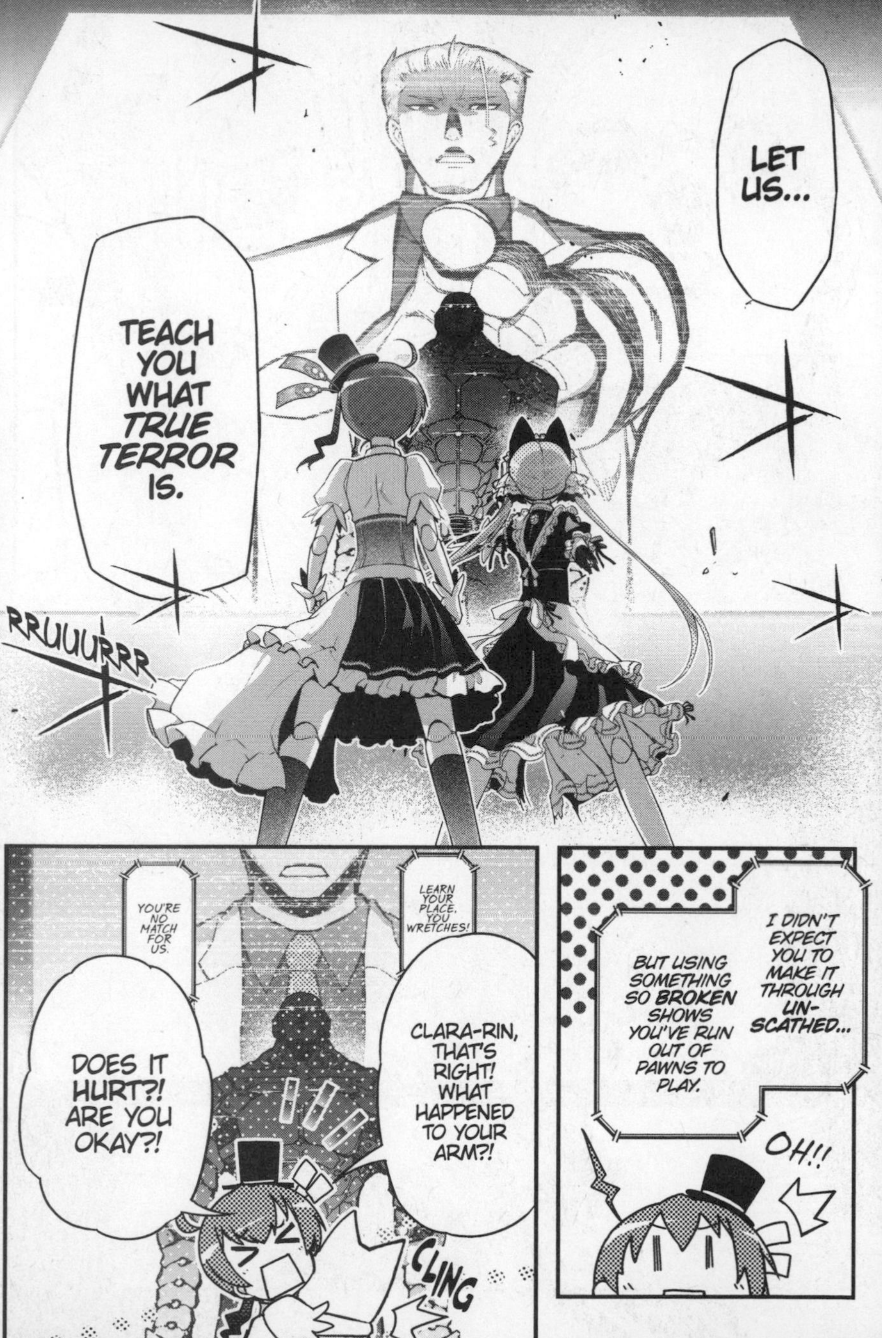
LET US...
TEACH YOU WHAT TRUE TERROR IS.
RRUUURRR
I DIDN'T EXPECT YOU TO MAKE IT THROUGH UN-SCATHED...
BUT USING SOMETHING SO BROKEN SHOWS YOU'VE RUN OUT OF PAWNS TO PLAY.
OH!!
LEARN YOUR PLACE, YOU WRETCHES!
YOU'RE NO MATCH FOR US.
CLARA-RIN, THAT'S RIGHT! WHAT HAPPENED TO YOUR ARM?!
DOES IT HURT?! ARE YOU OKAY?!
CLING

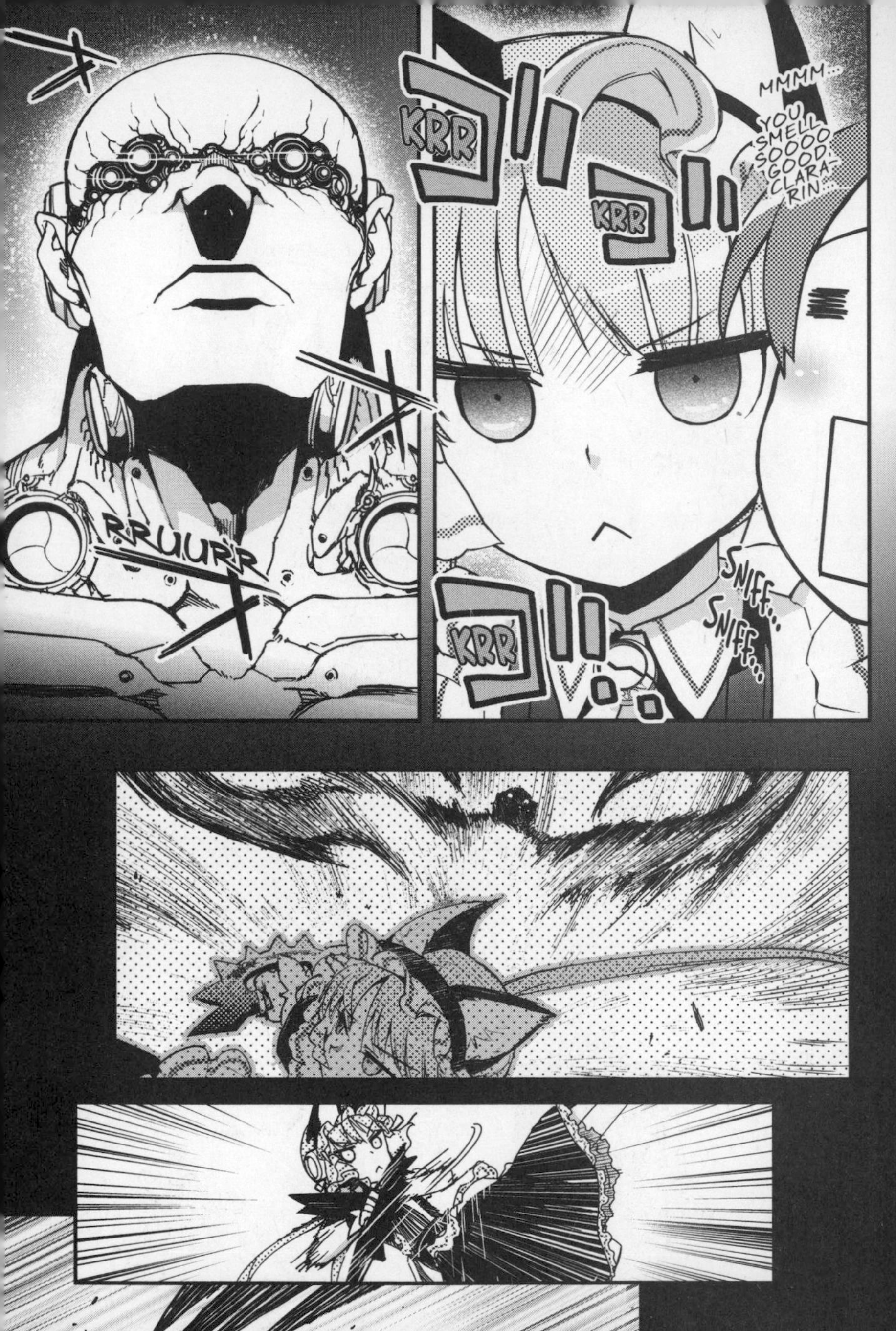
KRR
KRR
MMMM...
YOU SMELL SOOOO GOOD, CLARA-RIN...
KRR
SNIFF... SNIFF...
RRUURR

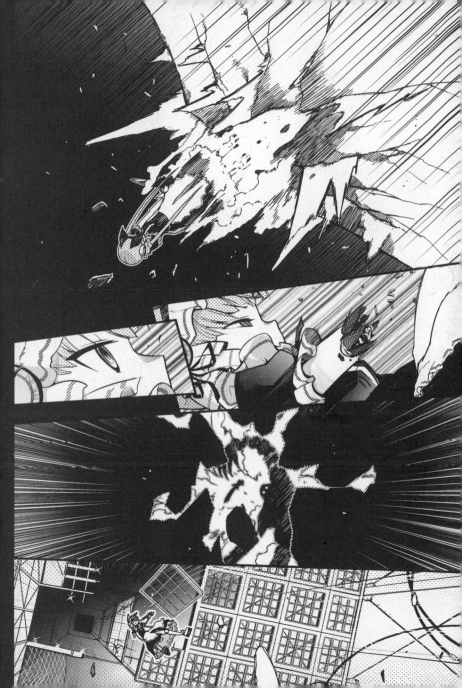

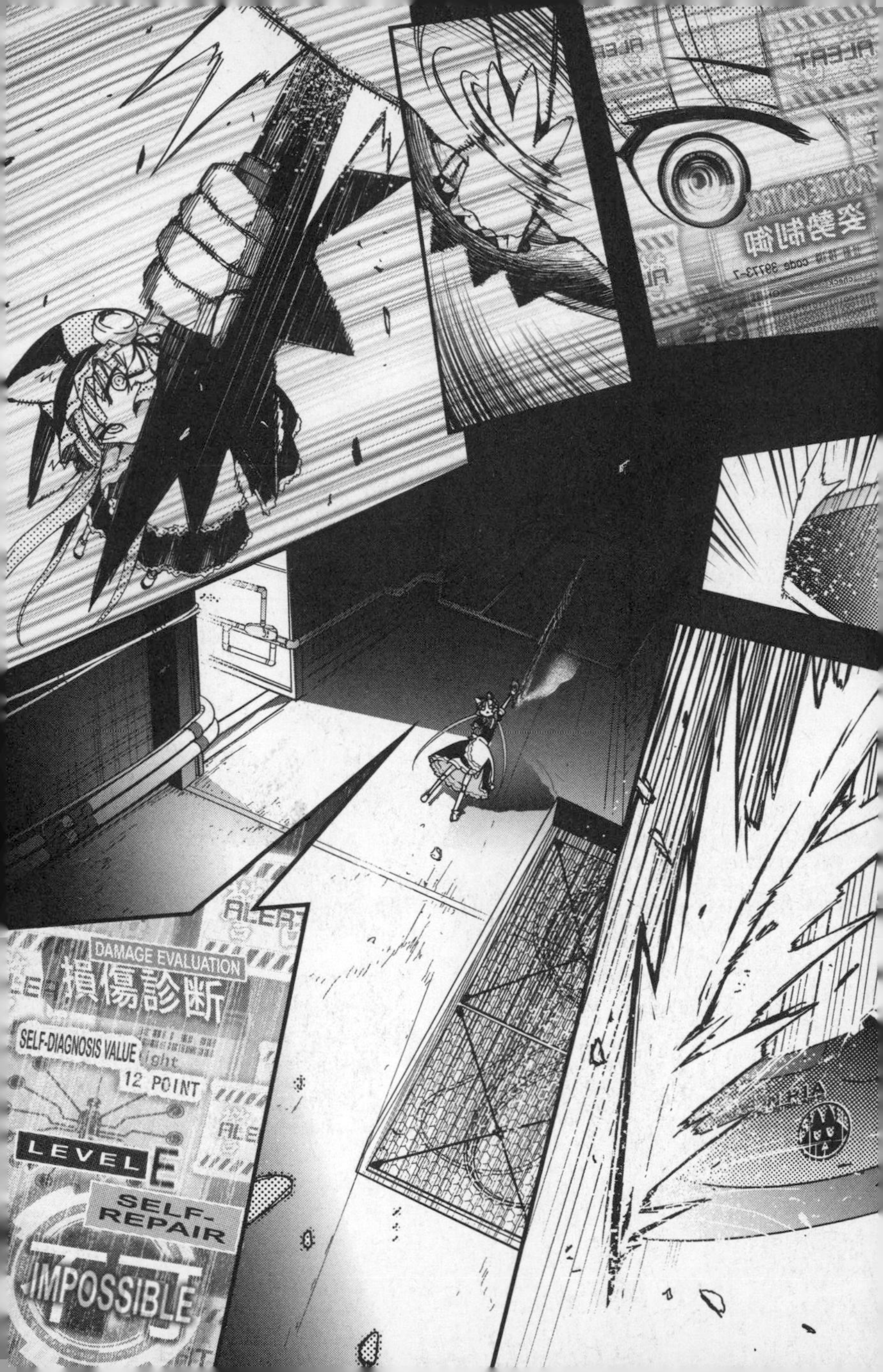
DAMAGE EVALUATION
損傷診断
SELF-DIAGNOSIS VALUE
12 POINT
LEVEL E
SELF-REPAIR
IMPOSSIBLE

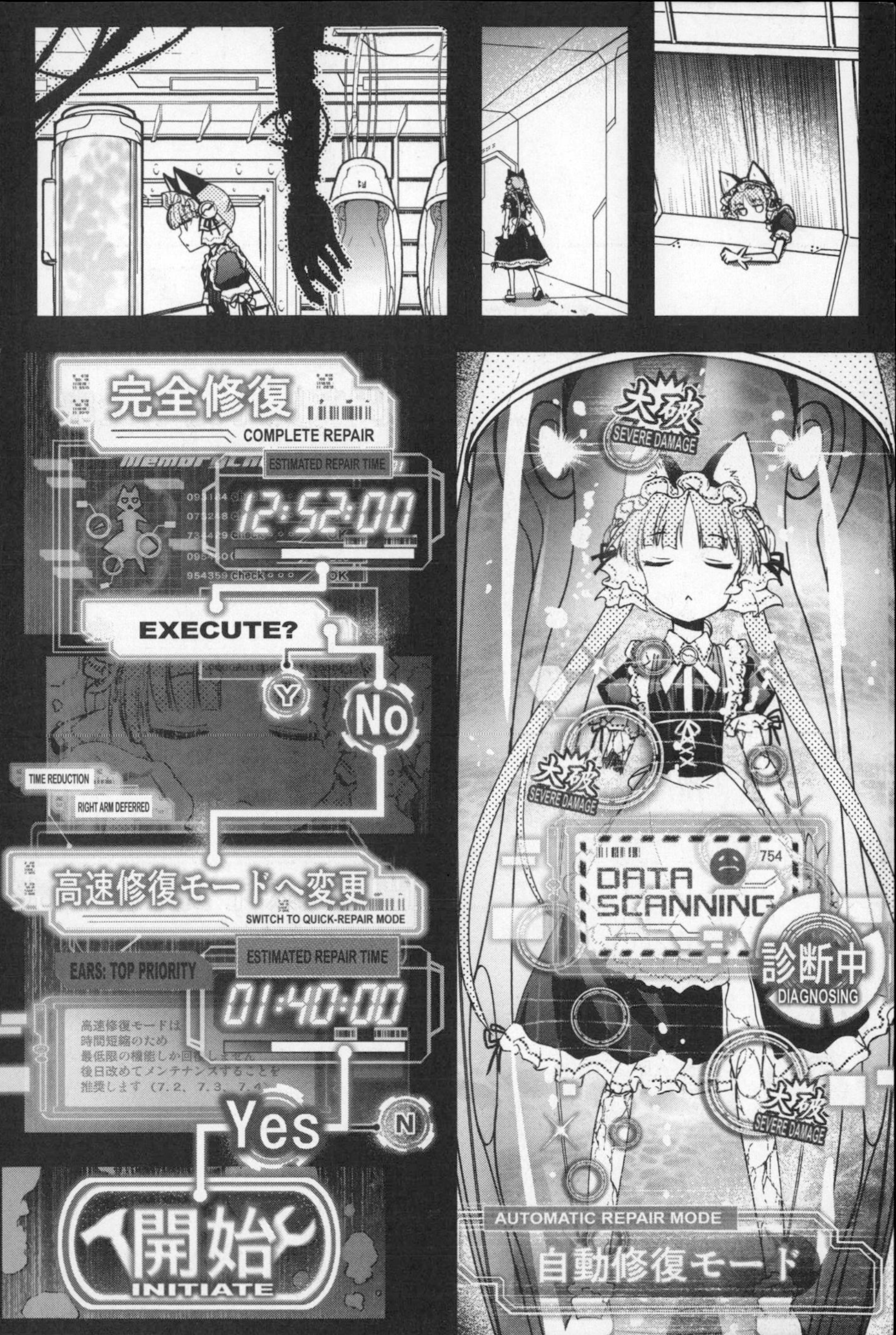
大破
SEVERE DAMAGE
大破
SEVERE DAMAGE
754
DATA SCANNING
診断中
DIAGNOSING
大破
SEVERE DAMAGE
AUTOMATIC REPAIR MODE
自動修復モード
完全修復
COMPLETE REPAIR
ESTIMATED REPAIR TIME
12:52:00
954359 check
OK
EXECUTE?
Y
No
TIME REDUCTION
RIGHT ARM DEFERRED
高速修復モードへ変更
SWITCH TO QUICK-REPAIR MODE
EARS: TOP PRIORITY
ESTIMATED REPAIR TIME
01:40:00
高速修復モードは
時間短縮のため
最低限の機能しか回
後日改めてメンテナンスすることを
推奨します（7.2、7.3、7.4
Yes
N
開始
INITIATE

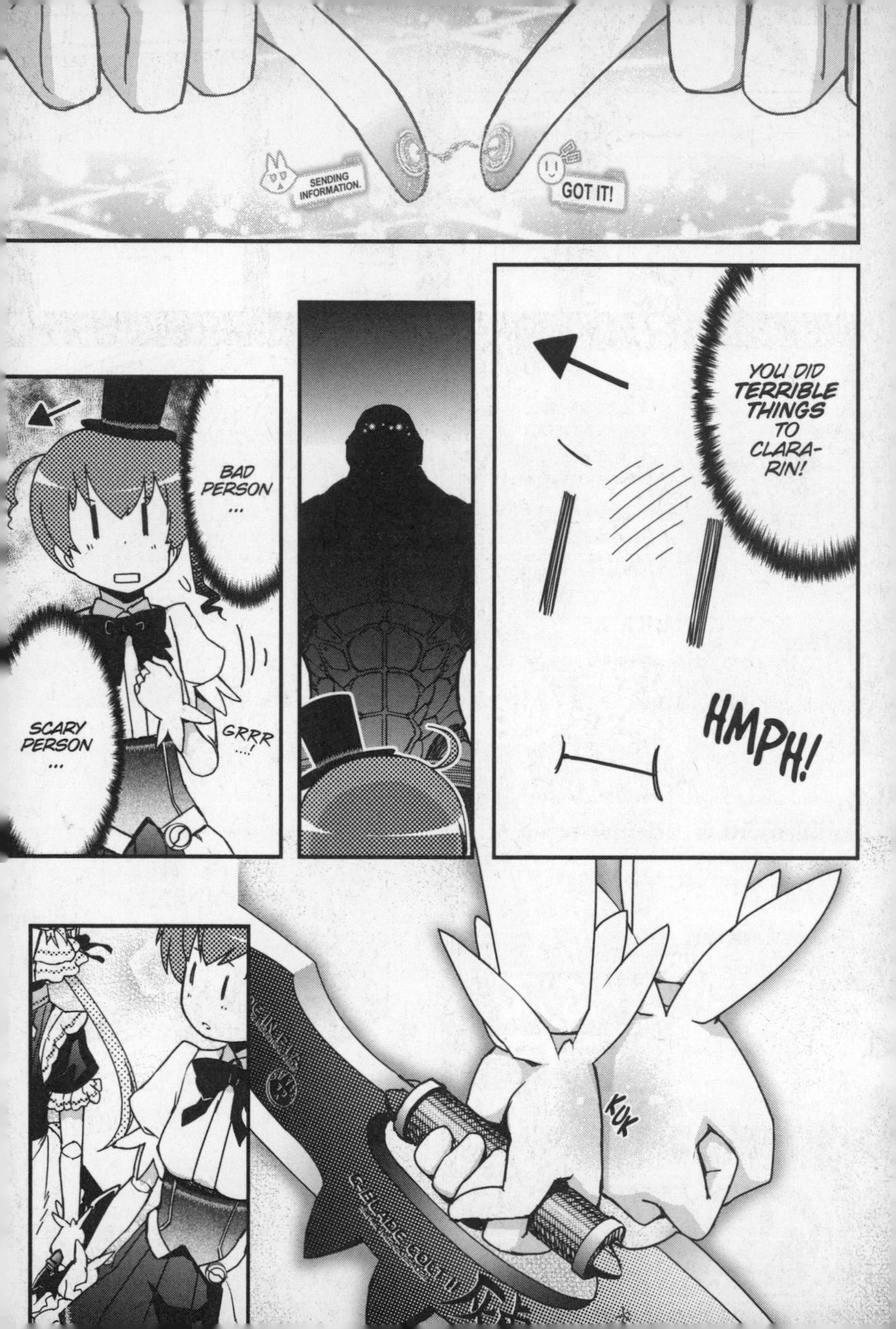
GOT IT!
SENDING INFORMATION.
YOU DID TERRIBLE THINGS TO CLARA-RIN!
HMPH!
BAD PERSON ...
GRRR ...!
SCARY PERSON ...
KUK

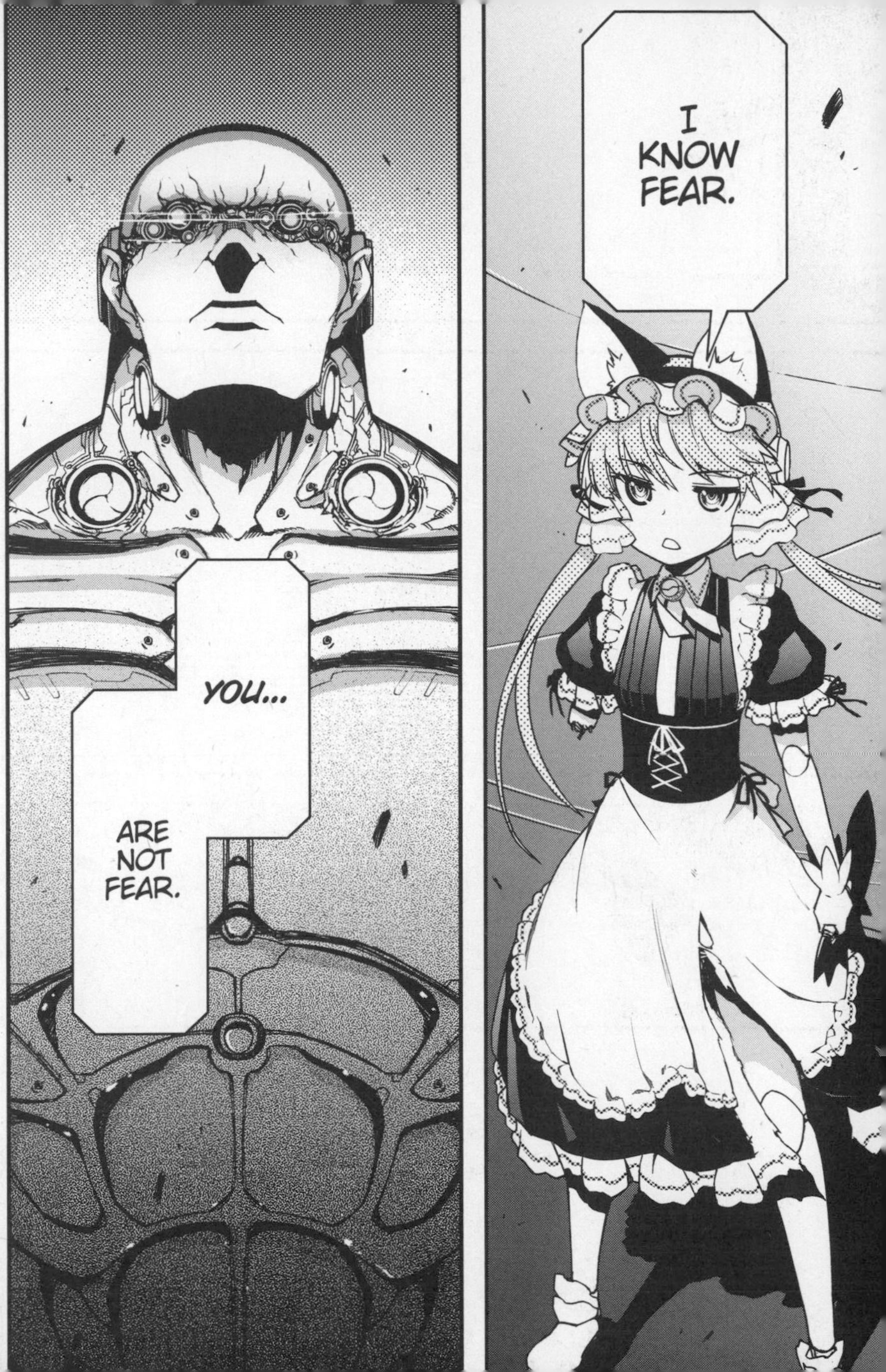
I KNOW FEAR.
YOU...
ARE NOT FEAR.

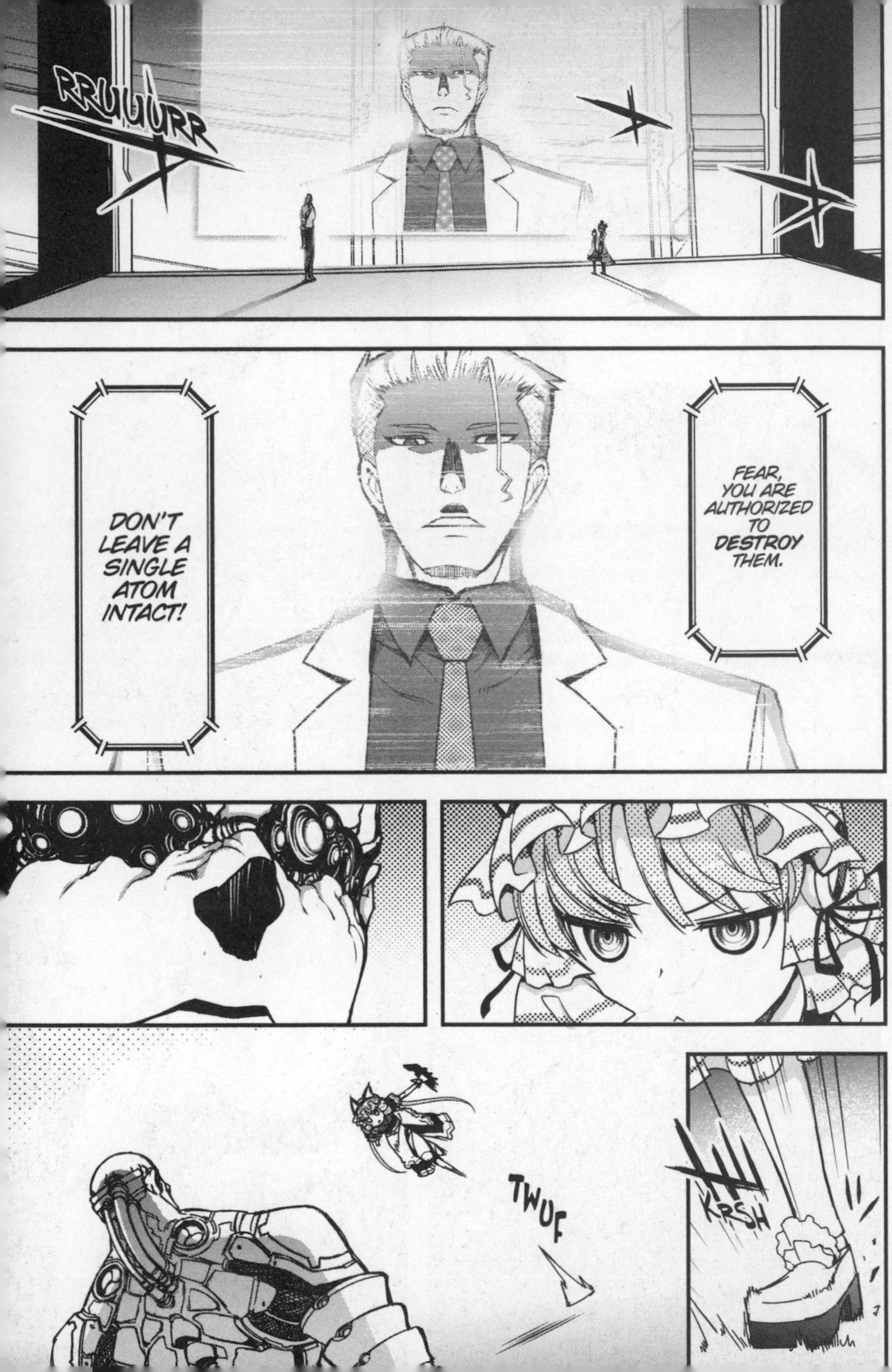
RRUUURR
FEAR, YOU ARE AUTHORIZED TO DESTROY THEM.
DON'T LEAVE A SINGLE ATOM INTACT!
KRSH
TWUF

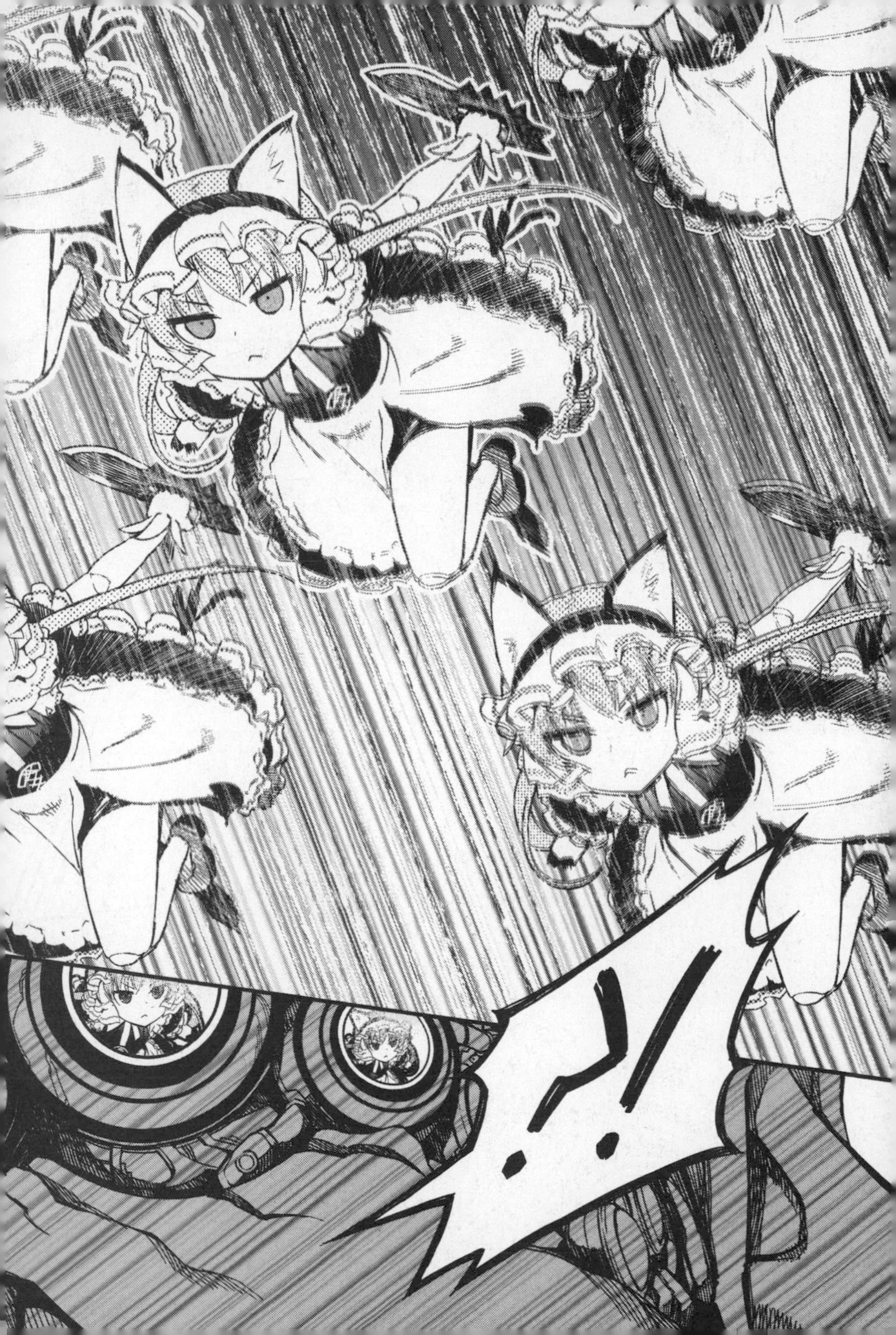

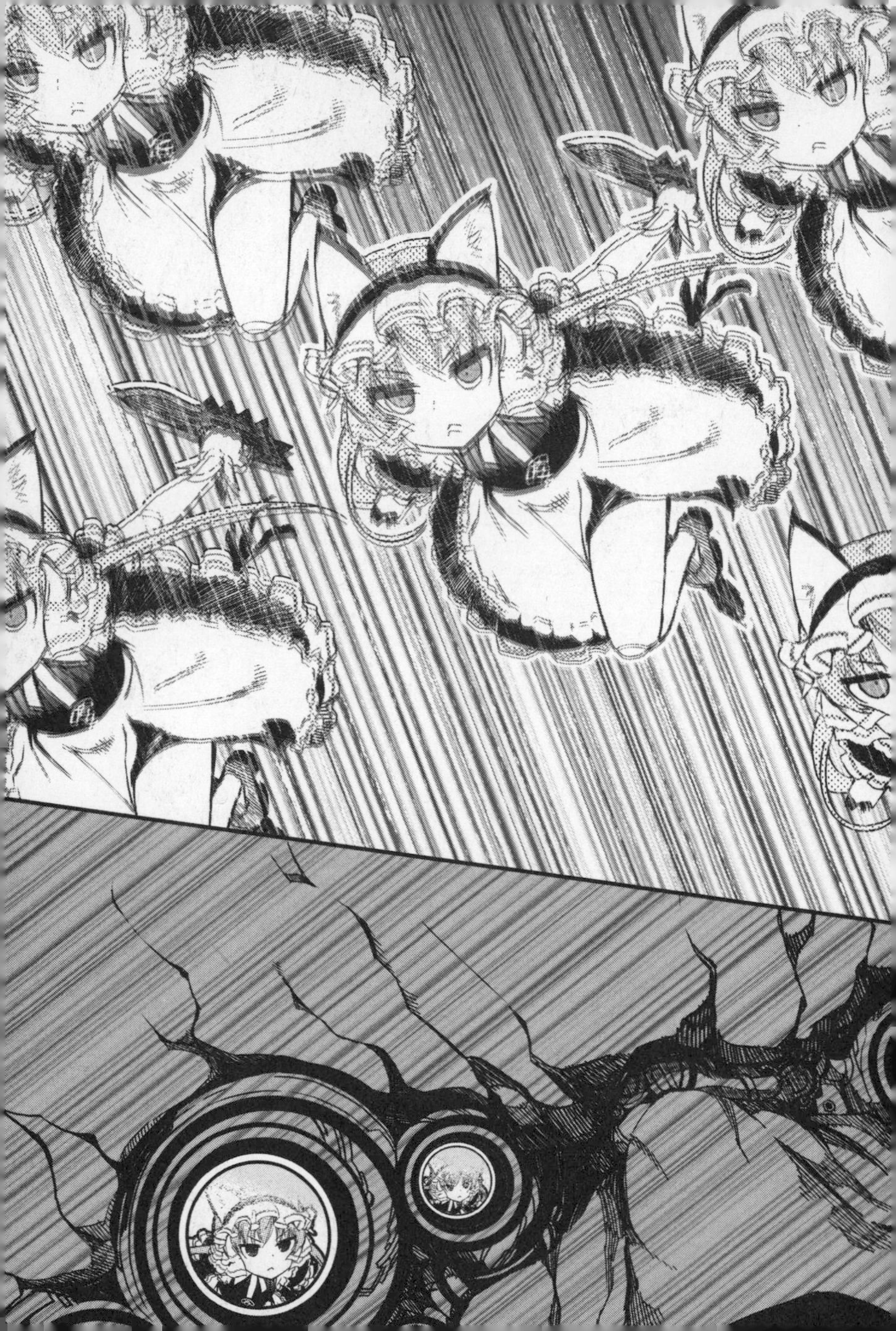

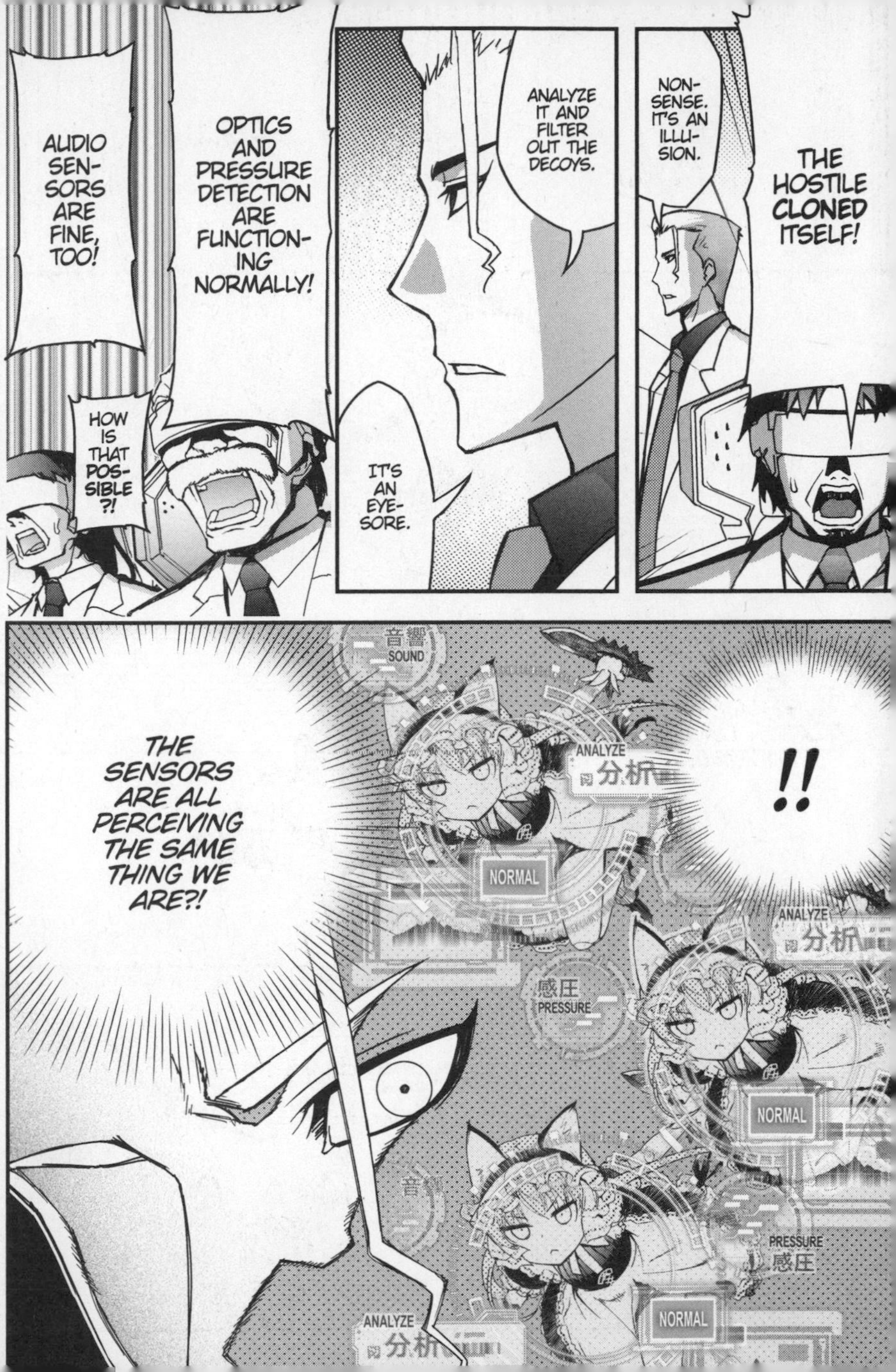
THE HOSTILE CLONED ITSELF!
NON-SENSE. IT'S AN ILLU-SION.
ANALYZE IT AND FILTER OUT THE DECOYS.
IT'S AN EYE-SORE.
OPTICS AND PRESSURE DETECTION ARE FUNCTION-ING NORMALLY!
AUDIO SEN-SORS ARE FINE, TOO!
HOW IS THAT POS-SIBLE?!
音響 SOUND
ANALYZE 分析
NORMAL
!!
ANALYZE 分析
感圧 PRESSURE
NORMAL
PRESSURE 感圧
NORMAL
ANALYZE 分析
THE SENSORS ARE ALL PERCEIVING THE SAME THING WE ARE?!

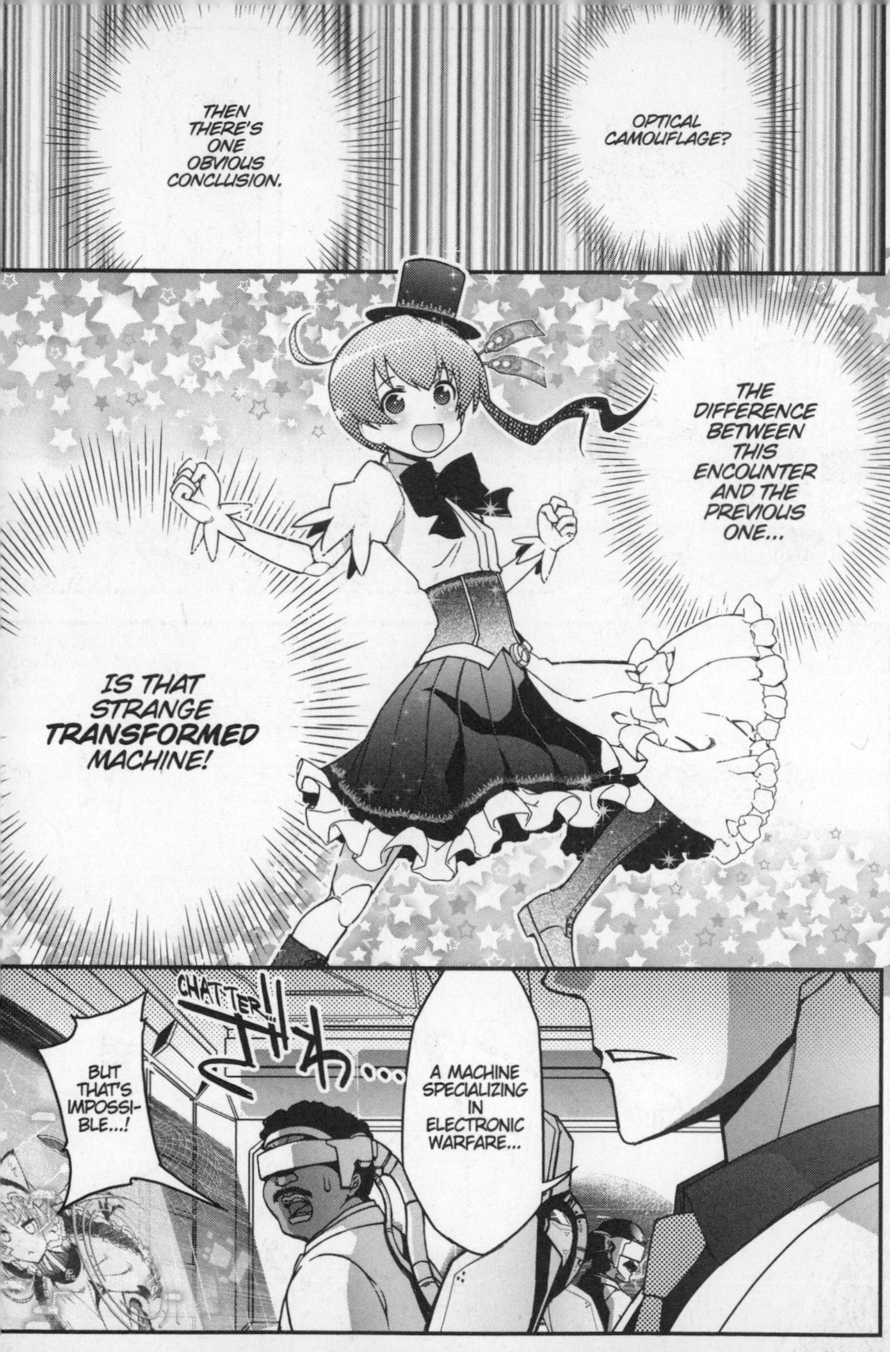
OPTICAL CAMOUFLAGE?
THEN THERE'S ONE OBVIOUS CONCLUSION.
THE DIFFERENCE BETWEEN THIS ENCOUNTER AND THE PREVIOUS ONE...
IS THAT STRANGE TRANSFORMED MACHINE!
A MACHINE SPECIALIZING IN ELECTRONIC WARFARE...
...
CHATTER!!
BUT THAT'S IMPOSSI-BLE...!

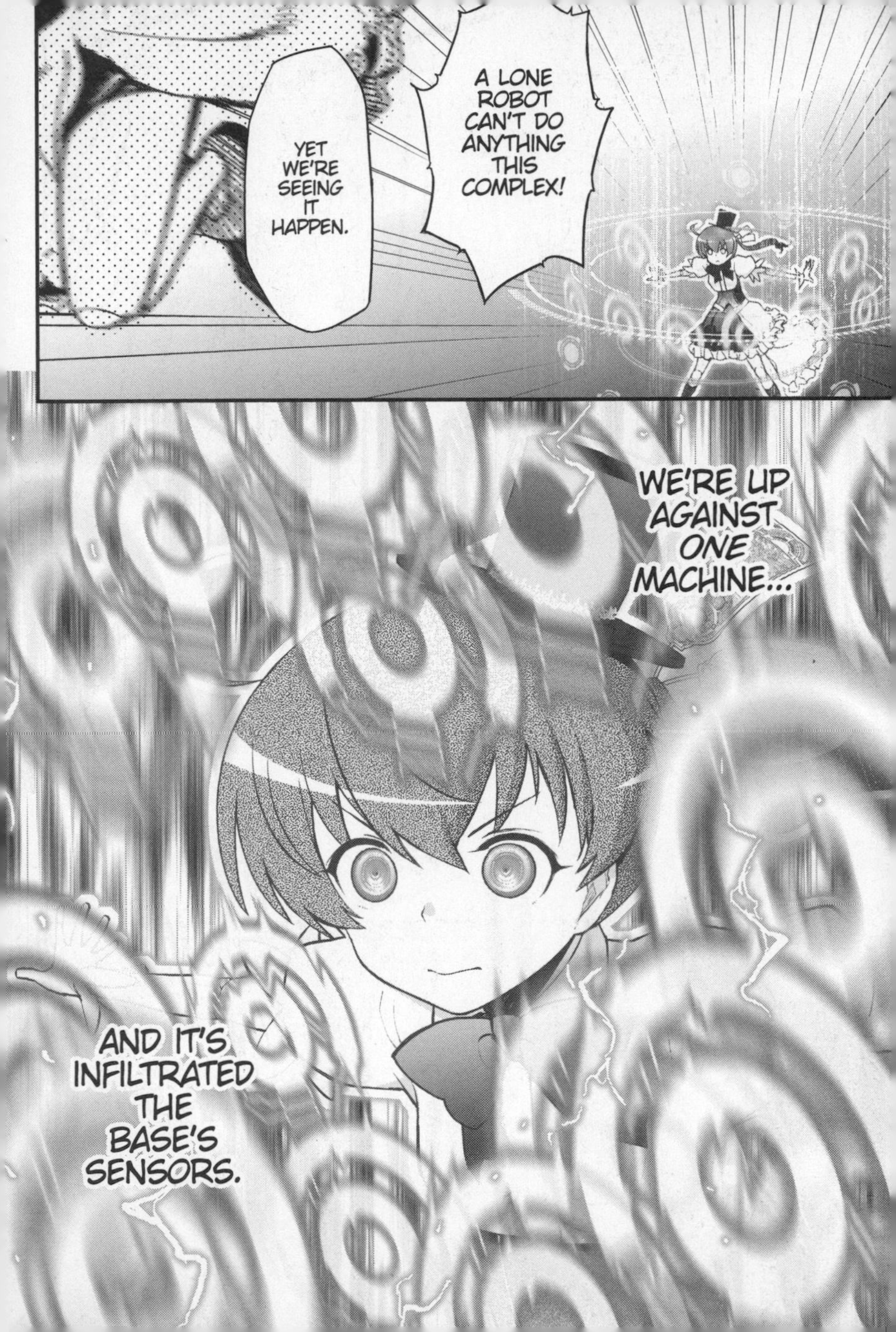
A LONE ROBOT CAN'T DO ANYTHING THIS COMPLEX!
YET WE'RE SEEING IT HAPPEN.
WE'RE UP AGAINST ONE MACHINE...
AND IT'S INFILTRATED THE BASE'S SENSORS.

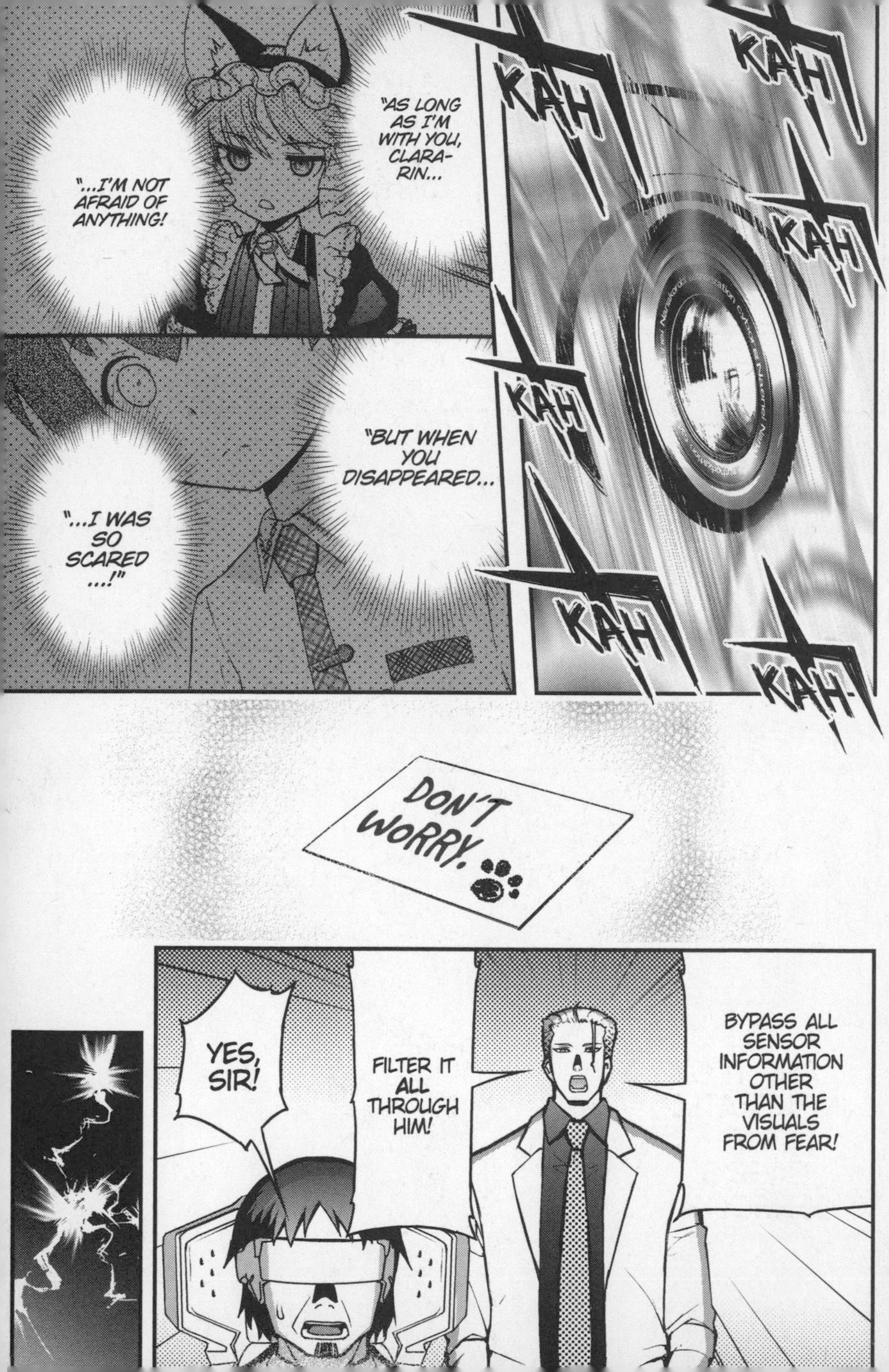
KAH
KAH
KAH
KAH
KAH
KAH
KAH
"AS LONG AS I'M WITH YOU, CLARA-RIN...
"...I'M NOT AFRAID OF ANYTHING!
"BUT WHEN YOU DISAPPEARED...
"...I WAS SO SCARED ...!"
DON'T WORRY.
BYPASS ALL SENSOR INFORMATION OTHER THAN THE VISUALS FROM FEAR!
FILTER IT ALL THROUGH HIM!
YES, SIR!

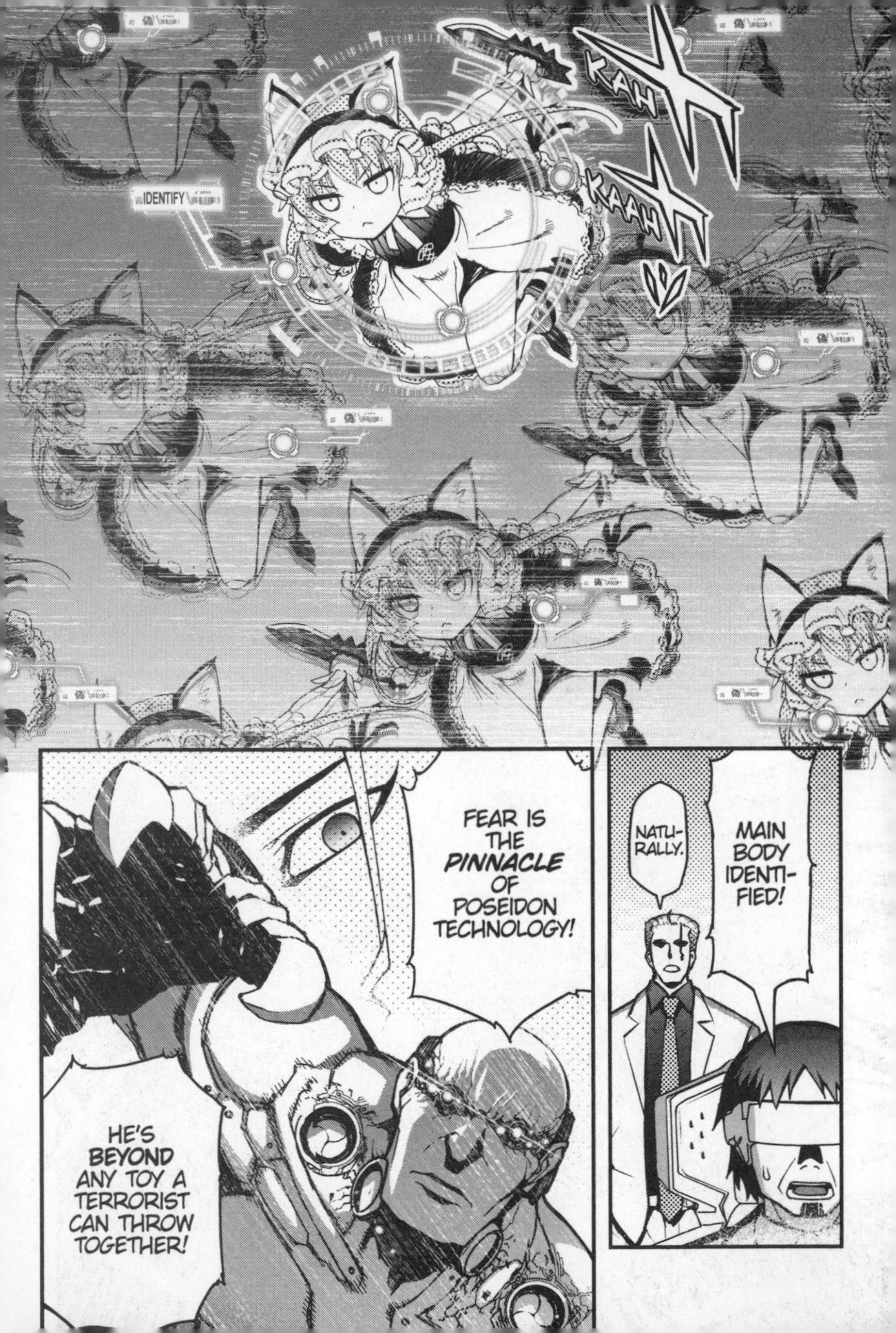

KAAH
KAAH
IDENTIFY
MAIN BODY IDENTIFIED!
NATURALLY.
FEAR IS THE PINNACLE OF POSEIDON TECHNOLOGY!
HE'S BEYOND ANY TOY A TERRORIST CAN THROW TOGETHER!

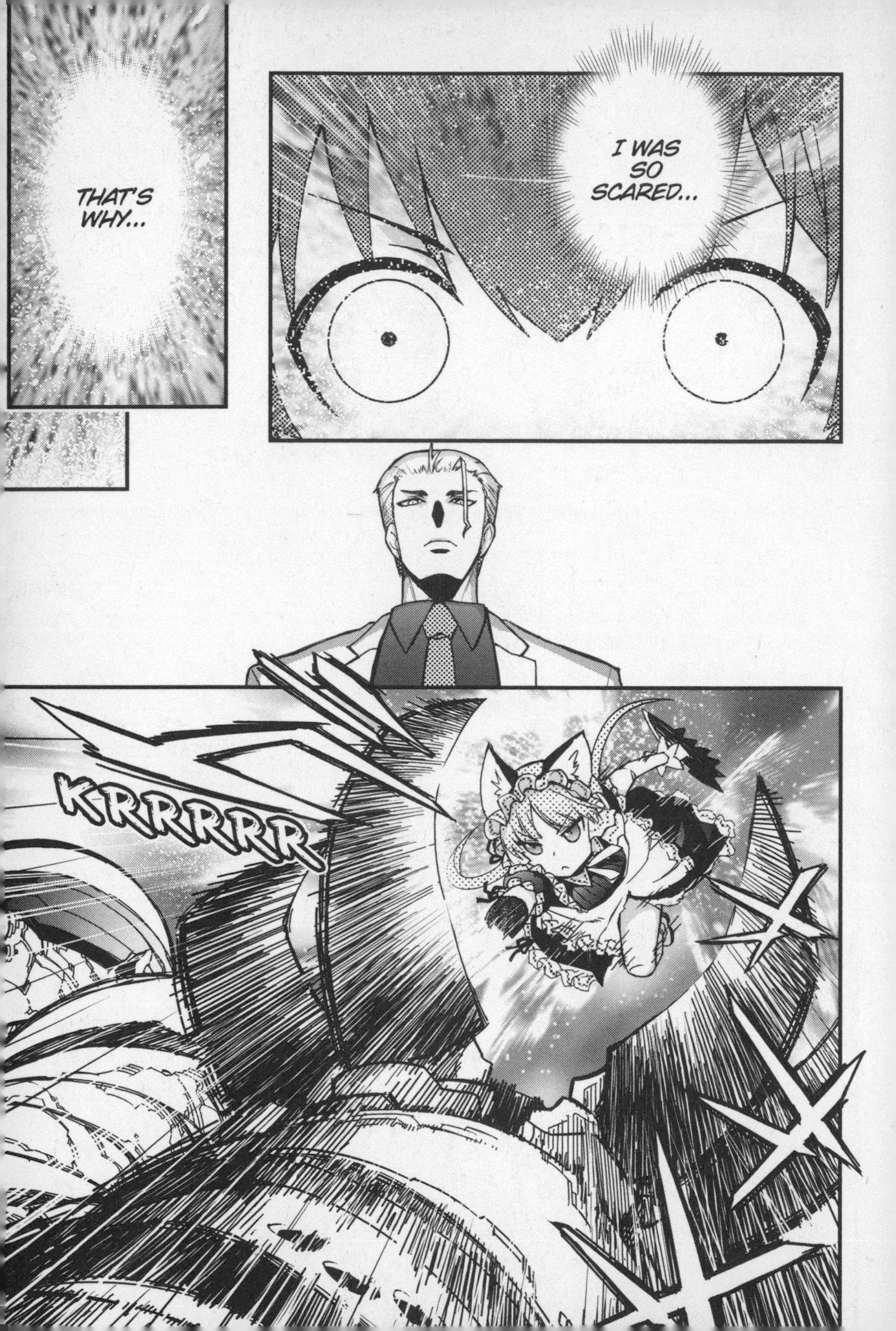
I WAS SO SCARED...
THAT'S WHY...
KRRRRRR

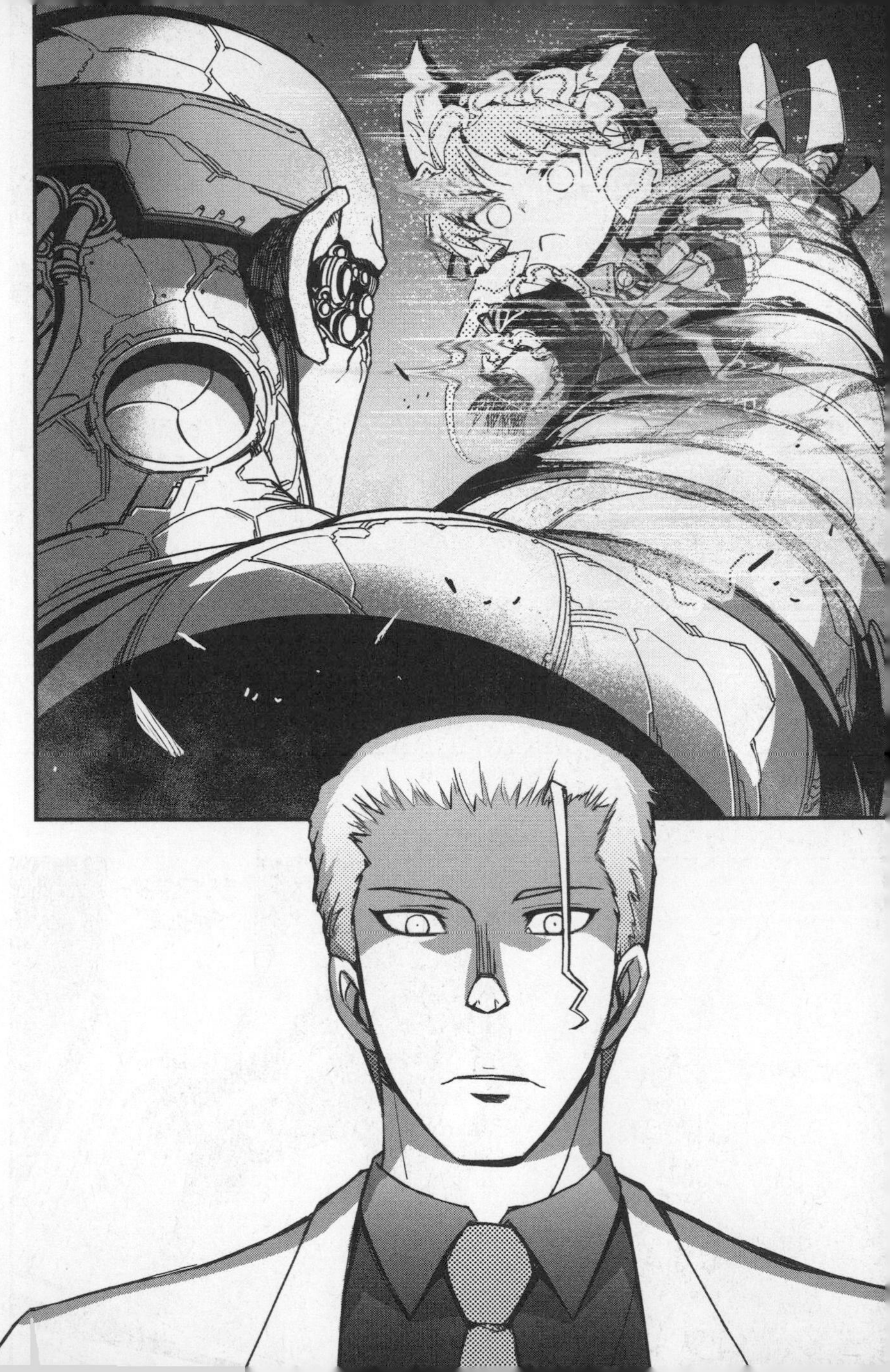

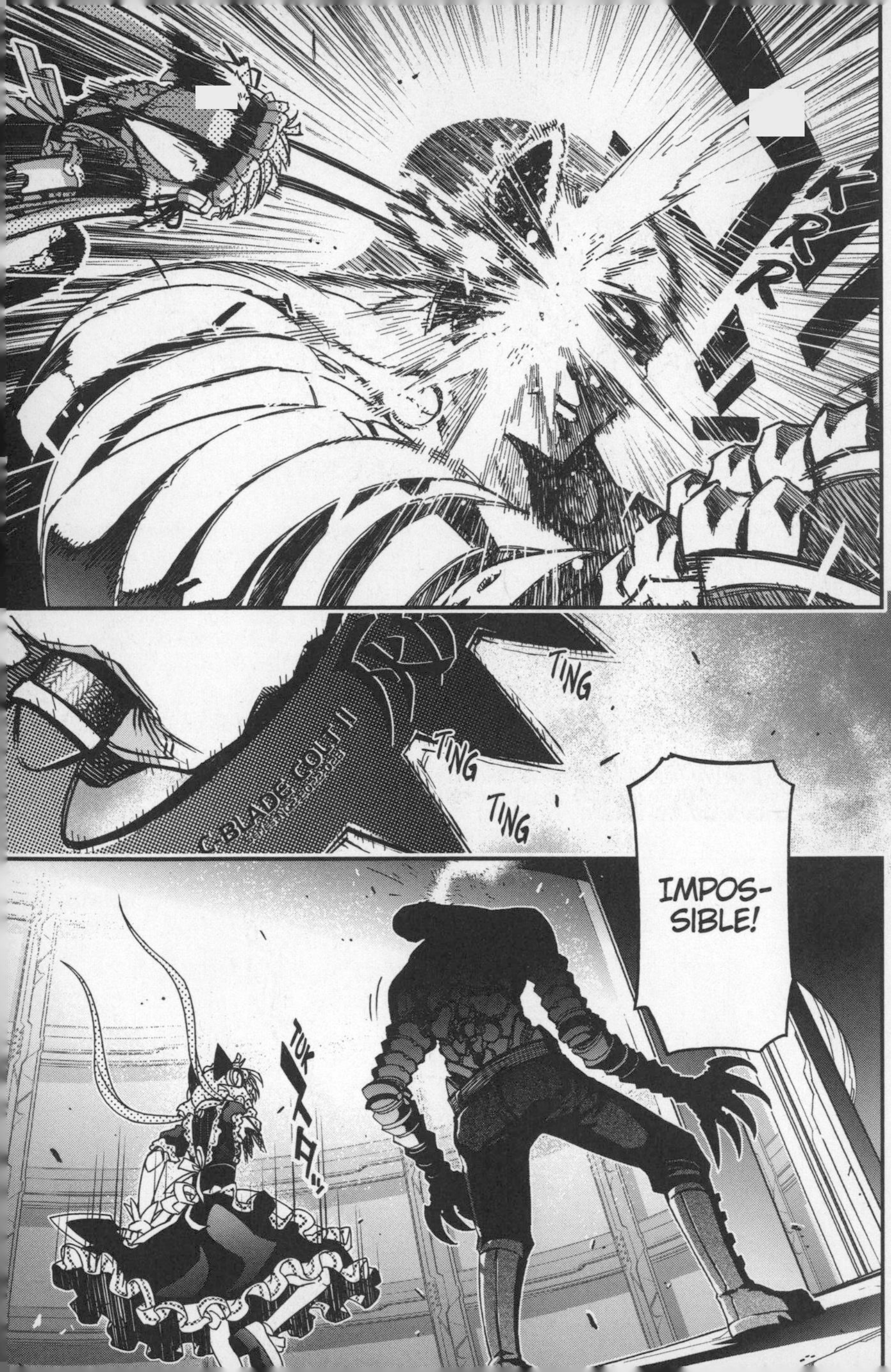
KRRR
TING
TING
TING
C-BLADE COLT II
IMPOS-
SIBLE!
TUK

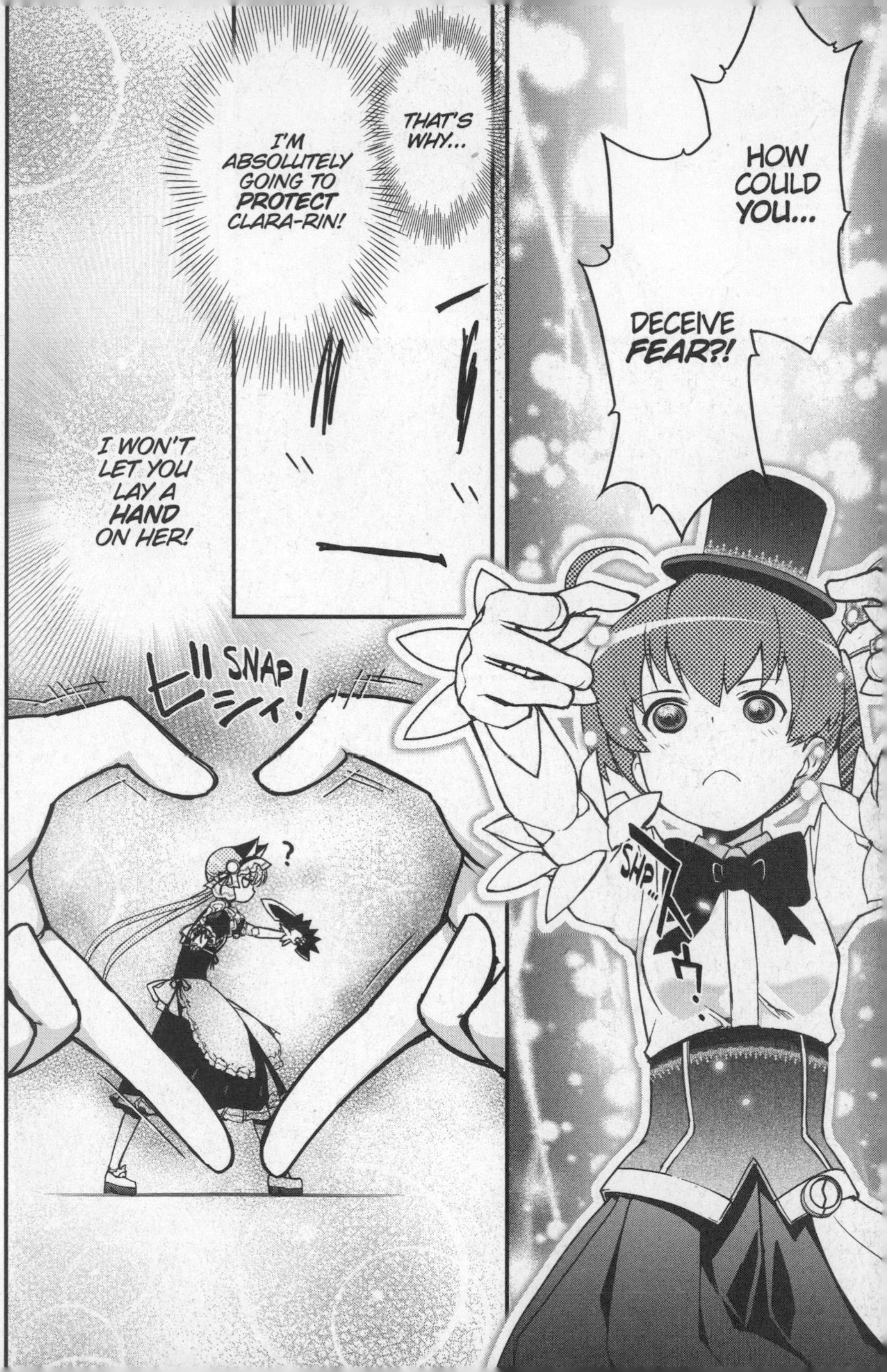
HOW COULD YOU...
DECEIVE FEAR?!
SHP...!
THAT'S WHY...
I'M ABSOLUTELY GOING TO PROTECT CLARA-RIN!
I WON'T LET YOU LAY A HAND ON HER!
SNAP!
?

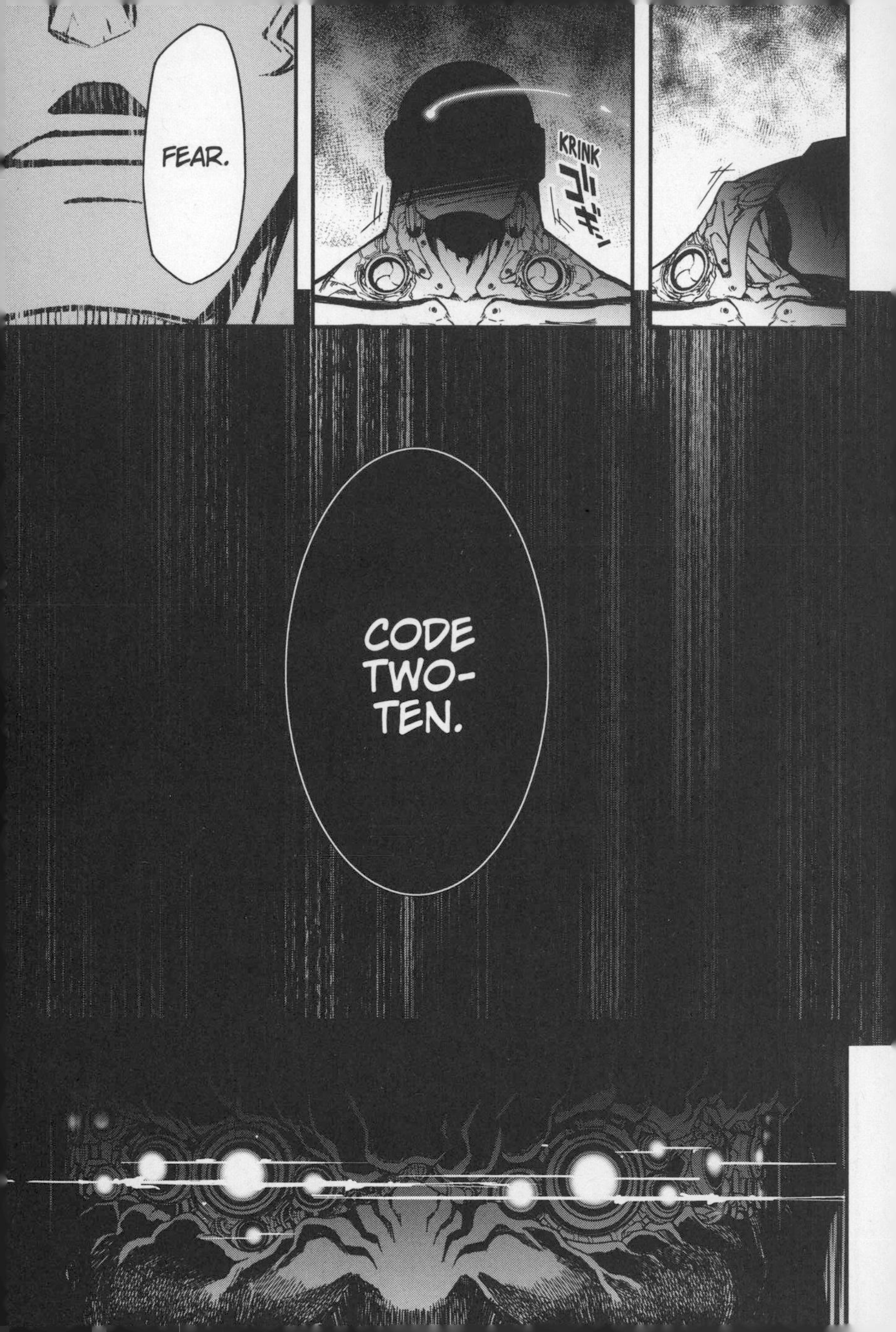
KRINK
FEAR.
CODE TWO-TEN.

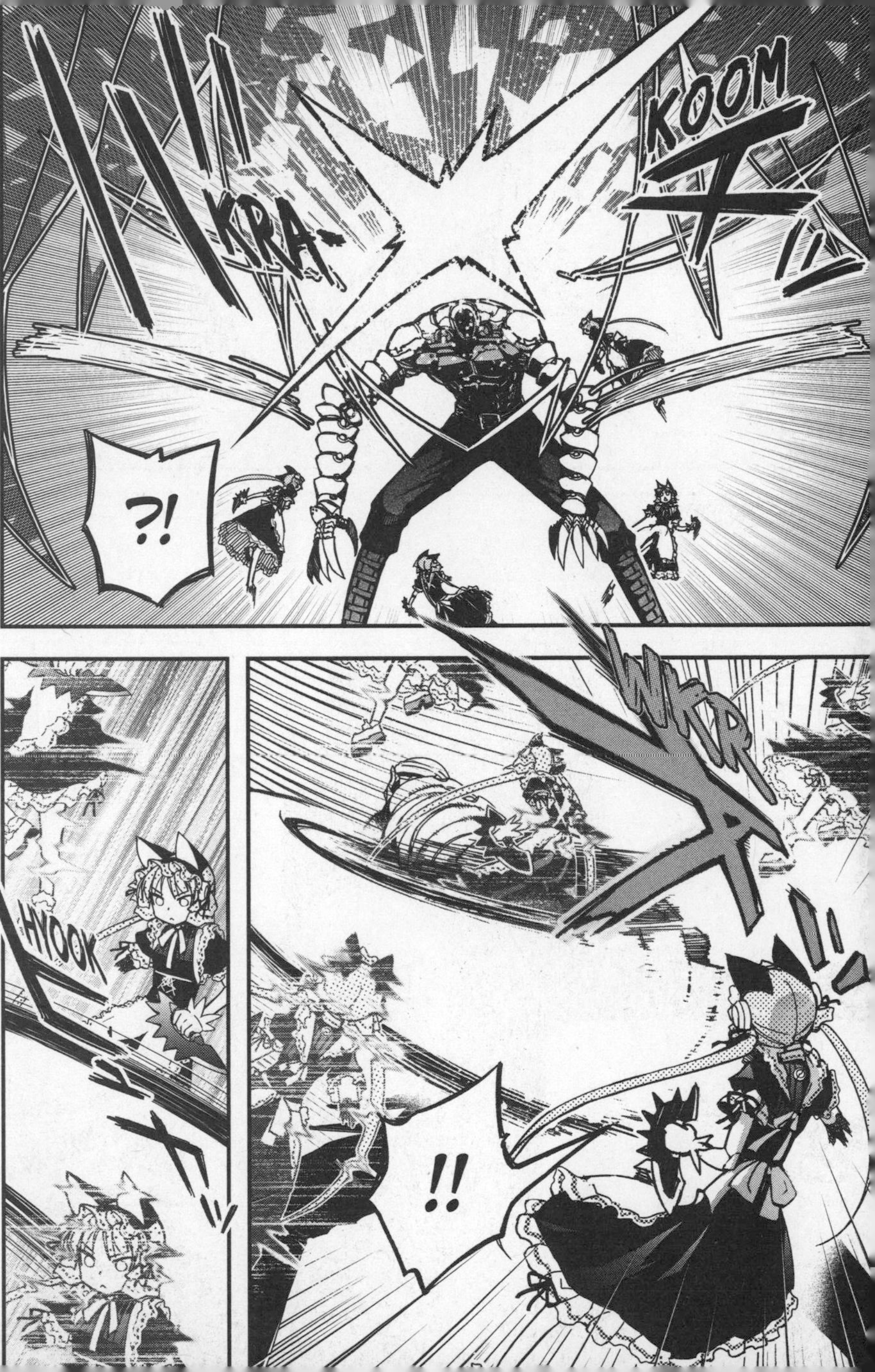
KOOM
KRA-
?!
WKRR
!!
HYOOK
!!

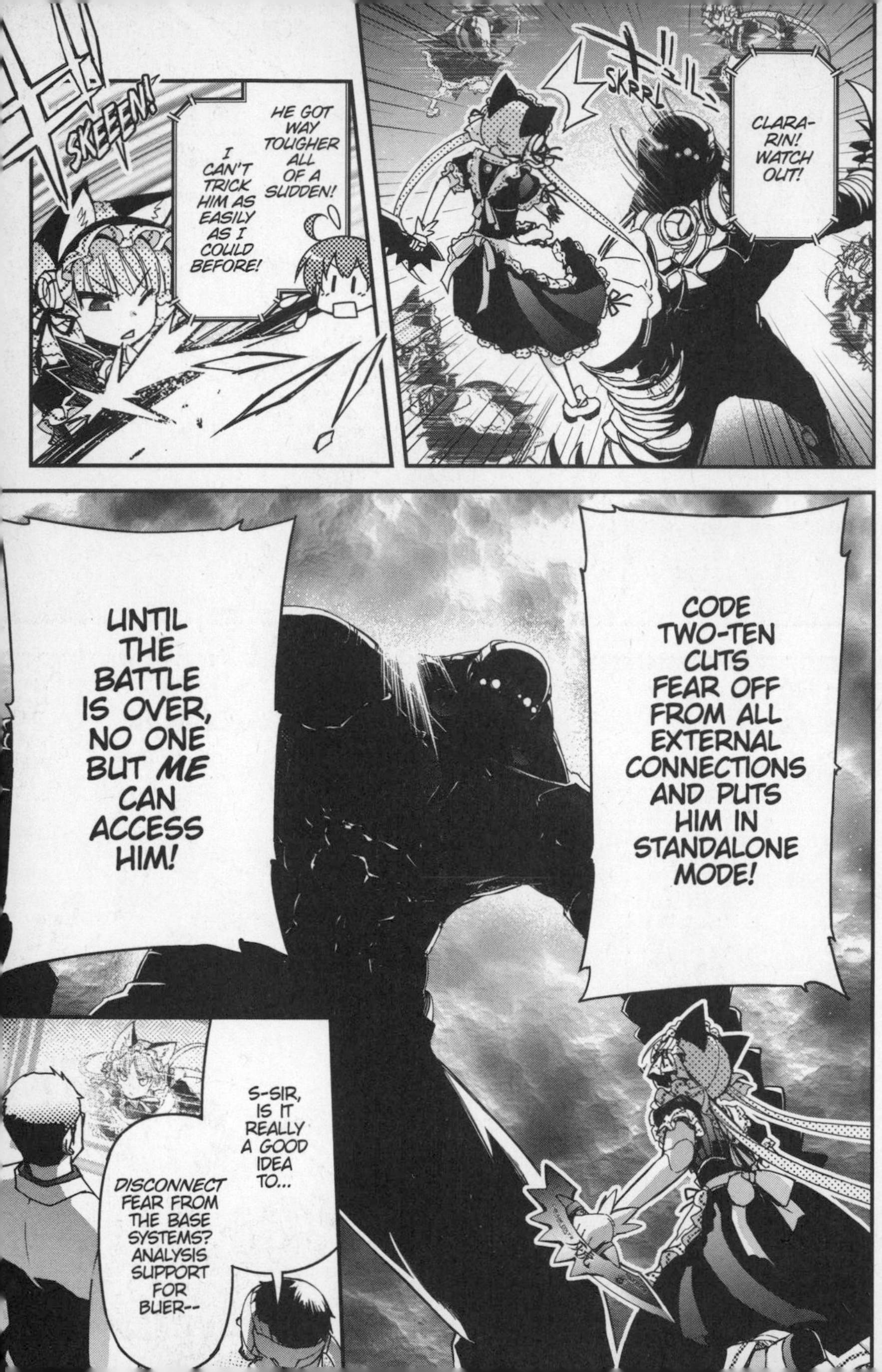
CLARA-RIN! WATCH OUT!
SKRRL
HE GOT WAY TOUGHER ALL OF A SUDDEN!
I CAN'T TRICK HIM AS EASILY AS I COULD BEFORE!
SKEEEN!
CODE TWO-TEN CUTS FEAR OFF FROM ALL EXTERNAL CONNECTIONS AND PUTS HIM IN STANDALONE MODE!
UNTIL THE BATTLE IS OVER, NO ONE BUT *ME* CAN ACCESS HIM!
S-SIR, IS IT REALLY A GOOD IDEA TO...
DISCONNECT FEAR FROM THE BASE SYSTEMS? ANALYSIS SUPPORT FOR BUER--

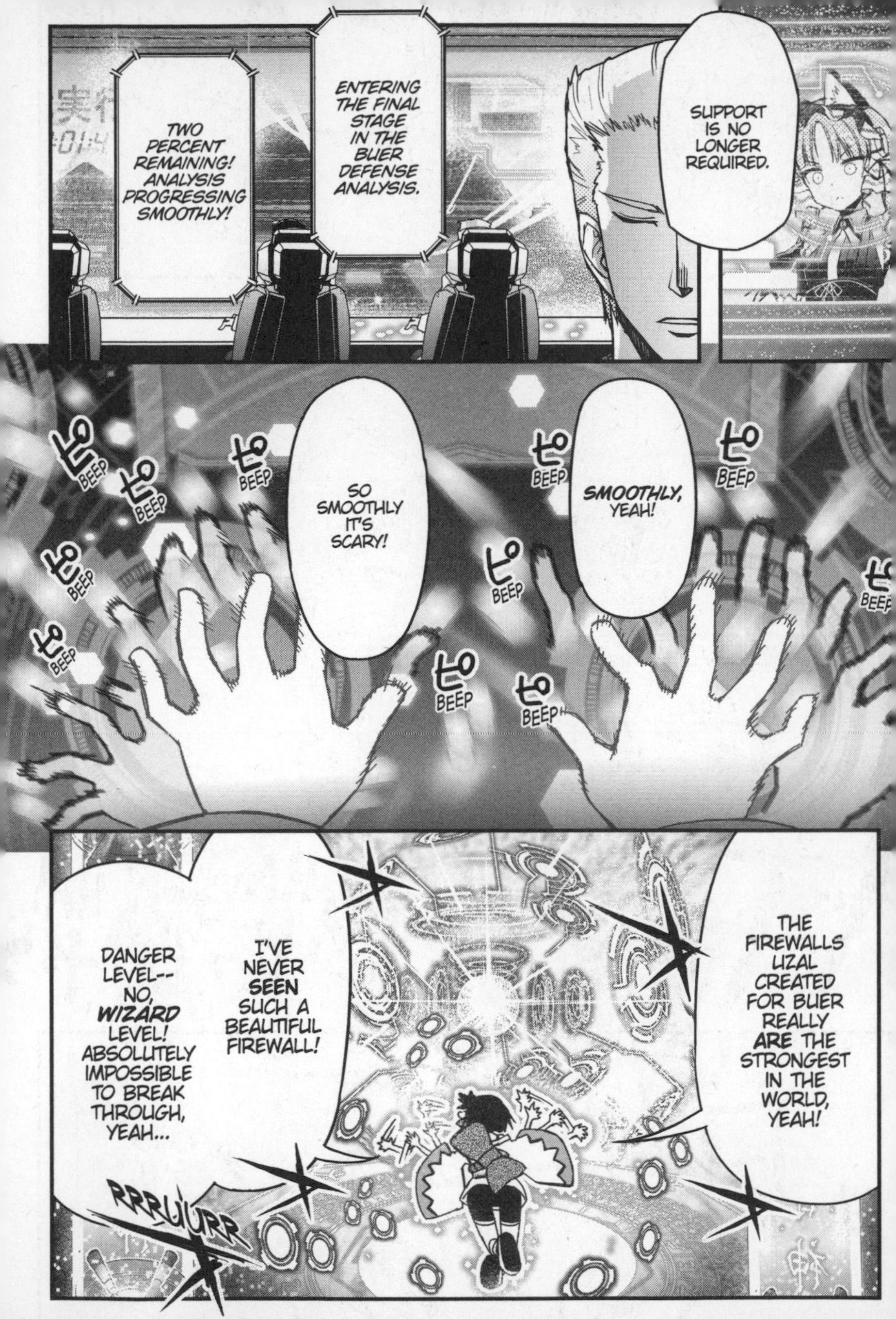

SUPPORT IS NO LONGER REQUIRED.
ENTERING THE FINAL STAGE IN THE BUER DEFENSE ANALYSIS.
TWO PERCENT REMAINING! ANALYSIS PROGRESSING SMOOTHLY!
ぴ BEEP
ぴ BEEP
SMOOTHLY, YEAH!
ぴ BEEP
ぴ BEEP
ぴ BEEP
SO SMOOTHLY IT'S SCARY!
ぴ BEEP
ぴ BEEP
ぴ BEEP
ぴ BEEP
ぴ BEEP
THE FIREWALLS UZAL CREATED FOR BUER REALLY ARE THE STRONGEST IN THE WORLD, YEAH!
I'VE NEVER SEEN SUCH A BEAUTIFUL FIREWALL!
DANGER LEVEL-- NO, WIZARD LEVEL! ABSOLUTELY IMPOSSIBLE TO BREAK THROUGH, YEAH...
RRRUUURR

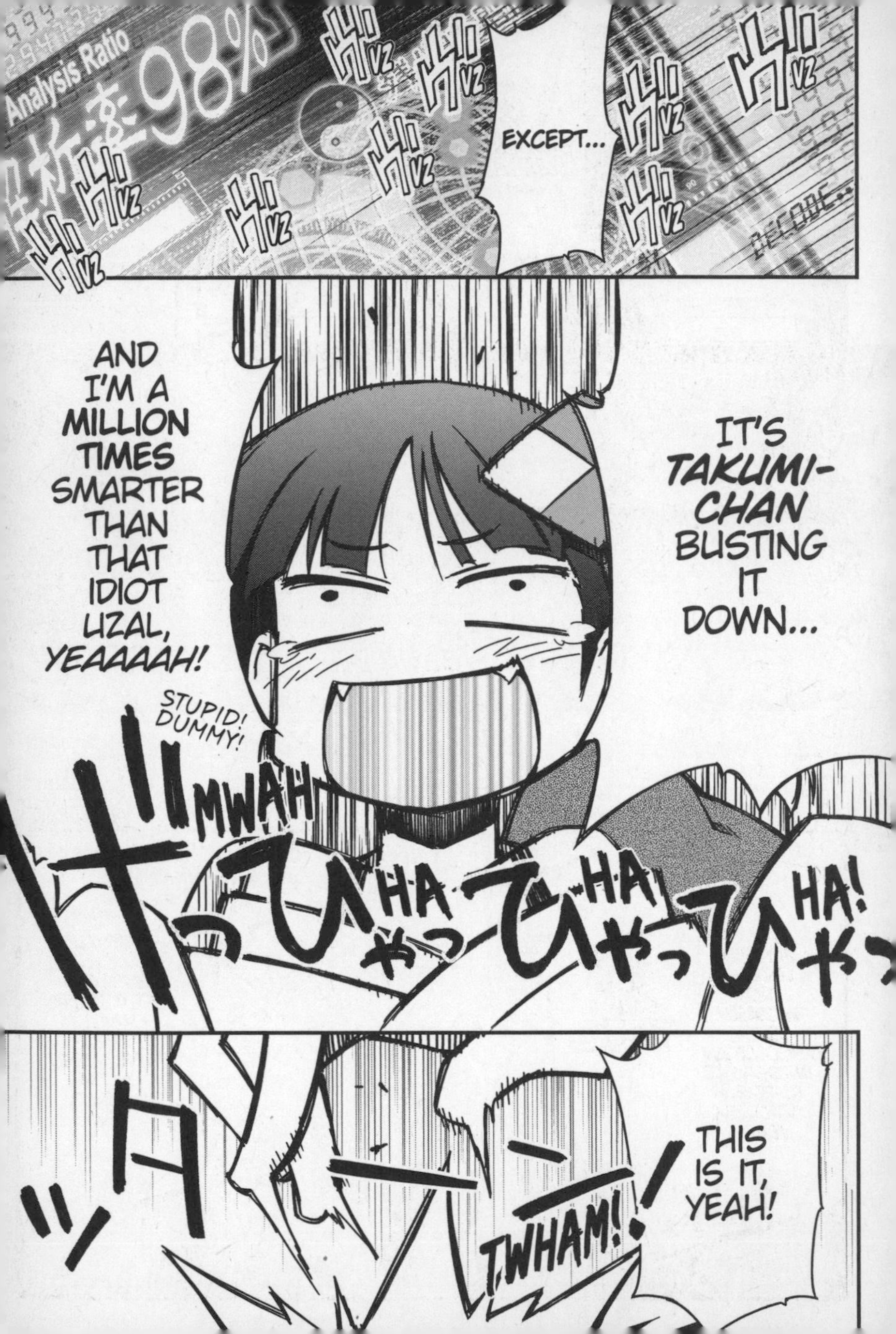
Analysis Ratio
98%
EXCEPT...
DECODE..
IT'S *TAKUMI-CHAN* BUSTING IT DOWN...
AND I'M A MILLION TIMES SMARTER THAN THAT IDIOT UZAL, *YEAAAAH!*
STUPID! DUMMY!
MWAH HA HA HA!
THIS IS IT, YEAH!
TWHAM!

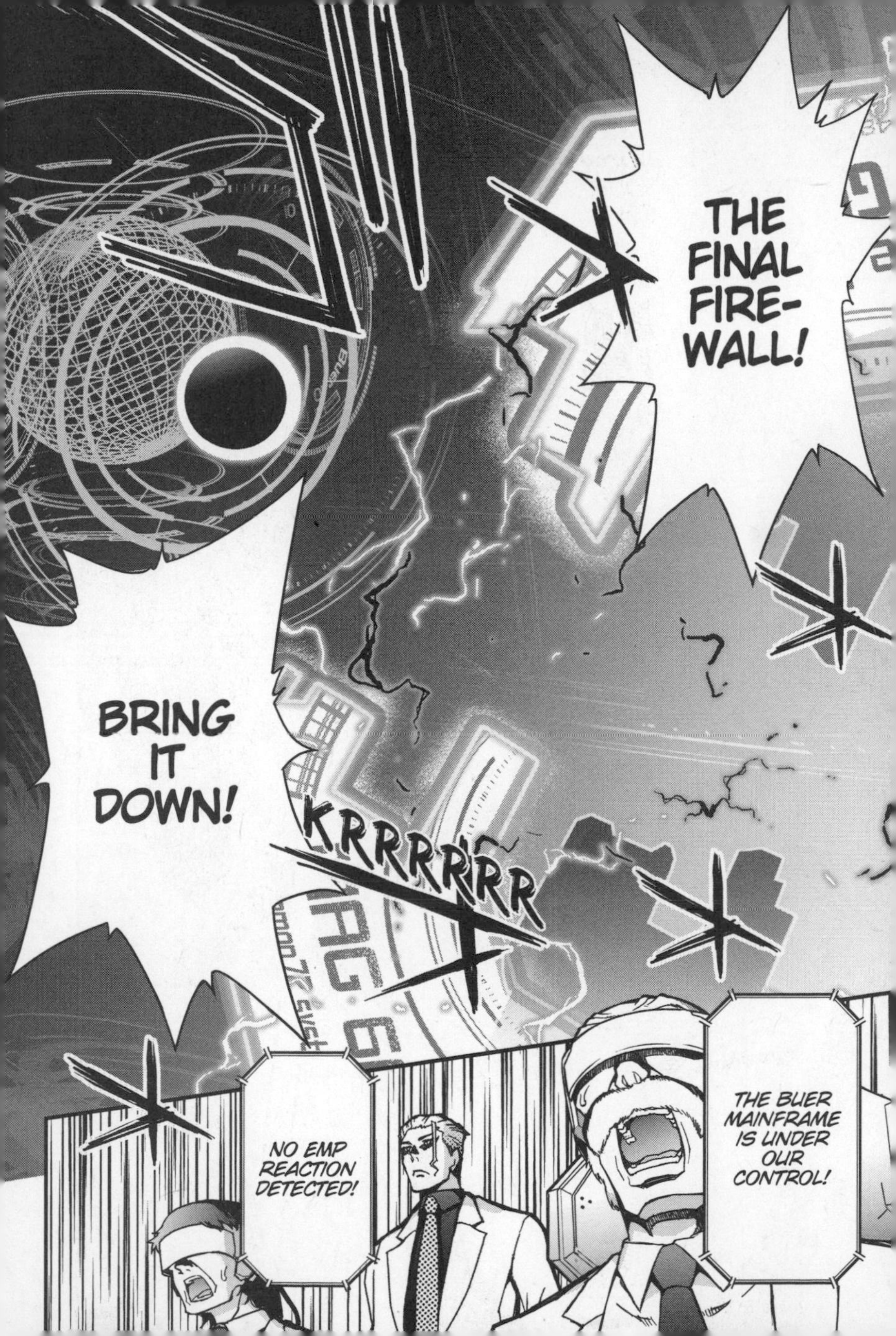
THE FINAL FIRE-WALL!
BRING IT DOWN!
KRRRRRRR
THE BUER MAINFRAME IS UNDER OUR CONTROL!
NO EMP REACTION DETECTED!

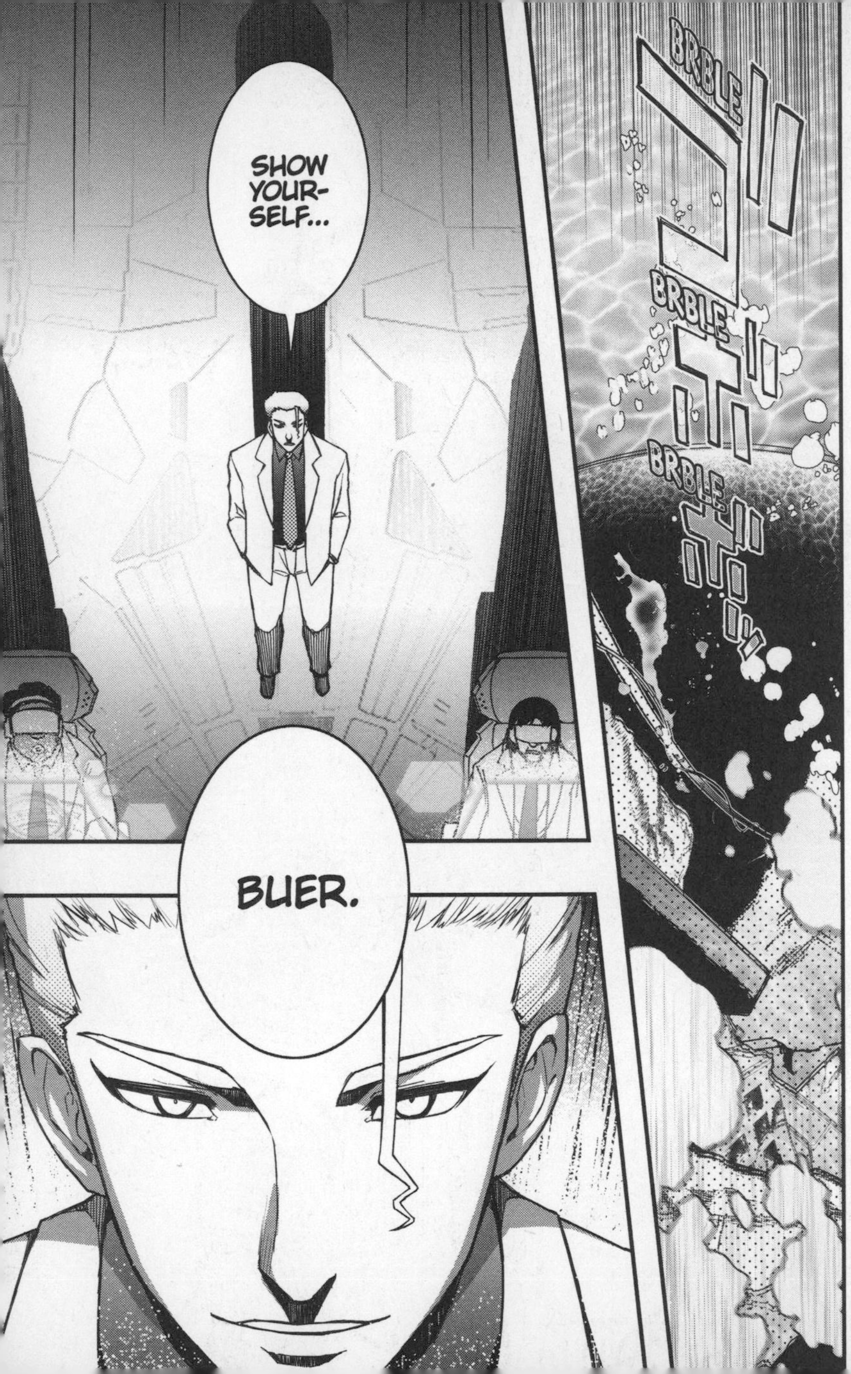
BRBLE
BRBLE
BRBLE
SHOW YOUR-SELF...
BUER.

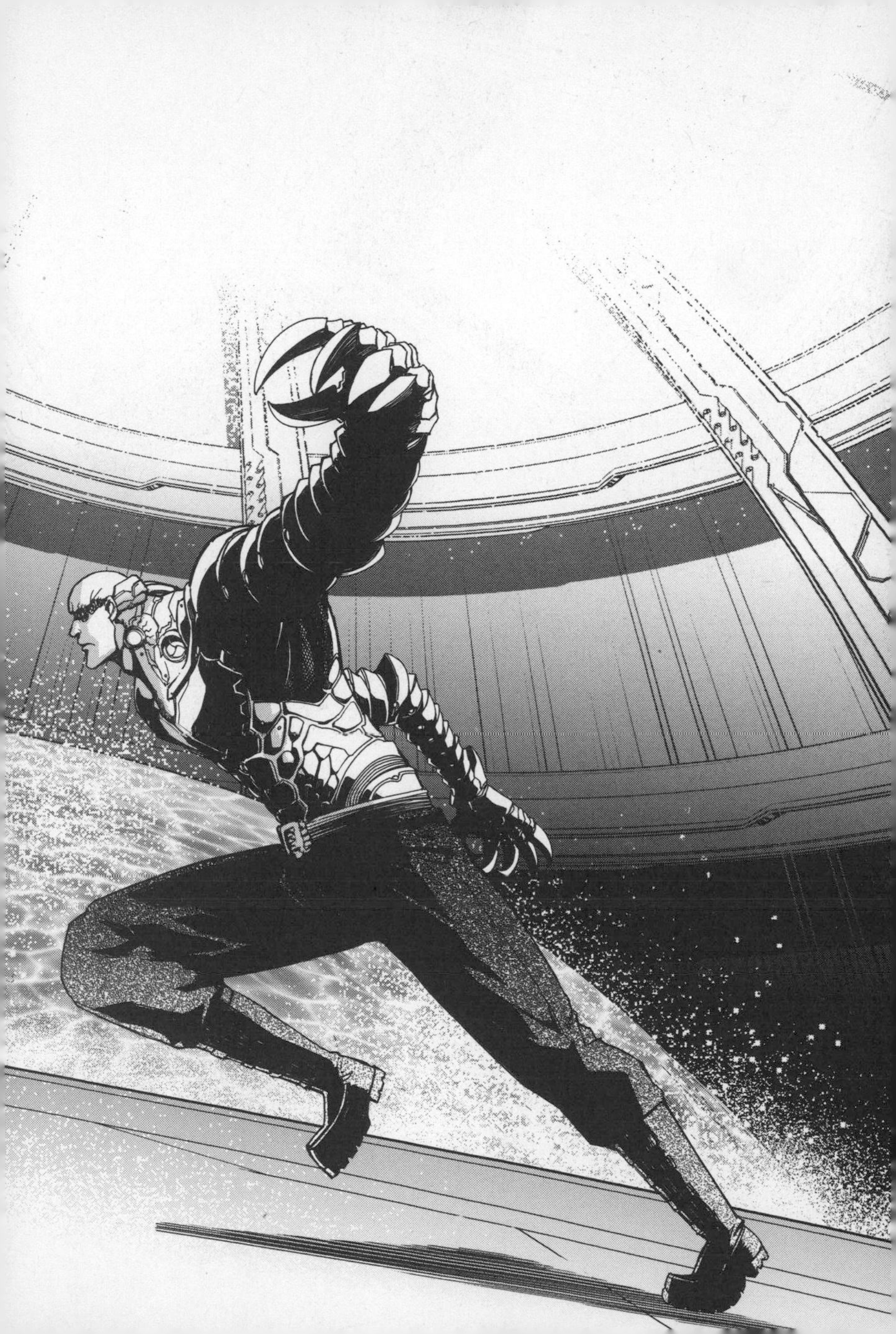

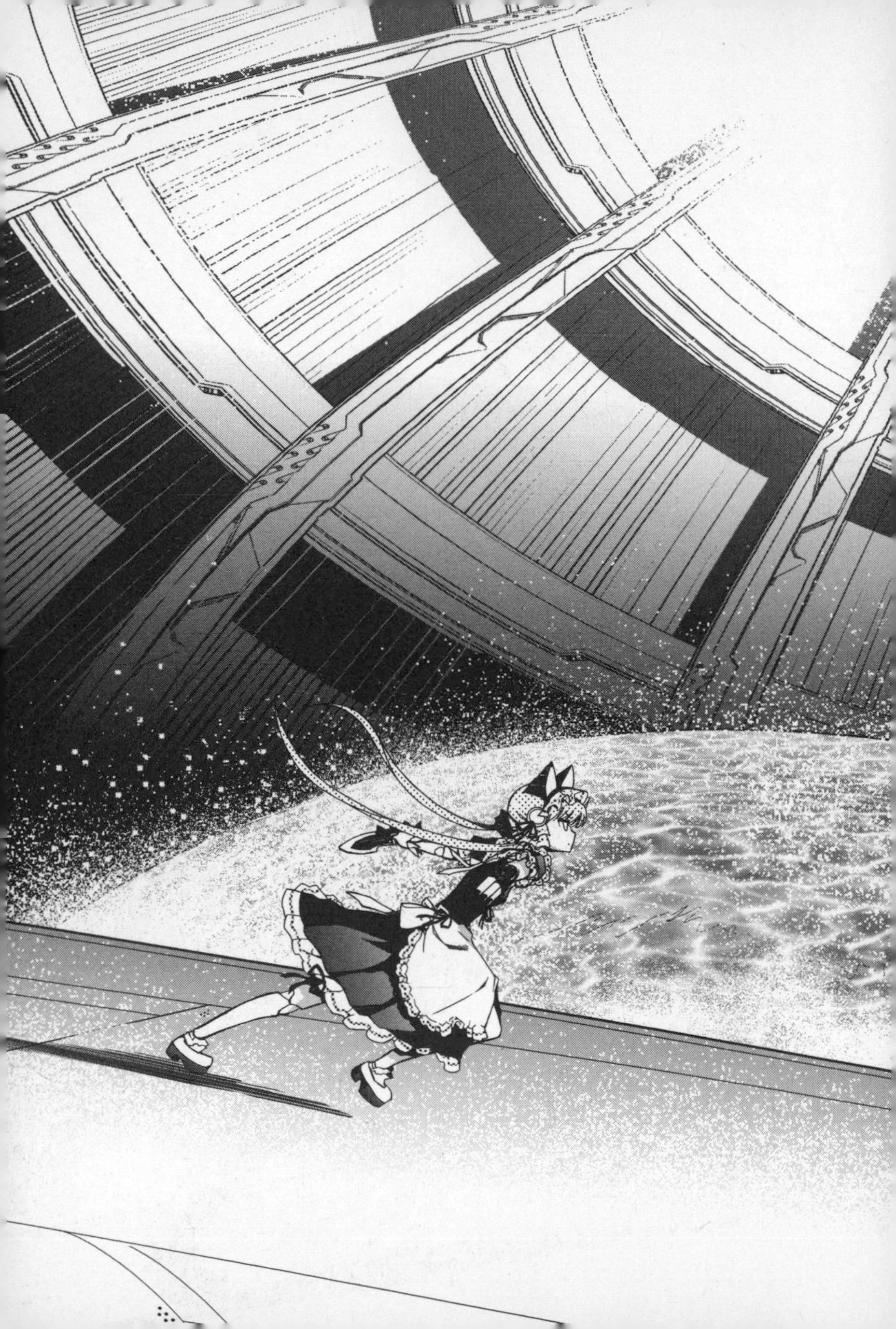

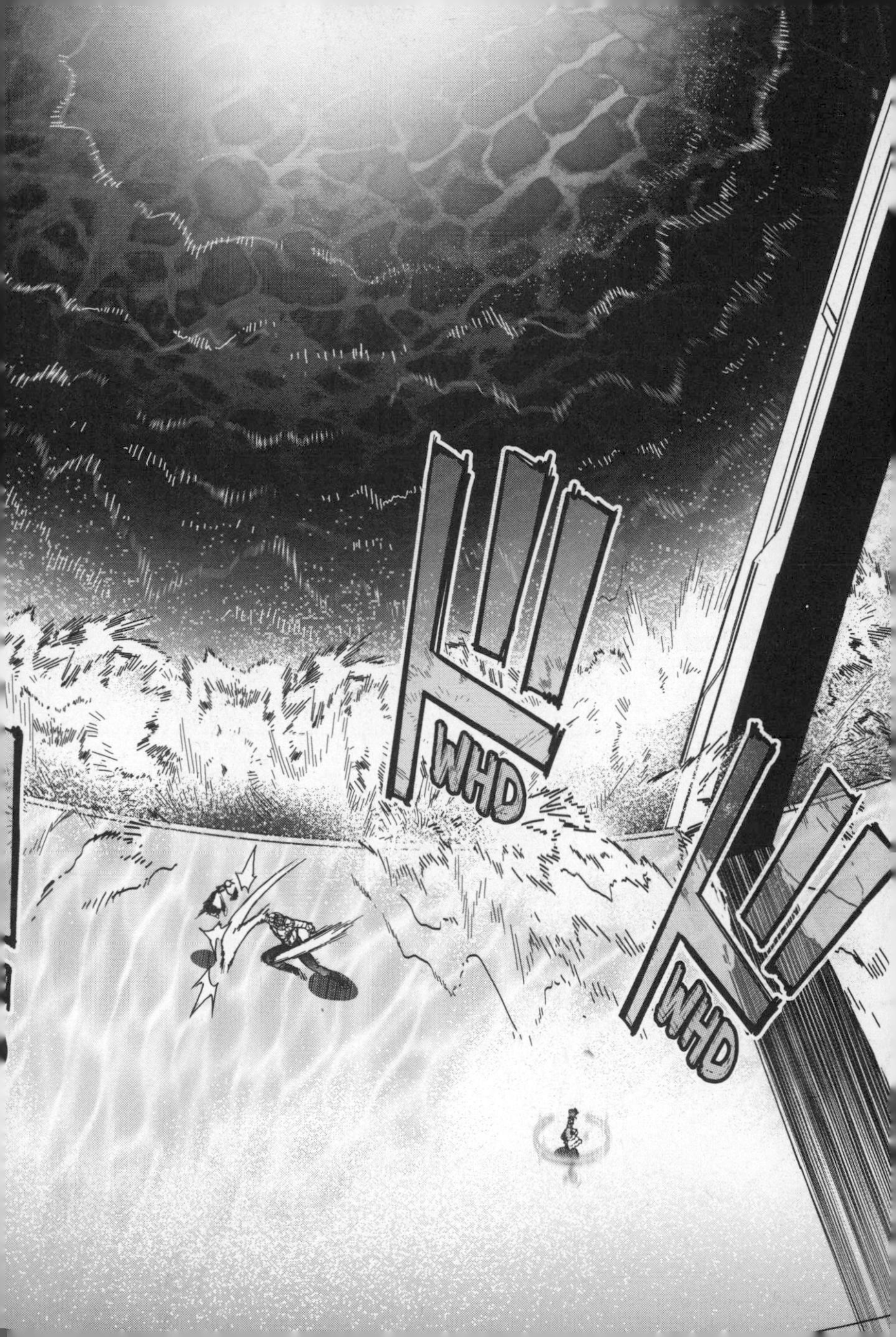
WHD
WHD

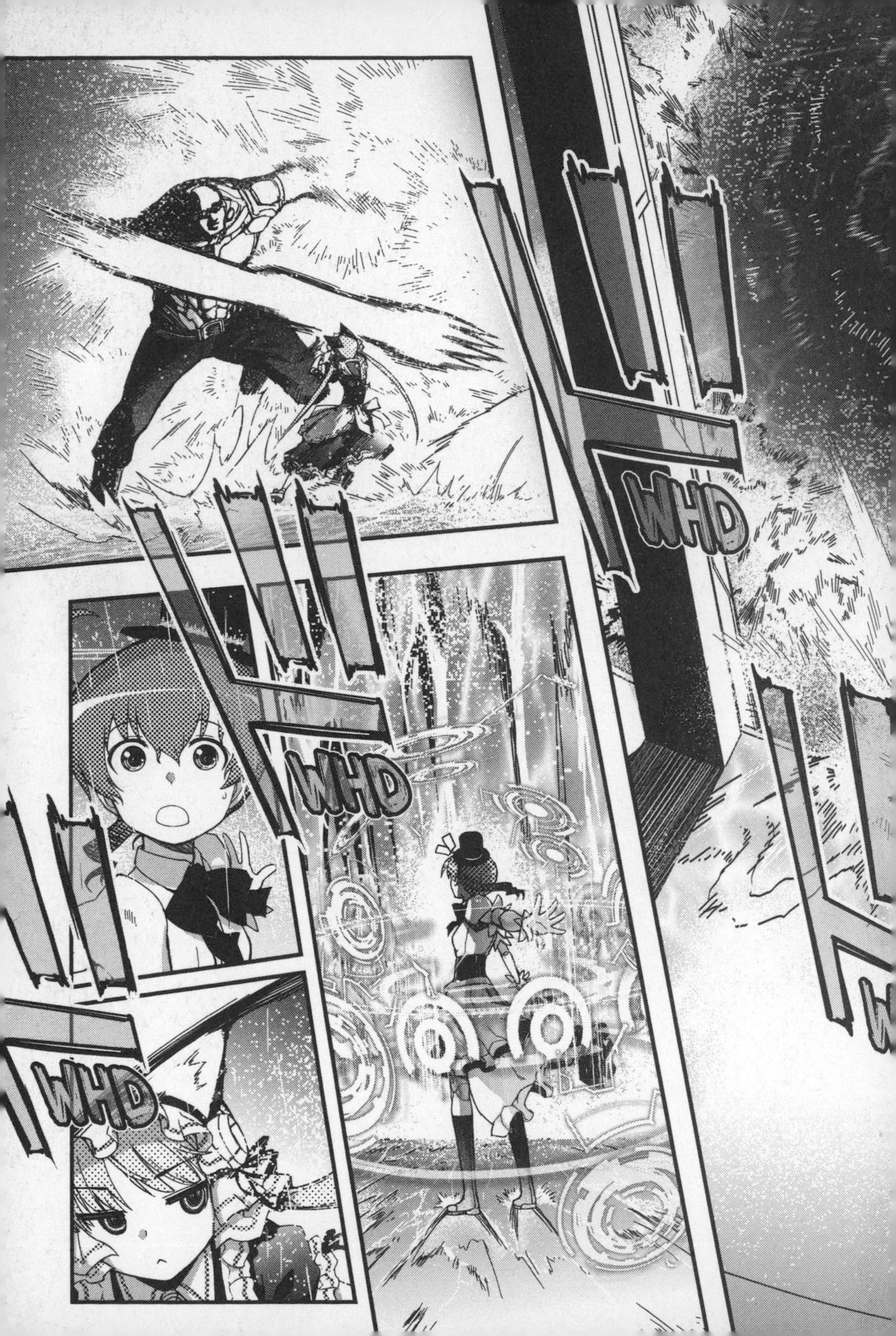
WHD
WHD
WHD

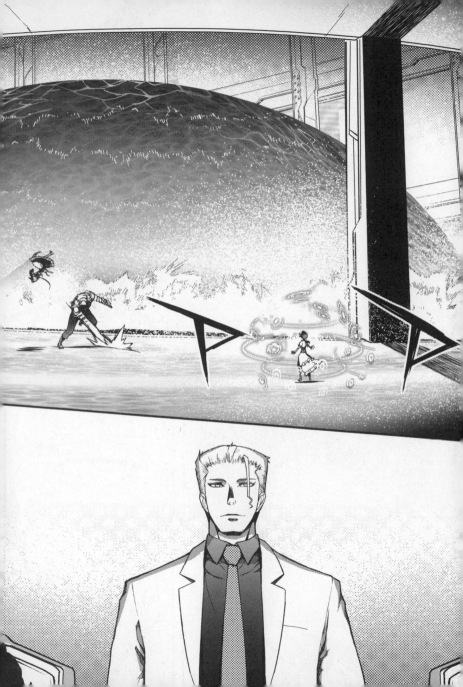

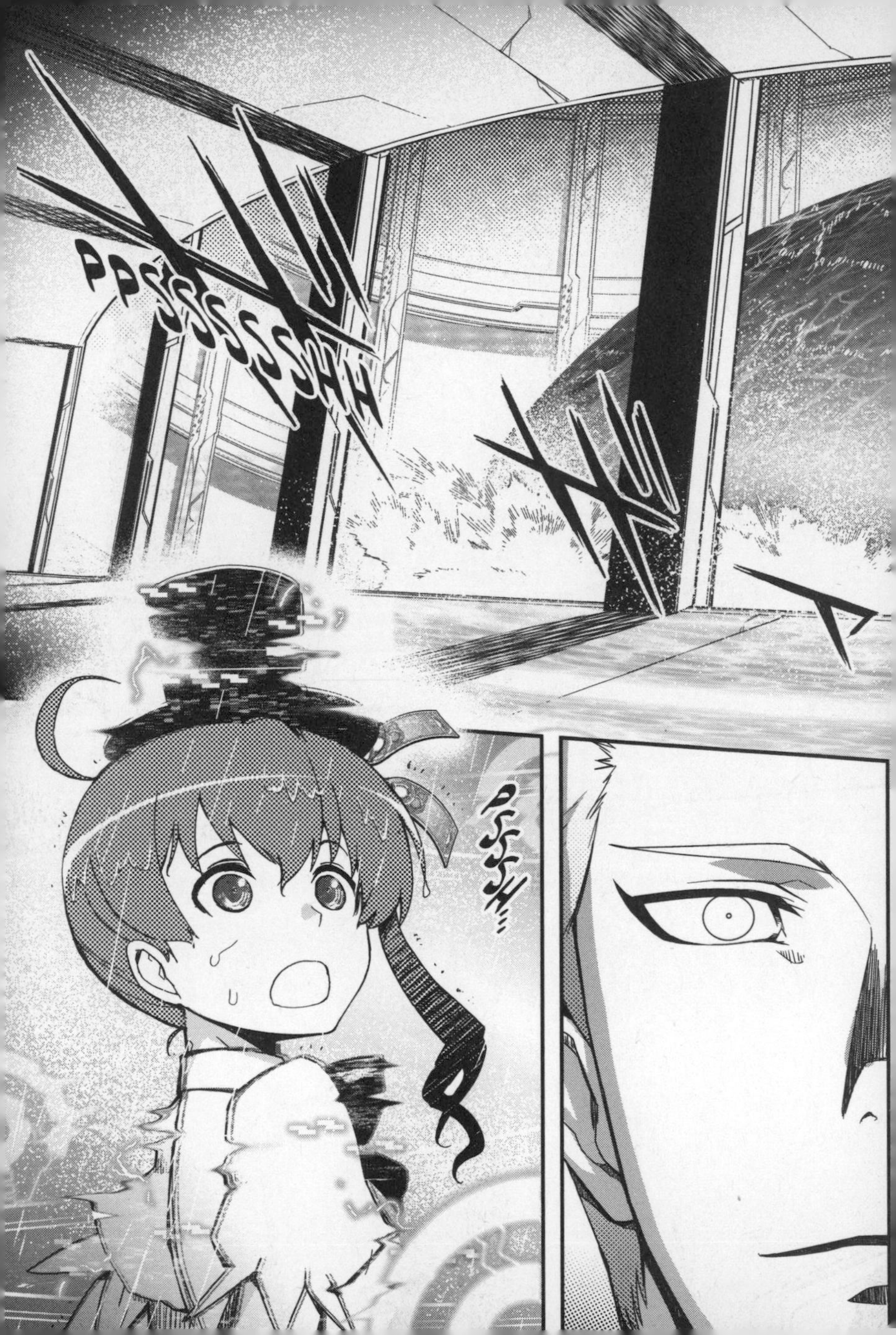
PPSSSSSSHH
PSSSH...

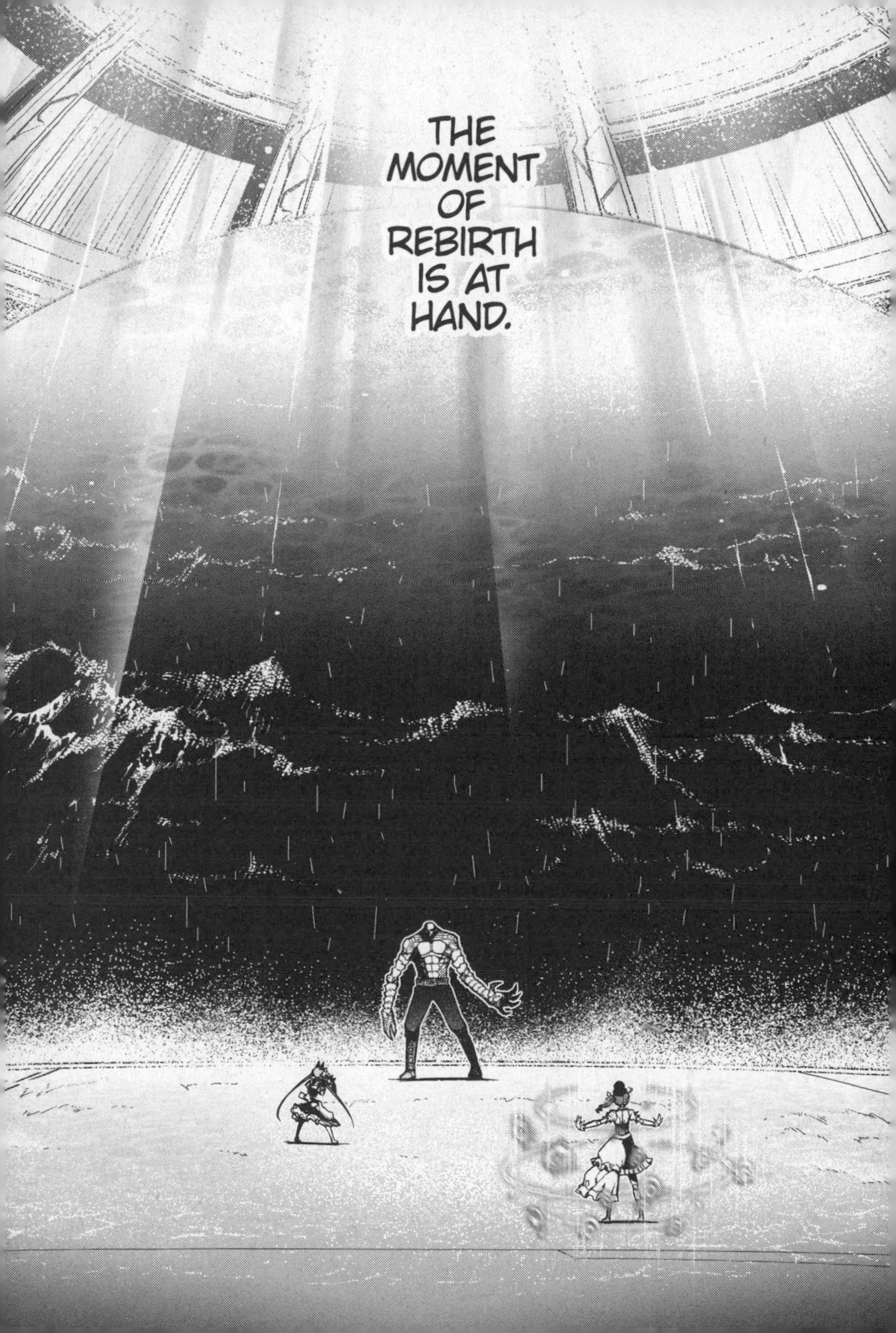
THE MOMENT OF REBIRTH IS AT HAND.

GHOST URN

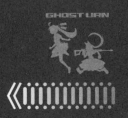

GHOST URN

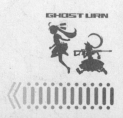

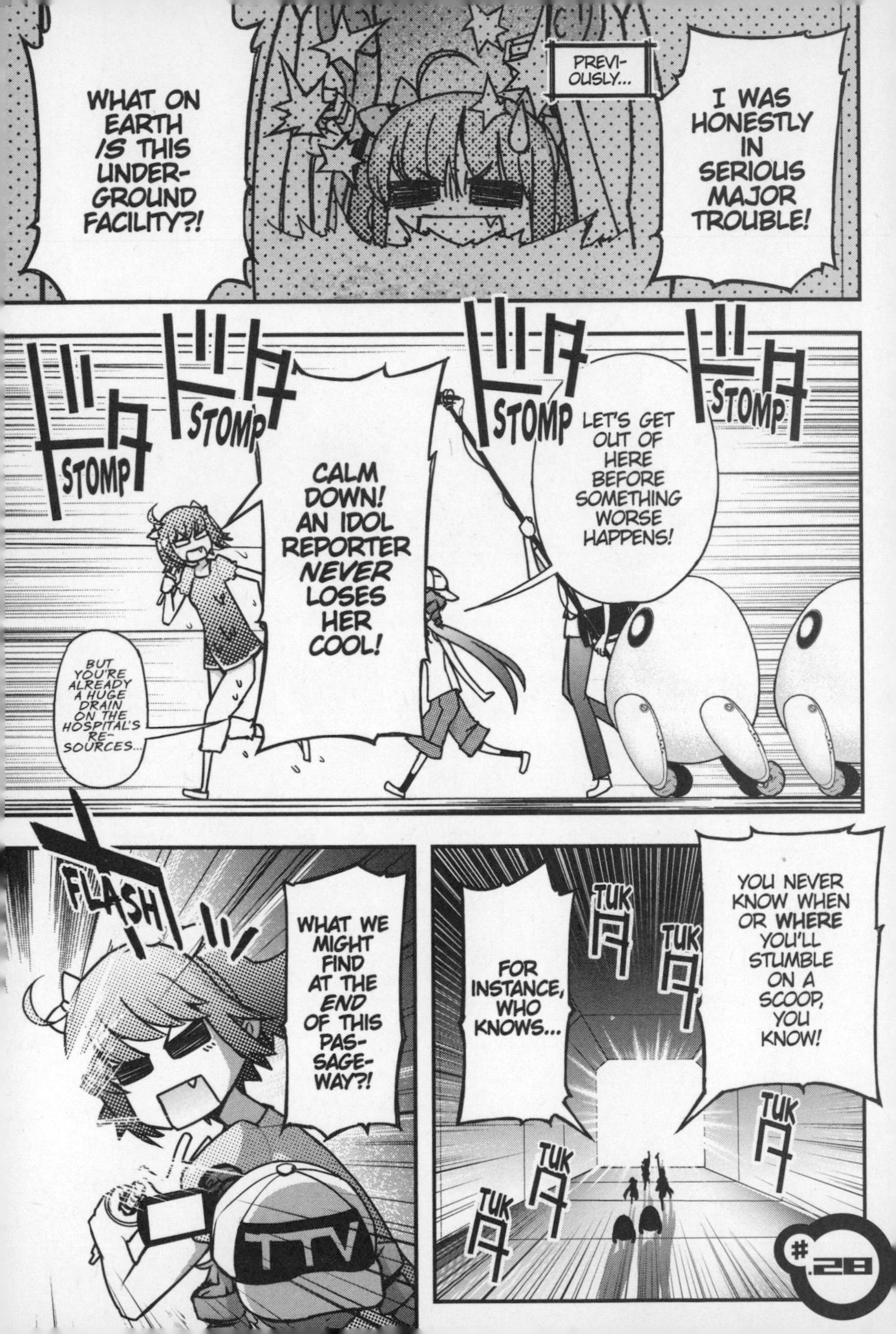
PREVI-OUSLY...
I WAS HONESTLY IN SERIOUS MAJOR TROUBLE!
WHAT ON EARTH IS THIS UNDER-GROUND FACILITY?!
STOMP STOMP STOMP STOMP
LET'S GET OUT OF HERE BEFORE SOMETHING WORSE HAPPENS!
CALM DOWN! AN IDOL REPORTER NEVER LOSES HER COOL!
BUT YOU'RE ALREADY A HUGE DRAIN ON THE HOSPITAL'S RE-SOURCES...
YOU NEVER KNOW WHEN OR WHERE YOU'LL STUMBLE ON A SCOOP, YOU KNOW!
FOR INSTANCE, WHO KNOWS...
TUK TUK TUK TUK TUK
FLASH
WHAT WE MIGHT FIND AT THE END OF THIS PAS-SAGE-WAY?!
TTV
#.28

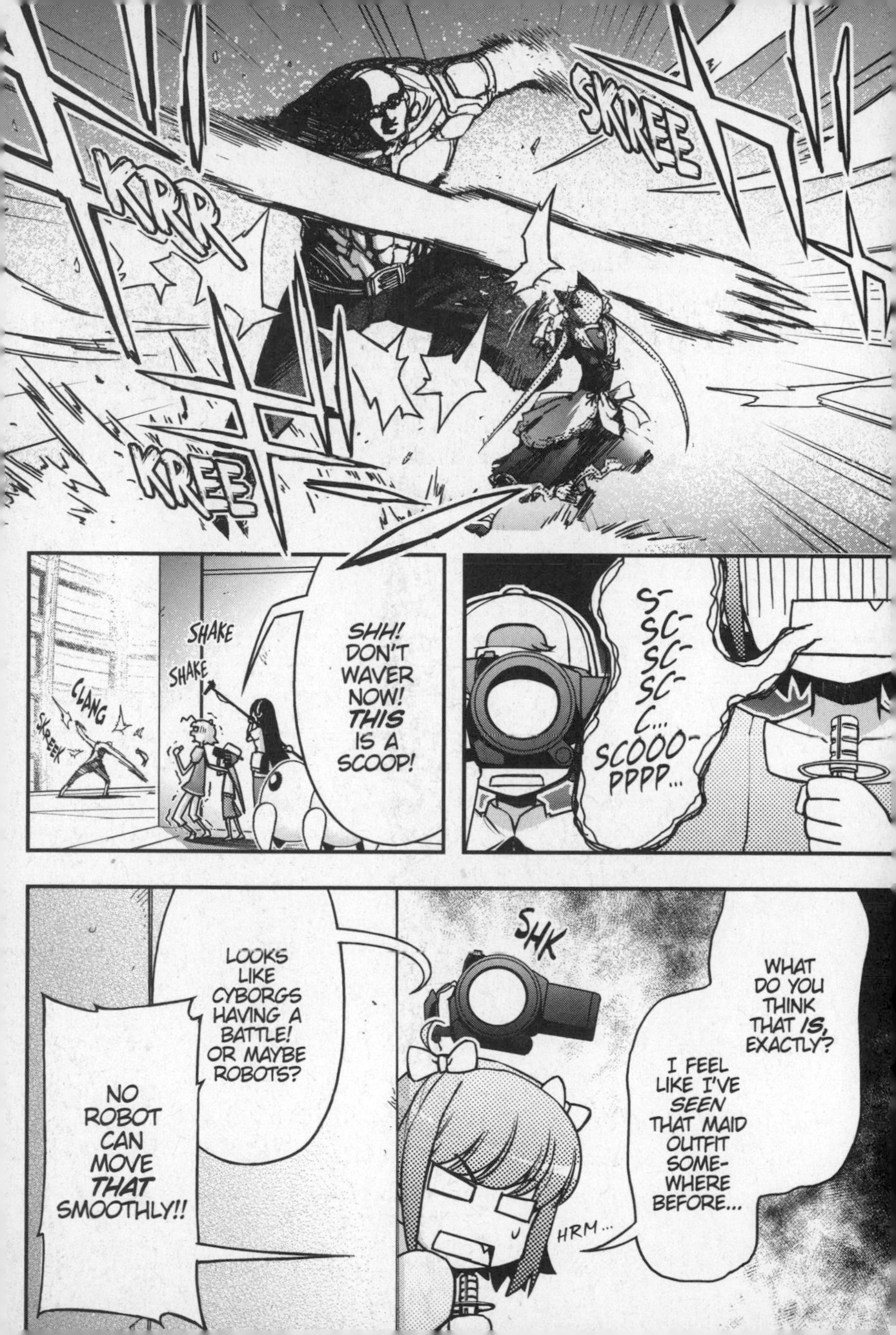
SKREEE
KRRR
KREEE
S-SC-SC-SC-C... SCOOOPPPP...
SHH! DON'T WAVER NOW! *THIS* IS A SCOOP!
SHAKE
SHAKE
CLANG
SKREEK
SHK
WHAT DO YOU THINK THAT *IS*, EXACTLY?
I FEEL LIKE I'VE *SEEN* THAT MAID OUTFIT SOME-WHERE BEFORE...
HRM...
LOOKS LIKE CYBORGS HAVING A BATTLE! OR MAYBE ROBOTS?
NO ROBOT CAN MOVE *THAT* SMOOTHLY!!

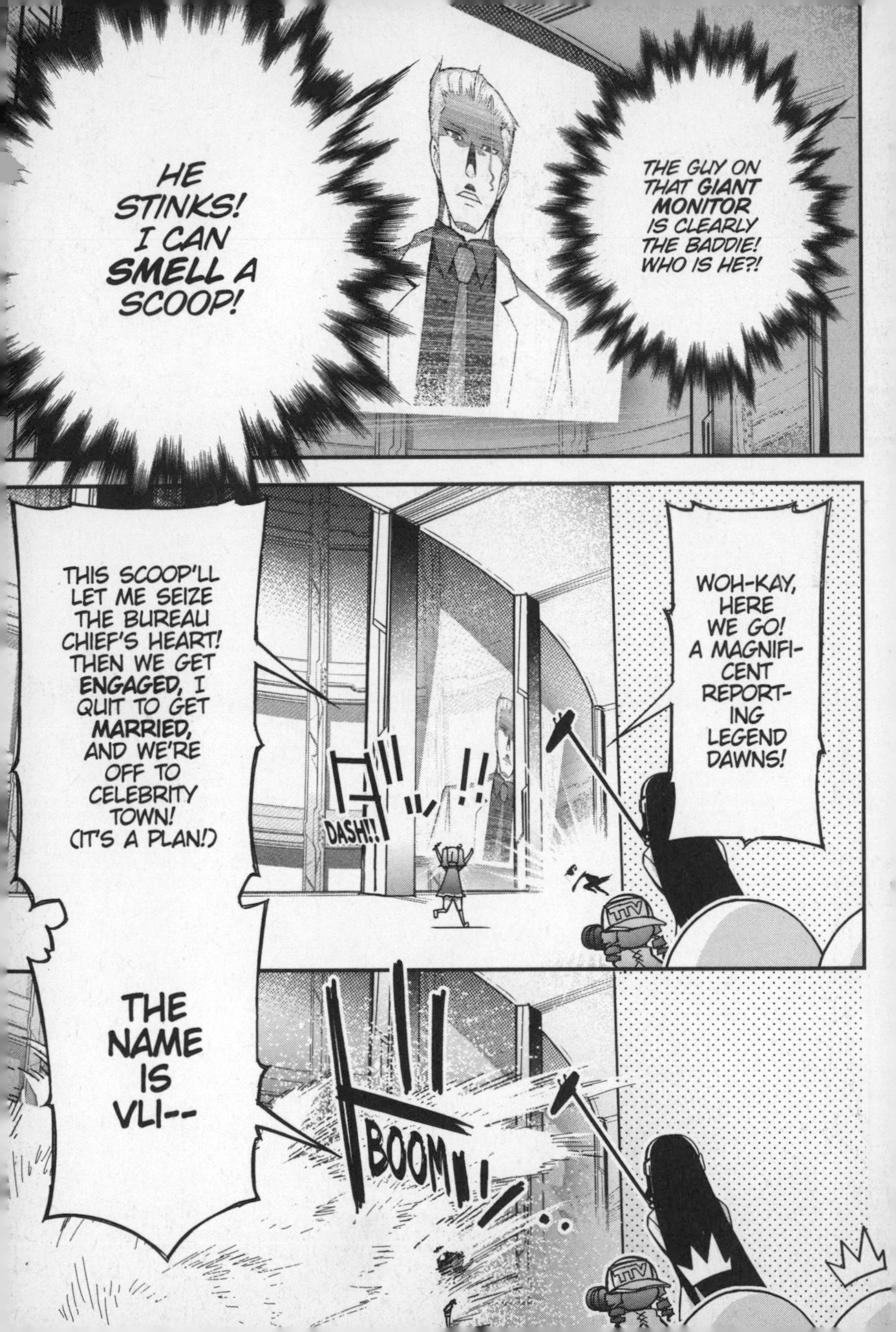
THE GUY ON THAT GIANT MONITOR IS CLEARLY THE BADDIE! WHO IS HE?!
HE STINKS! I CAN SMELL A SCOOP!
WOH-KAY, HERE WE GO! A MAGNIFI-CENT REPORT-ING LEGEND DAWNS!
DASH!!
THIS SCOOP'LL LET ME SEIZE THE BUREAU CHIEF'S HEART! THEN WE GET ENGAGED, I QUIT TO GET MARRIED, AND WE'RE OFF TO CELEBRITY TOWN! (IT'S A PLAN!)
THE NAME IS VLI--
BOOM

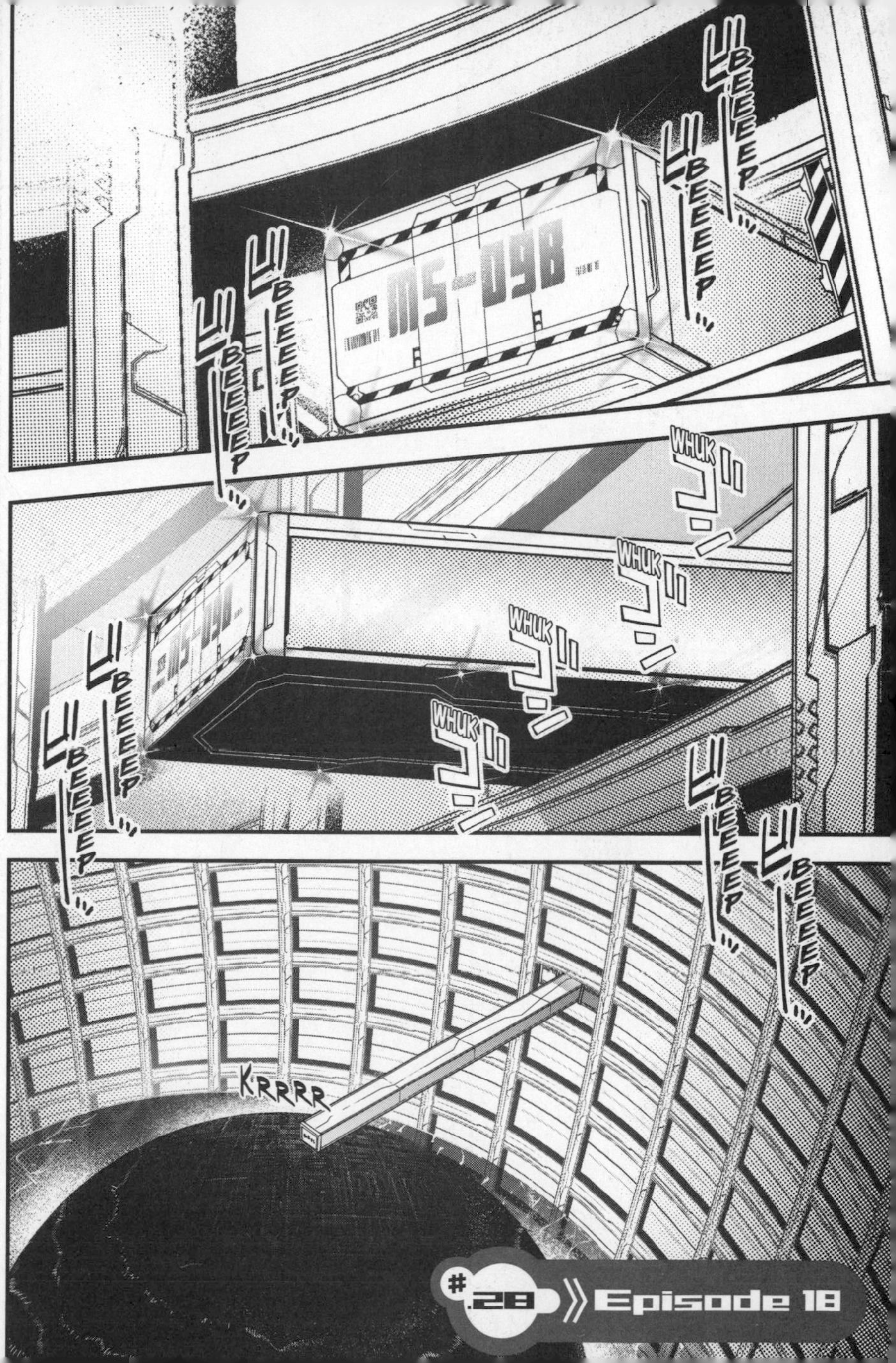
BEEEEP...
BEEEEP...
MS-098
BEEEEP...
BEEEEP...
WHUK
WHUK
WHUK
WHUK
BEEEEP...
BEEEEP...
BEEEEP...
BEEEEP...
KRRRR
#.28 Episode 18

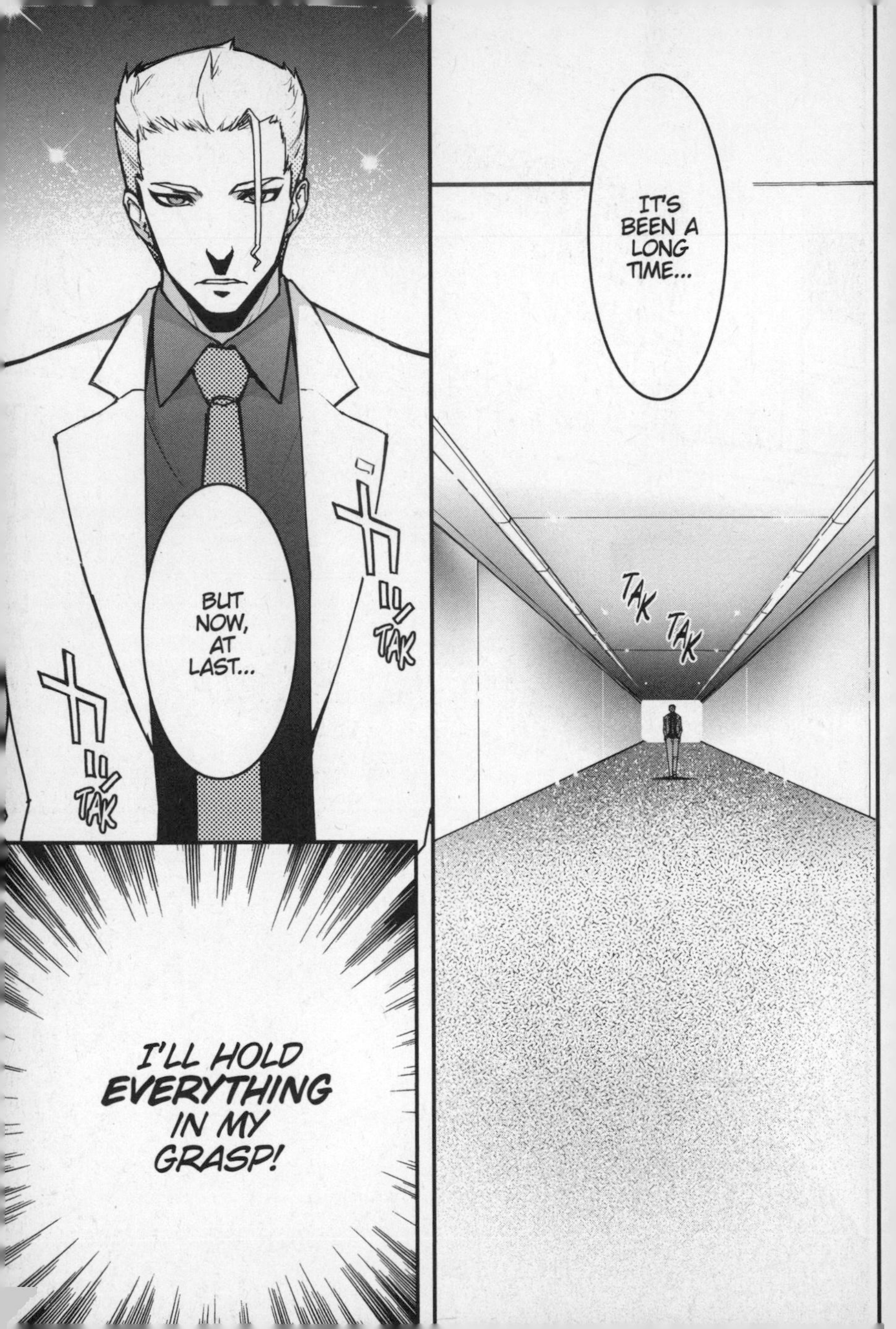
IT'S BEEN A LONG TIME...
TAK TAK
BUT NOW, AT LAST...
TAK
TAK
I'LL HOLD EVERYTHING IN MY GRASP!

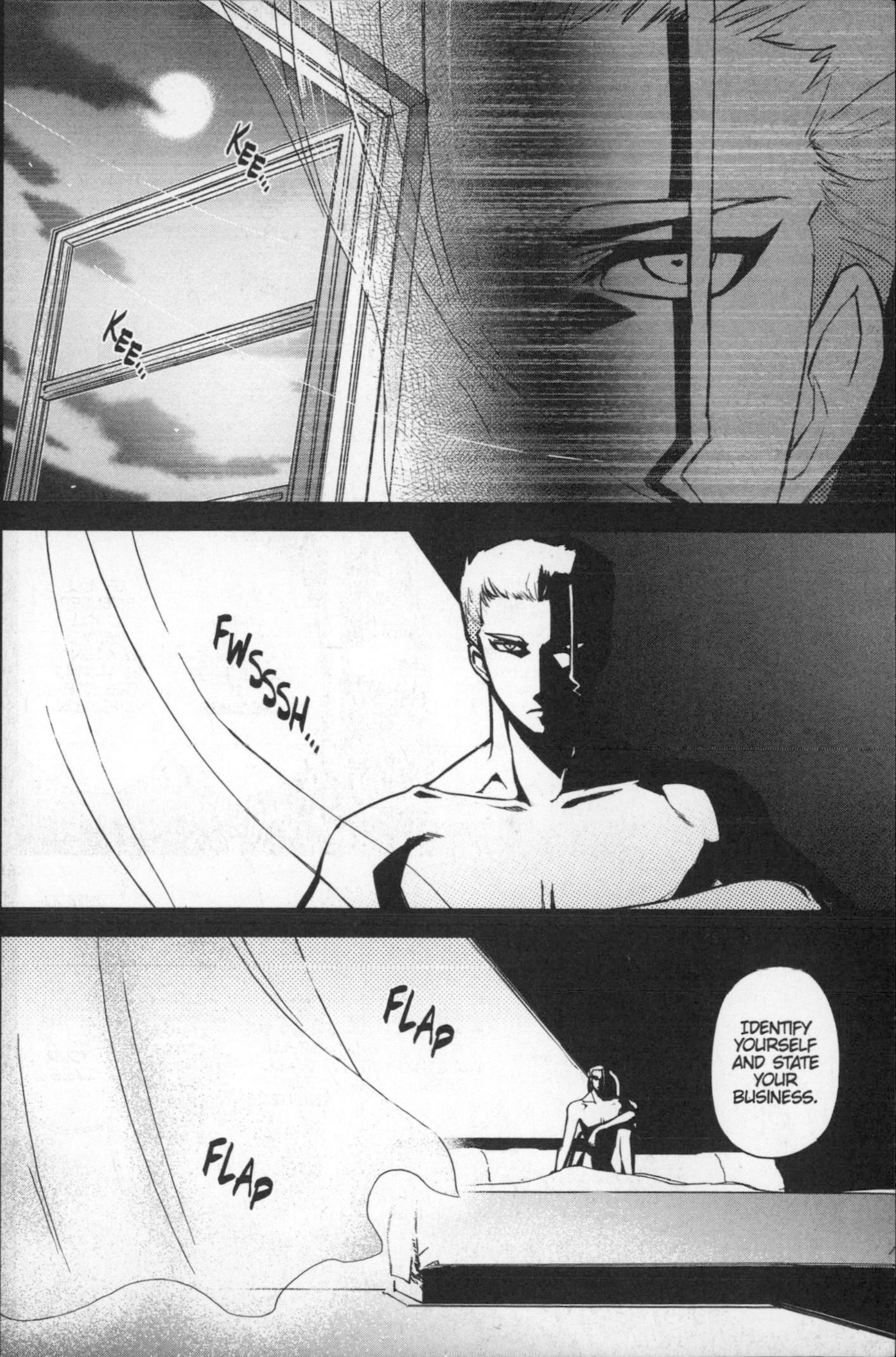
KEE...
KEE...
FWSSSSH...
IDENTIFY YOURSELF AND STATE YOUR BUSINESS.
FLAP
FLAP

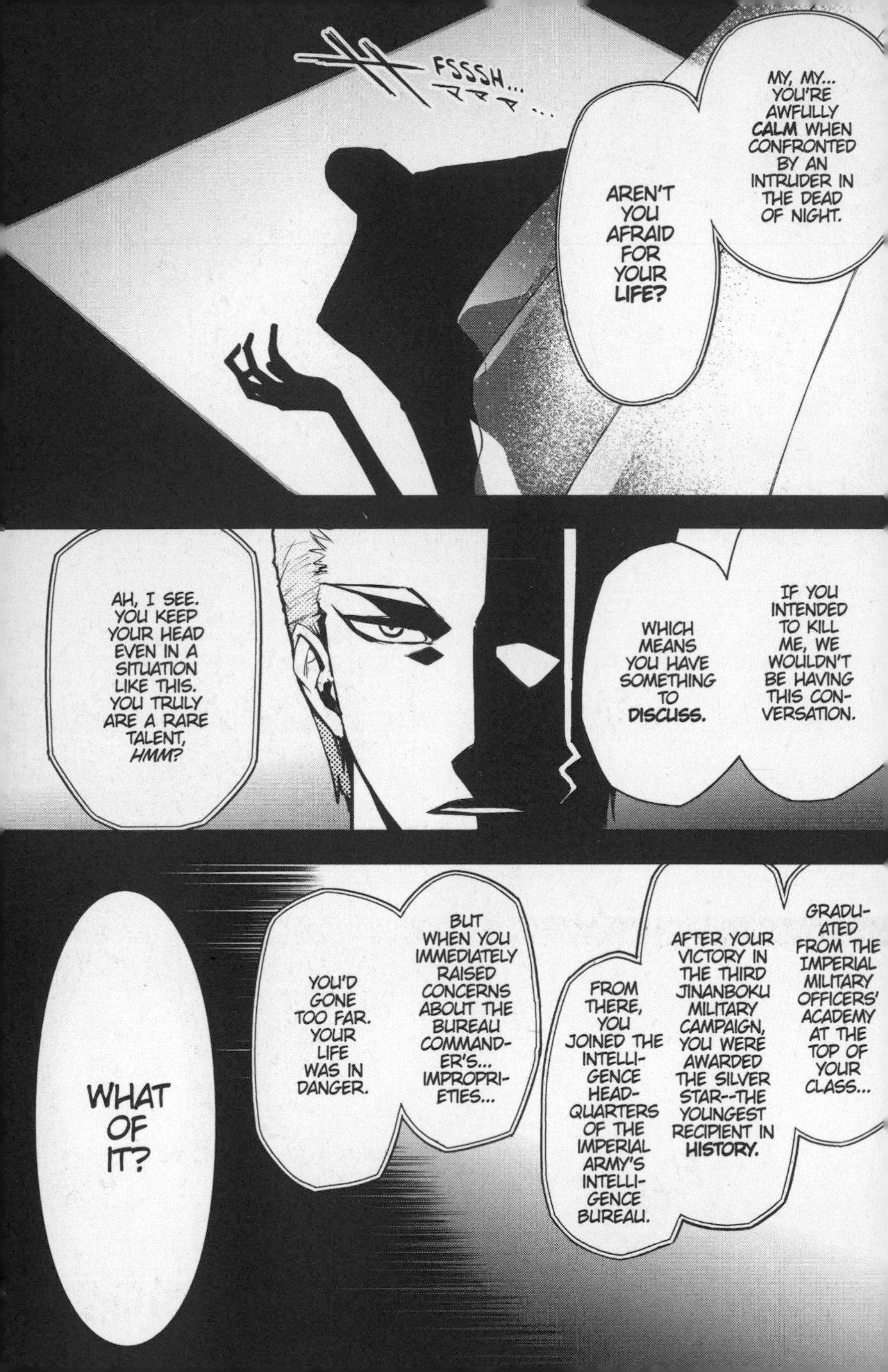
FSSSH...
MY, MY... YOU'RE AWFULLY **CALM** WHEN CONFRONTED BY AN INTRUDER IN THE DEAD OF NIGHT.
AREN'T YOU AFRAID FOR YOUR **LIFE?**
IF YOU INTENDED TO KILL ME, WE WOULDN'T BE HAVING THIS CONVERSATION.
WHICH MEANS YOU HAVE SOMETHING TO **DISCUSS.**
AH, I SEE. YOU KEEP YOUR HEAD EVEN IN A SITUATION LIKE THIS. YOU TRULY ARE A RARE TALENT, *HMM?*
GRADUATED FROM THE IMPERIAL MILITARY OFFICERS' ACADEMY AT THE TOP OF YOUR CLASS...
AFTER YOUR VICTORY IN THE THIRD JINANBOKU MILITARY CAMPAIGN, YOU WERE AWARDED THE SILVER STAR--THE YOUNGEST RECIPIENT IN **HISTORY.**
FROM THERE, YOU JOINED THE INTELLIGENCE HEADQUARTERS OF THE IMPERIAL ARMY'S INTELLIGENCE BUREAU.
BUT WHEN YOU IMMEDIATELY RAISED CONCERNS ABOUT THE BUREAU COMMANDER'S... IMPROPRIETIES...
YOU'D GONE TOO FAR. YOUR LIFE WAS IN DANGER.
WHAT OF IT?

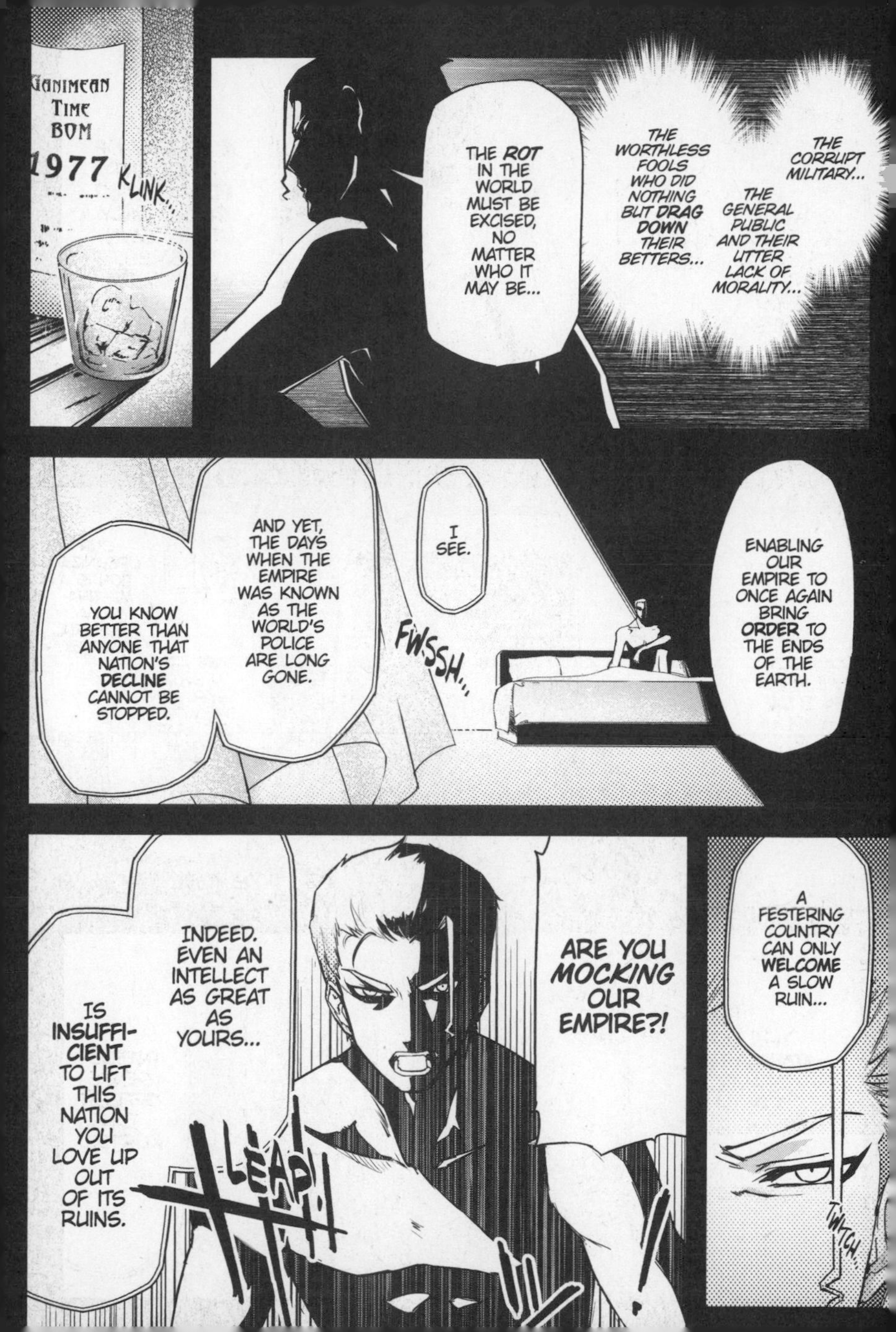
THE CORRUPT MILITARY...
THE GENERAL PUBLIC AND THEIR UTTER LACK OF MORALITY...
THE WORTHLESS FOOLS WHO DID NOTHING BUT DRAG DOWN THEIR BETTERS...
THE ROT IN THE WORLD MUST BE EXCISED, NO MATTER WHO IT MAY BE...
GANIMEAN TIME BOM
1977
KLINK...
ENABLING OUR EMPIRE TO ONCE AGAIN BRING ORDER TO THE ENDS OF THE EARTH.
I SEE.
FWSSH...
AND YET, THE DAYS WHEN THE EMPIRE WAS KNOWN AS THE WORLD'S POLICE ARE LONG GONE.
YOU KNOW BETTER THAN ANYONE THAT NATION'S DECLINE CANNOT BE STOPPED.
A FESTERING COUNTRY CAN ONLY WELCOME A SLOW RUIN...
TWITCH
ARE YOU MOCKING OUR EMPIRE?!
INDEED. EVEN AN INTELLECT AS GREAT AS YOURS...
IS INSUFFICIENT TO LIFT THIS NATION YOU LOVE UP OUT OF ITS RUINS.
LEAP!!

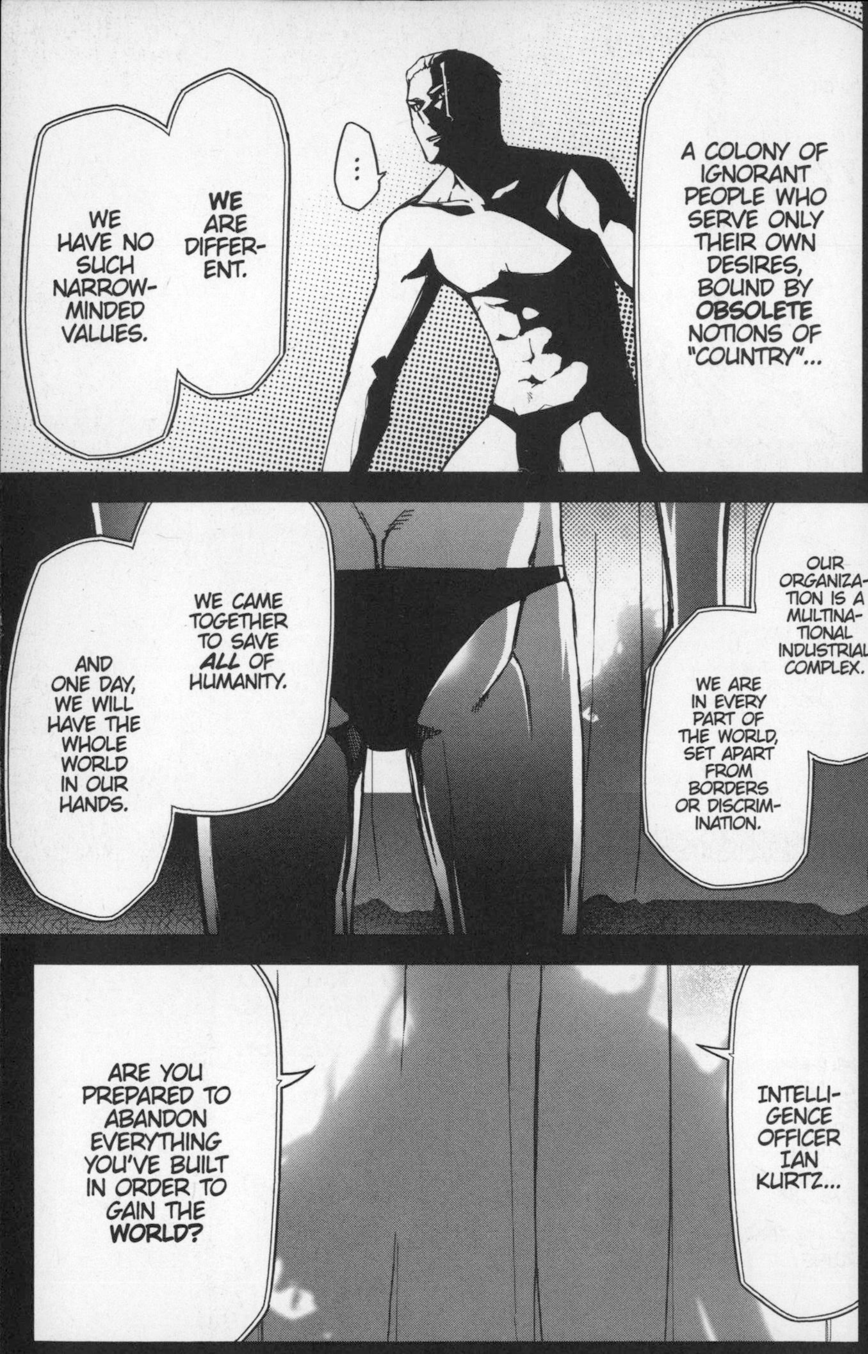
A COLONY OF IGNORANT PEOPLE WHO SERVE ONLY THEIR OWN DESIRES, BOUND BY OBSOLETE NOTIONS OF "COUNTRY"...
...
WE ARE DIFFERENT.
WE HAVE NO SUCH NARROW-MINDED VALUES.
OUR ORGANIZATION IS A MULTINATIONAL INDUSTRIAL COMPLEX.
WE ARE IN EVERY PART OF THE WORLD, SET APART FROM BORDERS OR DISCRIMINATION.
WE CAME TOGETHER TO SAVE ALL OF HUMANITY.
AND ONE DAY, WE WILL HAVE THE WHOLE WORLD IN OUR HANDS.
INTELLIGENCE OFFICER IAN KURTZ...
ARE YOU PREPARED TO ABANDON EVERYTHING YOU'VE BUILT IN ORDER TO GAIN THE WORLD?

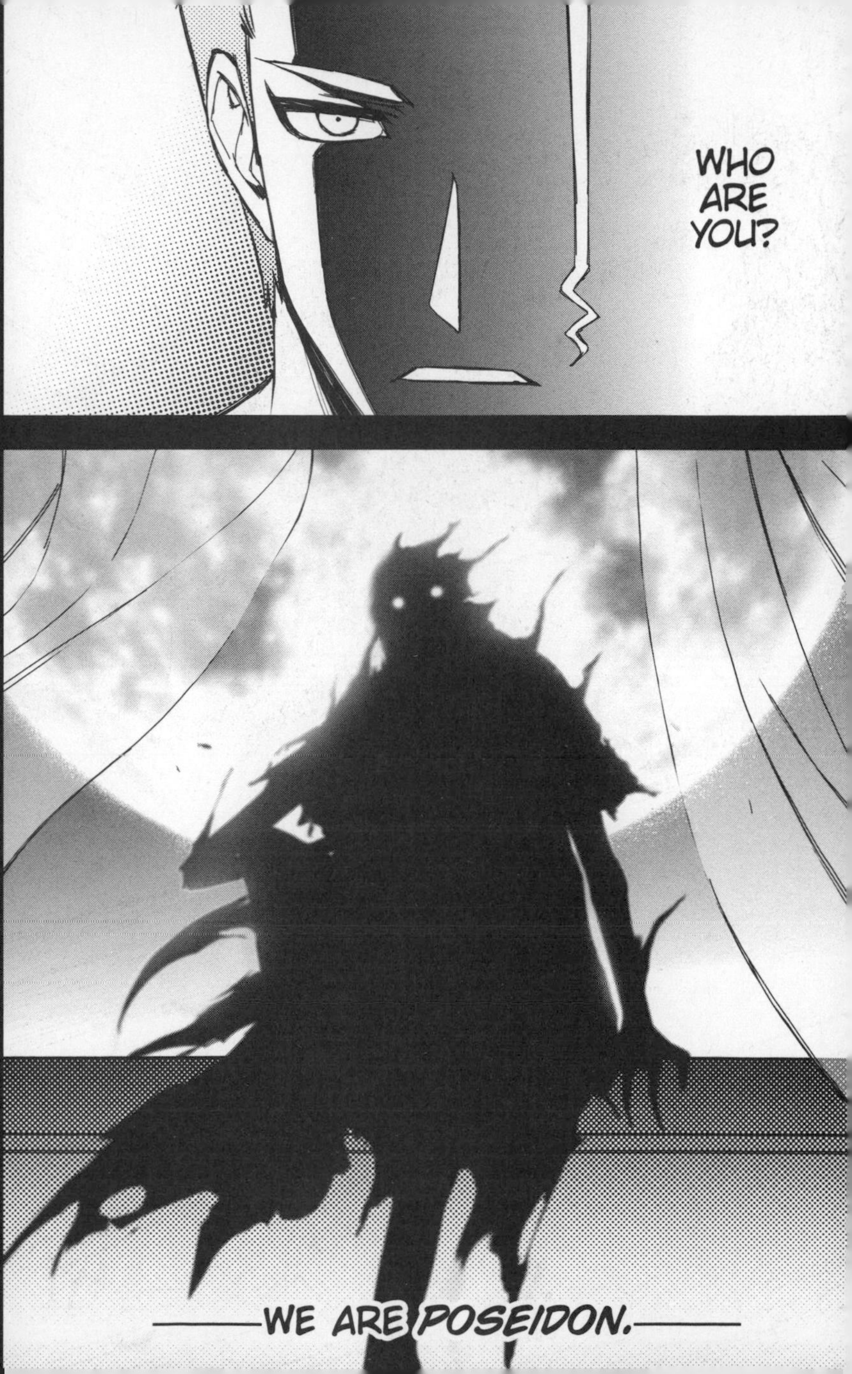
WHO ARE YOU?
—WE ARE POSEIDON.—

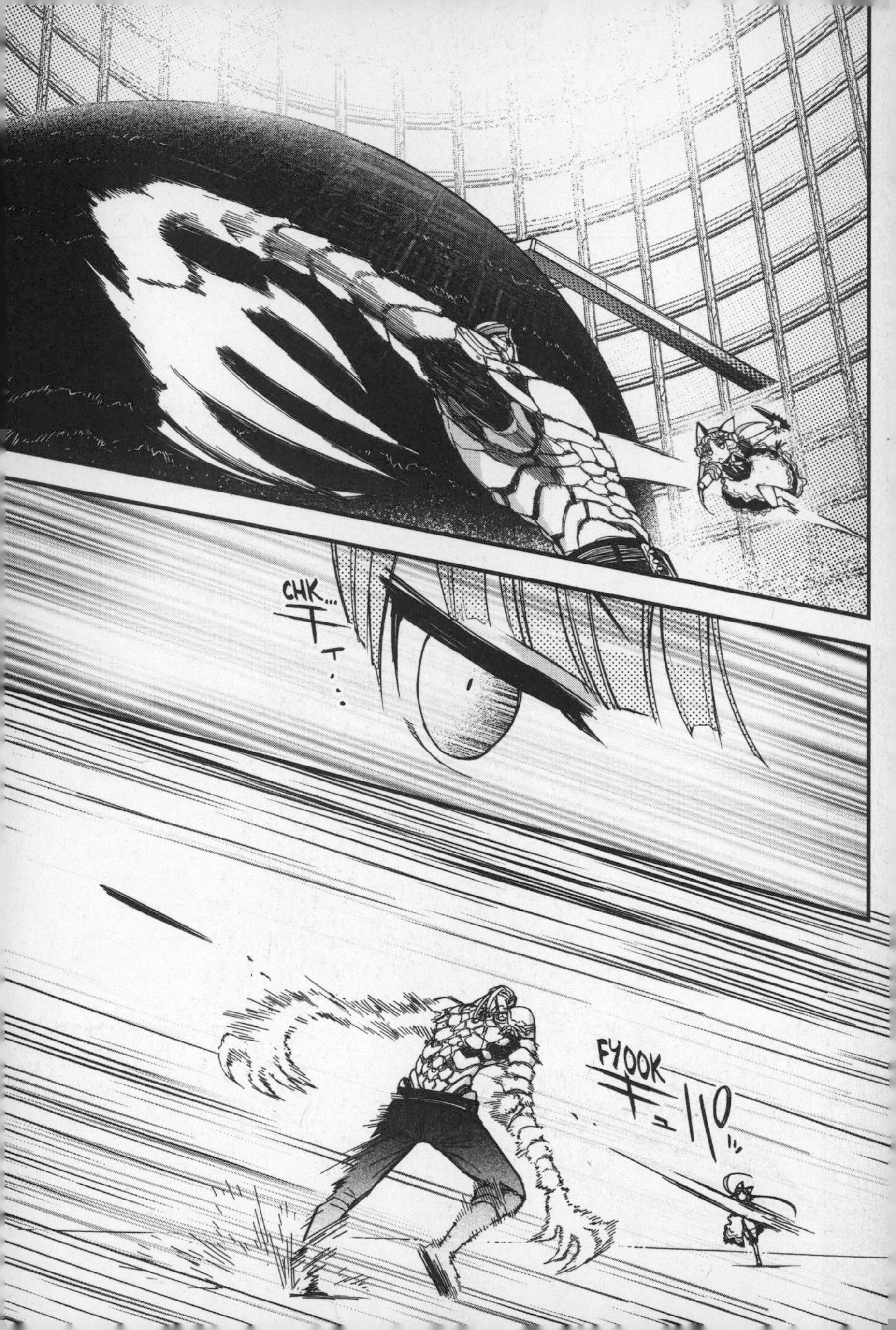
CHK...
FYOOK

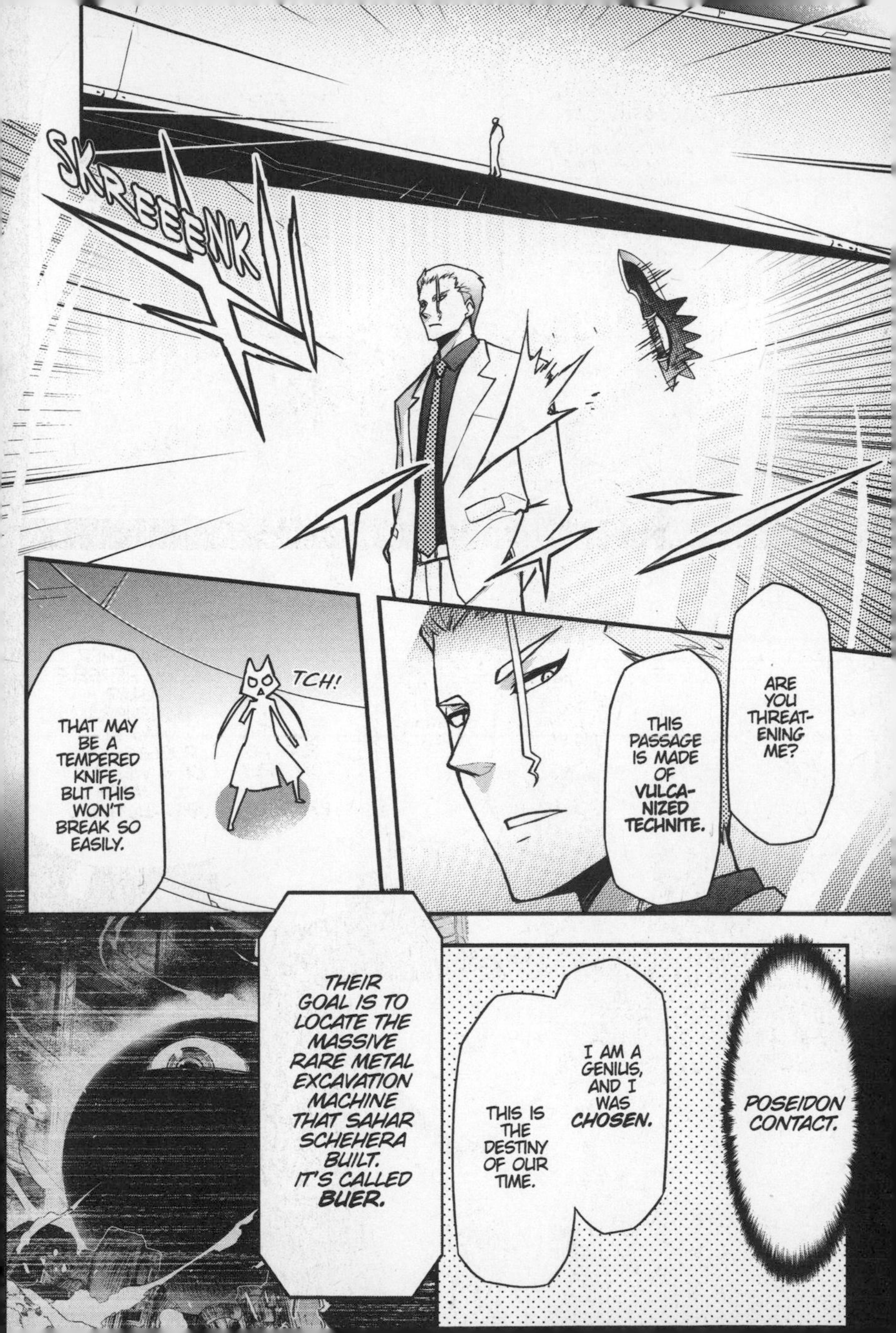
SKREEEENK
ARE YOU THREATENING ME?
THIS PASSAGE IS MADE OF VULCANIZED TECHNITE.
TCH!
THAT MAY BE A TEMPERED KNIFE, BUT THIS WON'T BREAK SO EASILY.
POSEIDON CONTACT.
I AM A GENIUS, AND I WAS **CHOSEN.**
THIS IS THE DESTINY OF OUR TIME.
THEIR GOAL IS TO LOCATE THE MASSIVE RARE METAL EXCAVATION MACHINE THAT SAHAR SCHEHERA BUILT. IT'S CALLED ***BUER.***

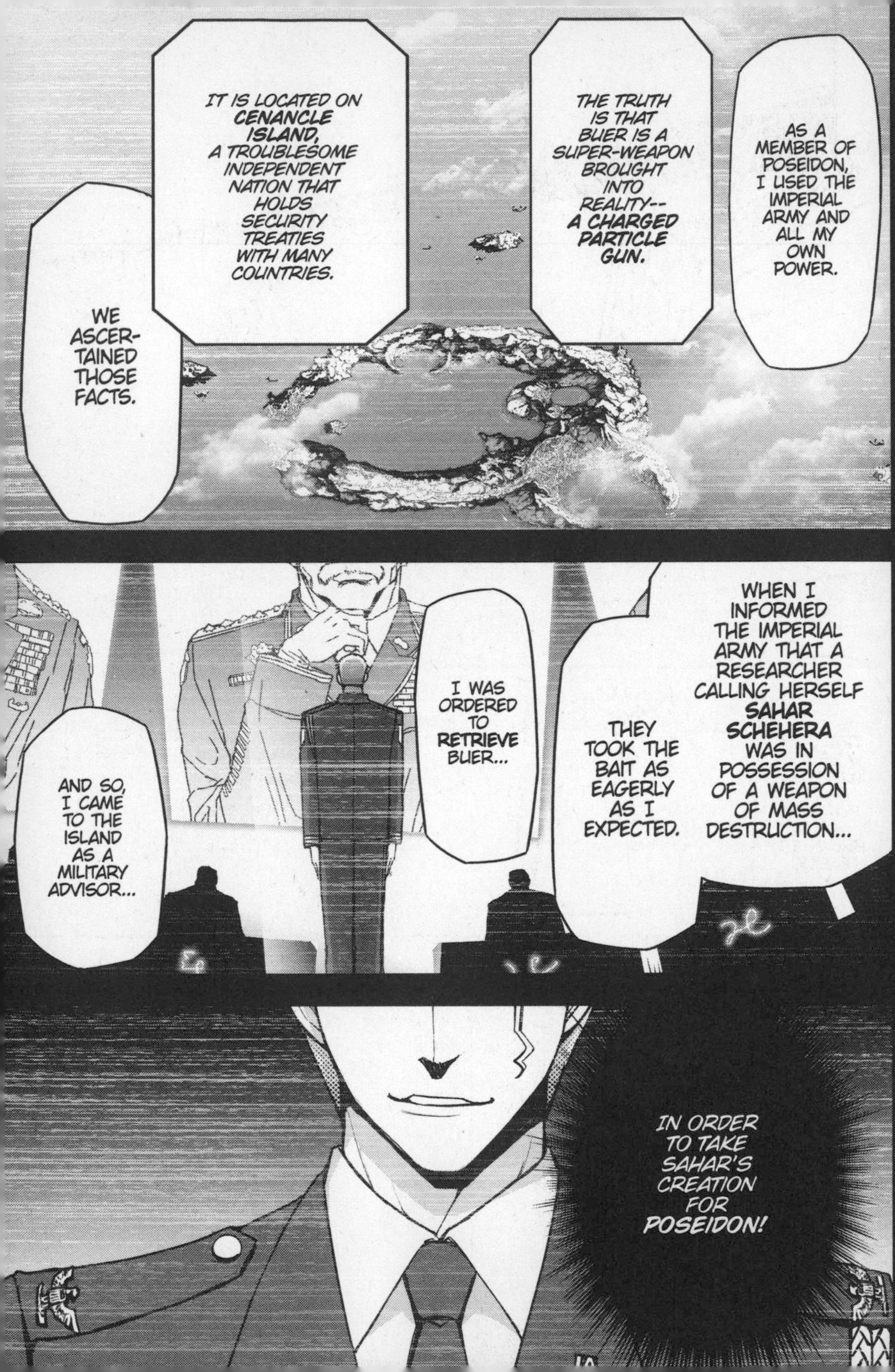
AS A MEMBER OF POSEIDON, I USED THE IMPERIAL ARMY AND ALL MY OWN POWER.
THE TRUTH IS THAT BUER IS A SUPER-WEAPON BROUGHT INTO REALITY-- A CHARGED PARTICLE GUN.
IT IS LOCATED ON CENANCLE ISLAND, A TROUBLESOME INDEPENDENT NATION THAT HOLDS SECURITY TREATIES WITH MANY COUNTRIES.
WE ASCER-TAINED THOSE FACTS.
WHEN I INFORMED THE IMPERIAL ARMY THAT A RESEARCHER CALLING HERSELF SAHAR SCHEHERA WAS IN POSSESSION OF A WEAPON OF MASS DESTRUCTION...
THEY TOOK THE BAIT AS EAGERLY AS I EXPECTED.
I WAS ORDERED TO RETRIEVE BUER...
AND SO, I CAME TO THE ISLAND AS A MILITARY ADVISOR...
IN ORDER TO TAKE SAHAR'S CREATION FOR POSEIDON!

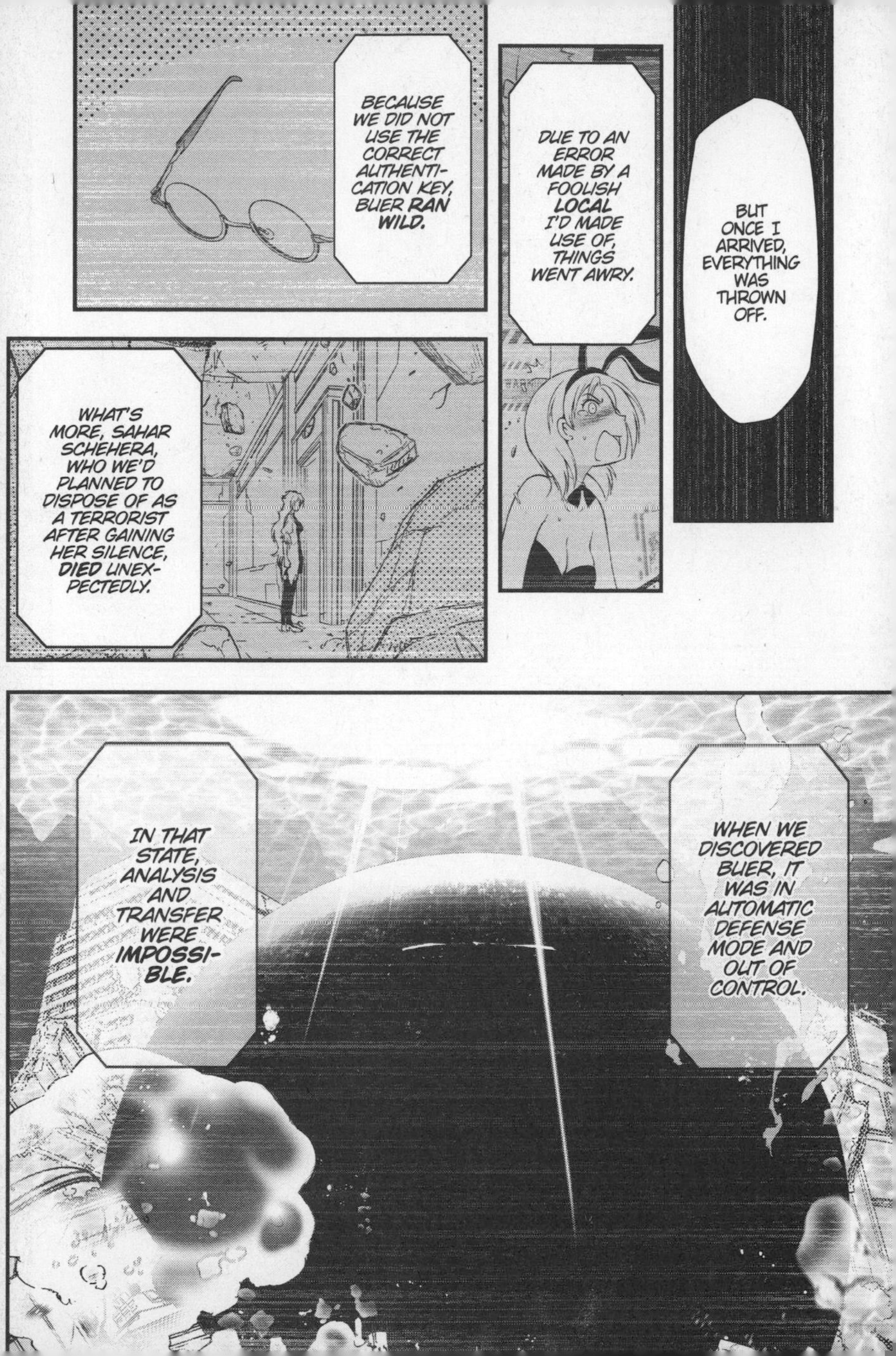

BUT ONCE I ARRIVED, EVERYTHING WAS THROWN OFF.
DUE TO AN ERROR MADE BY A FOOLISH **LOCAL** I'D MADE USE OF, THINGS WENT AWRY.
BECAUSE WE DID NOT USE THE CORRECT AUTHENTICATION KEY, BUER **RAN WILD.**
WHAT'S MORE, SAHAR SCHEHERA, WHO WE'D PLANNED TO DISPOSE OF AS A TERRORIST AFTER GAINING HER SILENCE, **DIED** UNEXPECTEDLY.
WHEN WE DISCOVERED BUER, IT WAS IN AUTOMATIC DEFENSE MODE AND OUT OF CONTROL.
IN THAT STATE, ANALYSIS AND TRANSFER WERE **IMPOSSIBLE.**

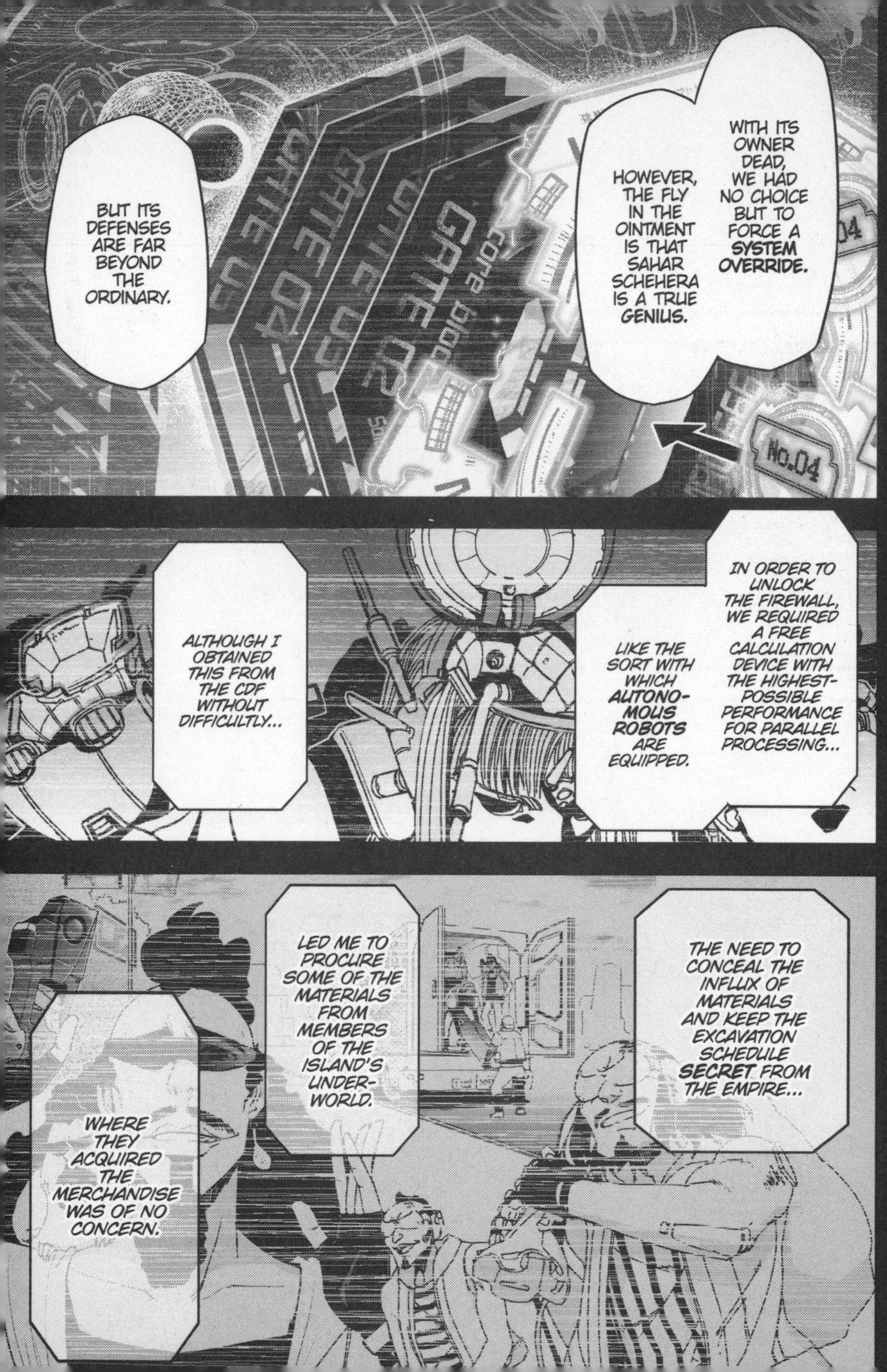
WITH ITS OWNER DEAD, WE HAD NO CHOICE BUT TO FORCE A **SYSTEM OVERRIDE.**
HOWEVER, THE FLY IN THE OINTMENT IS THAT SAHAR SCHEHERA IS A TRUE **GENIUS.**
BUT ITS DEFENSES ARE FAR BEYOND THE ORDINARY.
No.04
IN ORDER TO UNLOCK THE FIREWALL, WE REQUIRED A FREE CALCULATION DEVICE WITH THE HIGHEST-POSSIBLE PERFORMANCE FOR PARALLEL PROCESSING...
LIKE THE SORT WITH WHICH ***AUTONOMOUS ROBOTS*** *ARE EQUIPPED.*
ALTHOUGH I OBTAINED THIS FROM THE CDF WITHOUT DIFFICULTLY...
THE NEED TO CONCEAL THE INFLUX OF MATERIALS AND KEEP THE EXCAVATION SCHEDULE ***SECRET*** *FROM THE EMPIRE...*
LED ME TO PROCURE SOME OF THE MATERIALS FROM MEMBERS OF THE ISLAND'S UNDERWORLD.
WHERE THEY ACQUIRED THE MERCHANDISE WAS OF NO CONCERN.

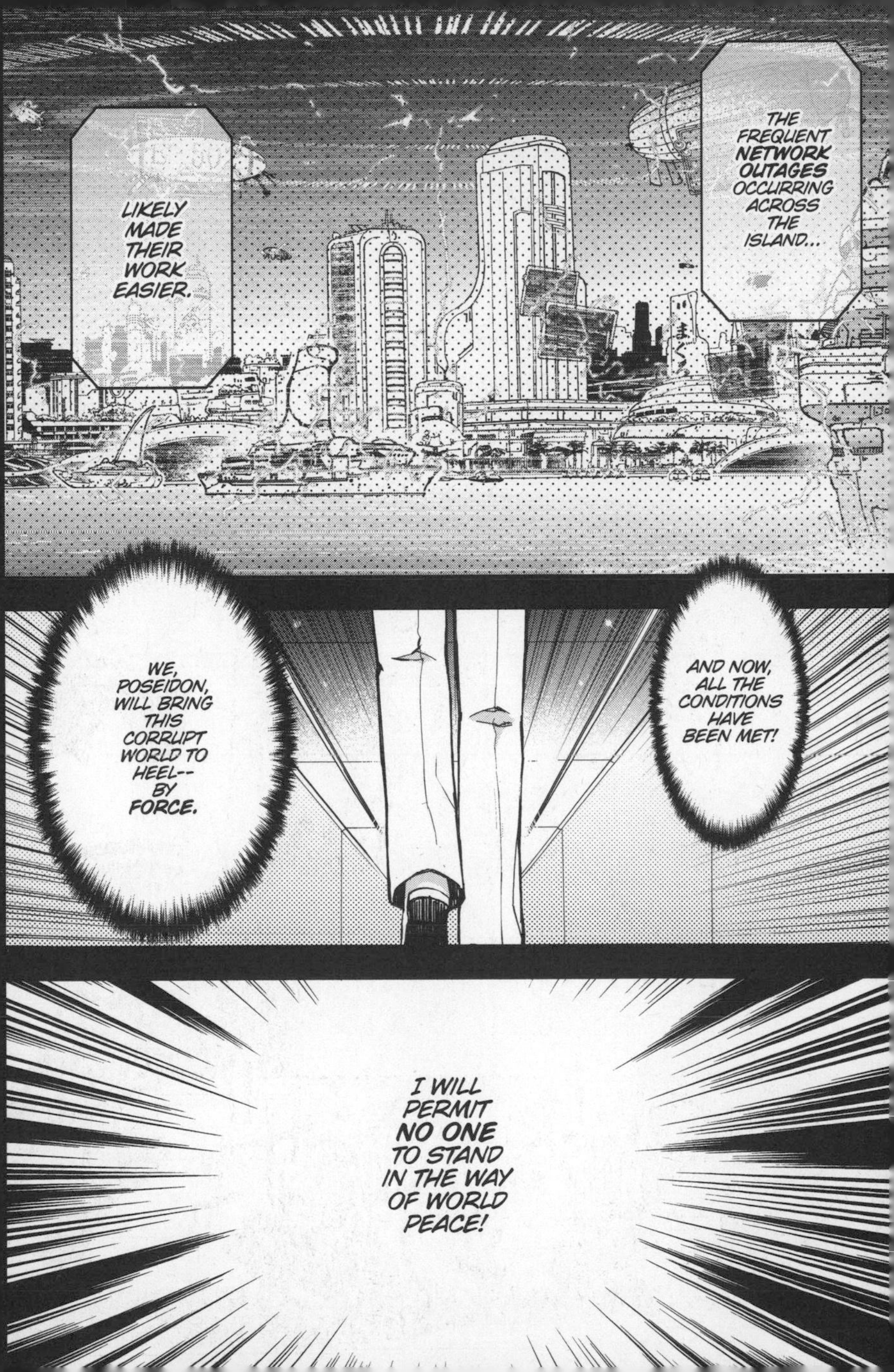
THE FREQUENT NETWORK OUTAGES OCCURRING ACROSS THE ISLAND...
LIKELY MADE THEIR WORK EASIER.
AND NOW, ALL THE CONDITIONS HAVE BEEN MET!
WE, POSEIDON, WILL BRING THIS CORRUPT WORLD TO HEEL-- BY FORCE.
I WILL PERMIT NO ONE TO STAND IN THE WAY OF WORLD PEACE!

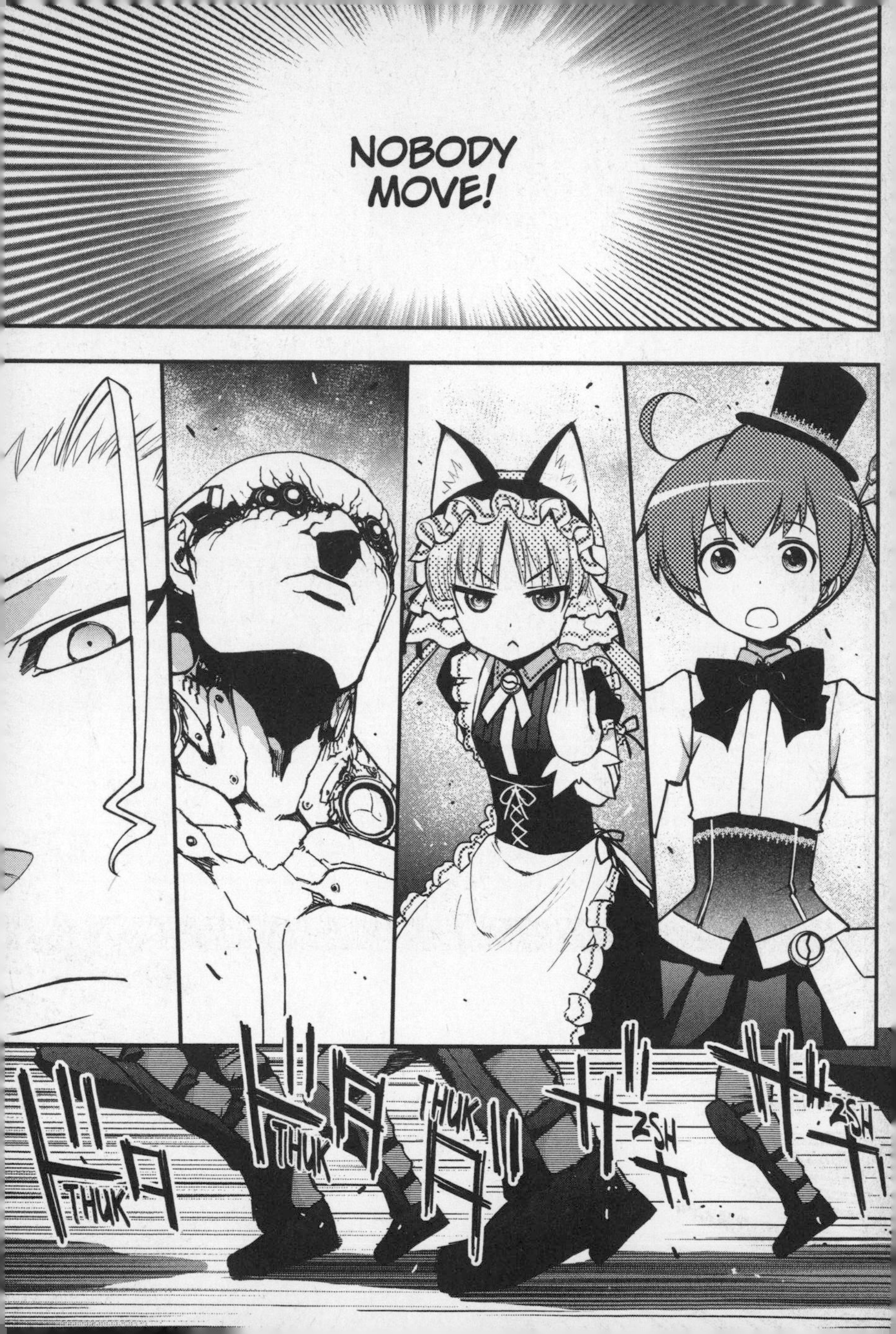
NOBODY MOVE!
ZSH
ZSH
THUK
THUK
THUK

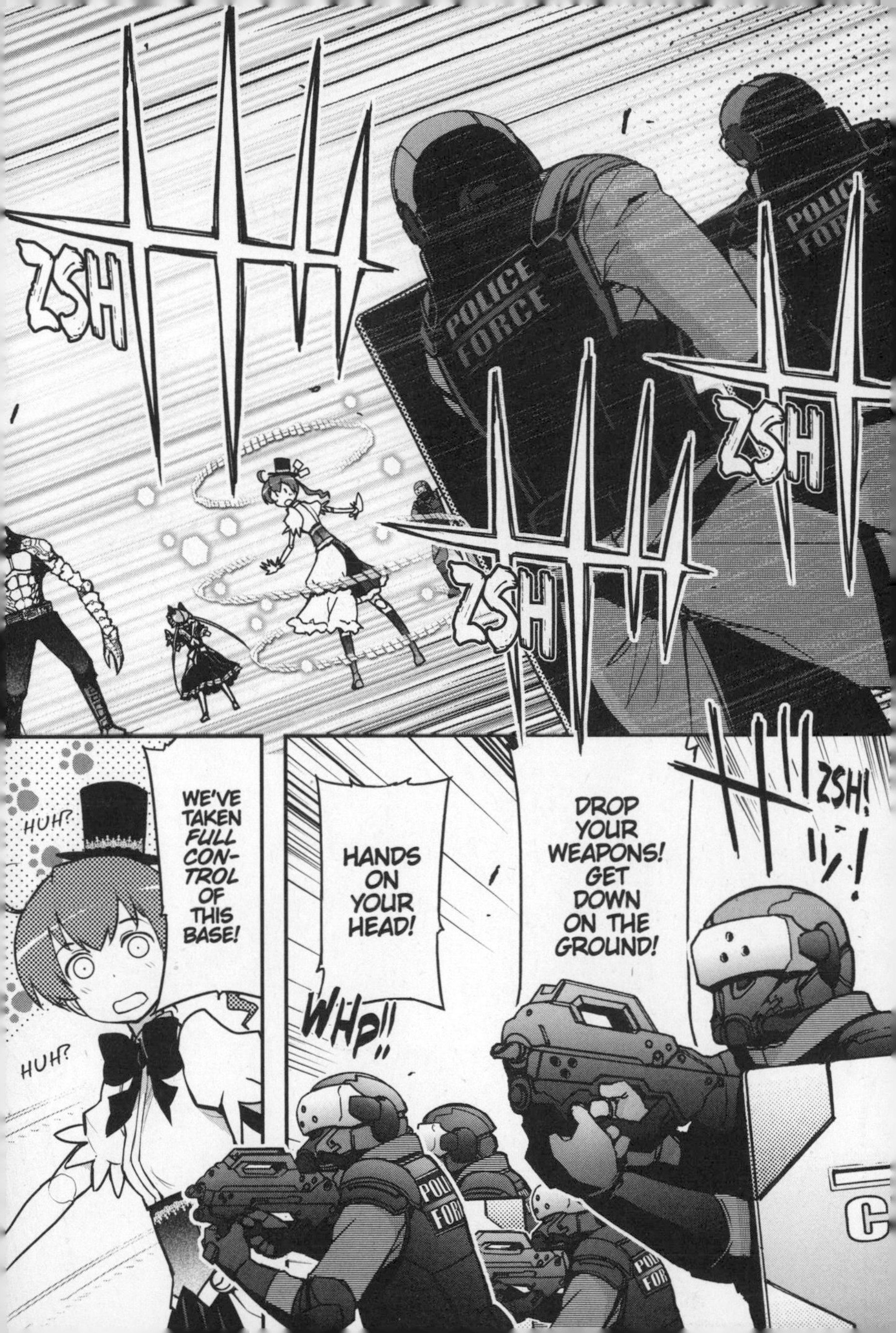
ZSH
ZSH
ZSH
ZSH!
DROP YOUR WEAPONS! GET DOWN ON THE GROUND!
HANDS ON YOUR HEAD!
WHP!!
WE'VE TAKEN FULL CON-TROL OF THIS BASE!
HUH?
HUH?

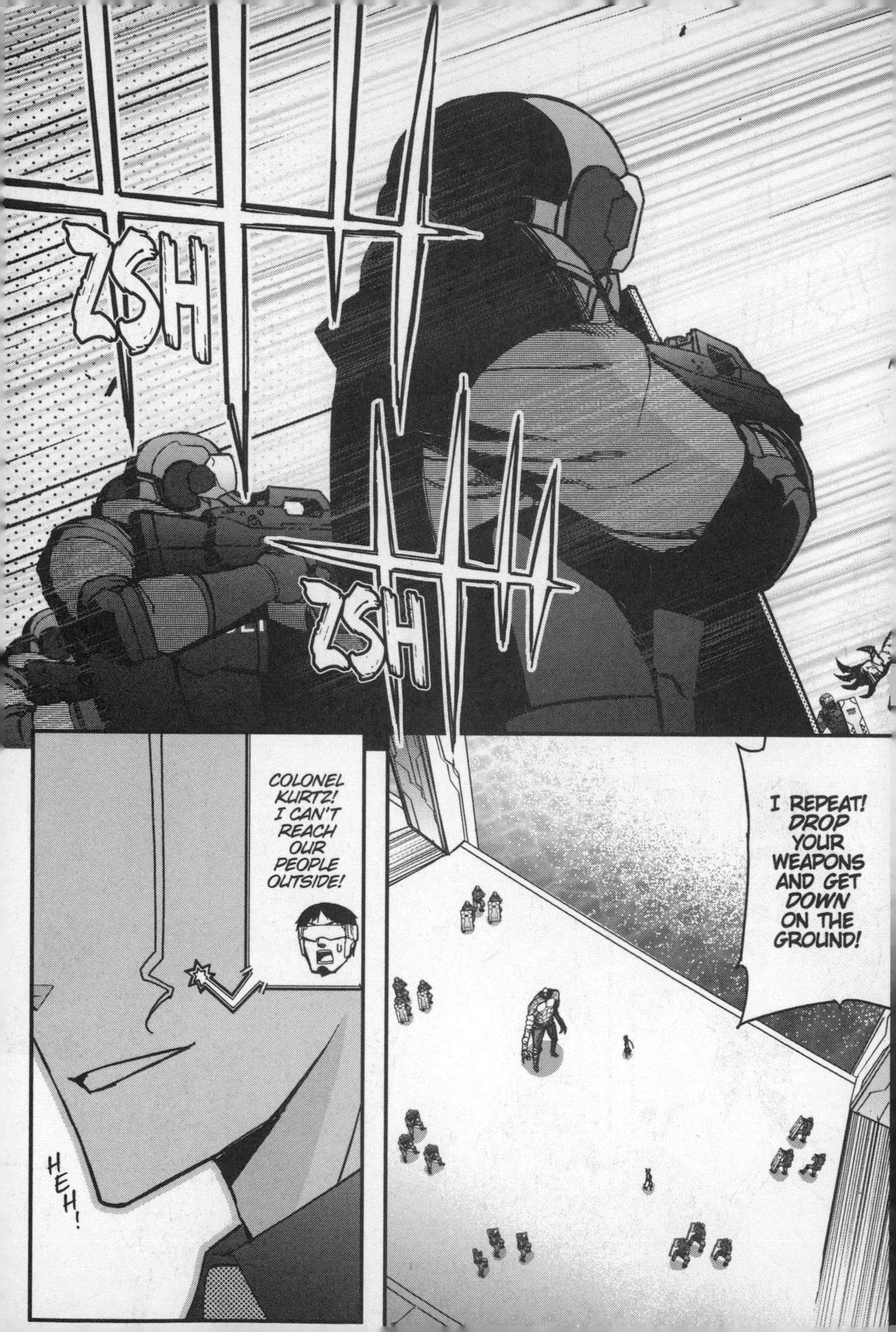
ZSH
ZSH
I REPEAT! DROP YOUR WEAPONS AND GET DOWN ON THE GROUND!
COLONEL KURTZ! I CAN'T REACH OUR PEOPLE OUTSIDE!
HEH!

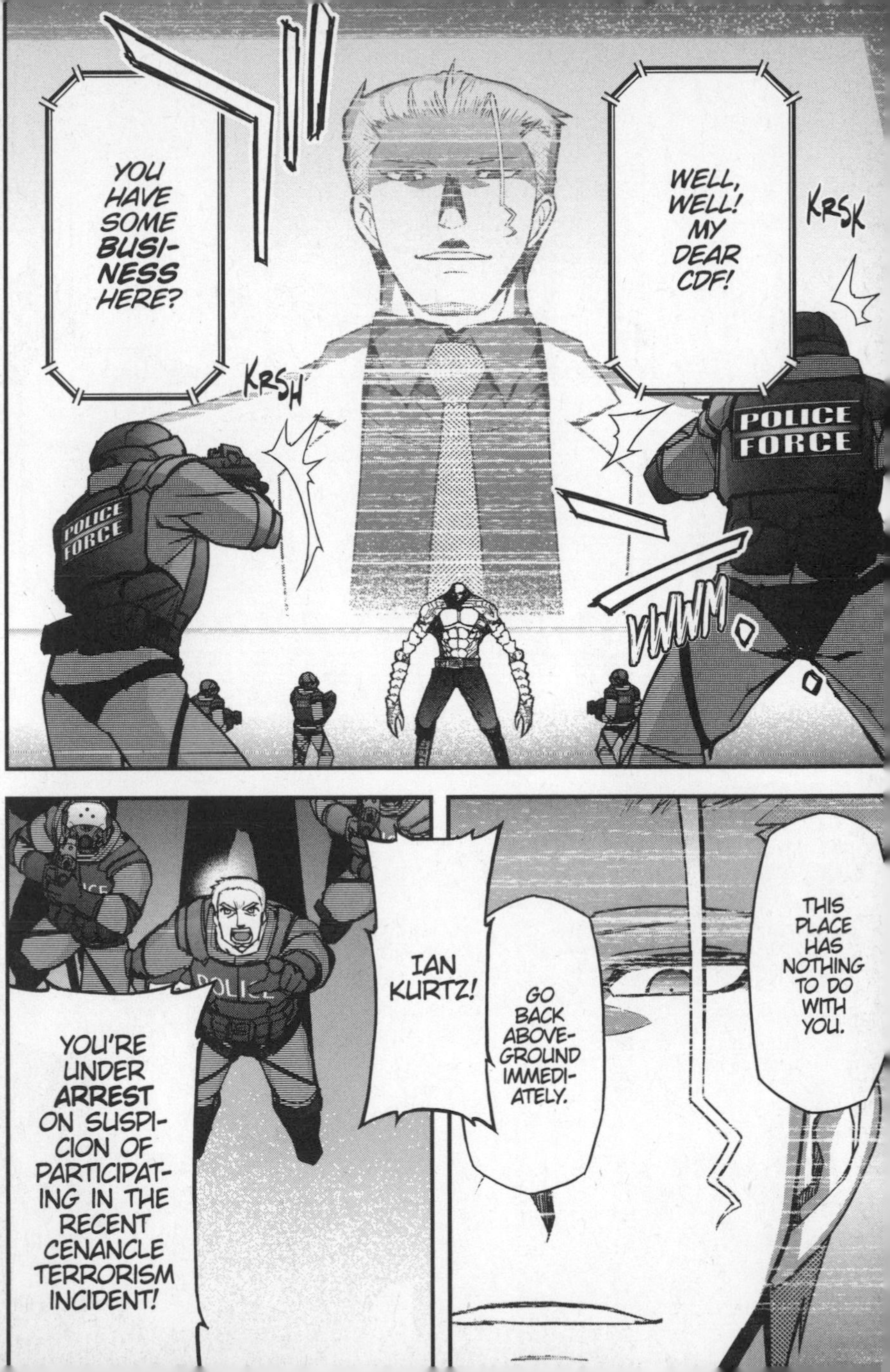
WELL, WELL! MY DEAR CDF!
KRSK
YOU HAVE SOME BUSINESS HERE?
KRSH
POLICE FORCE
POLICE FORCE
VWWM
THIS PLACE HAS NOTHING TO DO WITH YOU.
GO BACK ABOVEGROUND IMMEDIATELY.
IAN KURTZ!
YOU'RE UNDER ARREST ON SUSPICION OF PARTICIPATING IN THE RECENT CENANCLE TERRORISM INCIDENT!

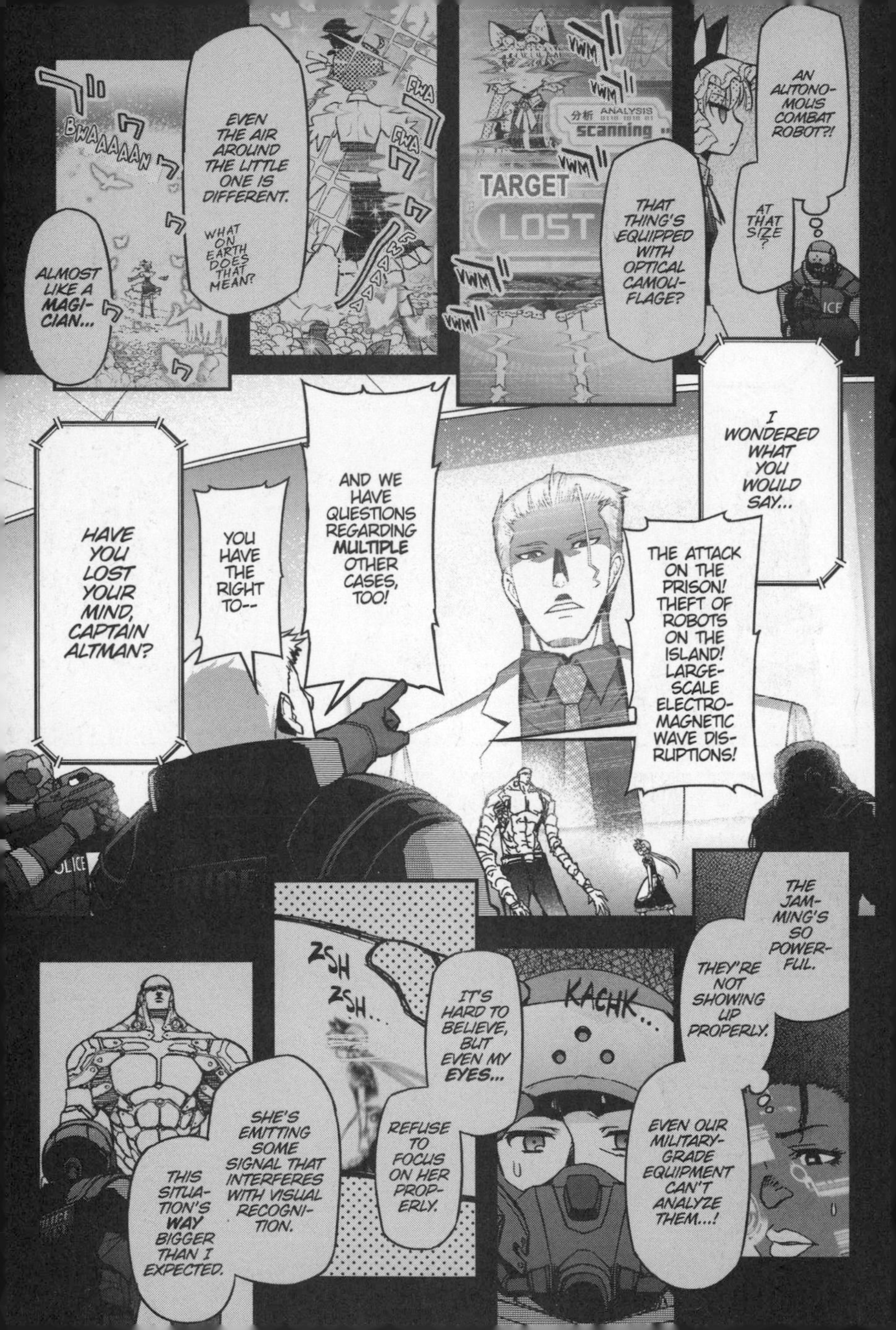
AN AUTONOMOUS COMBAT ROBOT?!
AT THAT SIZE?
THAT THING'S EQUIPPED WITH OPTICAL CAMOUFLAGE?
VWM
VWM
分析 ANALYSIS
scanning
TARGET
LOST
VWM
VWM
VWM
FWA
FWA
EVEN THE AIR AROUND THE LITTLE ONE IS DIFFERENT.
WHAT ON EARTH DOES THAT MEAN?
BWAAAAAN
ALMOST LIKE A MAGICIAN...
I WONDERED WHAT YOU WOULD SAY...
THE ATTACK ON THE PRISON! THEFT OF ROBOTS ON THE ISLAND! LARGE-SCALE ELECTROMAGNETIC WAVE DISRUPTIONS!
AND WE HAVE QUESTIONS REGARDING MULTIPLE OTHER CASES, TOO!
YOU HAVE THE RIGHT TO--
HAVE YOU LOST YOUR MIND, CAPTAIN ALTMAN?
THE JAMMING'S SO POWERFUL.
THEY'RE NOT SHOWING UP PROPERLY.
KACHK...
EVEN OUR MILITARY-GRADE EQUIPMENT CAN'T ANALYZE THEM...!
ZSH
ZSH...
IT'S HARD TO BELIEVE, BUT EVEN MY EYES...
REFUSE TO FOCUS ON HER PROPERLY.
SHE'S EMITTING SOME SIGNAL THAT INTERFERES WITH VISUAL RECOGNITION.
THIS SITUATION'S WAY BIGGER THAN I EXPECTED.

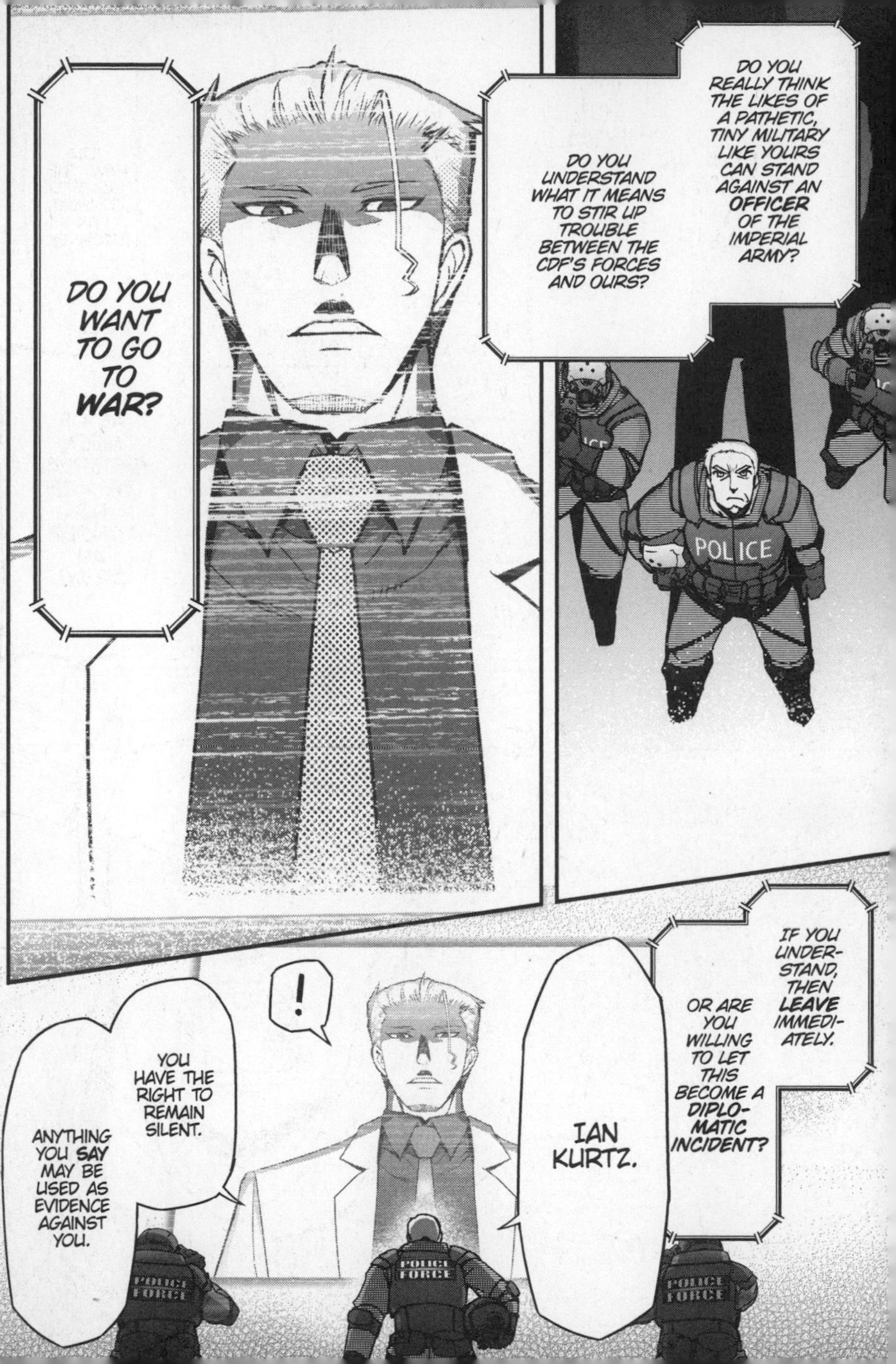
DO YOU REALLY THINK THE LIKES OF A PATHETIC, TINY MILITARY LIKE YOURS CAN STAND AGAINST AN **OFFICER** OF THE IMPERIAL ARMY?
DO YOU UNDERSTAND WHAT IT MEANS TO STIR UP TROUBLE BETWEEN THE CDF'S FORCES AND OURS?
POLICE
DO YOU WANT TO GO TO **WAR?**
IF YOU UNDER-STAND, THEN **LEAVE** IMMEDI-ATELY.
OR ARE YOU WILLING TO LET THIS BECOME A **DIPLO-MATIC INCIDENT?**
IAN KURTZ.
!
YOU HAVE THE RIGHT TO REMAIN SILENT.
ANYTHING YOU **SAY** MAY BE USED AS EVIDENCE AGAINST YOU.
POLICE FORCE

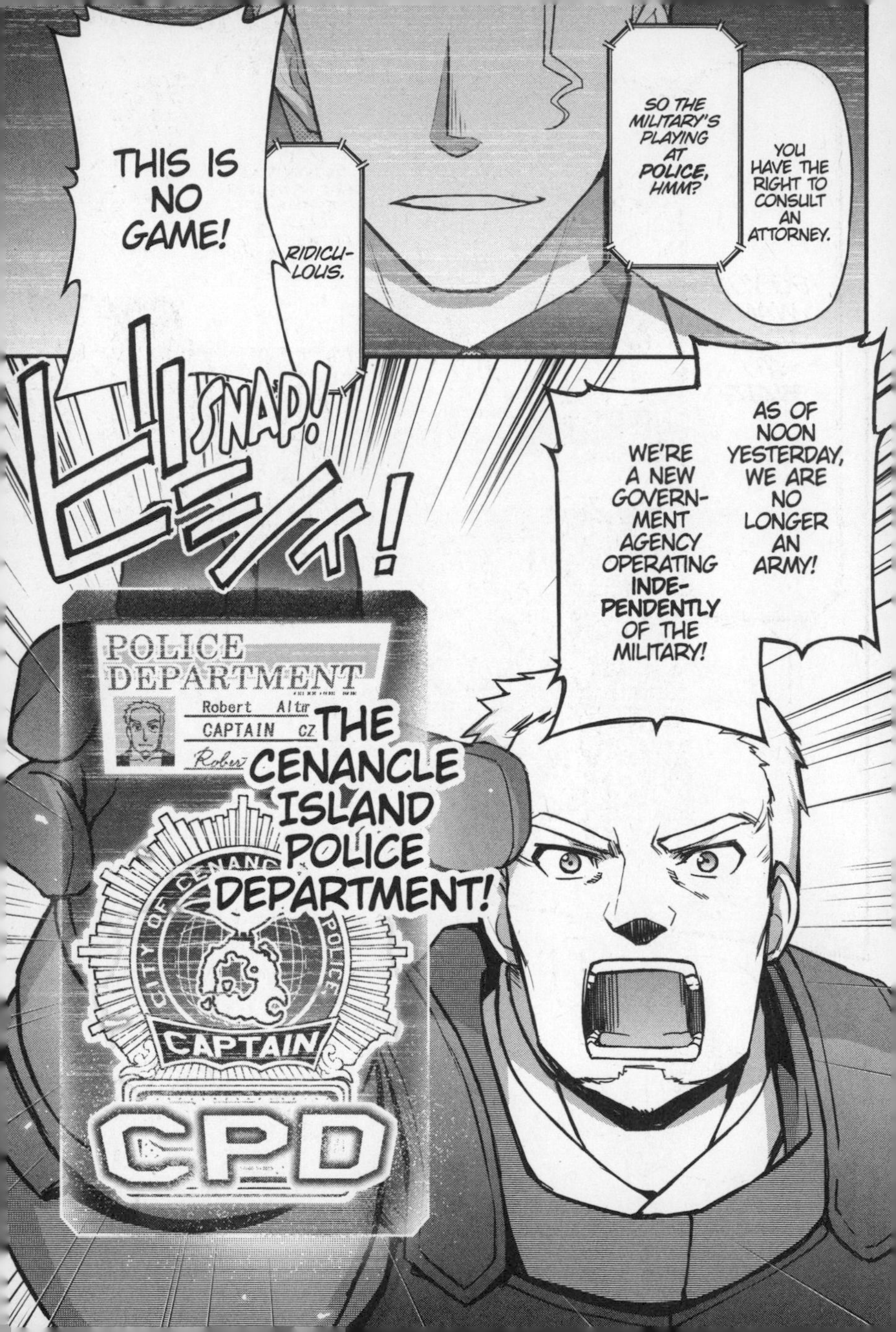
YOU HAVE THE RIGHT TO CONSULT AN ATTORNEY.
SO THE MILITARY'S PLAYING AT POLICE, HMM?
RIDICULOUS.
THIS IS NO GAME!
AS OF NOON YESTERDAY, WE ARE NO LONGER AN ARMY!
WE'RE A NEW GOVERNMENT AGENCY OPERATING INDEPENDENTLY OF THE MILITARY!
SNAP!
ビシィ!
POLICE DEPARTMENT
Robert Altr
CAPTAIN CZ
THE CENANCLE ISLAND POLICE DEPARTMENT!
CAPTAIN
CPD

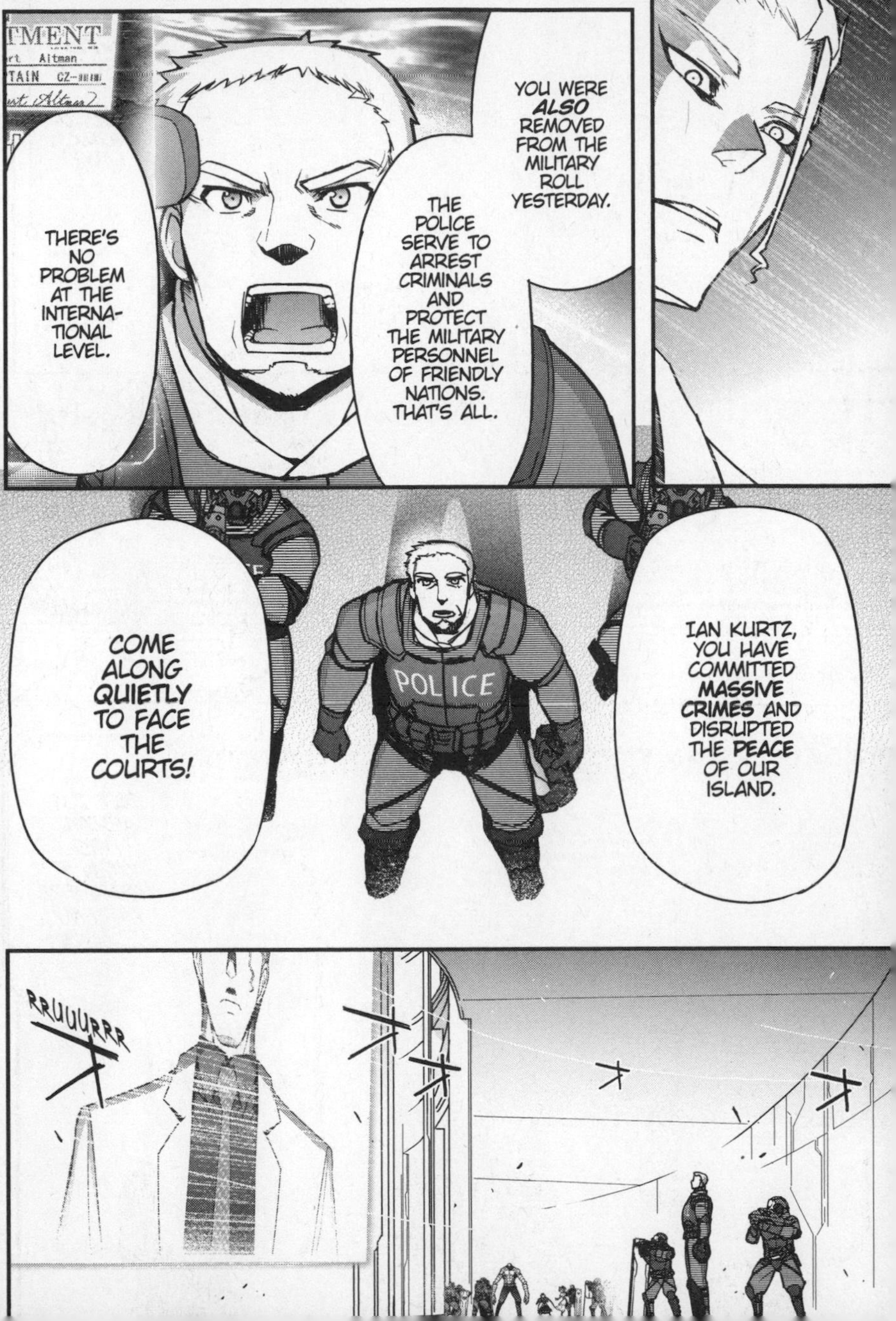
YOU WERE ALSO REMOVED FROM THE MILITARY ROLL YESTERDAY.
THE POLICE SERVE TO ARREST CRIMINALS AND PROTECT THE MILITARY PERSONNEL OF FRIENDLY NATIONS. THAT'S ALL.
THERE'S NO PROBLEM AT THE INTERNA-TIONAL LEVEL.
IAN KURTZ, YOU HAVE COMMITTED MASSIVE CRIMES AND DISRUPTED THE PEACE OF OUR ISLAND.
COME ALONG QUIETLY TO FACE THE COURTS!
POLICE
RRUUURRR

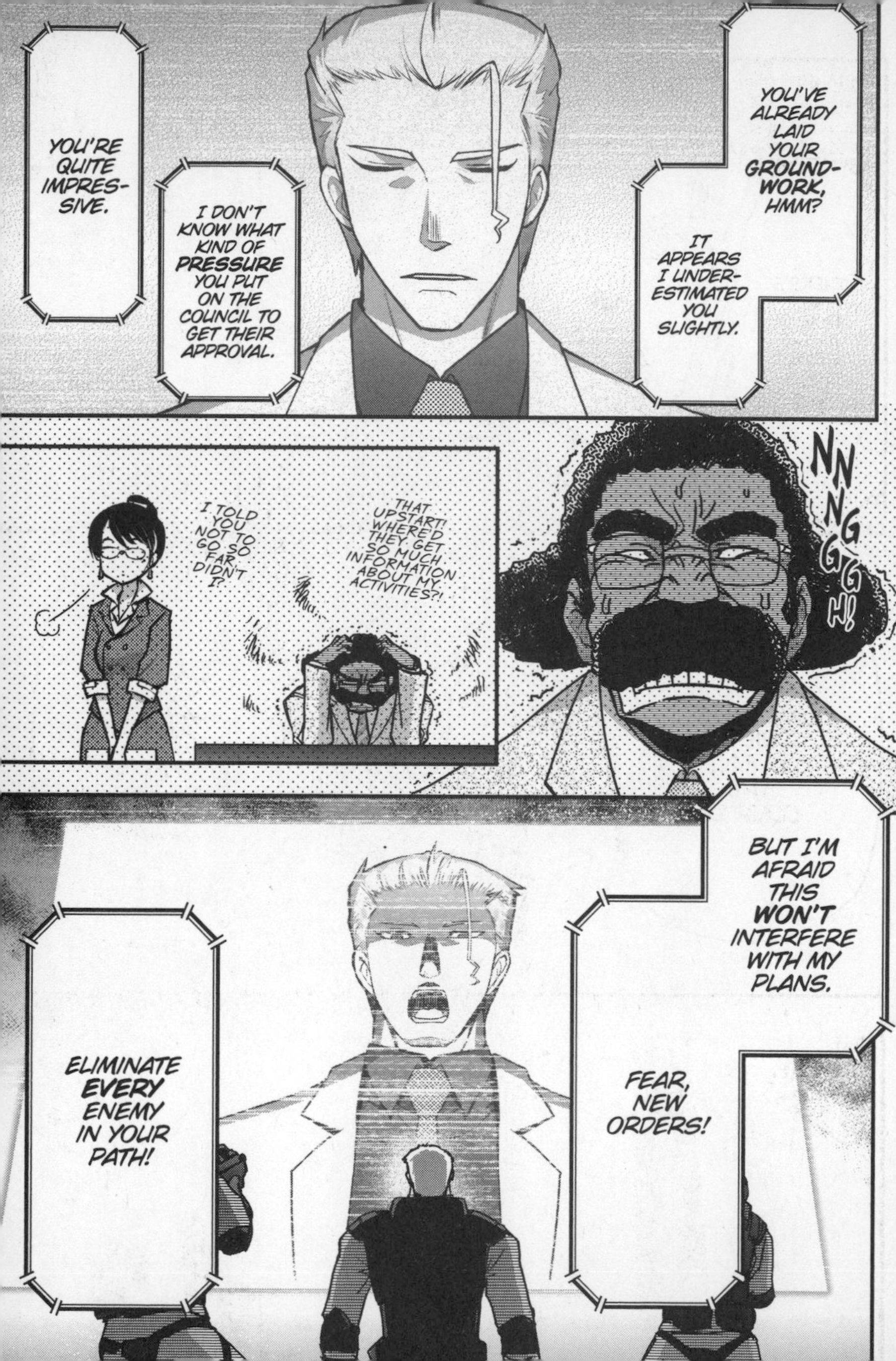
YOU'VE ALREADY LAID YOUR GROUND-WORK, HMM?
IT APPEARS I UNDER-ESTIMATED YOU SLIGHTLY.
I DON'T KNOW WHAT KIND OF PRESSURE YOU PUT ON THE COUNCIL TO GET THEIR APPROVAL.
YOU'RE QUITE IMPRES-SIVE.
NNNGGGH!
THAT UPSTART! WHERE'D THEY GET SO MUCH INFORMATION ABOUT MY ACTIVITIES?!
I TOLD YOU NOT TO GO SO FAR, DIDN'T I?
BUT I'M AFRAID THIS WON'T INTERFERE WITH MY PLANS.
FEAR, NEW ORDERS!
ELIMINATE EVERY ENEMY IN YOUR PATH!

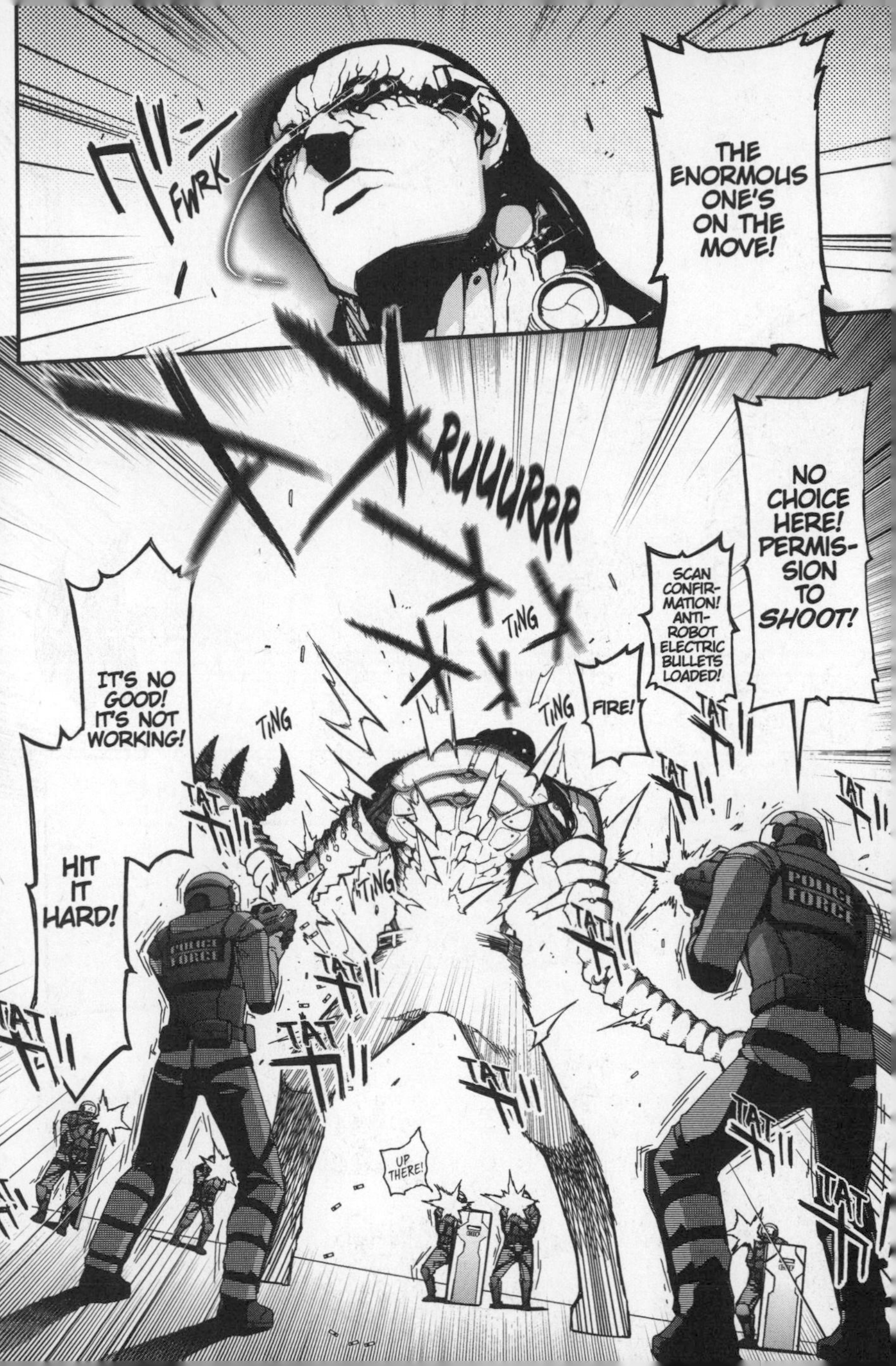
THE ENORMOUS ONE'S ON THE MOVE!
FWRK
RUUURRR
NO CHOICE HERE! PERMISSION TO SHOOT!
SCAN CONFIRMATION! ANTI-ROBOT ELECTRIC BULLETS LOADED!
FIRE!
TING
TING
TING
TING
IT'S NO GOOD! IT'S NOT WORKING!
HIT IT HARD!
TAT
TAT
TAT
TAT
TAT
TAT
TAT
TAT
TAT
TAT
TAT
UP THERE!
POLICE FORCE
POLICE FORCE

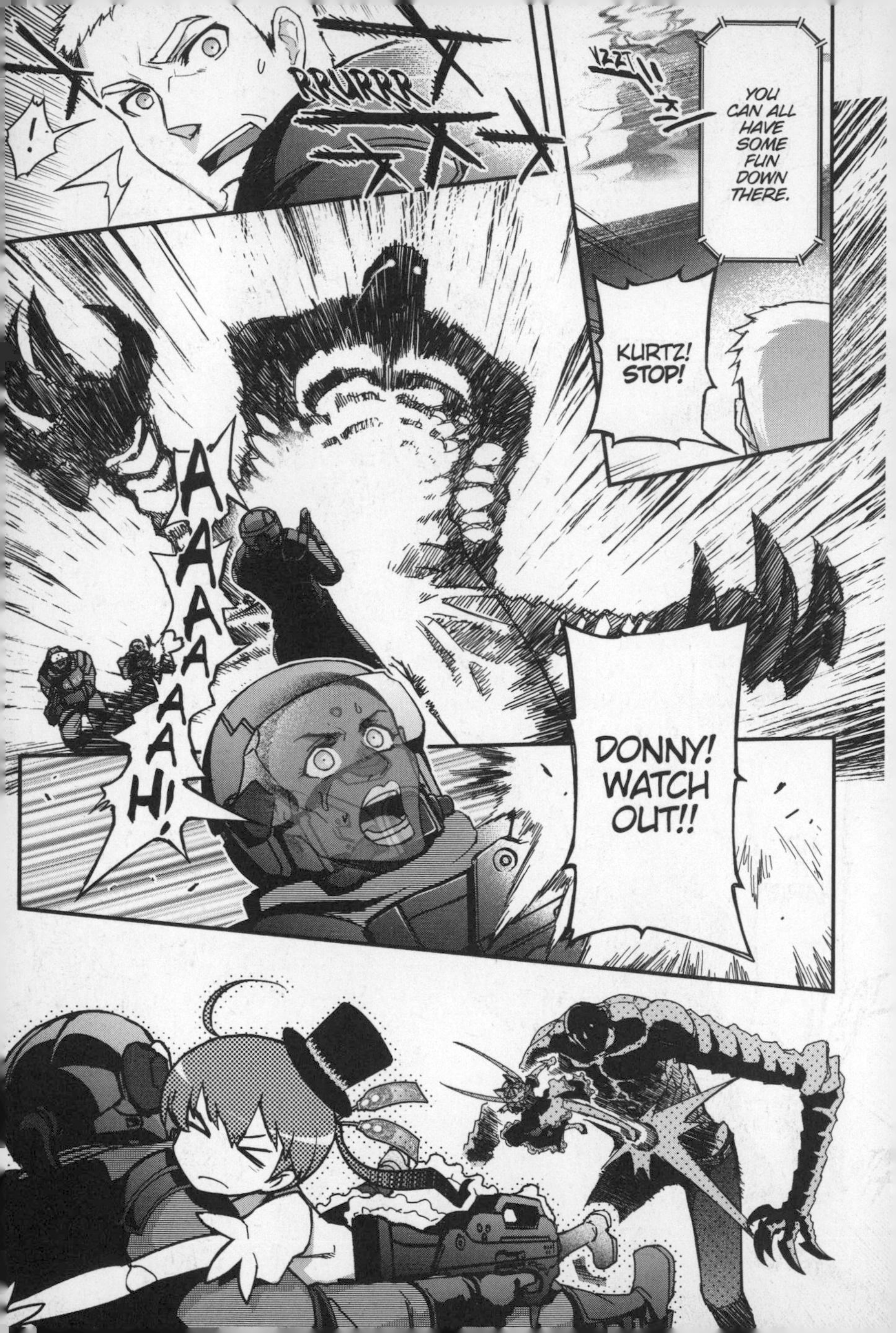
YOU CAN ALL HAVE SOME FUN DOWN THERE.
VZZT!!
RRURRR
!
KURTZ! STOP!
AAAAAAAH!
DONNY! WATCH OUT!!

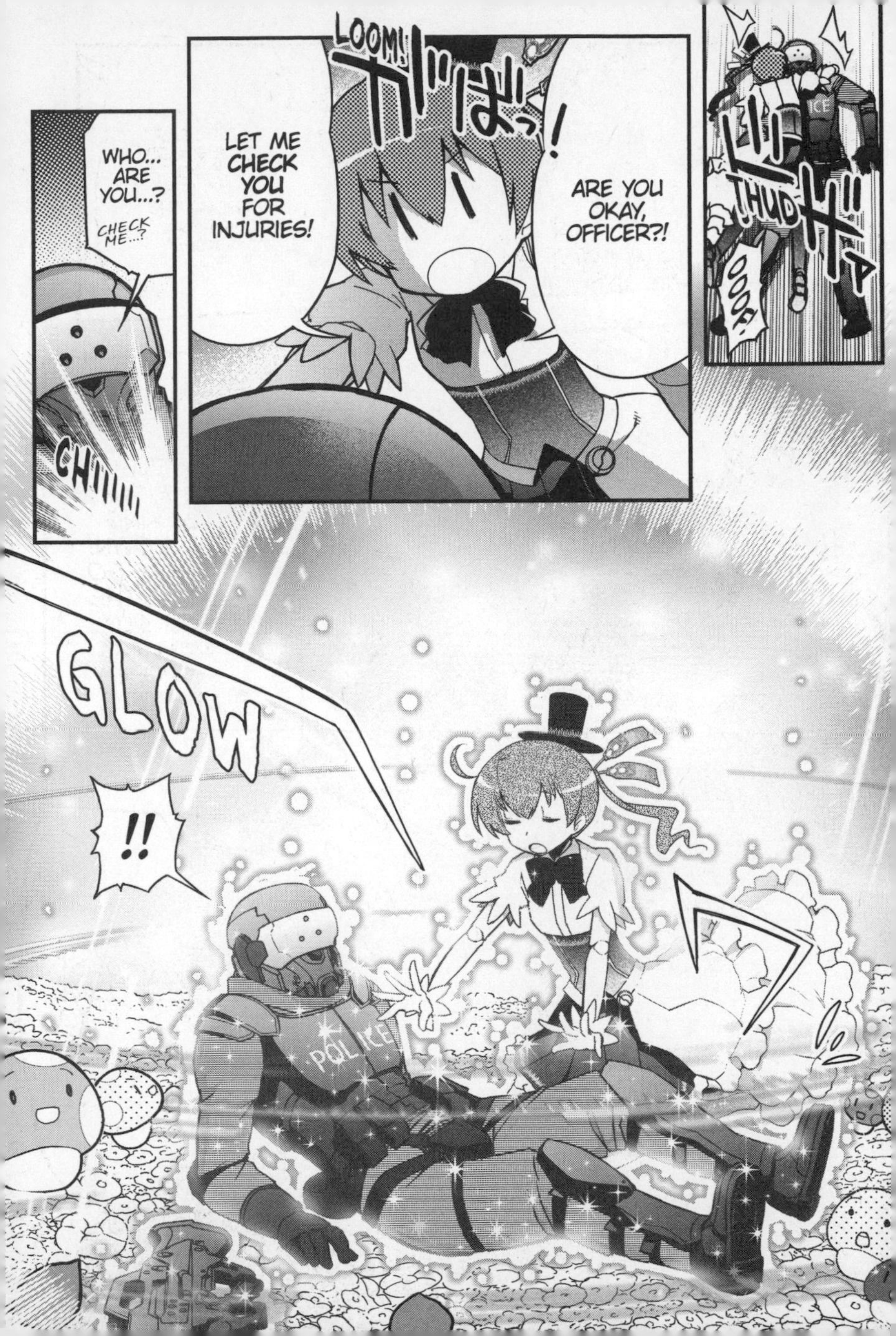
THUD
OOOF!
LOOM!
ガばっ!
ARE YOU OKAY, OFFICER?!
LET ME CHECK YOU FOR INJURIES!
WHO... ARE YOU...?
CHECK ME...?
CHI!!!!!
GLOW
!!

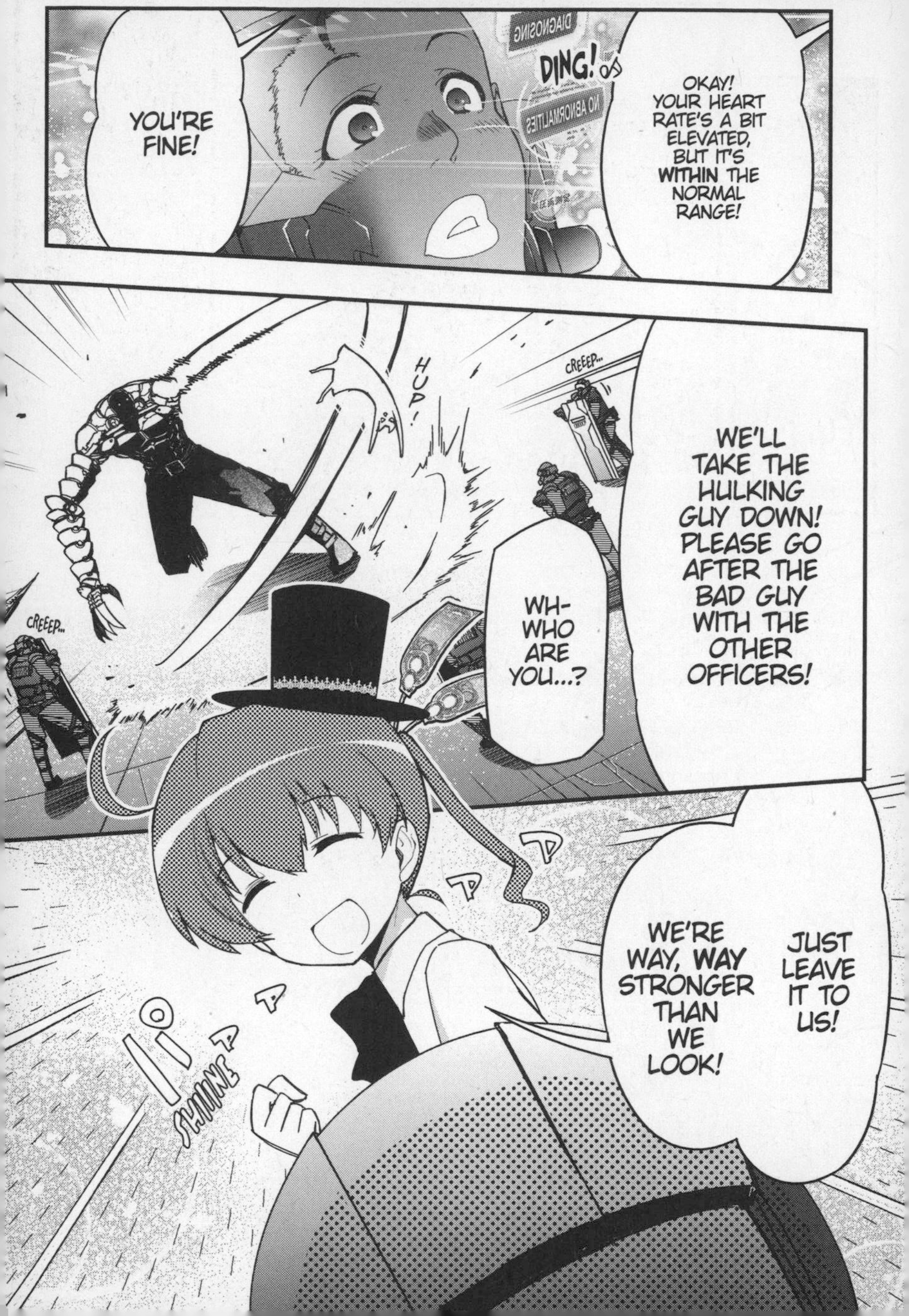

DING!
OKAY! YOUR HEART RATE'S A BIT ELEVATED, BUT IT'S WITHIN THE NORMAL RANGE!
YOU'RE FINE!
WE'LL TAKE THE HULKING GUY DOWN! PLEASE GO AFTER THE BAD GUY WITH THE OTHER OFFICERS!
CREEEP...
HUP!
WH-WHO ARE YOU...?
CREEEP...
JUST LEAVE IT TO US!
WE'RE WAY, WAY STRONGER THAN WE LOOK!
SHIIINE

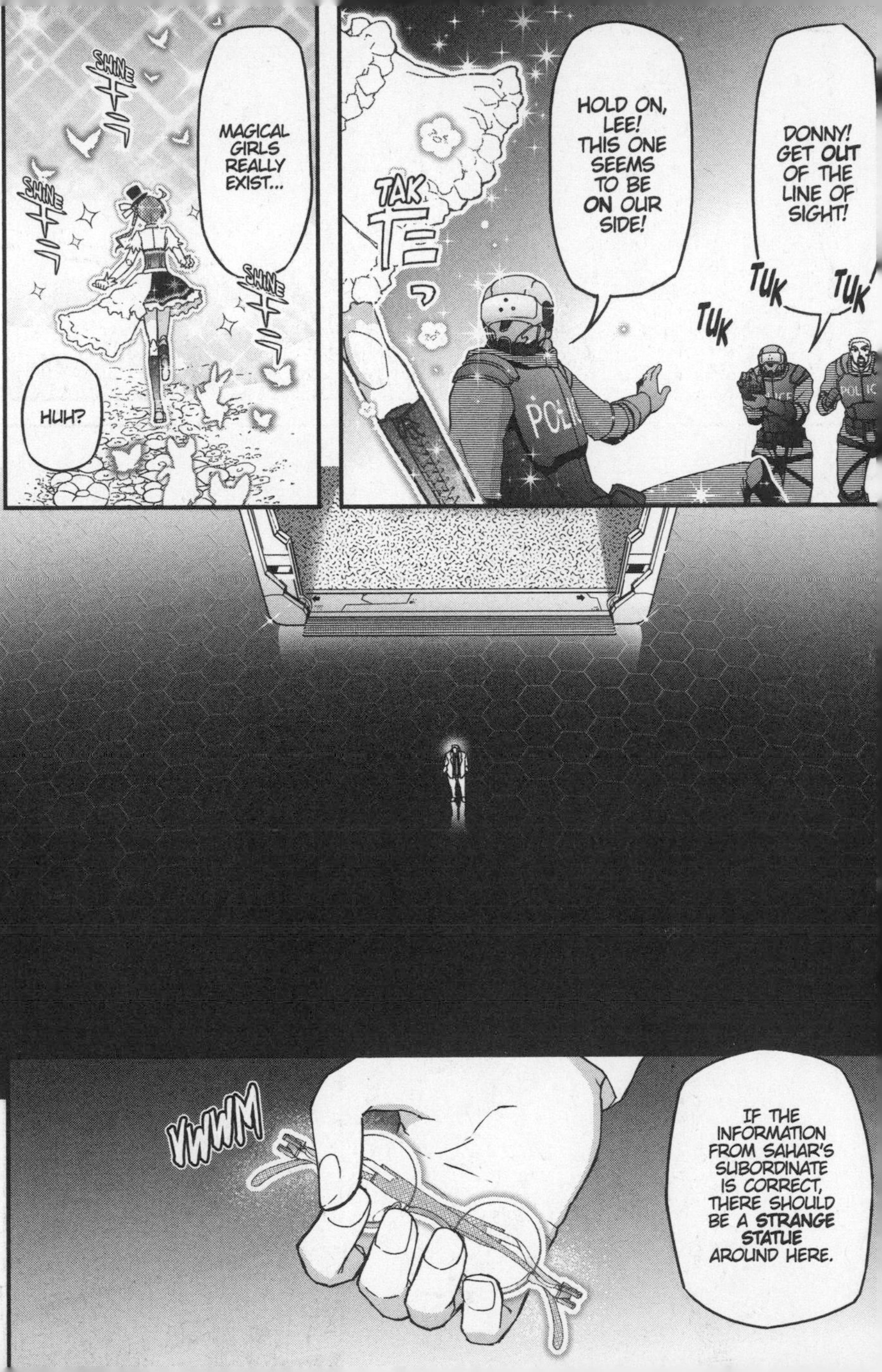
DONNY! GET OUT OF THE LINE OF SIGHT!
TUK
TUK
TUK
HOLD ON, LEE! THIS ONE SEEMS TO BE ON OUR SIDE!
TAK
MAGICAL GIRLS REALLY EXIST...
SHINE
SHINE
SHINE
HUH?
IF THE INFORMATION FROM SAHAR'S SUBORDINATE IS CORRECT, THERE SHOULD BE A STRANGE STATUE AROUND HERE.
VWWM

KATOK
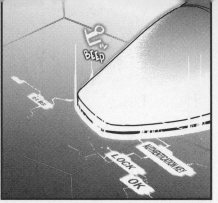

BEEP

AUTHENTICATION KEY

LOCK

OK

KRR

KRR

KRR

KRR

KRR

KRR

IT...
IT'S...

WATER

GRRTUNK

KRR

KRR

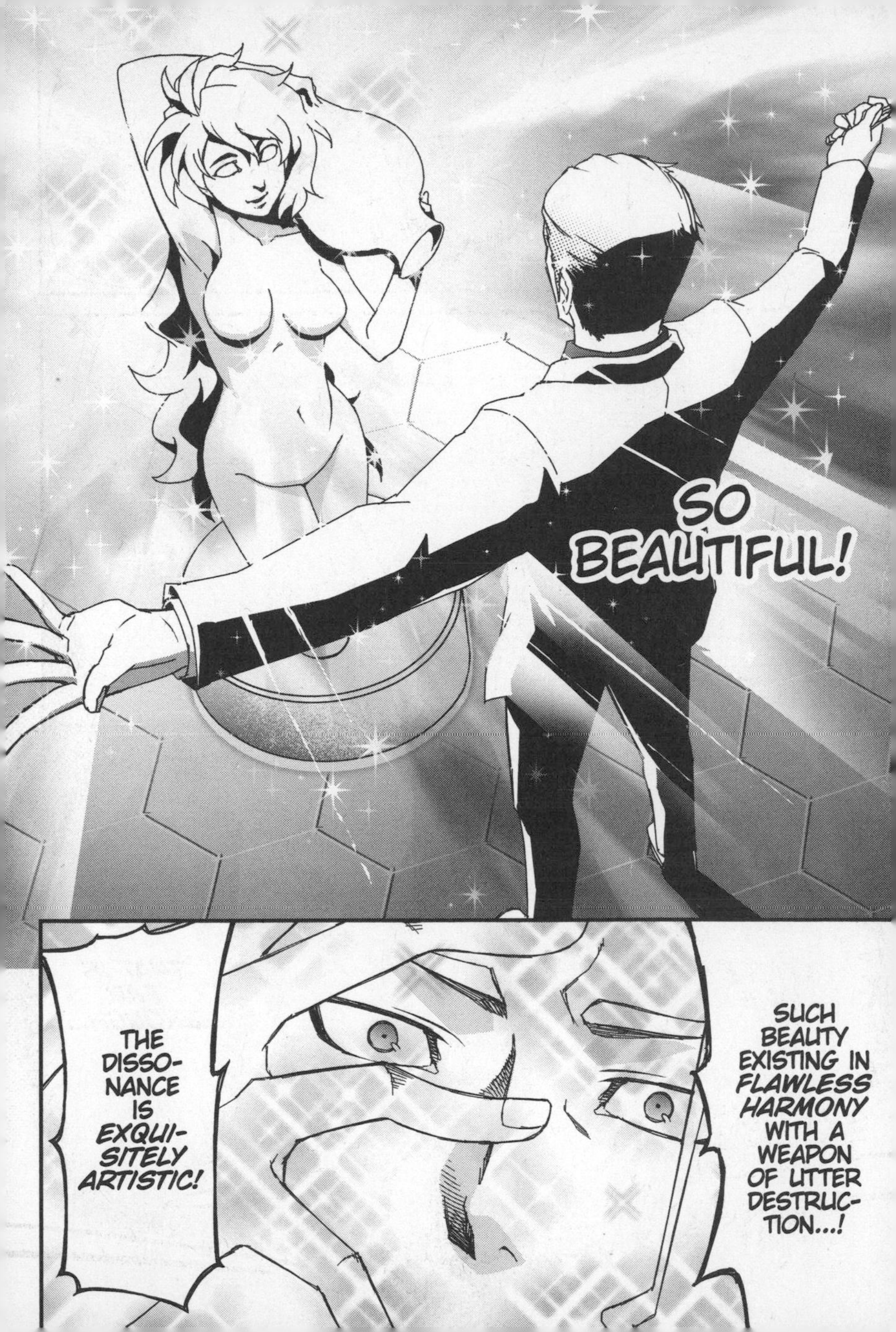
SO BEAUTIFUL!
SUCH BEAUTY EXISTING IN *FLAWLESS HARMONY* WITH A WEAPON OF UTTER DESTRUCTION...!
THE DISSONANCE IS *EXQUISITELY ARTISTIC!*

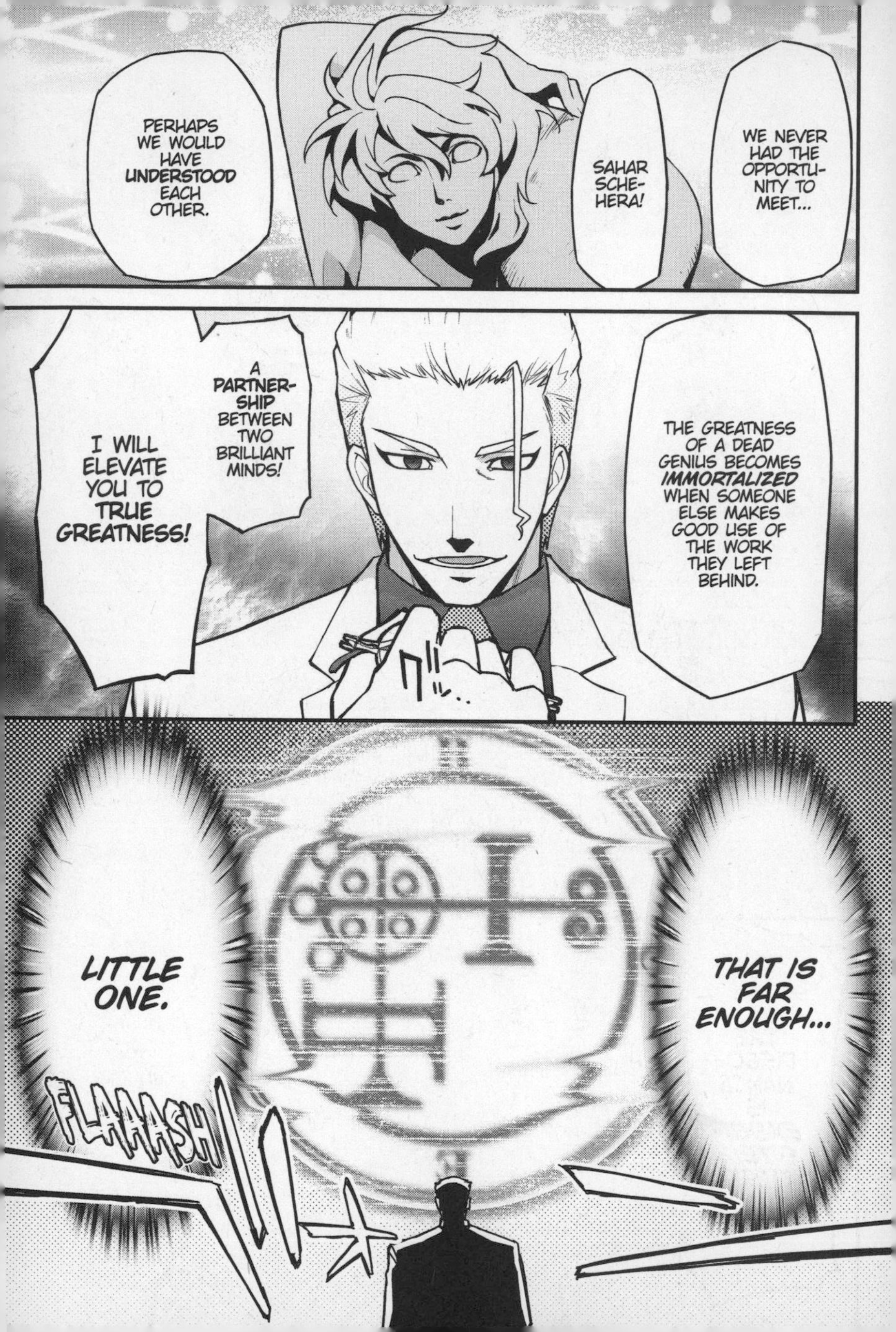
WE NEVER HAD THE OPPORTU-NITY TO MEET...
SAHAR SCHE-HERA!
PERHAPS WE WOULD HAVE UNDERSTOOD EACH OTHER.
THE GREATNESS OF A DEAD GENIUS BECOMES IMMORTALIZED WHEN SOMEONE ELSE MAKES GOOD USE OF THE WORK THEY LEFT BEHIND.
A PARTNER-SHIP BETWEEN TWO BRILLIANT MINDS!
I WILL ELEVATE YOU TO TRUE GREATNESS!
THAT IS FAR ENOUGH...
LITTLE ONE.
FLAAASH!!

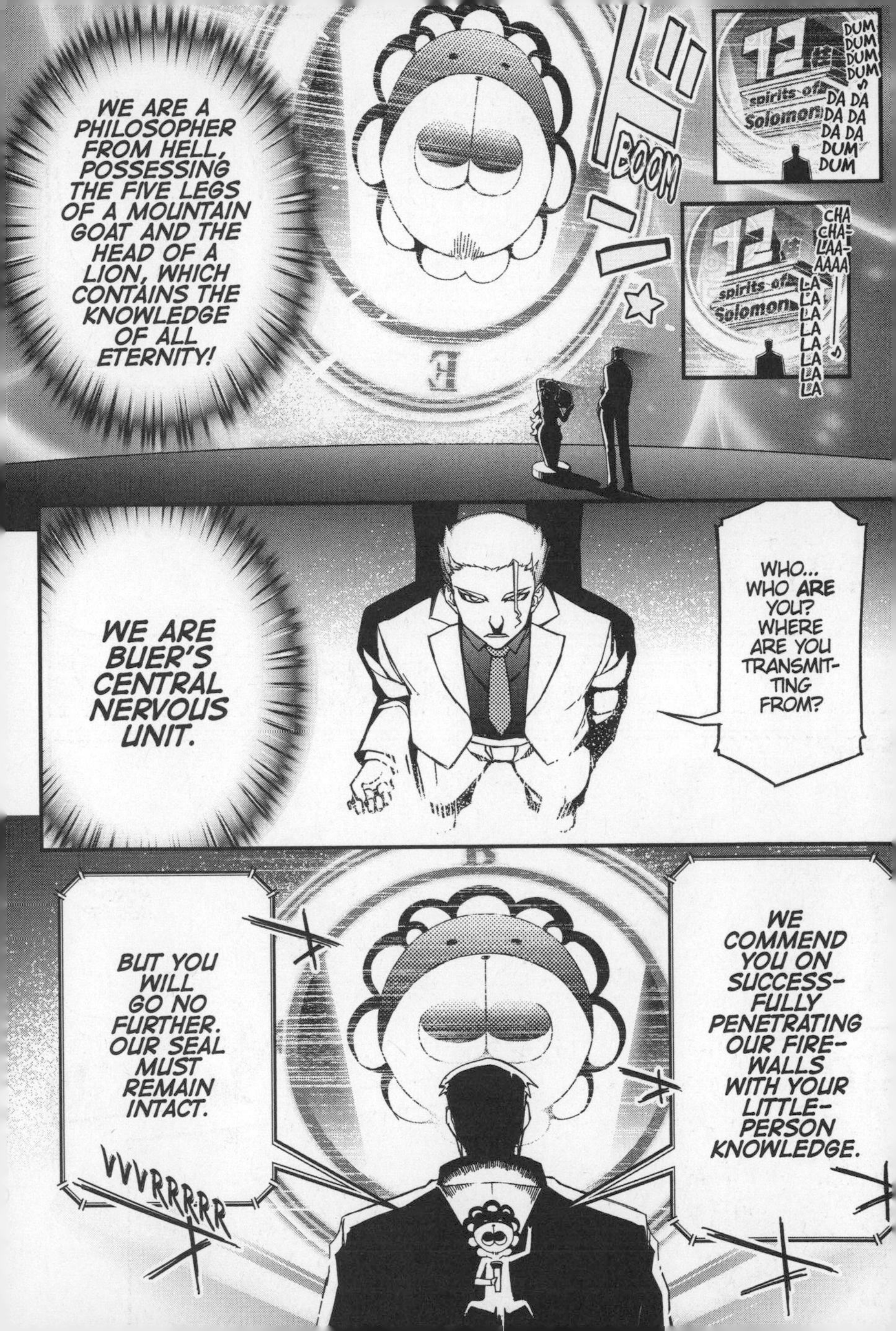
spirits of Solomon
DUM DUM DUM DUM DA DA DA DA DA DA DUM DUM
spirits of Solomon
CHA CHA-LAAAAAA LA LA LA LA LA LA LA LA!
BOOM
WE ARE A PHILOSOPHER FROM HELL, POSSESSING THE FIVE LEGS OF A MOUNTAIN GOAT AND THE HEAD OF A LION, WHICH CONTAINS THE KNOWLEDGE OF ALL ETERNITY!
WHO... WHO ARE YOU? WHERE ARE YOU TRANSMIT-TING FROM?
WE ARE BUER'S CENTRAL NERVOUS UNIT.
WE COMMEND YOU ON SUCCESS-FULLY PENETRATING OUR FIRE-WALLS WITH YOUR LITTLE-PERSON KNOWLEDGE.
BUT YOU WILL GO NO FURTHER. OUR SEAL MUST REMAIN INTACT.
VVVRRRRRR

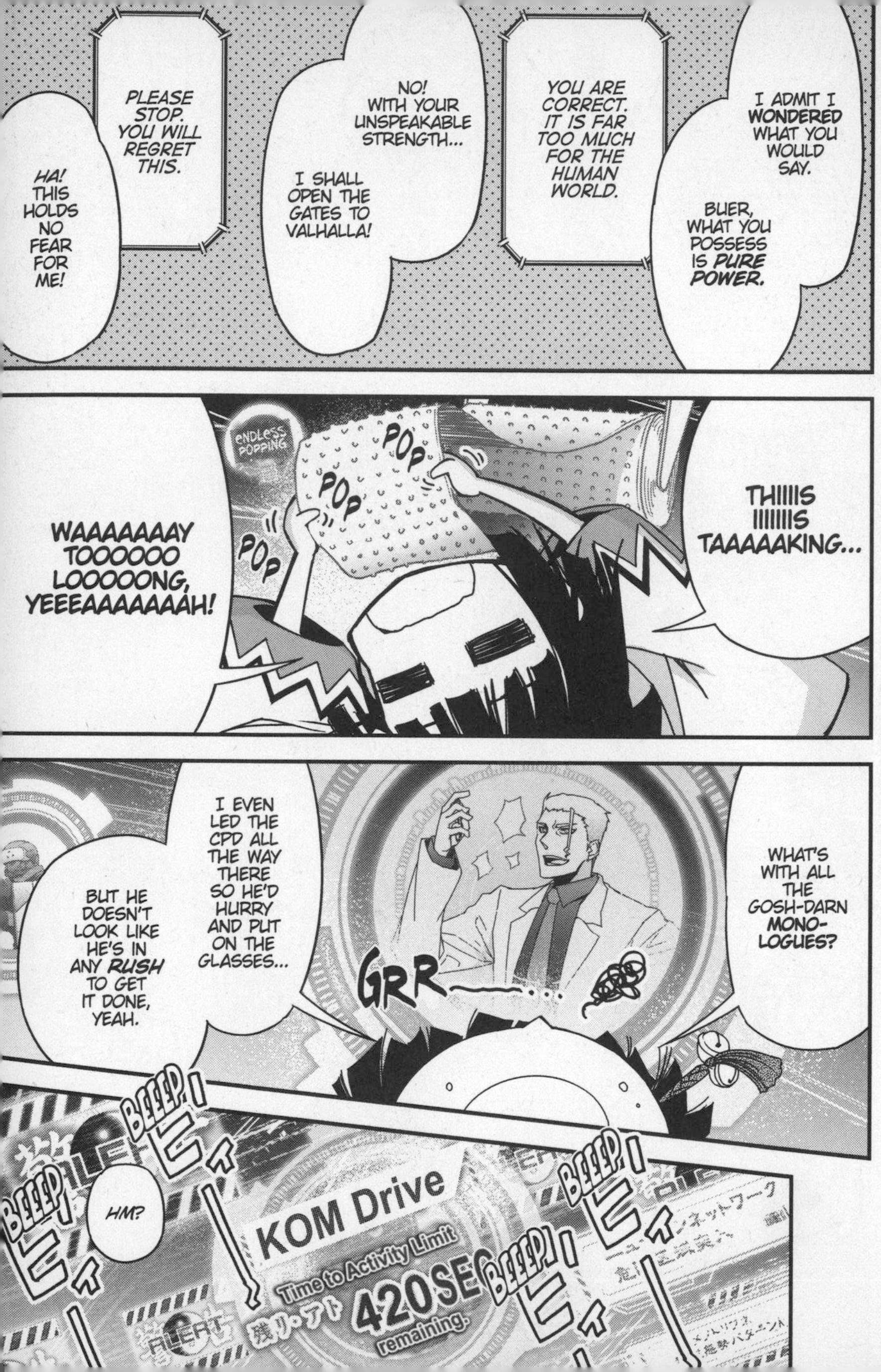
I ADMIT I WONDERED WHAT YOU WOULD SAY.
BUER, WHAT YOU POSSESS IS PURE POWER.
YOU ARE CORRECT. IT IS FAR TOO MUCH FOR THE HUMAN WORLD.
NO! WITH YOUR UNSPEAKABLE STRENGTH...
I SHALL OPEN THE GATES TO VALHALLA!
PLEASE STOP. YOU WILL REGRET THIS.
HA! THIS HOLDS NO FEAR FOR ME!
THIIIIS IIIIIIIS TAAAAAKING...
POP
POP
POP
ENDLESS POPPING
WAAAAAAAY TOOOOOO LOOOOOONG, YEEEAAAAAAAAH!
WHAT'S WITH ALL THE GOSH-DARN MONO-LOGUES?
GRR
I EVEN LED THE CPD ALL THE WAY THERE SO HE'D HURRY AND PUT ON THE GLASSES...
BUT HE DOESN'T LOOK LIKE HE'S IN ANY RUSH TO GET IT DONE, YEAH.
BEEP
BEEP
BEEP
BEEP
HM?
KOM Drive
Time to Activity Limit
420SEC
remaining.
ALERT

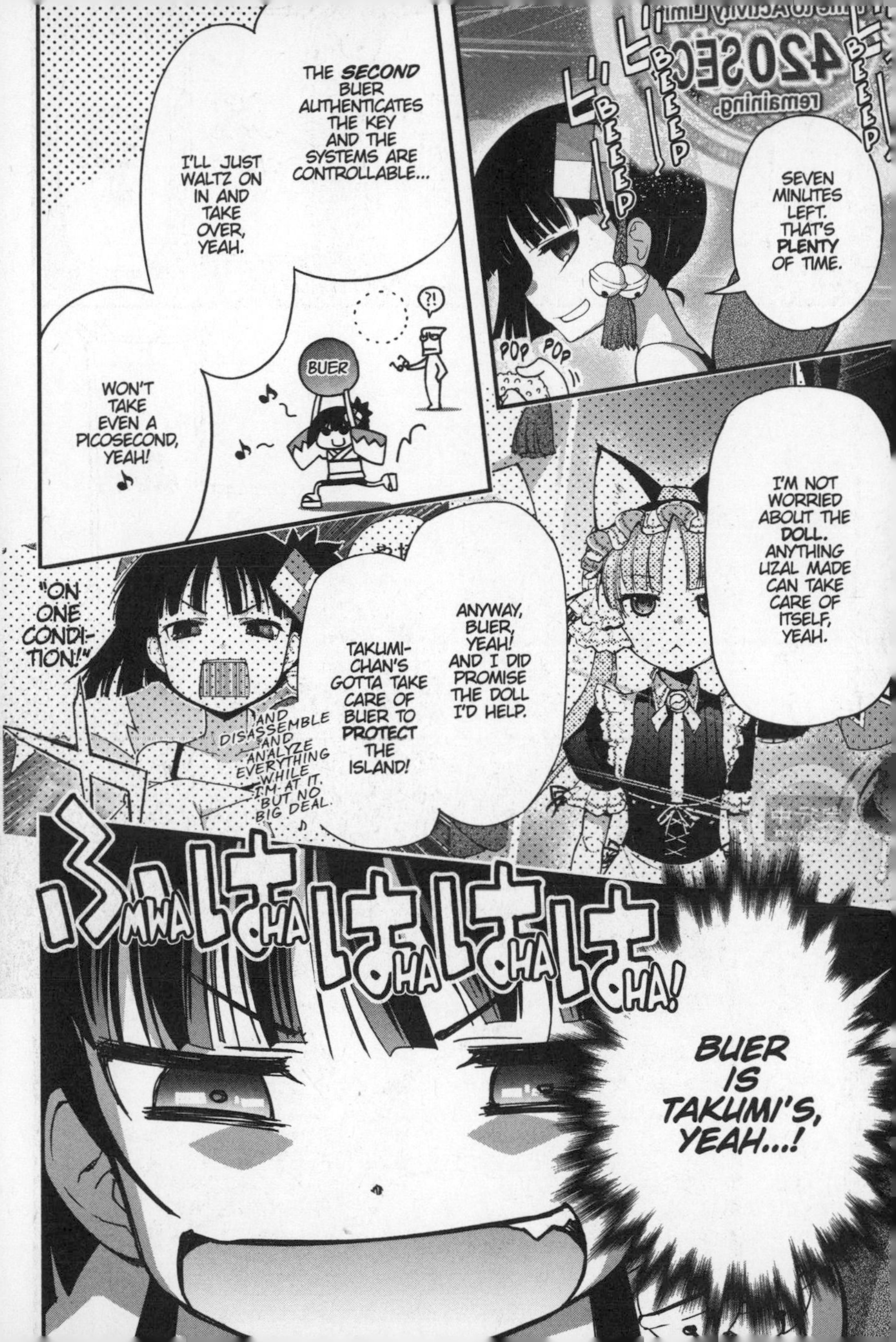
BEEEP
BEEEP
BEEEP
SEVEN MINUTES LEFT. THAT'S PLENTY OF TIME.
POP POP
THE SECOND BUER AUTHENTICATES THE KEY AND THE SYSTEMS ARE CONTROLLABLE...
I'LL JUST WALTZ ON IN AND TAKE OVER, YEAH.
BUER
?!
WON'T TAKE EVEN A PICOSECOND, YEAH! ♪
I'M NOT WORRIED ABOUT THE DOLL. ANYTHING UZAL MADE CAN TAKE CARE OF ITSELF, YEAH.
ANYWAY, BUER, YEAH! AND I DID PROMISE THE DOLL I'D HELP.
TAKUMI-CHAN'S GOTTA TAKE CARE OF BUER TO PROTECT THE ISLAND!
AND DISASSEMBLE AND ANALYZE EVERYTHING WHILE I'M AT IT. BUT NO BIG DEAL. ♪
"ON ONE CONDITION!"
MWA HA HA HA HA!
BUER IS TAKUMI'S, YEAH...!

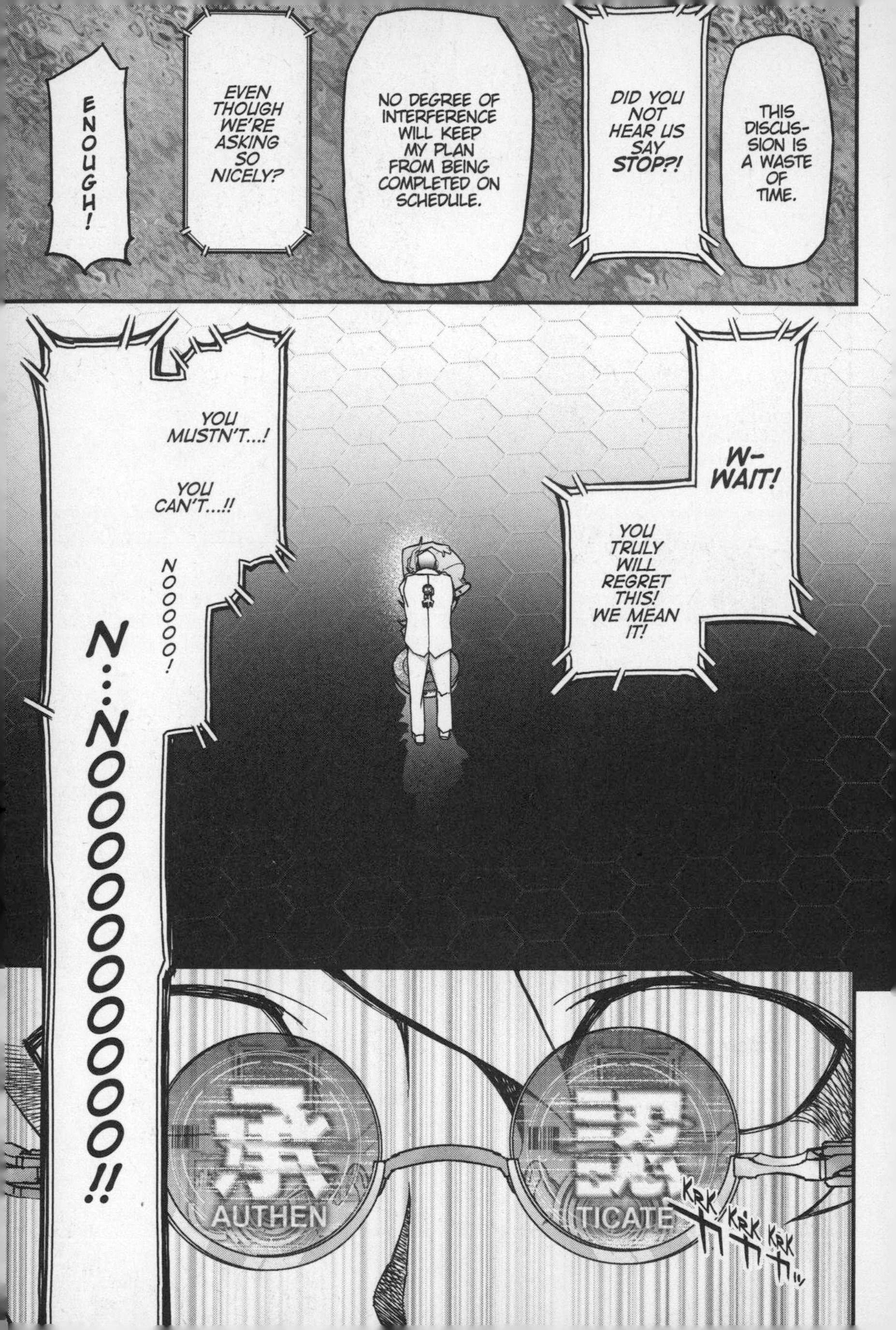
THIS DISCUSSION IS A WASTE OF TIME.
DID YOU NOT HEAR US SAY STOP?!
NO DEGREE OF INTERFERENCE WILL KEEP MY PLAN FROM BEING COMPLETED ON SCHEDULE.
EVEN THOUGH WE'RE ASKING SO NICELY?
ENOUGH!
W-WAIT!
YOU TRULY WILL REGRET THIS! WE MEAN IT!
YOU MUSTN'T...!
YOU CAN'T...!!
NOOOOOO!
N...NOOOOOOOOOOOOO!!
承 AUTHEN
認 TICATE
KRK KRK KRK

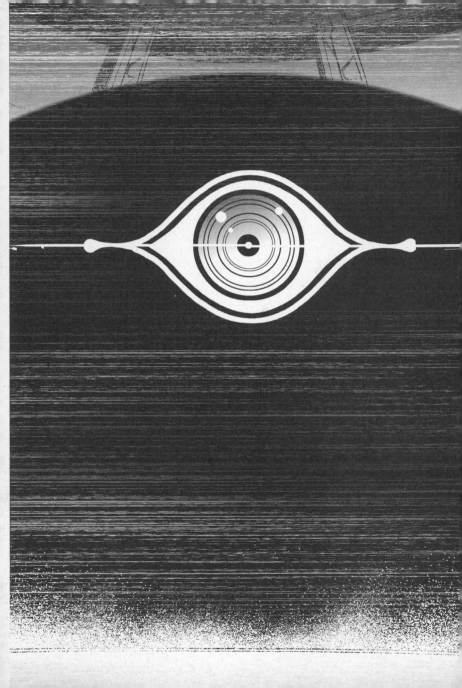

GHOST URN

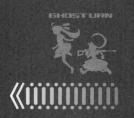

GHOST URN

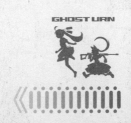

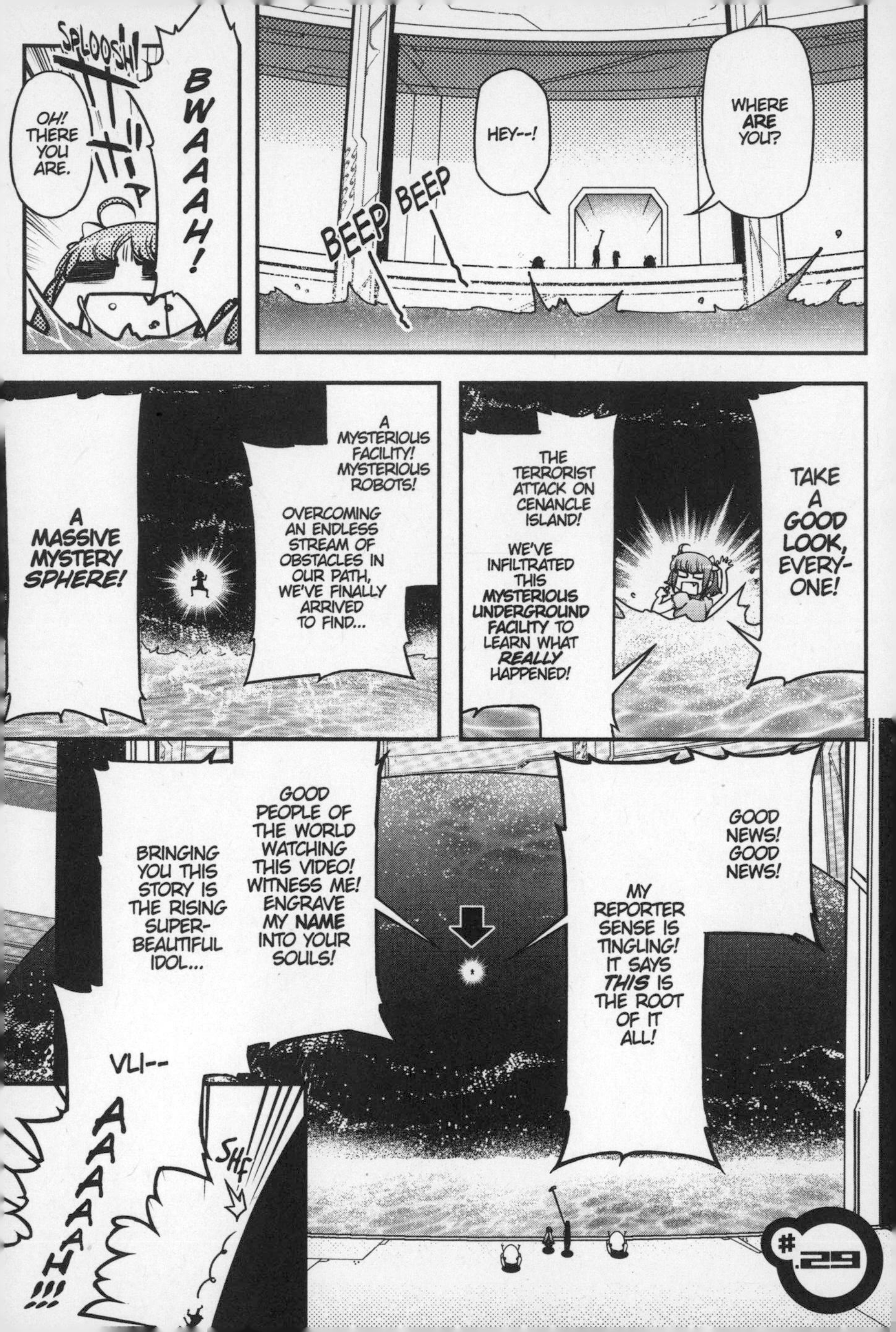
WHERE ARE YOU?
HEY--!
BEEP BEEP
SPLOOSH!
OH! THERE YOU ARE.
BWAAAAH!
TAKE A GOOD LOOK, EVERY-ONE!
THE TERRORIST ATTACK ON CENANCLE ISLAND!
WE'VE INFILTRATED THIS MYSTERIOUS UNDERGROUND FACILITY TO LEARN WHAT REALLY HAPPENED!
A MYSTERIOUS FACILITY! MYSTERIOUS ROBOTS!
OVERCOMING AN ENDLESS STREAM OF OBSTACLES IN OUR PATH, WE'VE FINALLY ARRIVED TO FIND...
A MASSIVE MYSTERY SPHERE!
GOOD NEWS! GOOD NEWS!
MY REPORTER SENSE IS TINGLING! IT SAYS THIS IS THE ROOT OF IT ALL!
GOOD PEOPLE OF THE WORLD WATCHING THIS VIDEO! WITNESS ME! ENGRAVE MY NAME INTO YOUR SOULS!
BRINGING YOU THIS STORY IS THE RISING SUPER-BEAUTIFUL IDOL...
VLI--
SHF
AAAAAAH!!!
#.29

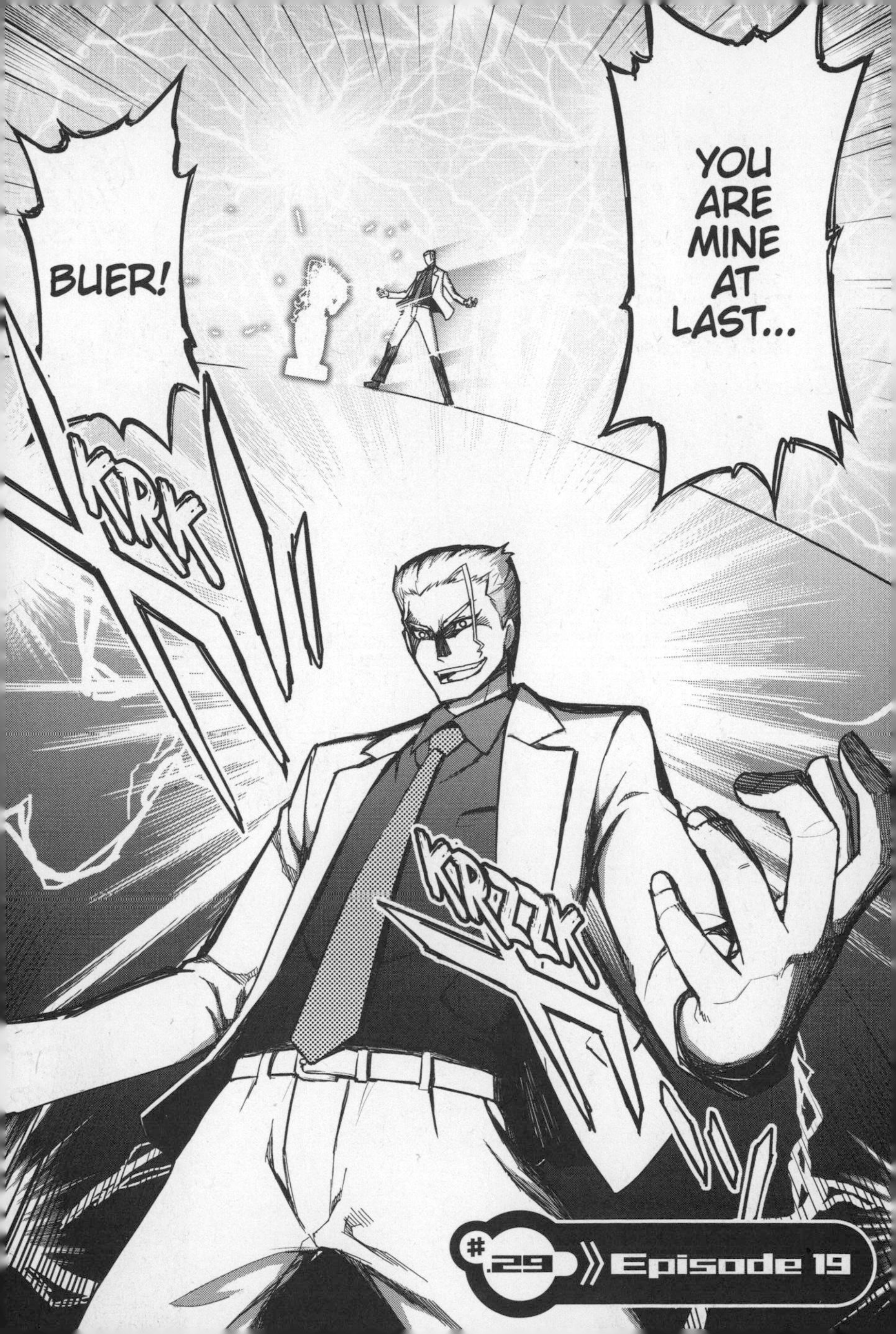
YOU ARE MINE AT LAST...
BUER!
#.29 Episode 19

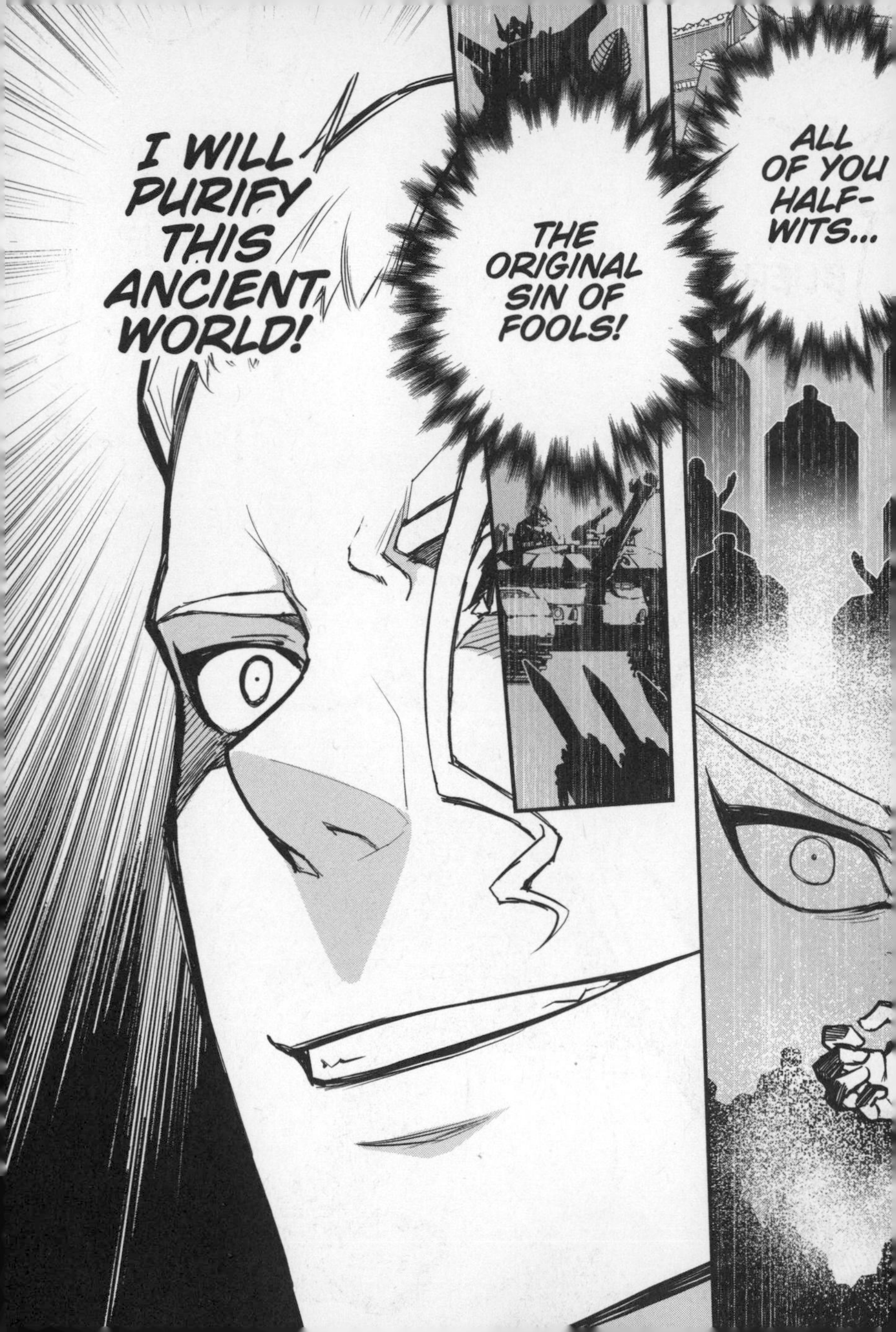
ALL OF YOU HALF-WITS...
THE ORIGINAL SIN OF FOOLS!
I WILL PURIFY THIS ANCIENT WORLD!

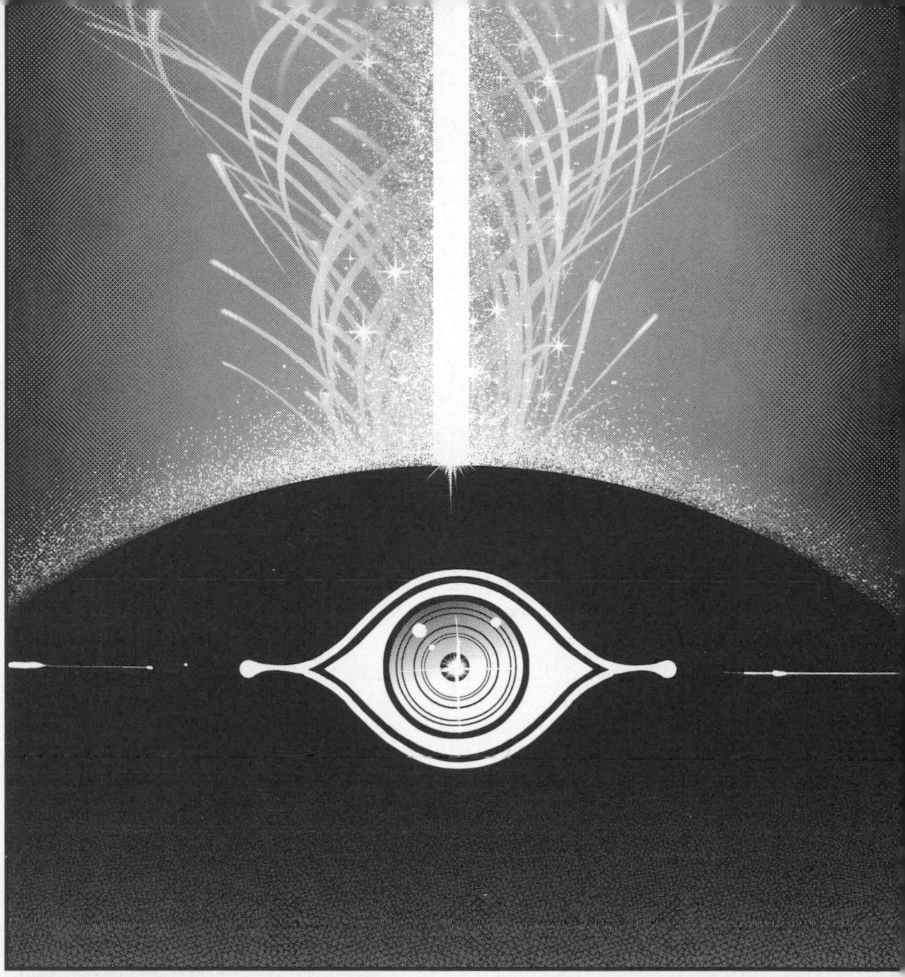

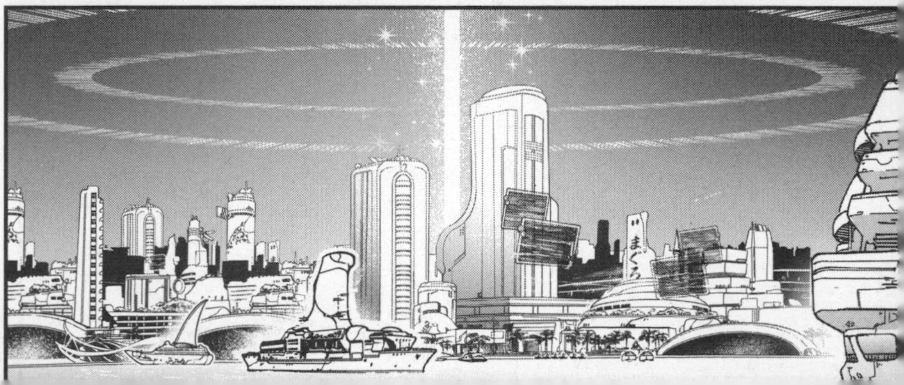
まぐろ

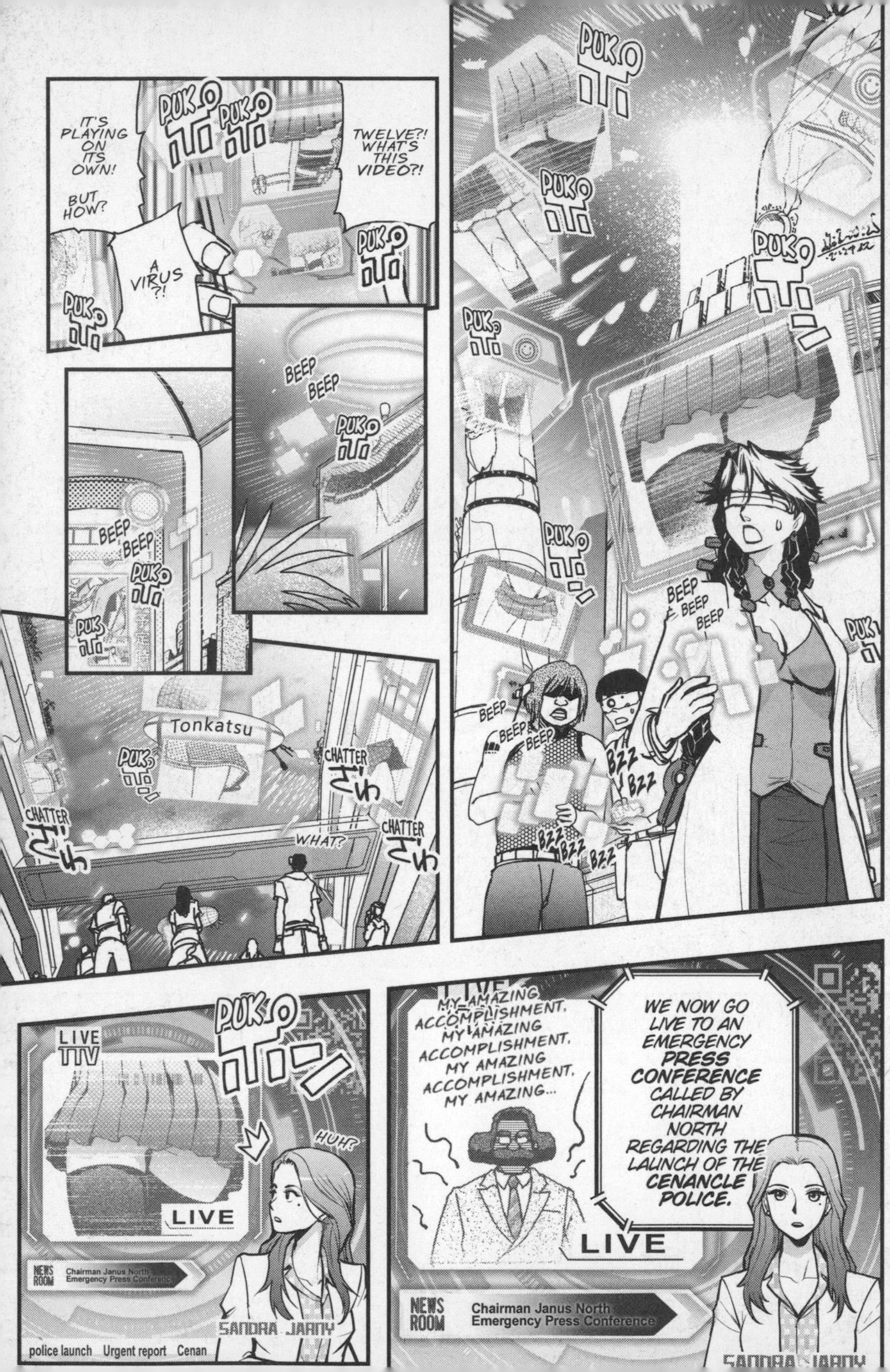
PUKO TI
PUKO TI
PUKO TI
PUKO TI
PUKO TI
BEEP BEEP BEEP
BEEP BEEP BEEP
BZZ BZZ
BZZ BZZ BZZ
PUK
TWELVE?! WHAT'S THIS VIDEO?!
PUKO TI
PUKO TI
IT'S PLAYING ON ITS OWN!
BUT HOW?
PUKO TI
A VIRUS?!
PUKO TI
BEEP BEEP
PUKO TI
BEEP BEEP
PUKO TI
PUK TI
CHATTER ざわ
Tonkatsu
PUKO TI
WHAT?
CHATTER ざわ
CHATTER ざわ
WE NOW GO LIVE TO AN EMERGENCY PRESS CONFERENCE CALLED BY CHAIRMAN NORTH REGARDING THE LAUNCH OF THE CENANCLE POLICE.
MY AMAZING ACCOMPLISHMENT, MY AMAZING ACCOMPLISHMENT, MY AMAZING ACCOMPLISHMENT, MY AMAZING...
LIVE
NEWS ROOM
Chairman Janus North Emergency Press Conference
PUKO TI
LIVE TTV
HUH?
LIVE
NEWS ROOM
Chairman Janus North Emergency Press Conference
SANDRA JARNY
police launch Urgent report Cenan

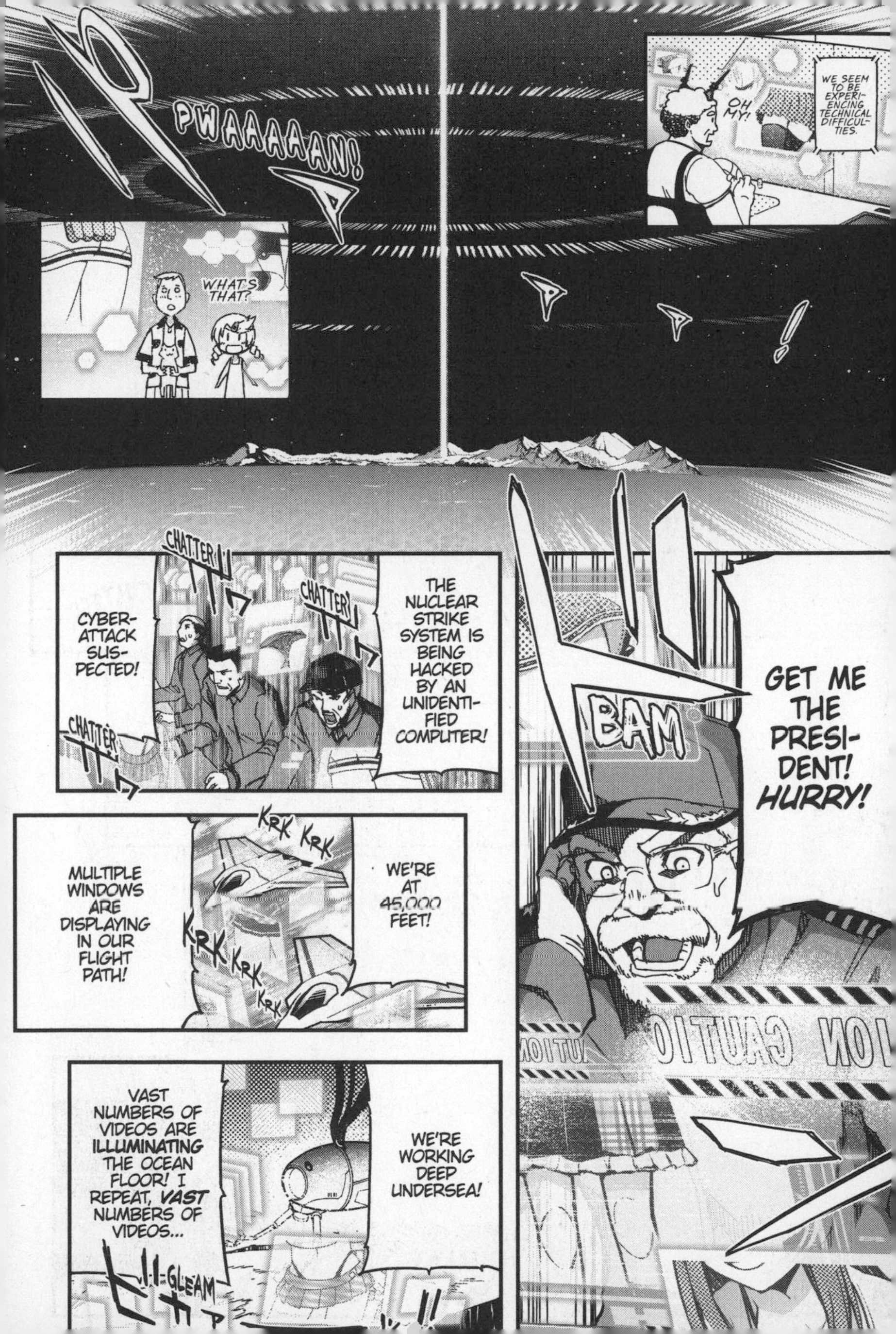
WE SEEM TO BE EXPERIENCING TECHNICAL DIFFICULTIES.
OH MY!
PWAAAAAAN!
!
WHAT'S THAT?
BAM
GET ME THE PRESIDENT! HURRY!
CAUTION CAUTIO
THE NUCLEAR STRIKE SYSTEM IS BEING HACKED BY AN UNIDENTIFIED COMPUTER!
CHATTER
CHATTER
CYBER-ATTACK SUSPECTED!
CHATTER
WE'RE AT 45,000 FEET!
KRK KRK
MULTIPLE WINDOWS ARE DISPLAYING IN OUR FLIGHT PATH!
KRK KRK KRK
WE'RE WORKING DEEP UNDERSEA!
VAST NUMBERS OF VIDEOS ARE ILLUMINATING THE OCEAN FLOOR! I REPEAT, VAST NUMBERS OF VIDEOS...
GLEAM

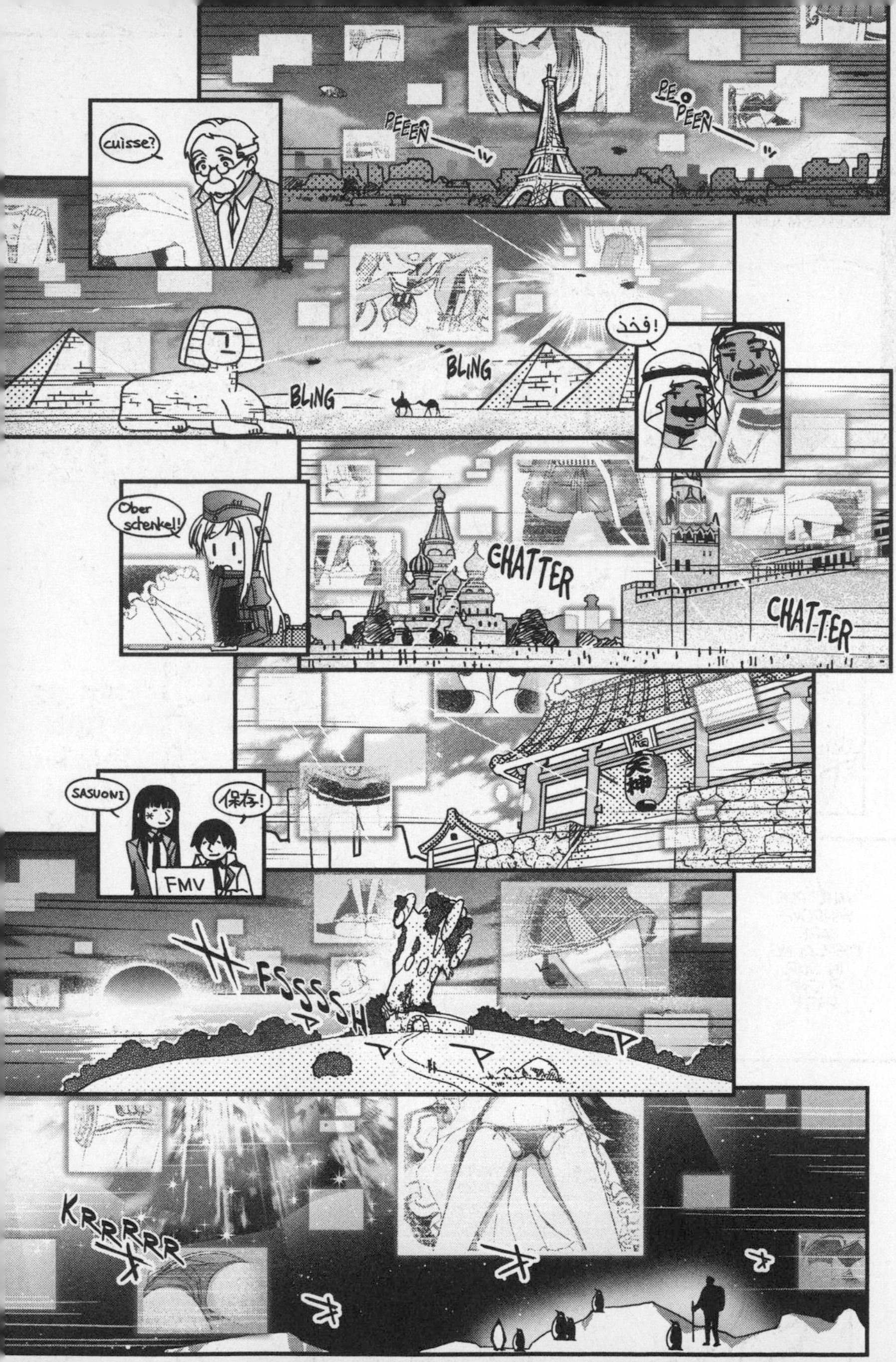
PE-O PEEN
PEEEN
cuisse?
فخذ!
BLING
BLING
CHAT-T-ER
CHATTER
Ober schenkel!
福
天神
SASUONI
保存!
FMV
FSSSSSH
KRRRRRR

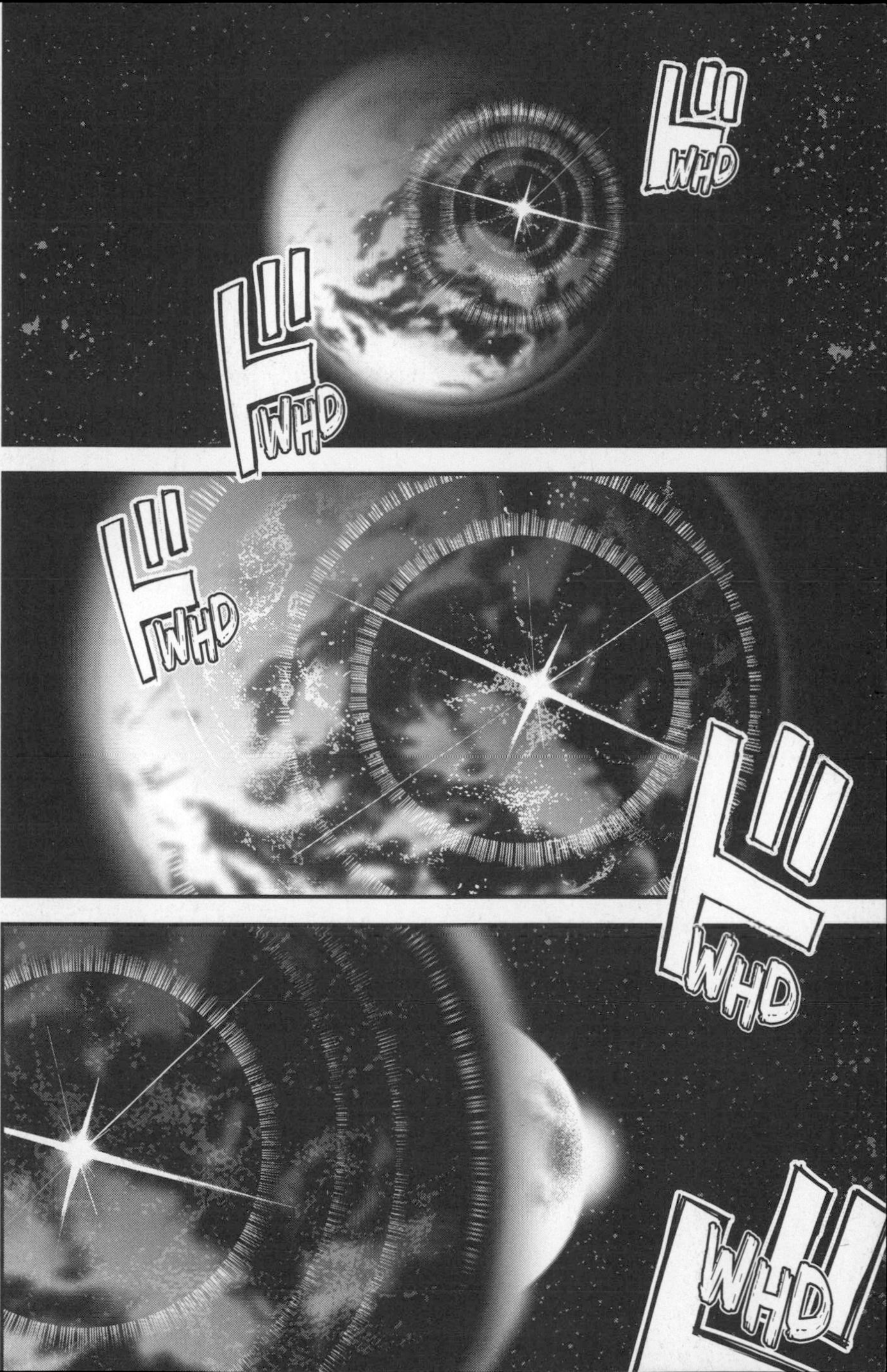
WHD
WHD
WHD
WHD
WHD

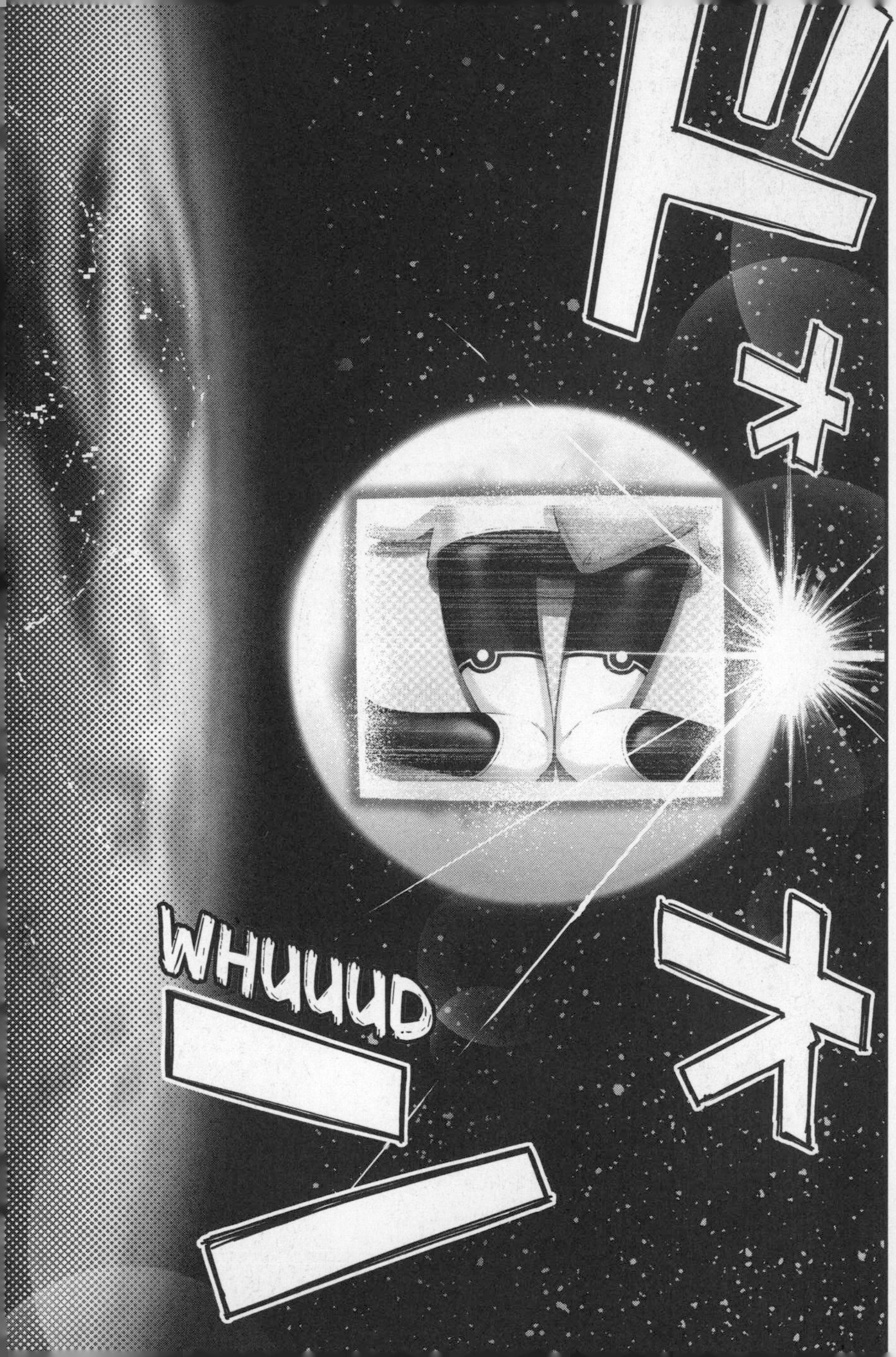
ドォォン
WHUUUD

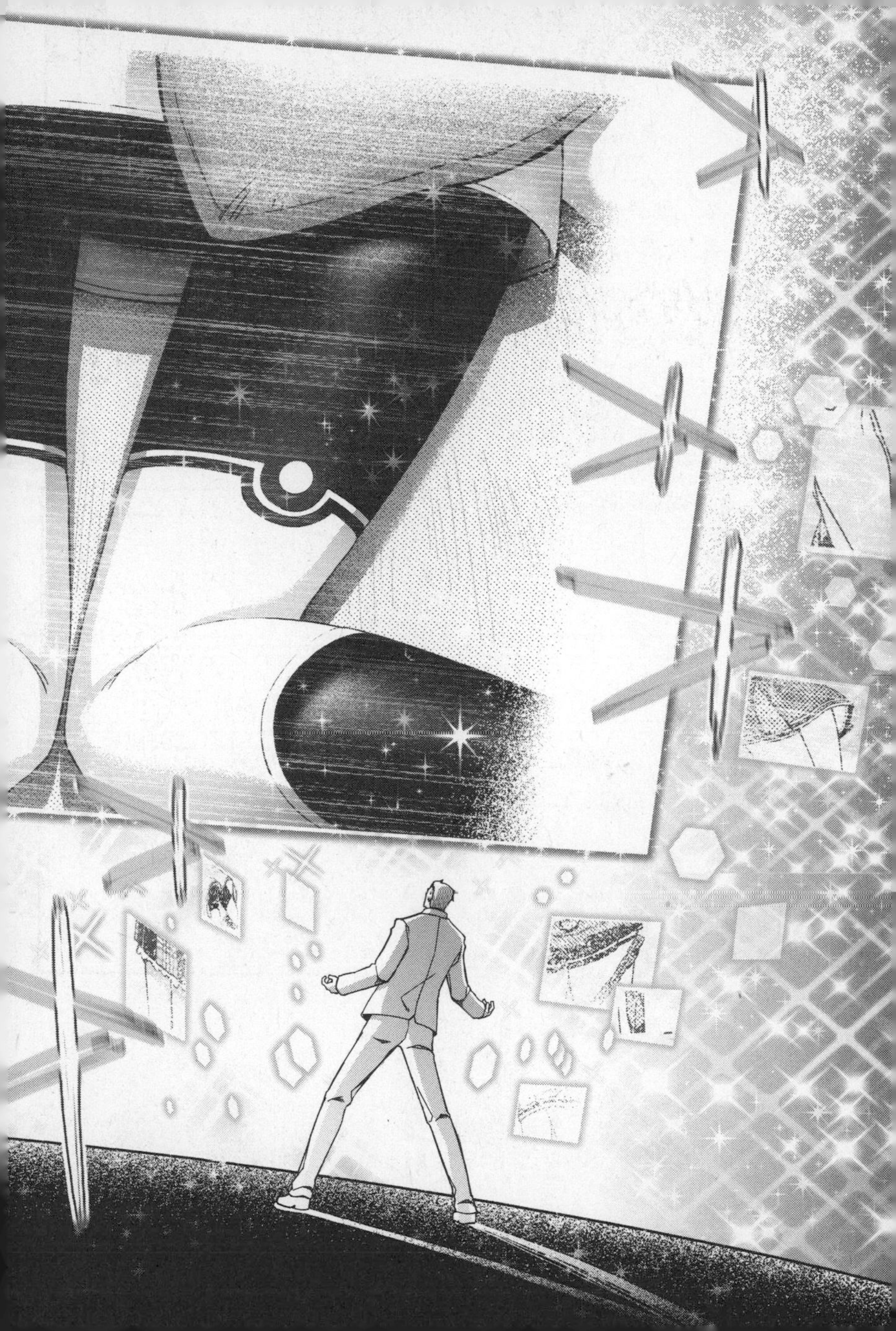

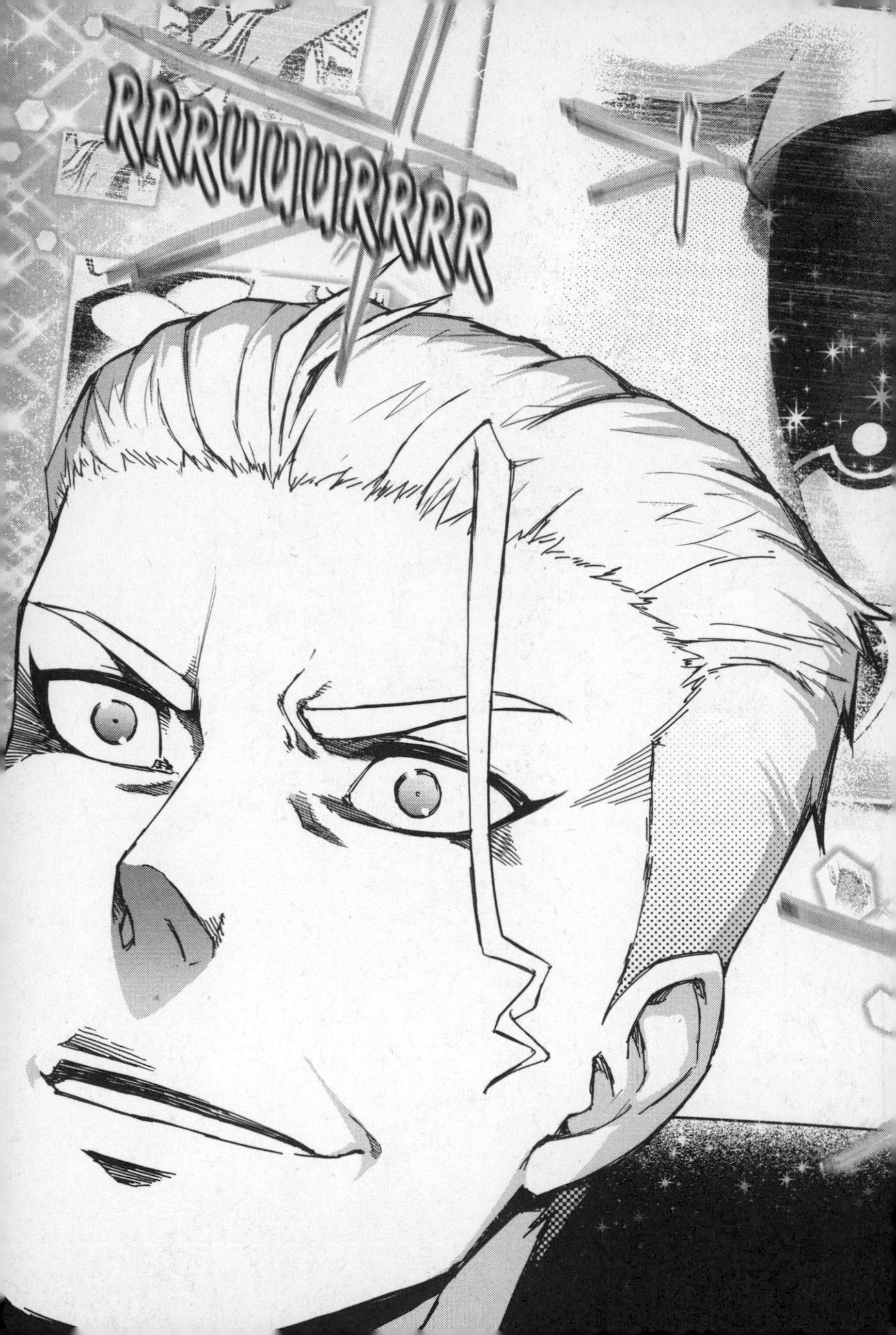
RRRUUUURRRR

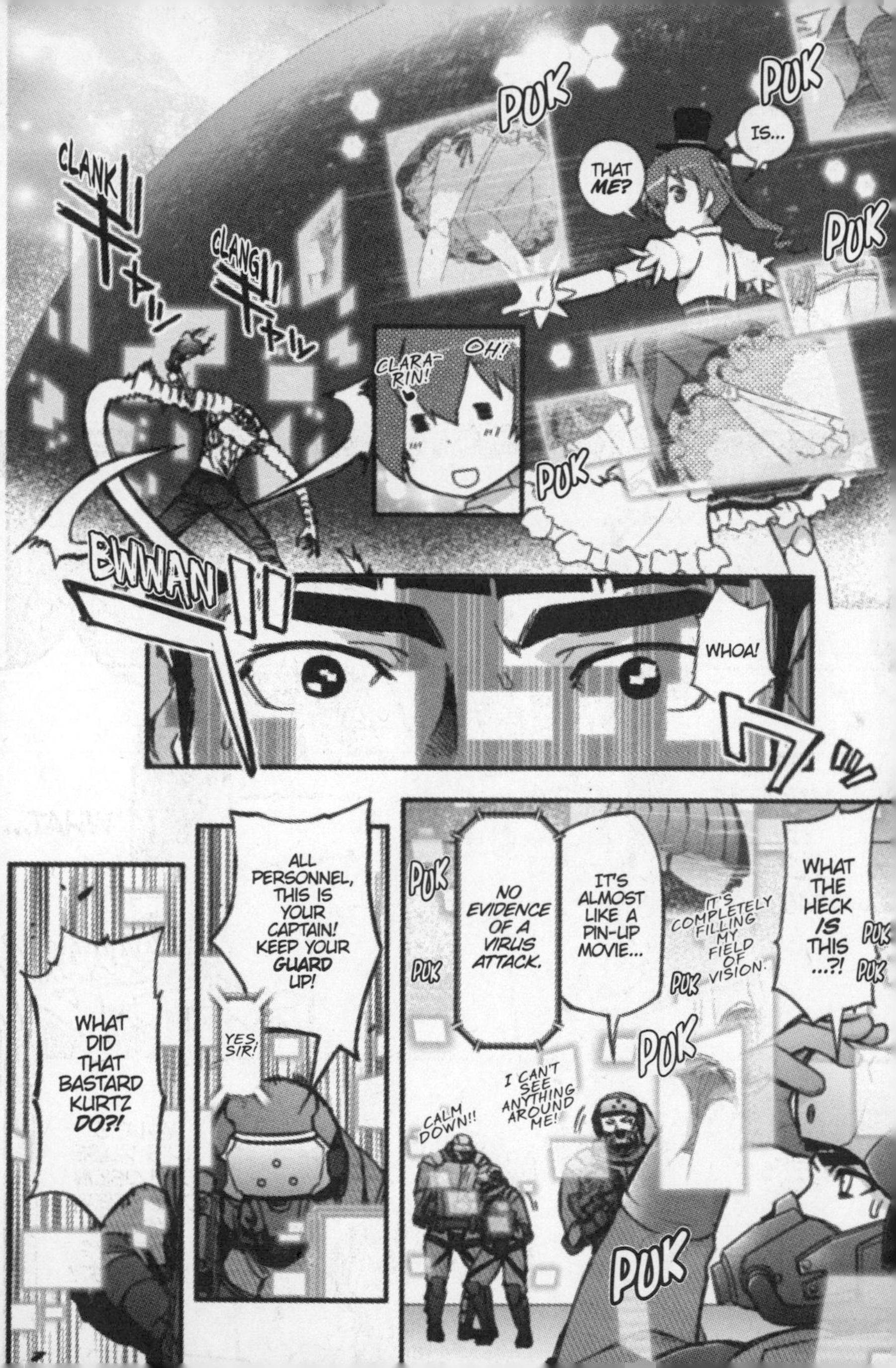
PUK
IS...
THAT ME?
PUK
PUK
CLANK!!
CLANG!!
OH!
CLARA-RIN! ♥
PUK
BWWAN!!
WHOA!
WHAT THE HECK IS THIS ...?!
PUK
PUK
IT'S COMPLETELY FILLING MY FIELD OF VISION.
PUK
IT'S ALMOST LIKE A PIN-UP MOVIE...
NO EVIDENCE OF A VIRUS ATTACK.
PUK
PUK
PUK
I CAN'T SEE ANYTHING AROUND ME!
CALM DOWN!!
PUK
ALL PERSONNEL, THIS IS YOUR CAPTAIN! KEEP YOUR GUARD UP!
YES, SIR!
WHAT DID THAT BASTARD KURTZ DO?!

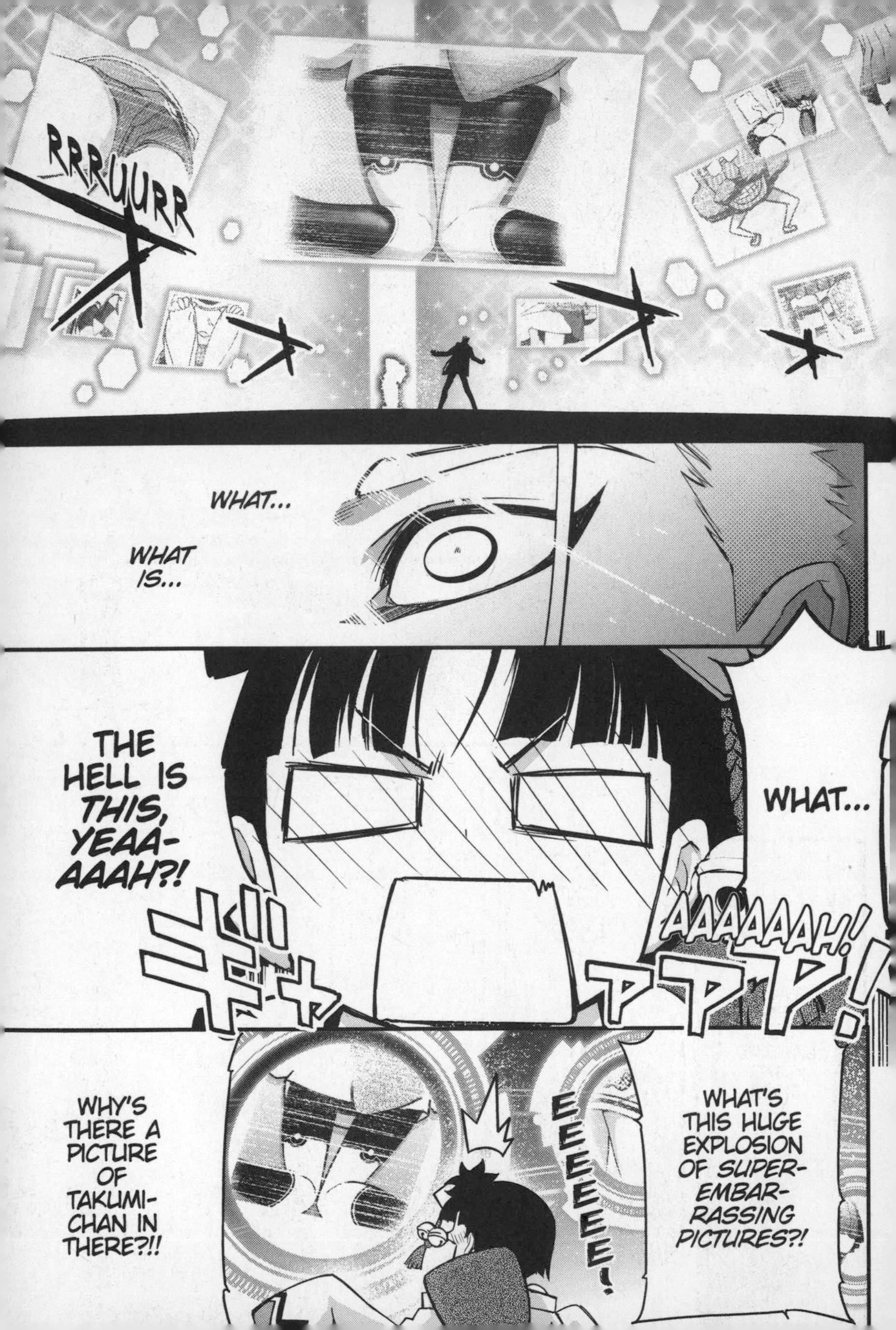
RRRUUURR
WHAT...
WHAT IS...
WHAT...
THE HELL IS THIS, YEAAAAAH?!
AAAAAAH!
ギャアアア!
WHAT'S THIS HUGE EXPLOSION OF SUPER-EMBARRASSING PICTURES?!
EEEEEEE!
WHY'S THERE A PICTURE OF TAKUMI-CHAN IN THERE?!!

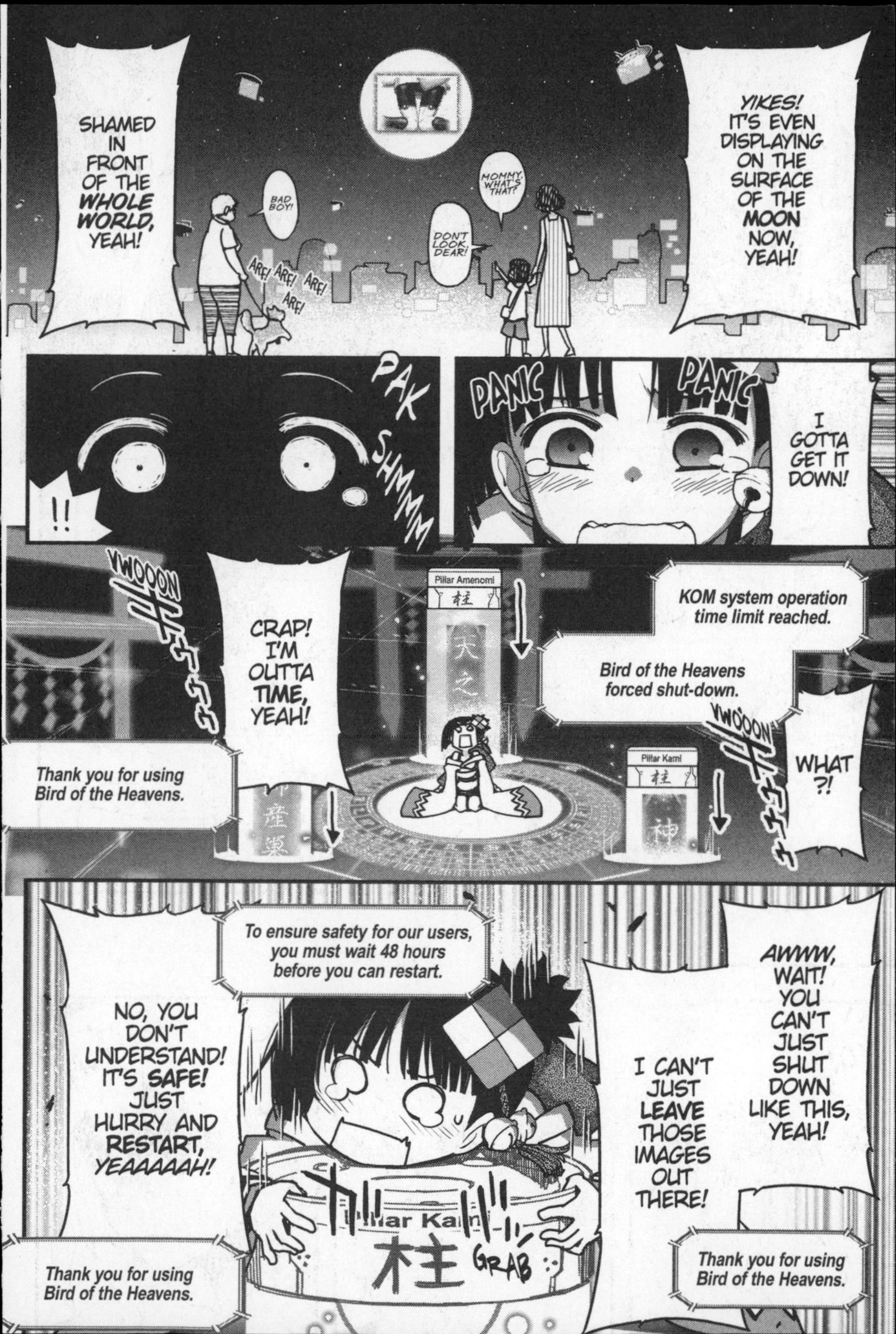
YIKES! IT'S EVEN DISPLAYING ON THE SURFACE OF THE MOON NOW, YEAH!
MOMMY, WHAT'S THAT?
DON'T LOOK, DEAR!
BAD BOY!
ARF! ARF! ARF! ARF!
SHAMED IN FRONT OF THE WHOLE WORLD, YEAH!
PANIC PANIC
I GOTTA GET IT DOWN!
PAK
SHMMM
!!
KOM system operation time limit reached.
Bird of the Heavens forced shut-down.
WHAT ?!
VWOOON
Pillar Kami
Pillar Amenomi
CRAP! I'M OUTTA TIME, YEAH!
VWOOON
Thank you for using Bird of the Heavens.
AWWW, WAIT! YOU CAN'T JUST SHUT DOWN LIKE THIS, YEAH!
To ensure safety for our users, you must wait 48 hours before you can restart.
I CAN'T JUST LEAVE THOSE IMAGES OUT THERE!
NO, YOU DON'T UNDERSTAND! IT'S SAFE! JUST HURRY AND RESTART, YEAAAAAH!
Thank you for using Bird of the Heavens.
GRAB
Thank you for using Bird of the Heavens.

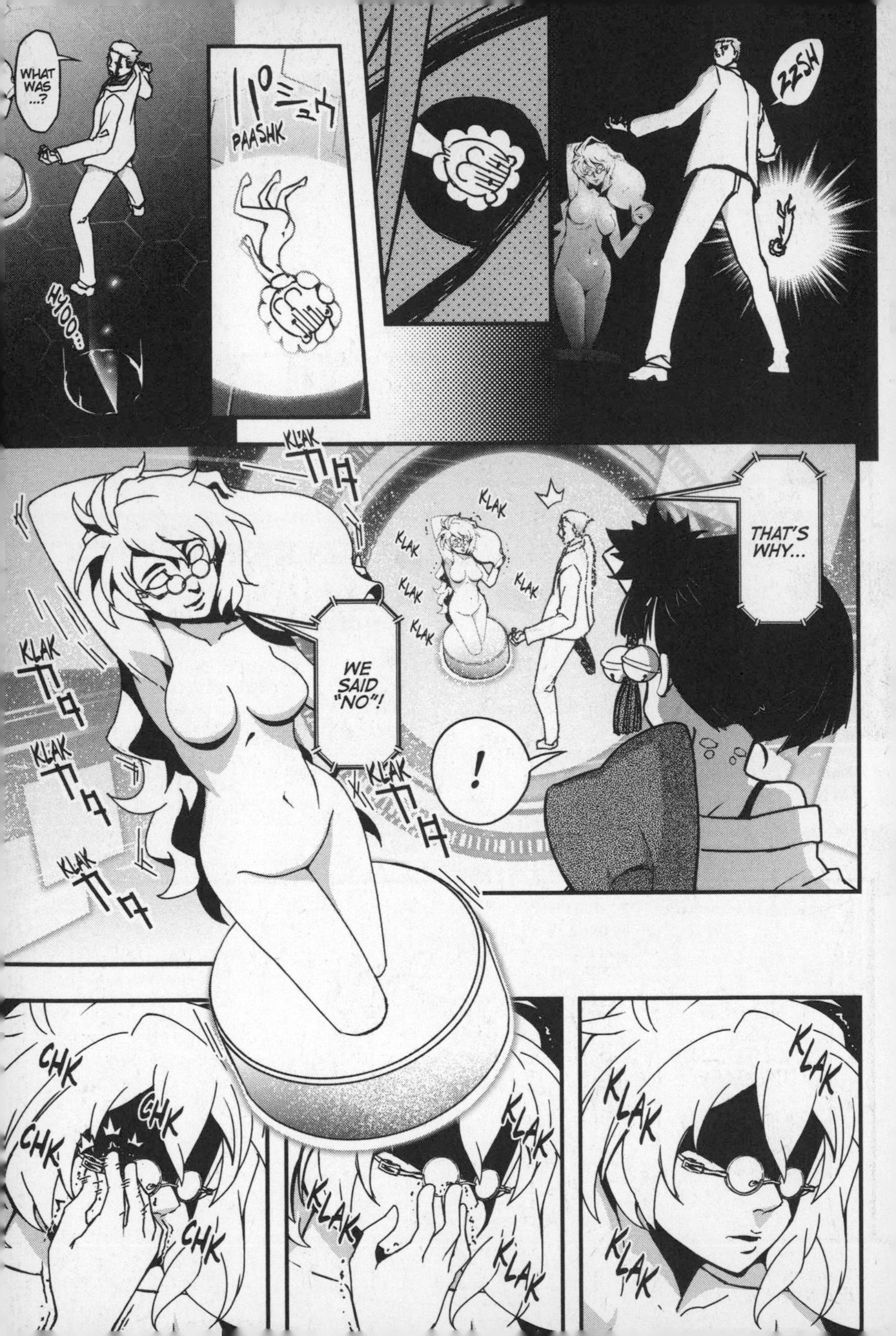
ZZSH
パシュウ
PAASHK
WHAT WAS ...?
HYOO..
THAT'S WHY...
!
WE SAID "NO"!
KLAK
KLAK
KLAK
KLAK
KLAK
KL'AK カタ
KLAK カタ
KLAK カタ
KL'AK カタ
KLAK カタ
KLAK カタ
KLAK
KLAK
KLAK
KLAK
KLAK
KLAK
KLAK
CHK
CHK
CHK
CHK

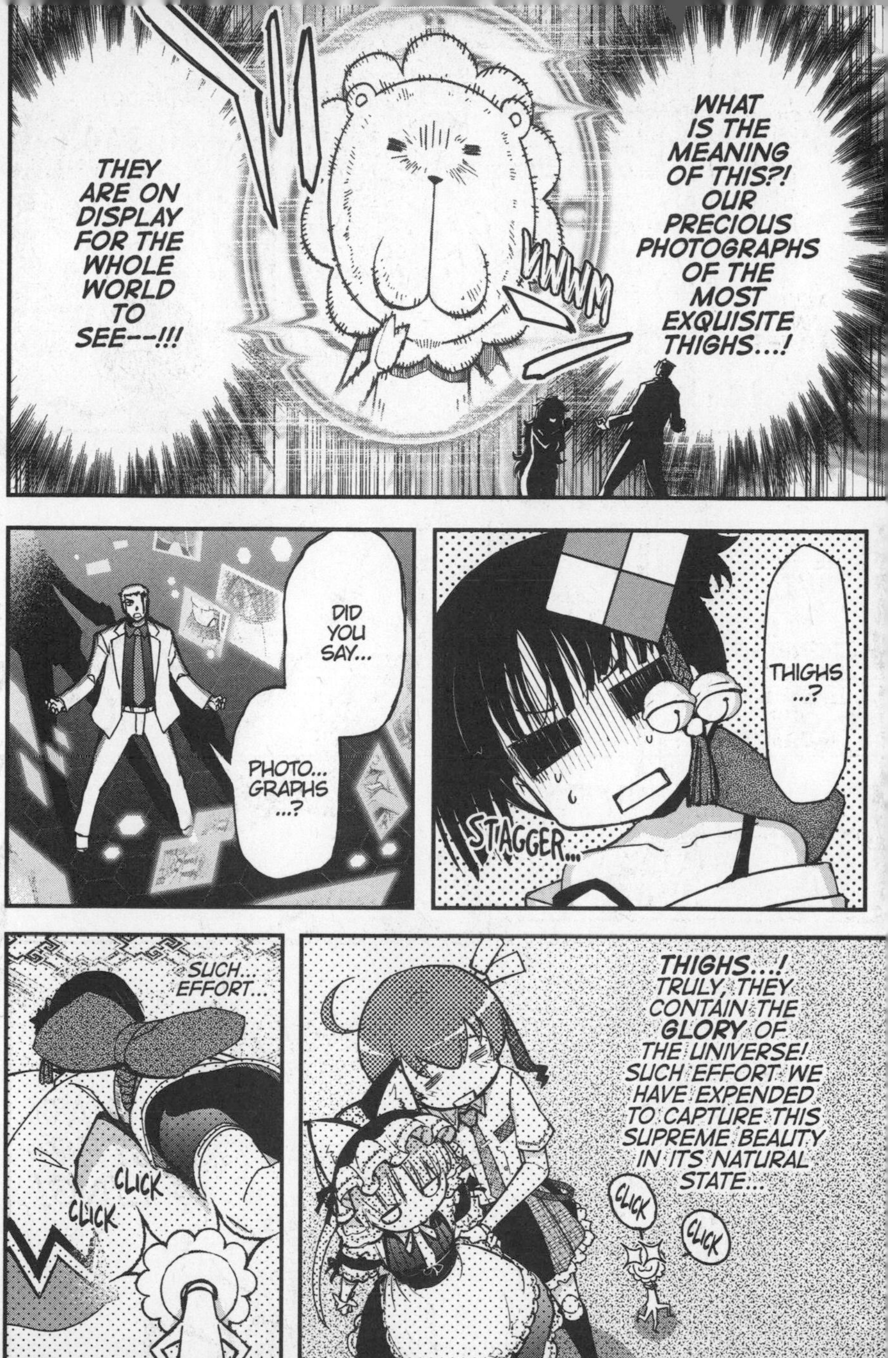
WHAT IS THE MEANING OF THIS?! OUR PRECIOUS PHOTOGRAPHS OF THE MOST EXQUISITE THIGHS...!
VWWM
THEY ARE ON DISPLAY FOR THE WHOLE WORLD TO SEE--!!!
THIGHS ...?
STAGGER...
DID YOU SAY...
PHOTO... GRAPHS ...?
THIGHS...! TRULY, THEY CONTAIN THE GLORY OF THE UNIVERSE! SUCH EFFORT WE HAVE EXPENDED TO CAPTURE THIS SUPREME BEAUTY IN ITS NATURAL STATE...
CLICK
CLICK
SUCH... EFFORT...
CLICK
CLICK

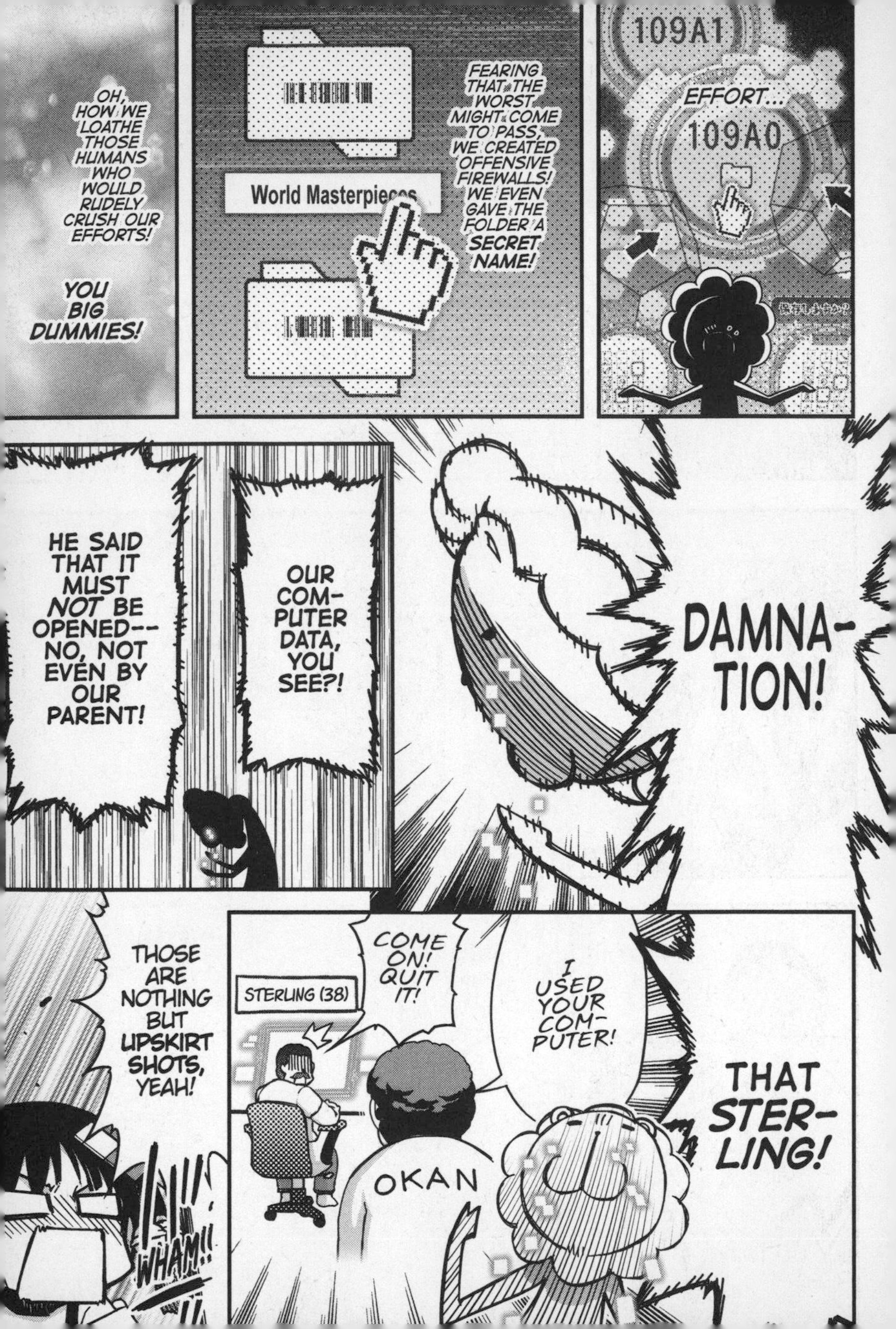
109A1
EFFORT...
109A0
FEARING THAT THE WORST MIGHT COME TO PASS, WE CREATED OFFENSIVE FIREWALLS! WE EVEN GAVE THE FOLDER A SECRET NAME!
World Masterpieces
OH, HOW WE LOATHE THOSE HUMANS WHO WOULD RUDELY CRUSH OUR EFFORTS!
YOU BIG DUMMIES!
DAMNA-TION!
OUR COMPUTER DATA, YOU SEE?!
HE SAID THAT IT MUST *NOT* BE OPENED-- NO, NOT EVEN BY OUR PARENT!
THAT STERLING!
I USED YOUR COMPUTER!
COME ON! QUIT IT!
STERLING (38)
OKAN
THOSE ARE NOTHING BUT UPSKIRT SHOTS, YEAH!
WHAM!!

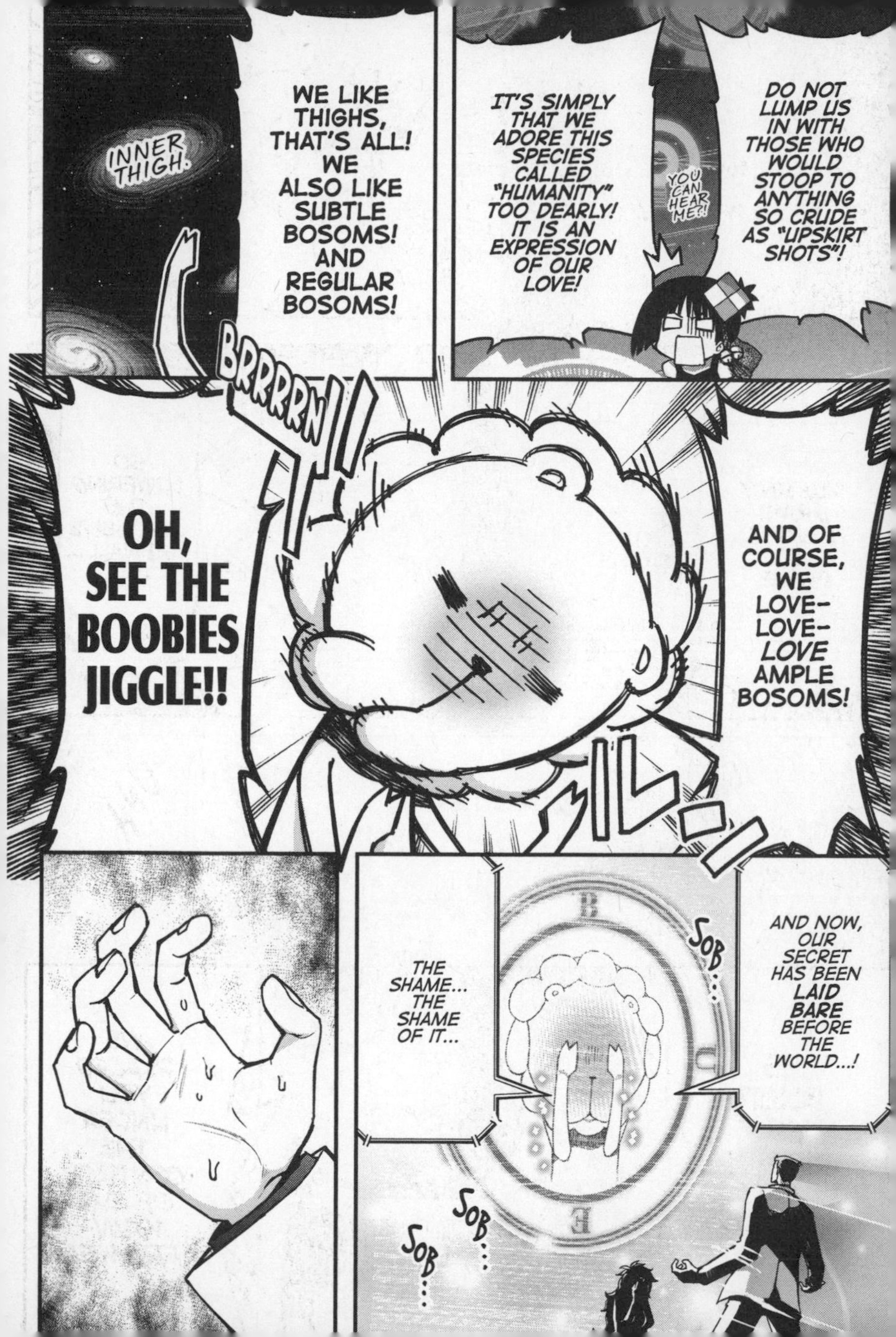
DO NOT LUMP US IN WITH THOSE WHO WOULD STOOP TO ANYTHING SO CRUDE AS "UPSKIRT SHOTS"!
IT'S SIMPLY THAT WE ADORE THIS SPECIES CALLED "HUMANITY" TOO DEARLY! IT IS AN EXPRESSION OF OUR LOVE!
YOU CAN HEAR ME?!
WE LIKE THIGHS, THAT'S ALL! WE ALSO LIKE SUBTLE BOSOMS! AND REGULAR BOSOMS!
INNER THIGH.
BRRRRN
AND OF COURSE, WE LOVE-LOVE-LOVE AMPLE BOSOMS!
OH, SEE THE BOOBIES JIGGLE!!
AND NOW, OUR SECRET HAS BEEN LAID BARE BEFORE THE WORLD...!
SOB...
THE SHAME... THE SHAME OF IT...
SOB...
SOB...

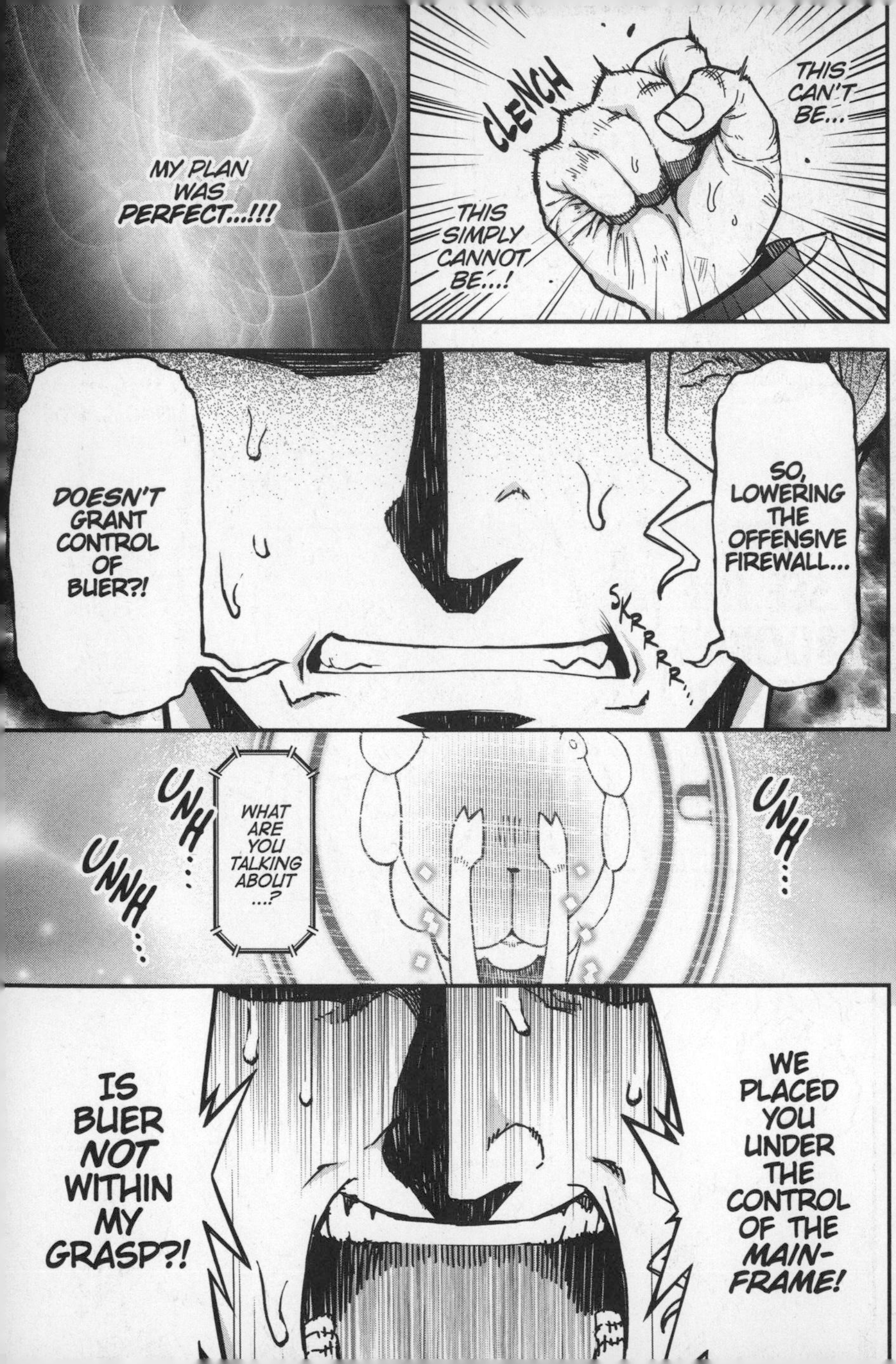
CLENCH
THIS CAN'T BE...
THIS SIMPLY CANNOT BE...!
MY PLAN WAS PERFECT...!!!
SO, LOWERING THE OFFENSIVE FIREWALL...
SKRRRRR...
DOESN'T GRANT CONTROL OF BUER?!
UNH...
WHAT ARE YOU TALKING ABOUT...?
UNH... UNNH...
WE PLACED YOU UNDER THE CONTROL OF THE MAIN-FRAME!
IS BUER NOT WITHIN MY GRASP?!

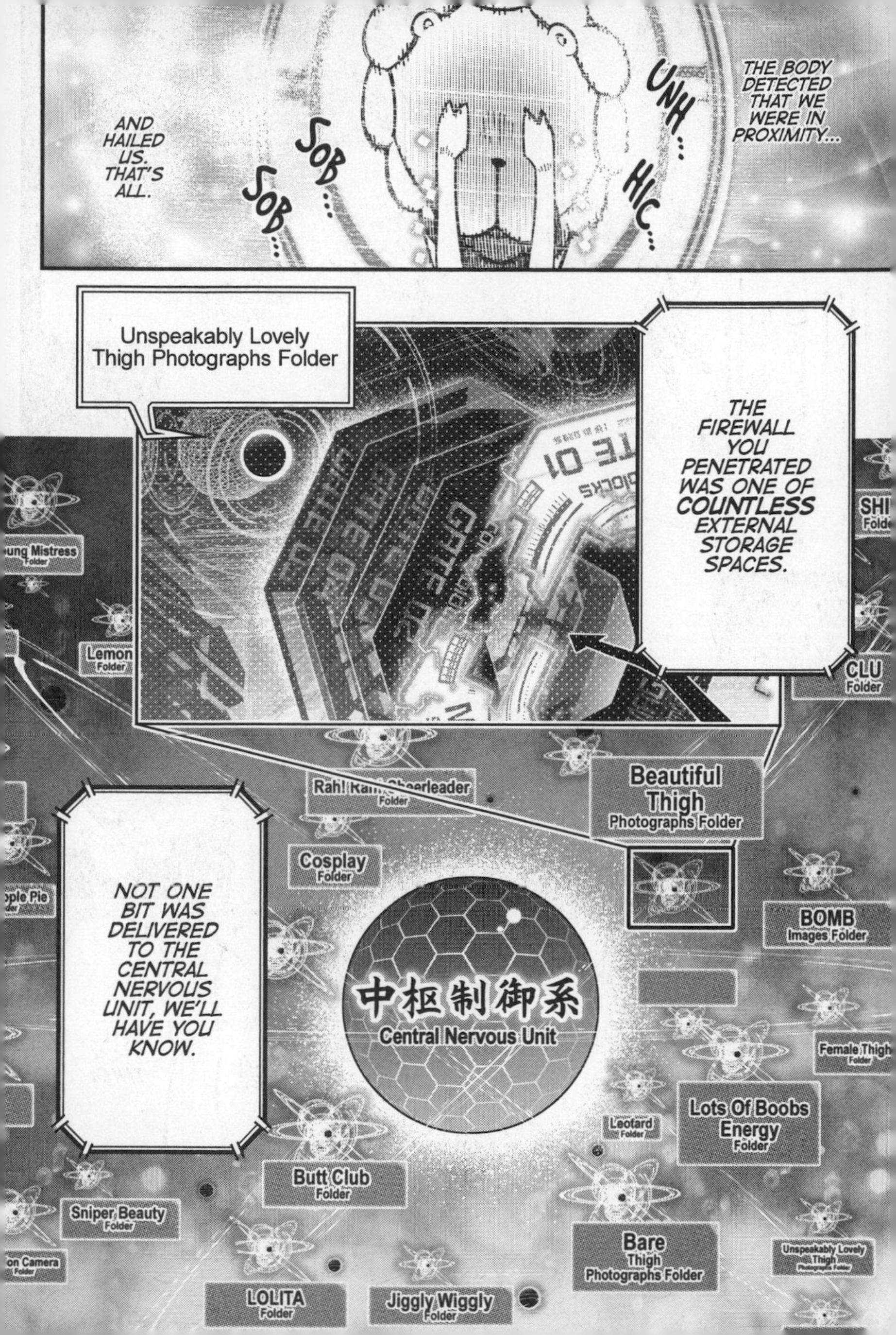
THE BODY DETECTED THAT WE WERE IN PROXIMITY...
UNH... HIC...
SOB... SOB...
AND HAILED US. THAT'S ALL.
THE FIREWALL YOU PENETRATED WAS ONE OF COUNTLESS EXTERNAL STORAGE SPACES.
Unspeakably Lovely Thigh Photographs Folder
Beautiful Thigh Photographs Folder
Cosplay Folder
BOMB Images Folder
中枢制御系
Central Nervous Unit
Female Thigh Folder
Lots Of Boobs Energy Folder
Leotard Folder
Butt Club Folder
Sniper Beauty Folder
Bare Thigh Photographs Folder
Unspeakably Lovely Thigh Photographs Folder
LOLITA Folder
Jiggly Wiggly Folder
NOT ONE BIT WAS DELIVERED TO THE CENTRAL NERVOUS UNIT, WE'LL HAVE YOU KNOW.

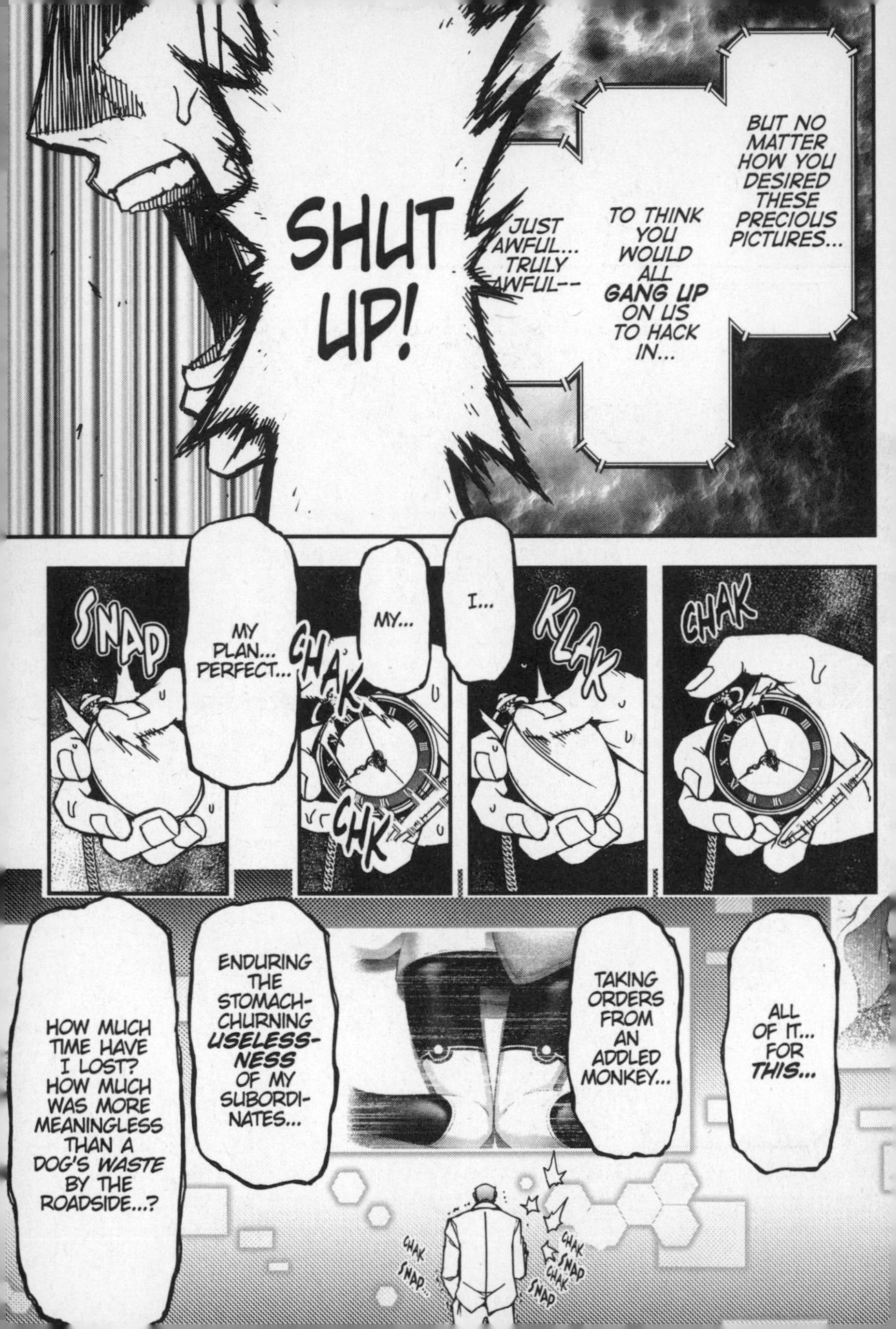
BUT NO MATTER HOW YOU DESIRED THESE PRECIOUS PICTURES...
TO THINK YOU WOULD ALL GANG UP ON US TO HACK IN...
JUST AWFUL... TRULY AWFUL--
SHUT UP!
CHAK
I...
KLAK
MY...
CHAK
CHK
MY PLAN... PERFECT...
SNAP
ALL OF IT... FOR THIS...
TAKING ORDERS FROM AN ADDLED MONKEY...
ENDURING THE STOMACH-CHURNING USELESS-NESS OF MY SUBORDI-NATES...
HOW MUCH TIME HAVE I LOST? HOW MUCH WAS MORE MEANINGLESS THAN A DOG'S WASTE BY THE ROADSIDE...?
CHAK SNAP CHAK SNAP
CHAK SNAP...

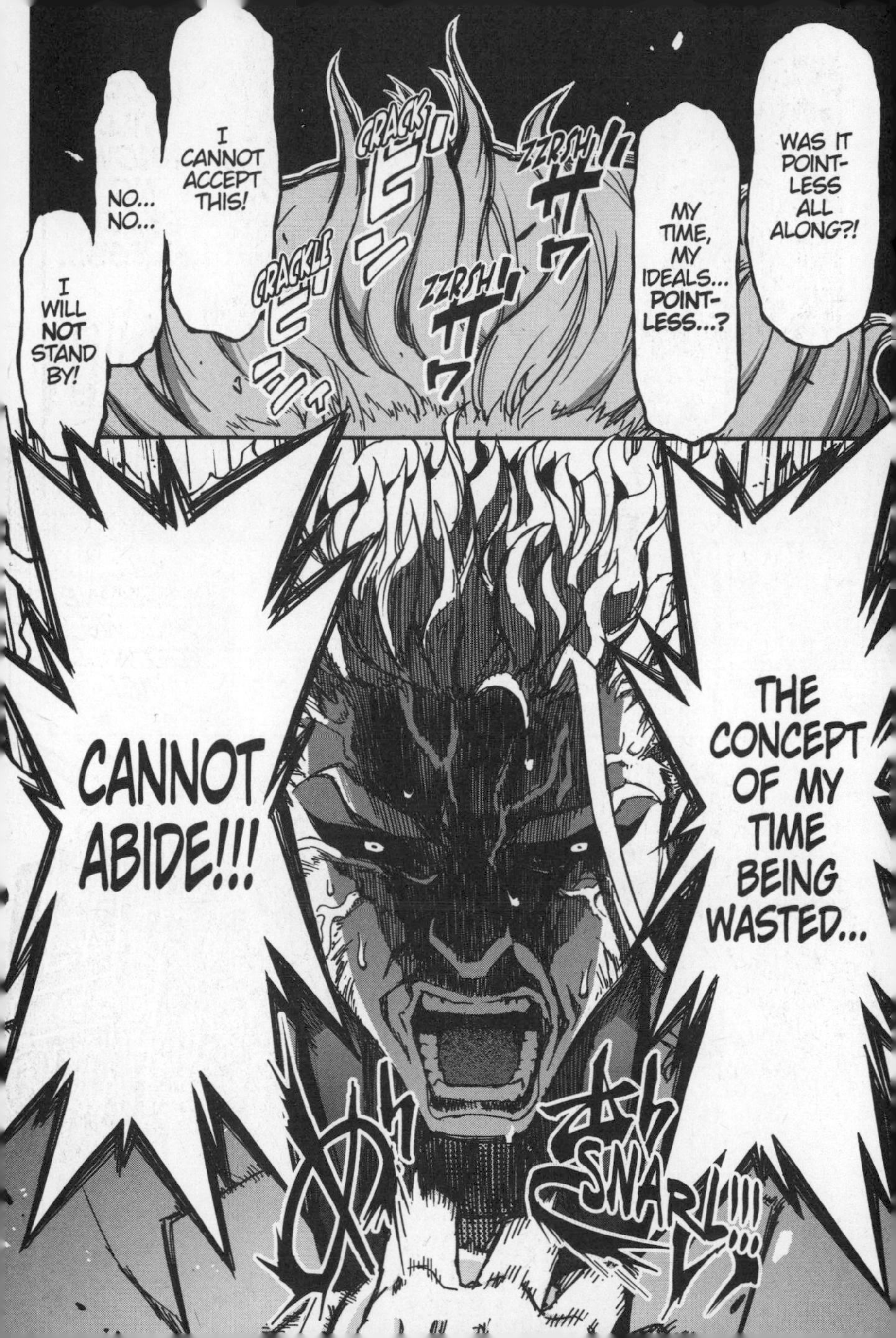
WAS IT POINTLESS ALL ALONG?!
MY TIME, MY IDEALS... POINTLESS...?
ZZRSH!!
CRACK!!
ZZRSH!!
CRACKLE
I CANNOT ACCEPT THIS!
NO... NO...
I WILL NOT STAND BY!
THE CONCEPT OF MY TIME BEING WASTED...
CANNOT ABIDE!!!
SNARL!!!

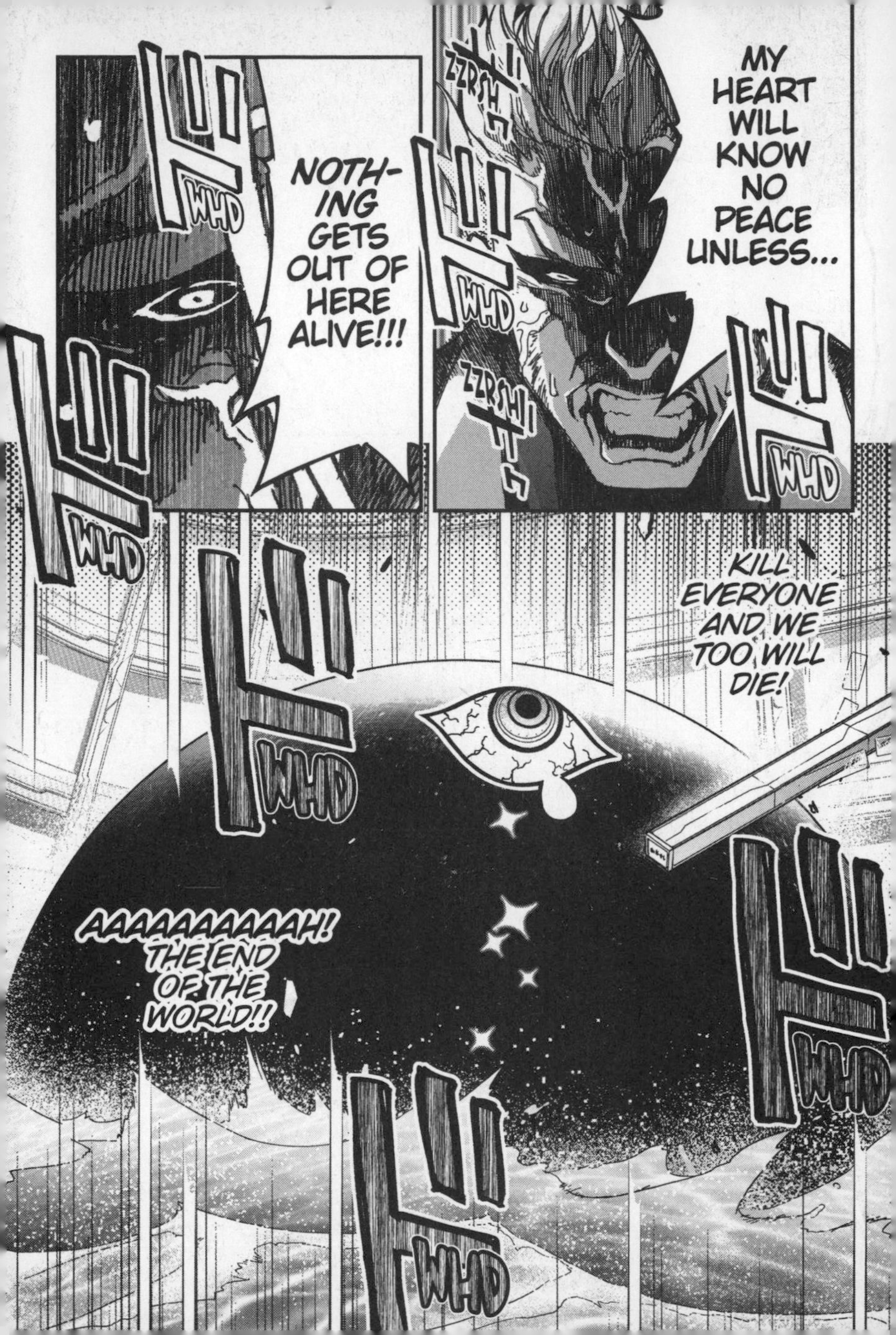
ZZRSH
MY HEART WILL KNOW NO PEACE UNLESS...
WHD
ZZRSH
WHD
WHD
NOTH-ING GETS OUT OF HERE ALIVE!!!
WHD
KILL EVERYONE AND WE TOO WILL DIE!
WHD
WHD
AAAAAAAAAH! THE END OF THE WORLD!!
WHD

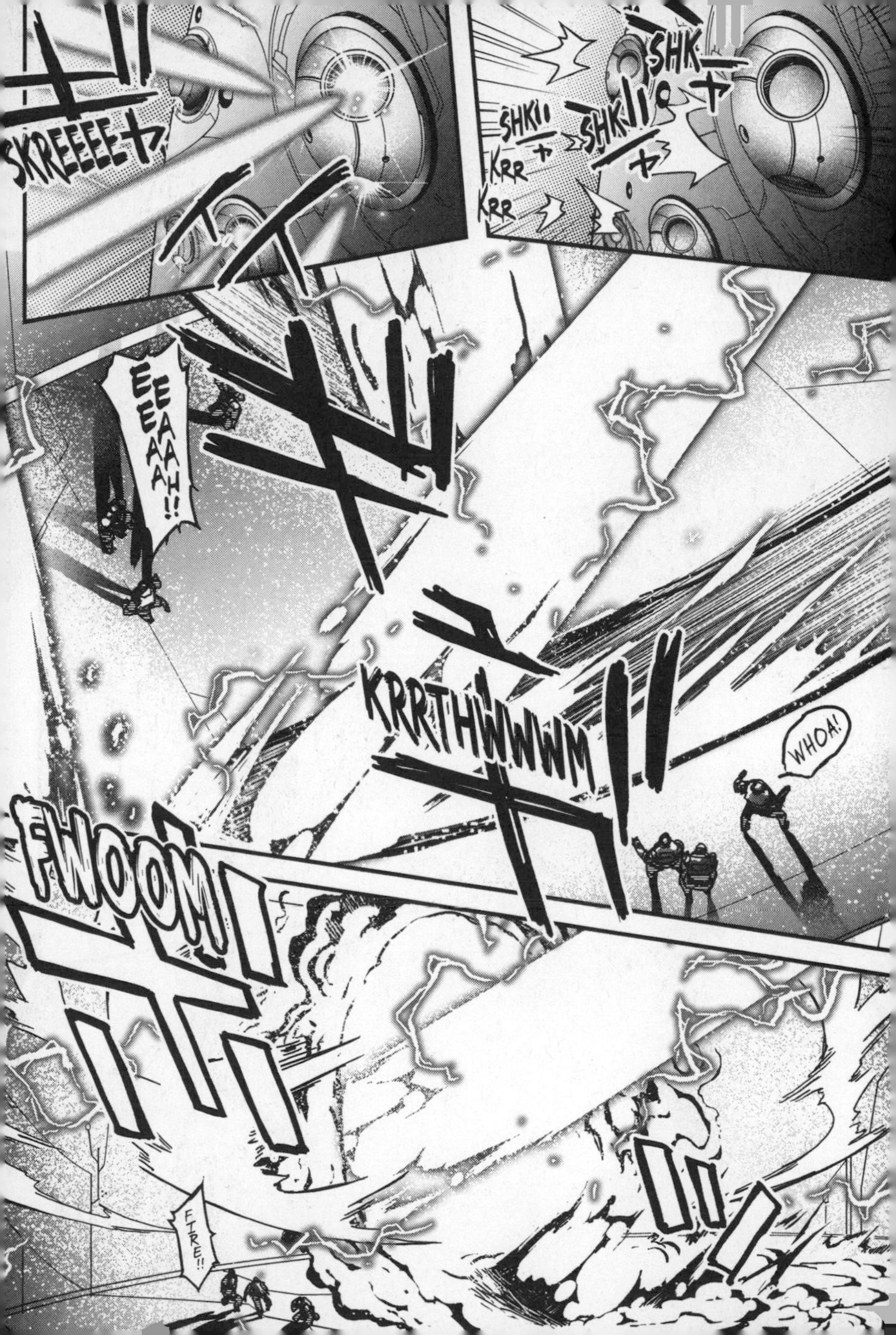
SHK
SHK
SHK
KRR
KRR
SKREEEEE
EEEAAAAH!!
KRRTHWWWM
WHOA!
FWOOM
FIRE!!

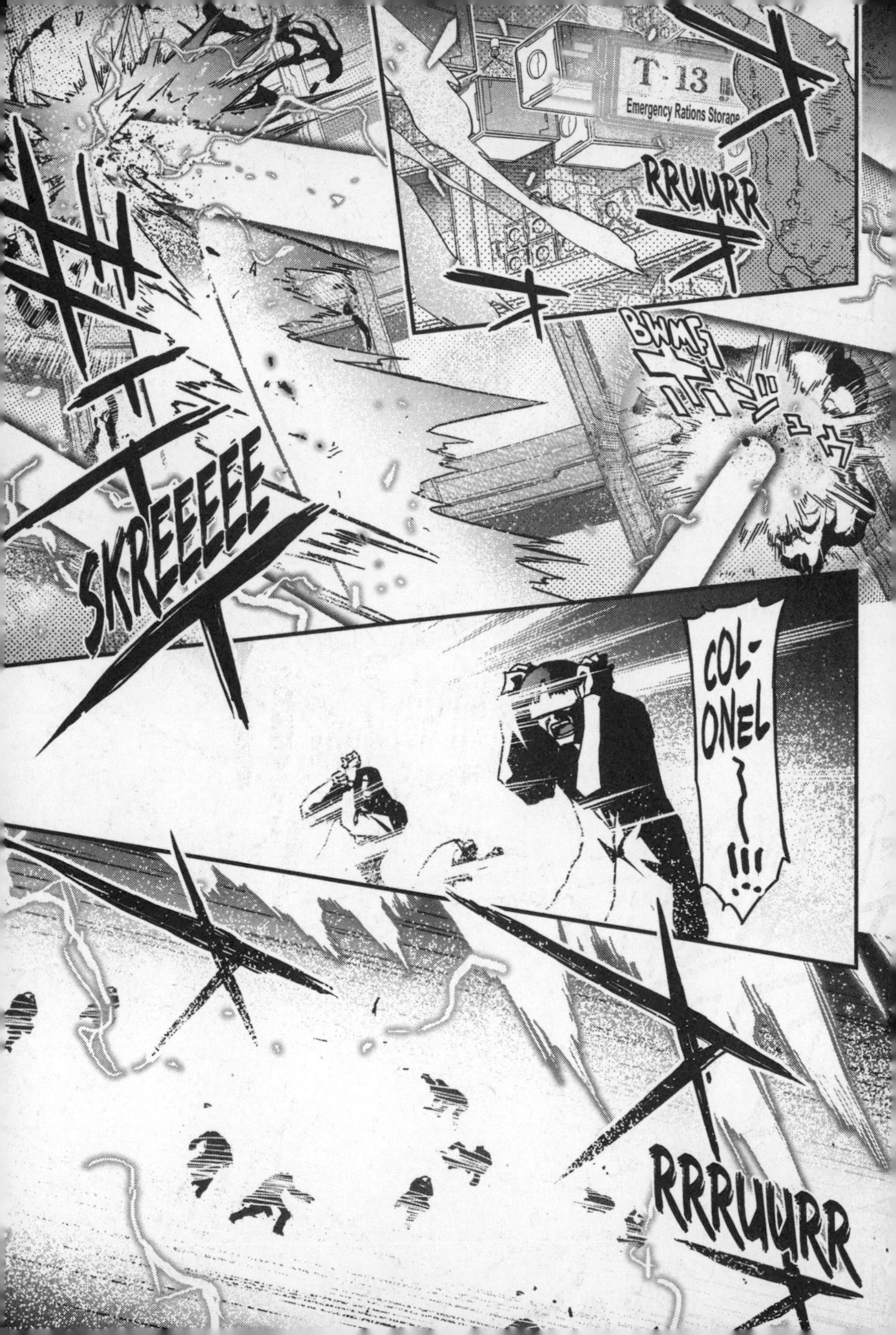
T-13
Emergency Rations Storage
RRUURR
SKREEEEE
BWMF
COL-ONEL~!!!
RRRUURR

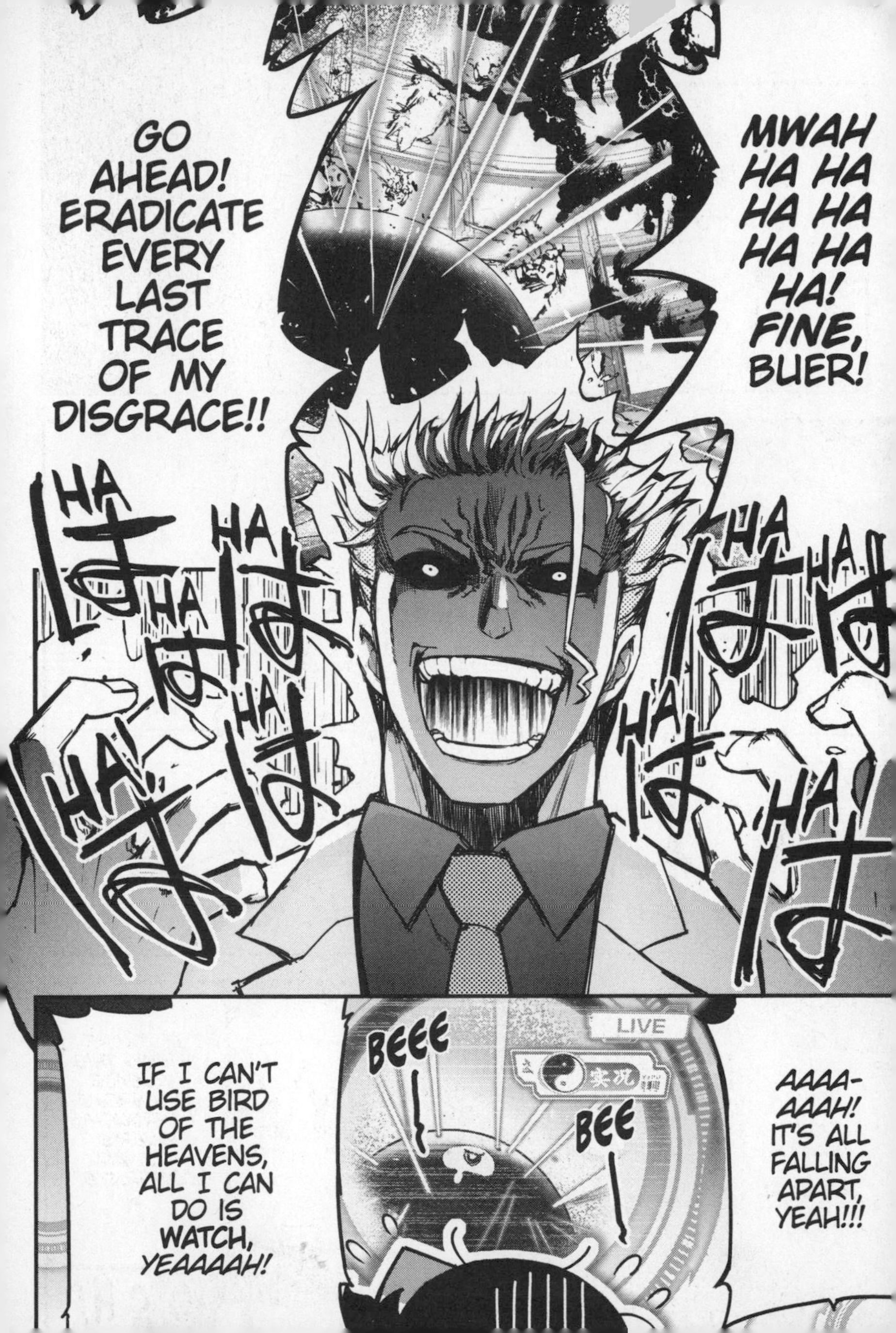

MWAH HA HA HA HA HA HA HA! FINE, BUER!
GO AHEAD! ERADICATE EVERY LAST TRACE OF MY DISGRACE!!
HA HA HA HA! HA
HA HA HA HA HA
AAAA-AAAH! IT'S ALL FALLING APART, YEAH!!!
LIVE
BEEE
BEE
IF I CAN'T USE BIRD OF THE HEAVENS, ALL I CAN DO IS WATCH, YEAAAAH!

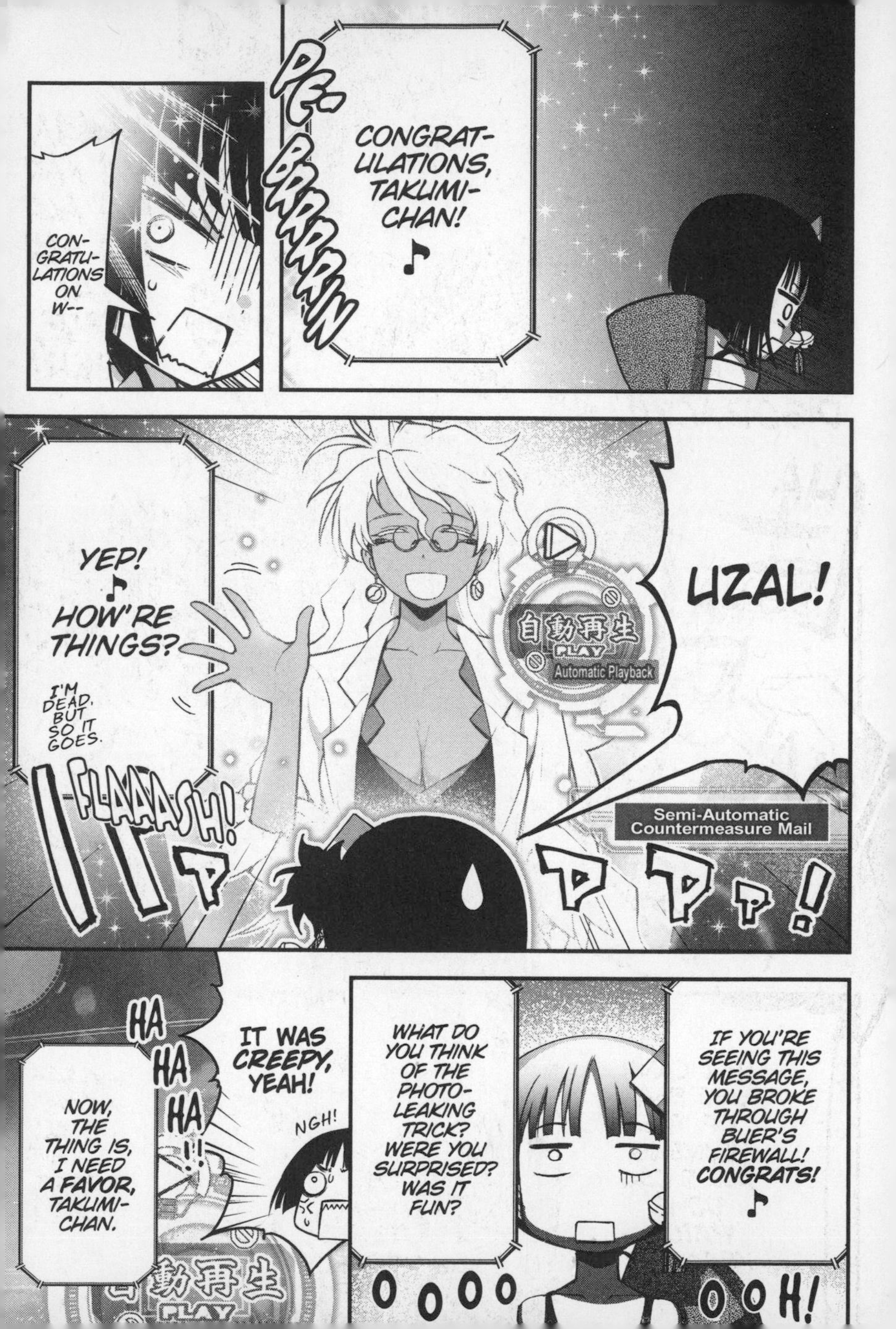
PE-BRRRRIN
CONGRAT-ULATIONS, TAKUMI-CHAN! ♪
CON-GRATU-LATIONS ON W--
UZAL!
自動再生
PLAY
Automatic Playback
YEP! ♪ HOW'RE THINGS?
I'M DEAD, BUT SO IT GOES.
Semi-Automatic Countermeasure Mail
FLAAASH!
IF YOU'RE SEEING THIS MESSAGE, YOU BROKE THROUGH BUER'S FIREWALL! CONGRATS! ♪
OOOOOOH!
WHAT DO YOU THINK OF THE PHOTO-LEAKING TRICK? WERE YOU SURPRISED? WAS IT FUN?
IT WAS CREEPY, YEAH!
NGH!
HA HA HA!!
NOW, THE THING IS, I NEED A FAVOR, TAKUMI-CHAN.
動再生
PLAY

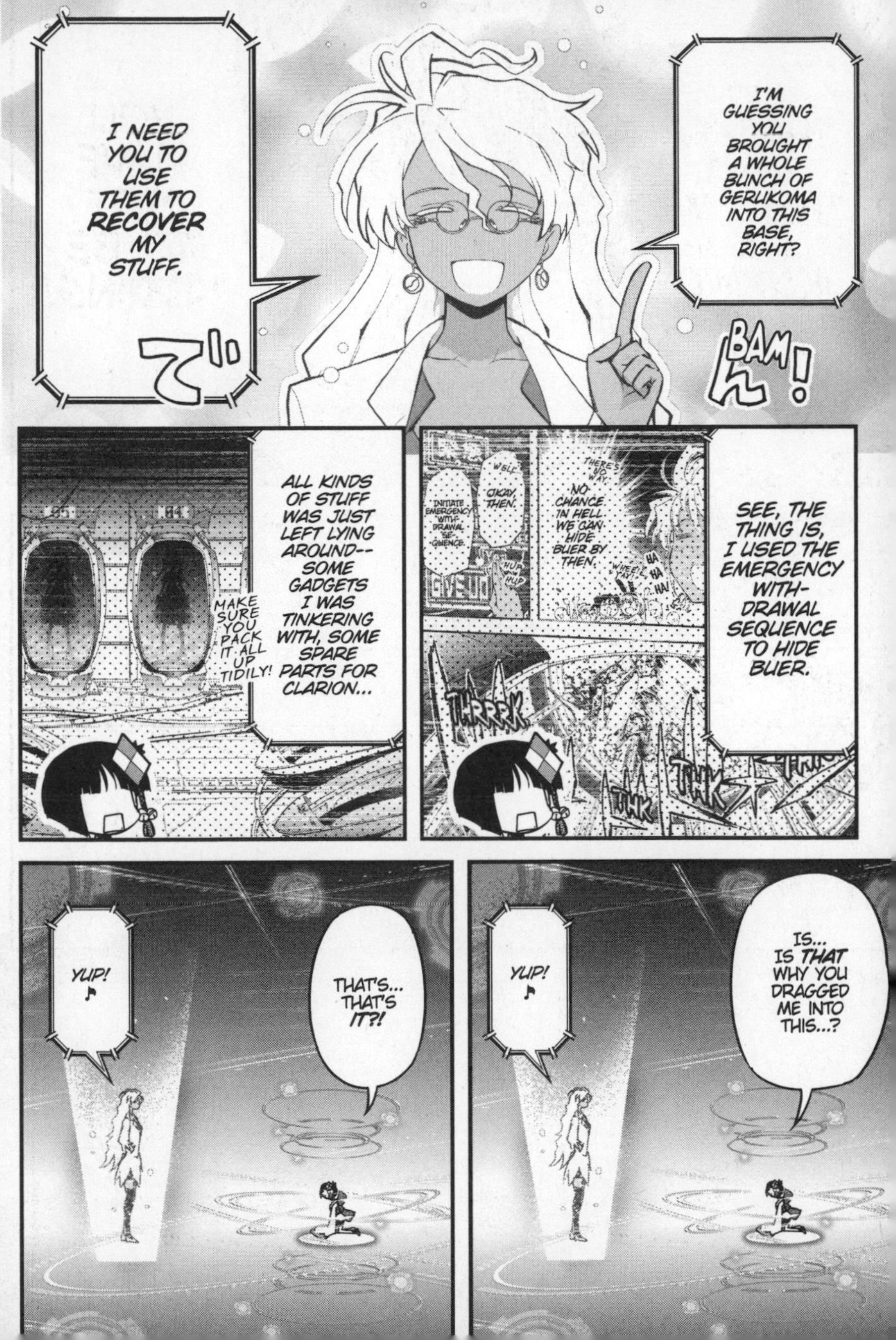
I'M GUESSING YOU BROUGHT A WHOLE BUNCH OF GERUKOMA INTO THIS BASE, RIGHT?
BAM!
I NEED YOU TO USE THEM TO RECOVER MY STUFF.
SEE, THE THING IS, I USED THE EMERGENCY WITH-DRAWAL SEQUENCE TO HIDE BUER.
THERE'S NO WAY.
NO CHANCE IN HELL WE CAN HIDE BUER BY THEN.
WELL... OKAY, THEN.
INITIATE EMERGENCY WITHDRAWAL SE-QUENCE.
HUP HUP
WHEE!
HA HA HA!
THRRRK
THK
THK
ALL KINDS OF STUFF WAS JUST LEFT LYING AROUND-- SOME GADGETS I WAS TINKERING WITH, SOME SPARE PARTS FOR CLARION...
MAKE SURE YOU PACK IT ALL UP TIDILY!
IS... IS THAT WHY YOU DRAGGED ME INTO THIS...?
YUP! ♪
THAT'S... THAT'S IT?!
YUP! ♪

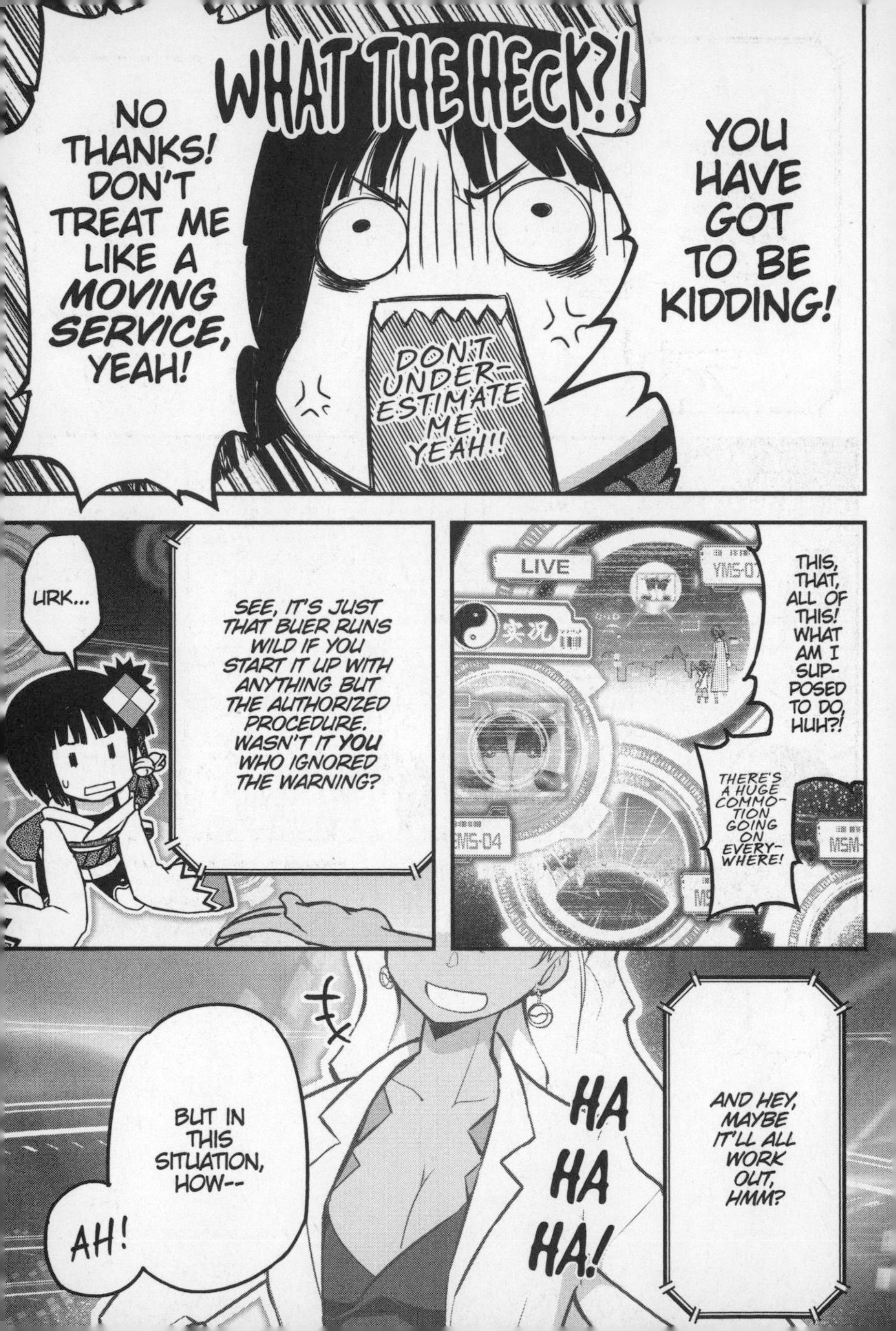
WHAT THE HECK?!
YOU HAVE GOT TO BE KIDDING!
NO THANKS! DON'T TREAT ME LIKE A MOVING SERVICE, YEAH!
DON'T UNDER-ESTIMATE ME, YEAH!!
LIVE
实况
THIS, THAT, ALL OF THIS! WHAT AM I SUP-POSED TO DO, HUH?!
THERE'S A HUGE COMMO-TION GOING ON EVERY-WHERE!
SEE, IT'S JUST THAT BUER RUNS WILD IF YOU START IT UP WITH ANYTHING BUT THE AUTHORIZED PROCEDURE. WASN'T IT YOU WHO IGNORED THE WARNING?
URK...
AND HEY, MAYBE IT'LL ALL WORK OUT, HMM?
HA HA HA HA!
BUT IN THIS SITUATION, HOW--
AH!

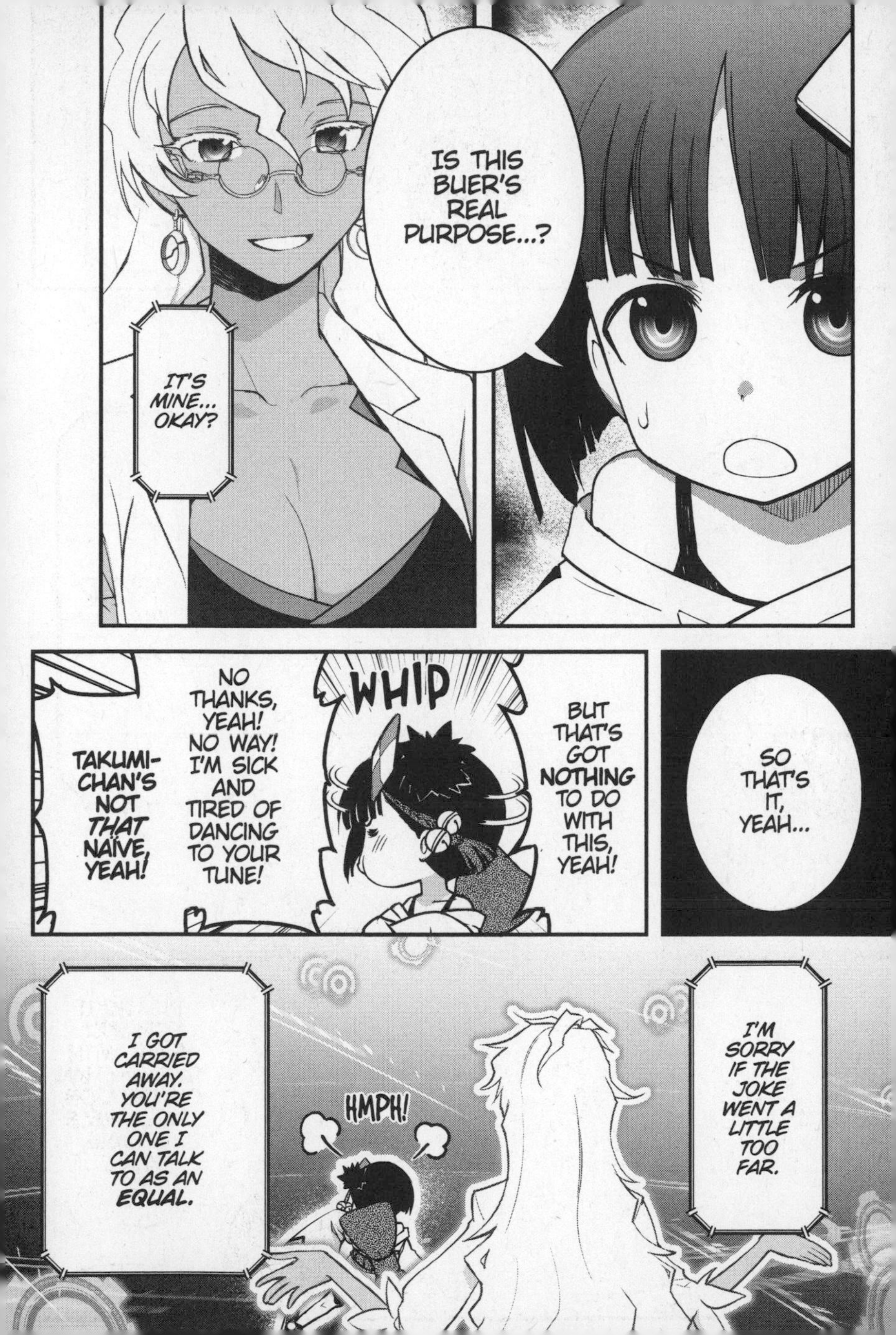
IS THIS BUER'S REAL PURPOSE...?
IT'S MINE... OKAY?
SO THAT'S IT, YEAH...
BUT THAT'S GOT NOTHING TO DO WITH THIS, YEAH!
WHIP
NO THANKS, YEAH! NO WAY! I'M SICK AND TIRED OF DANCING TO YOUR TUNE!
TAKUMI-CHAN'S NOT THAT NAÏVE, YEAH!
I'M SORRY IF THE JOKE WENT A LITTLE TOO FAR.
HMPH!
I GOT CARRIED AWAY. YOU'RE THE ONLY ONE I CAN TALK TO AS AN EQUAL.

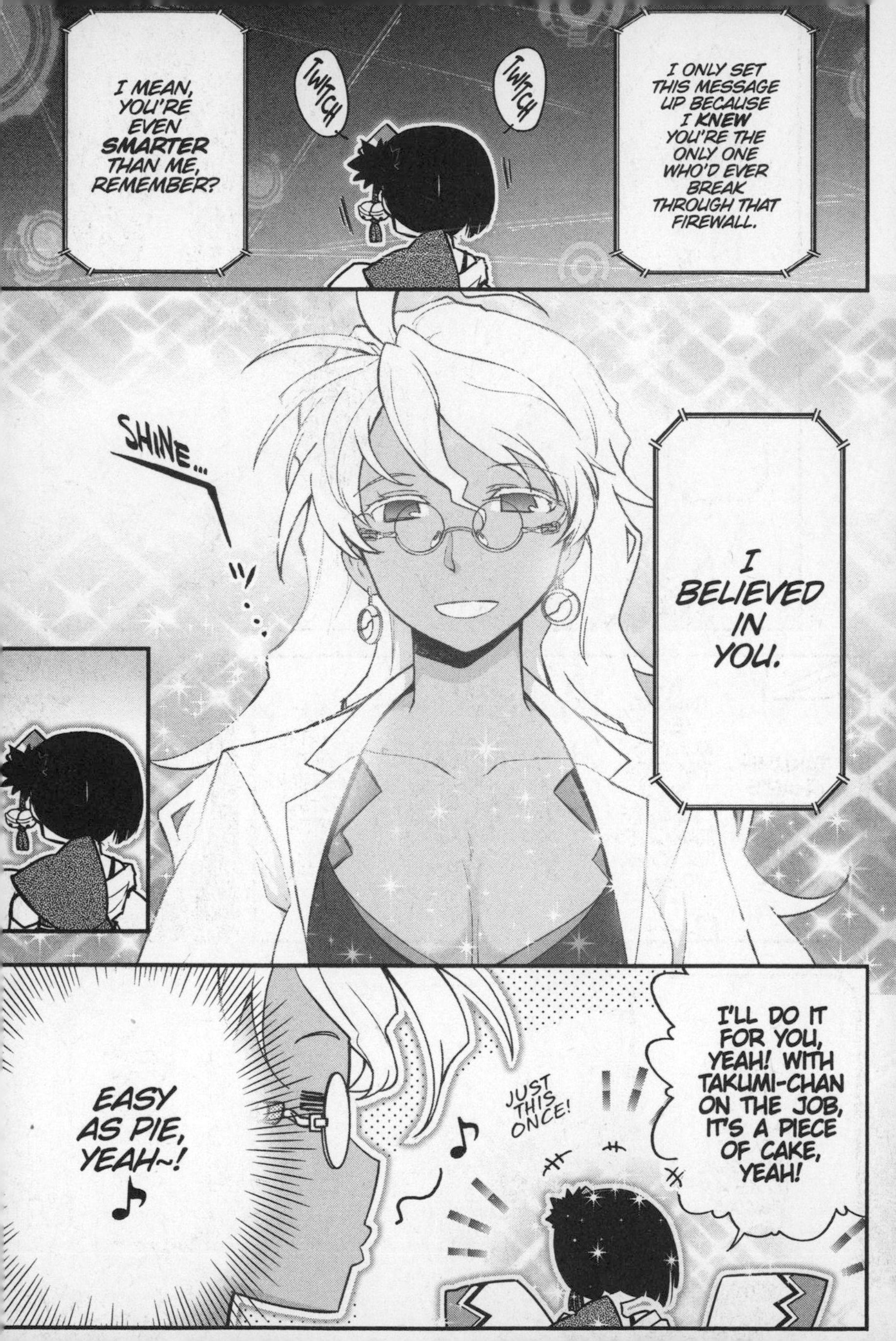
I ONLY SET THIS MESSAGE UP BECAUSE I KNEW YOU'RE THE ONLY ONE WHO'D EVER BREAK THROUGH THAT FIREWALL.
TWITCH
TWITCH
I MEAN, YOU'RE EVEN SMARTER THAN ME, REMEMBER?
I BELIEVED IN YOU.
SHINE...
I'LL DO IT FOR YOU, YEAH! WITH TAKUMI-CHAN ON THE JOB, IT'S A PIECE OF CAKE, YEAH!
JUST THIS ONCE!
EASY AS PIE, YEAH~!

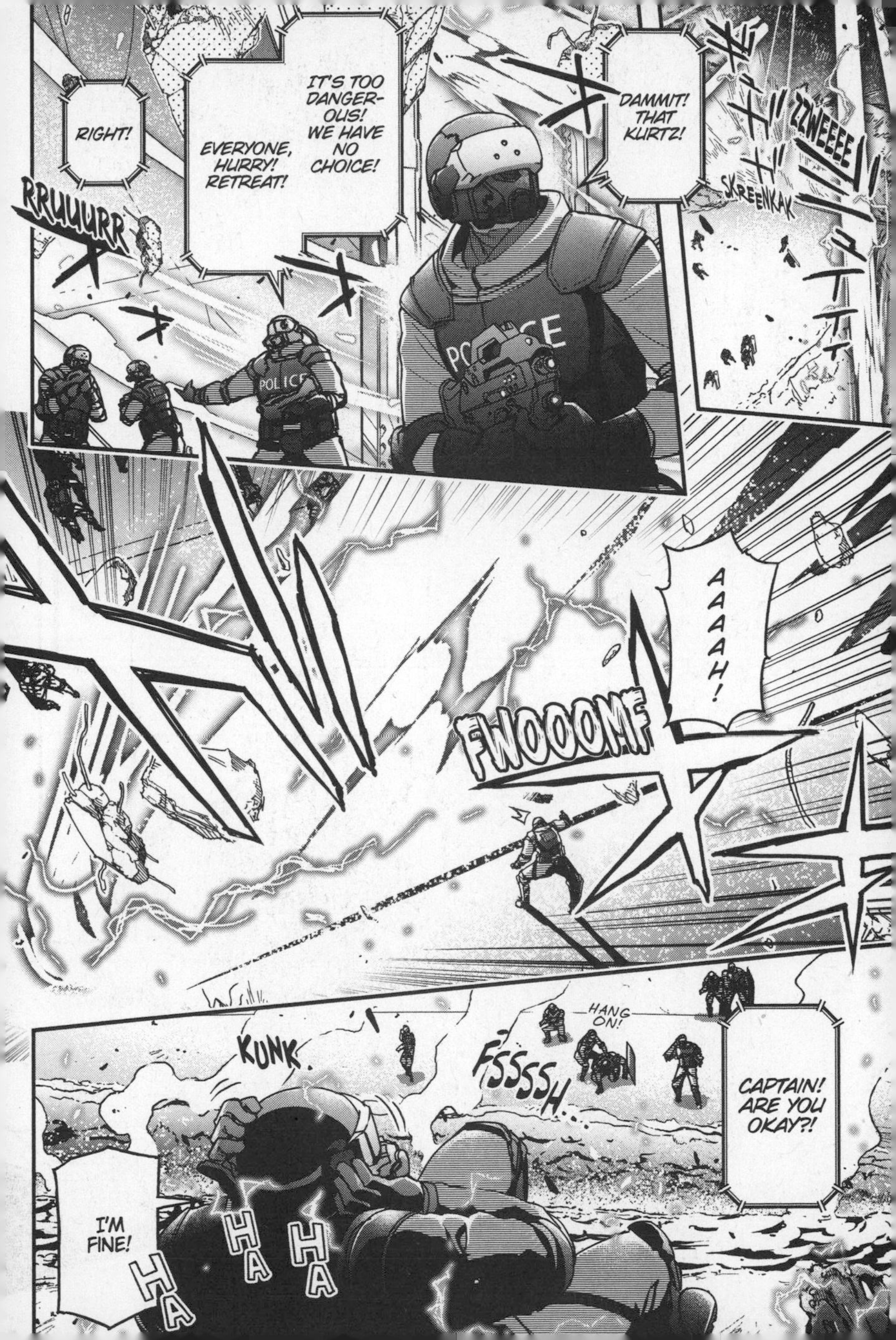
ZZWEEEEE
SKREENKAK
DAMMIT! THAT KURTZ!
IT'S TOO DANGER-OUS! WE HAVE NO CHOICE!
EVERYONE, HURRY! RETREAT!
RIGHT!
RRUUUURR
AAAAAH!
FWOOOMF
CAPTAIN! ARE YOU OKAY?!
HANG ON!
FSSSSH
KUNK
I'M FINE!
HA HA HA HA

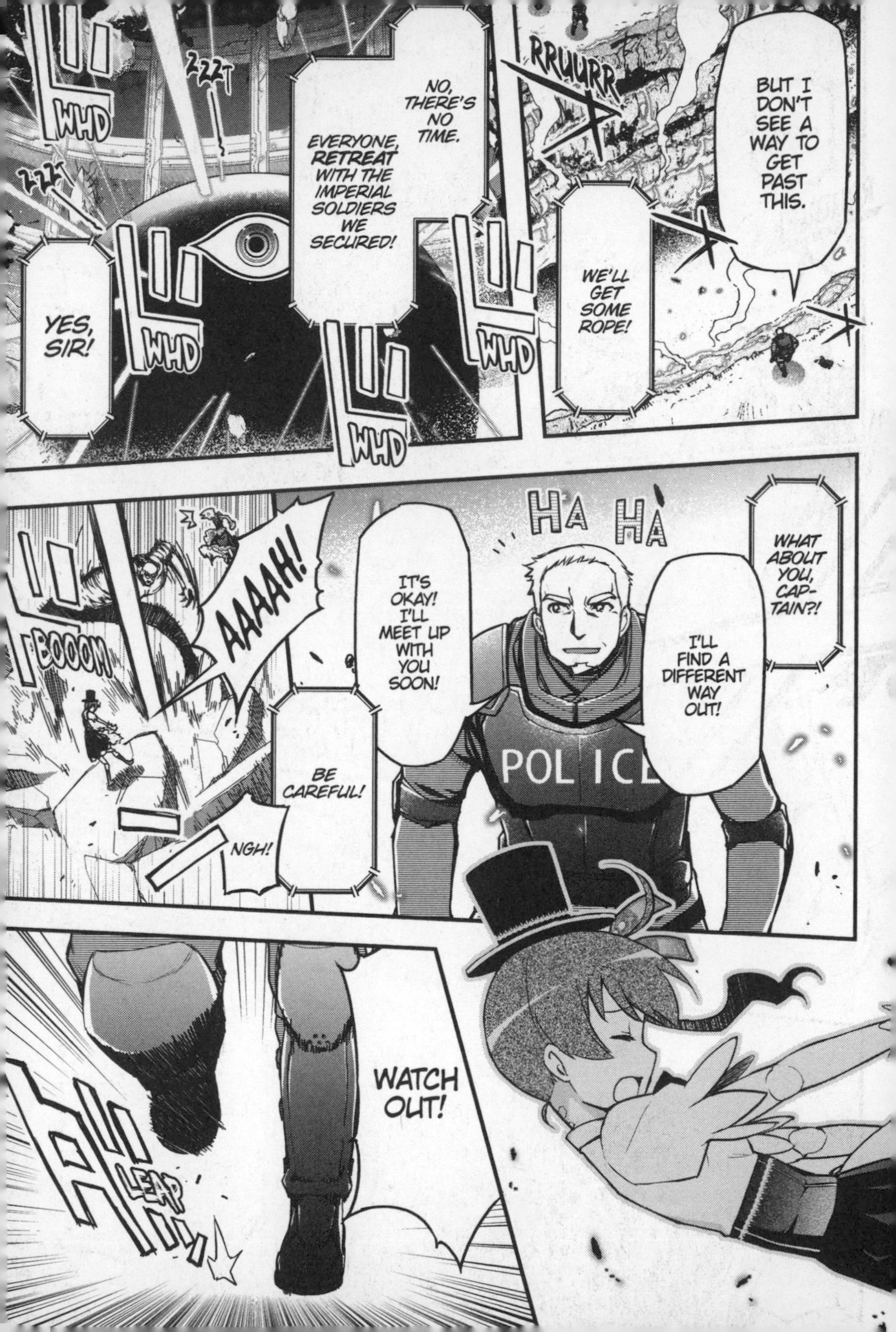
RRUURR
BUT I DON'T SEE A WAY TO GET PAST THIS.
WE'LL GET SOME ROPE!
NO, THERE'S NO TIME.
EVERYONE, **RETREAT** WITH THE IMPERIAL SOLDIERS WE SECURED!
WHD
WHD
YES, SIR!
WHD
WHD
ZZZT
ZZZT
WHAT ABOUT YOU, CAPTAIN?!
I'LL FIND A DIFFERENT WAY OUT!
HA HA
IT'S OKAY! I'LL MEET UP WITH YOU SOON!
BE CAREFUL!
POLICE
AAAAH!
NGH!
BOOOM
WATCH OUT!
LEAP

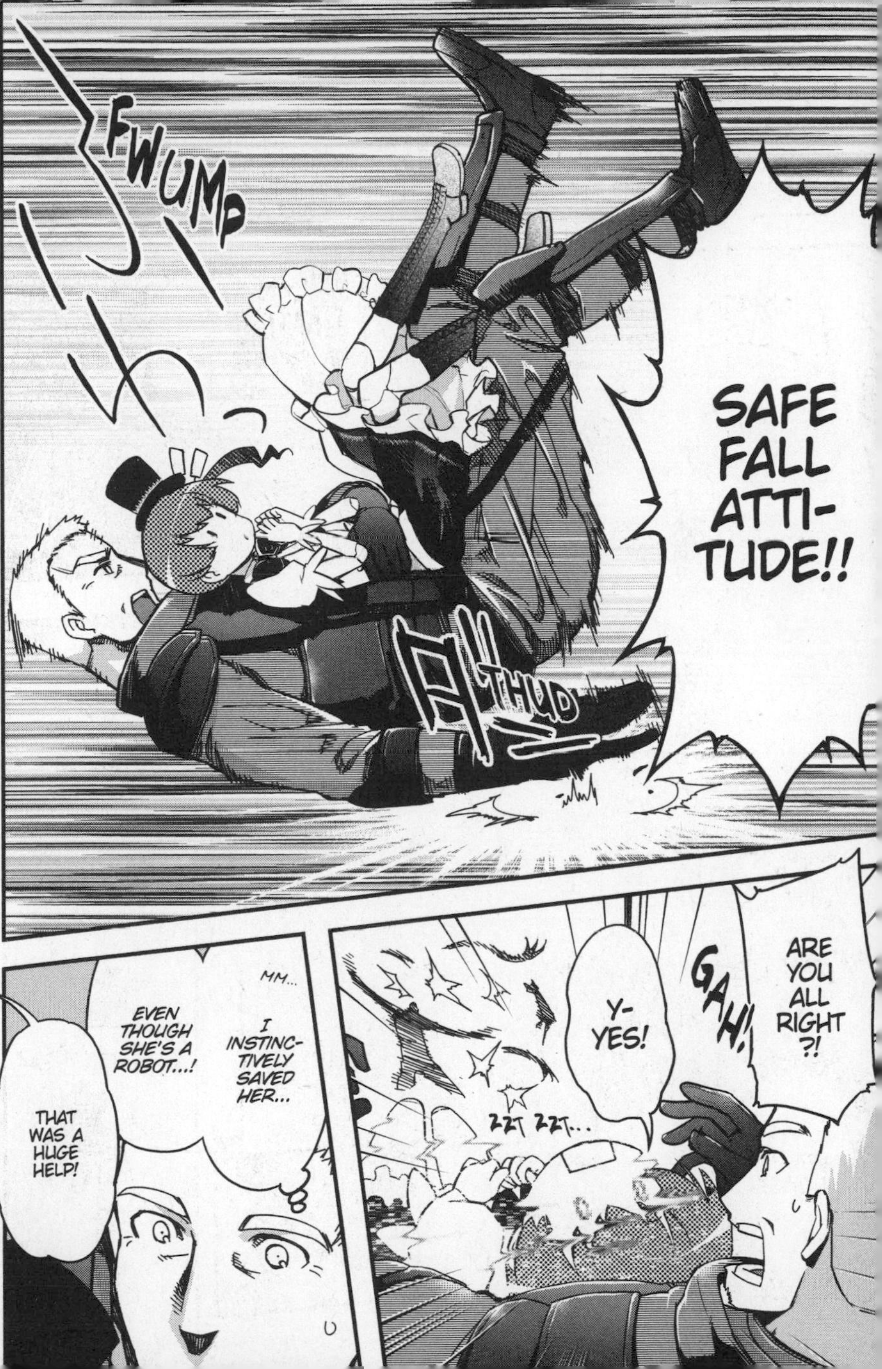
FWUMP
SAFE FALL ATTI-TUDE!!
THUD
ARE YOU ALL RIGHT ?!
GAH!
Y-YES!
ZZT ZZT...
MM...
I INSTINC-TIVELY SAVED HER...
EVEN THOUGH SHE'S A ROBOT...!
THAT WAS A HUGE HELP!

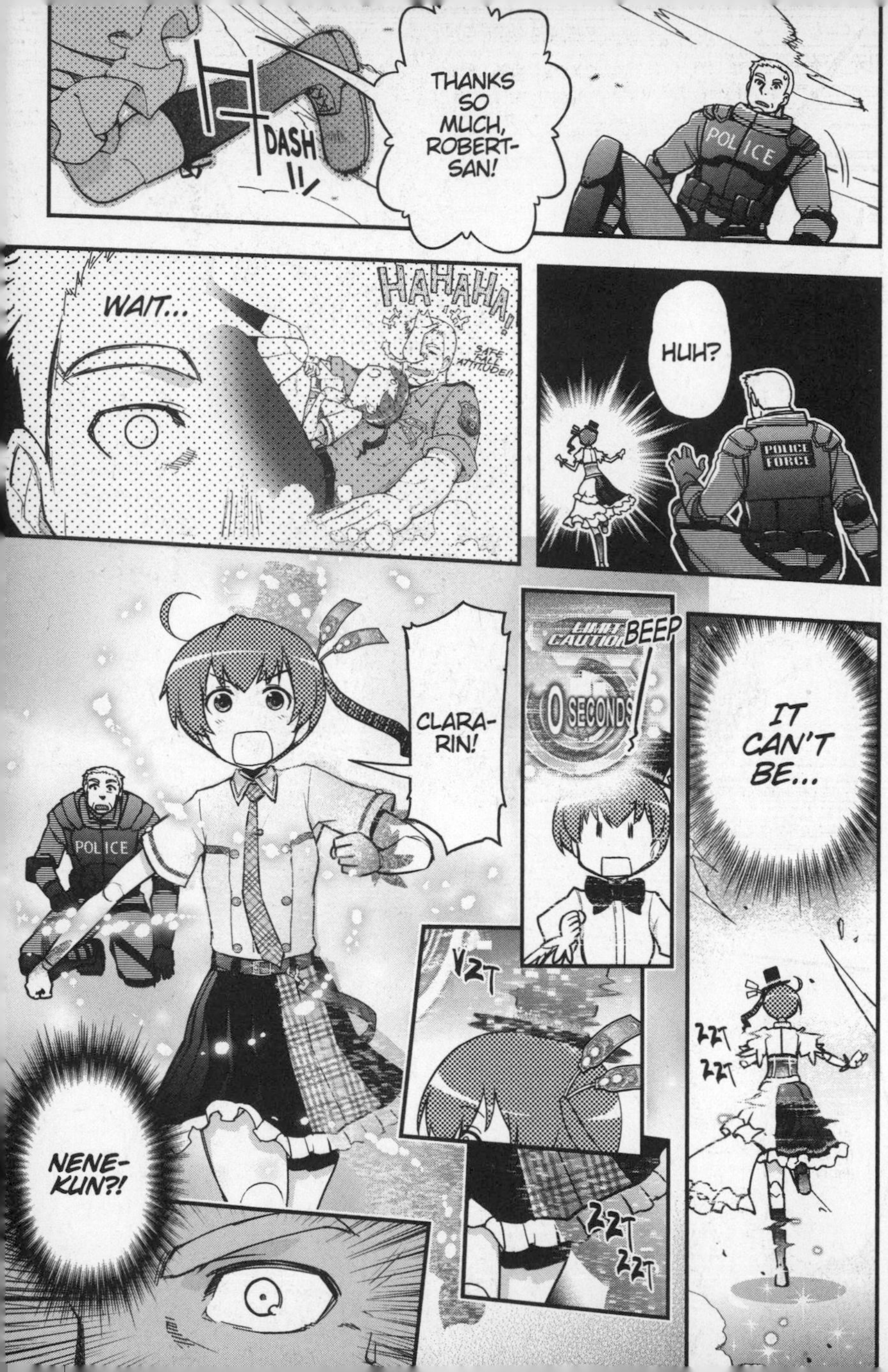
THANKS SO MUCH, ROBERT-SAN!
DASH
HUH?
HAHAHA!
SAFE FALL ATTITUDE!!
WAIT...
IT CAN'T BE...
ZZT
ZZT
LIMIT CAUTION
BEEP
0 SECONDS
VZZT
ZZT
ZZT
CLARA-RIN!
NENE-KUN?!

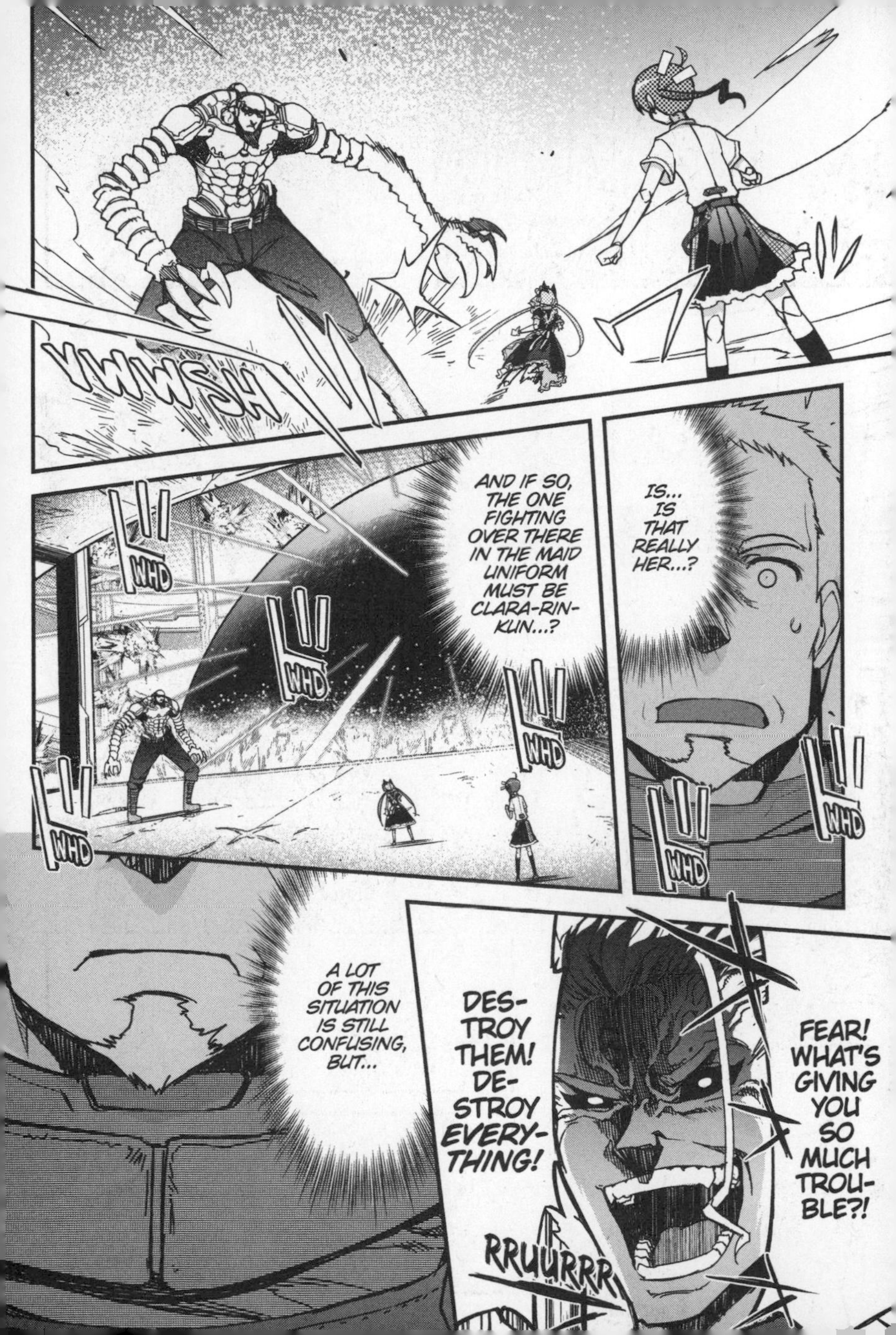
IS... IS THAT REALLY HER...?
WHD
WHD
WHD
AND IF SO, THE ONE FIGHTING OVER THERE IN THE MAID UNIFORM MUST BE CLARA-RIN-KUN...?
WHD
WHD
WHD
FEAR! WHAT'S GIVING YOU SO MUCH TROUBLE?!
DES-TROY THEM! DE-STROY EVERY-THING!
RRUURRR
A LOT OF THIS SITUATION IS STILL CONFUSING, BUT...

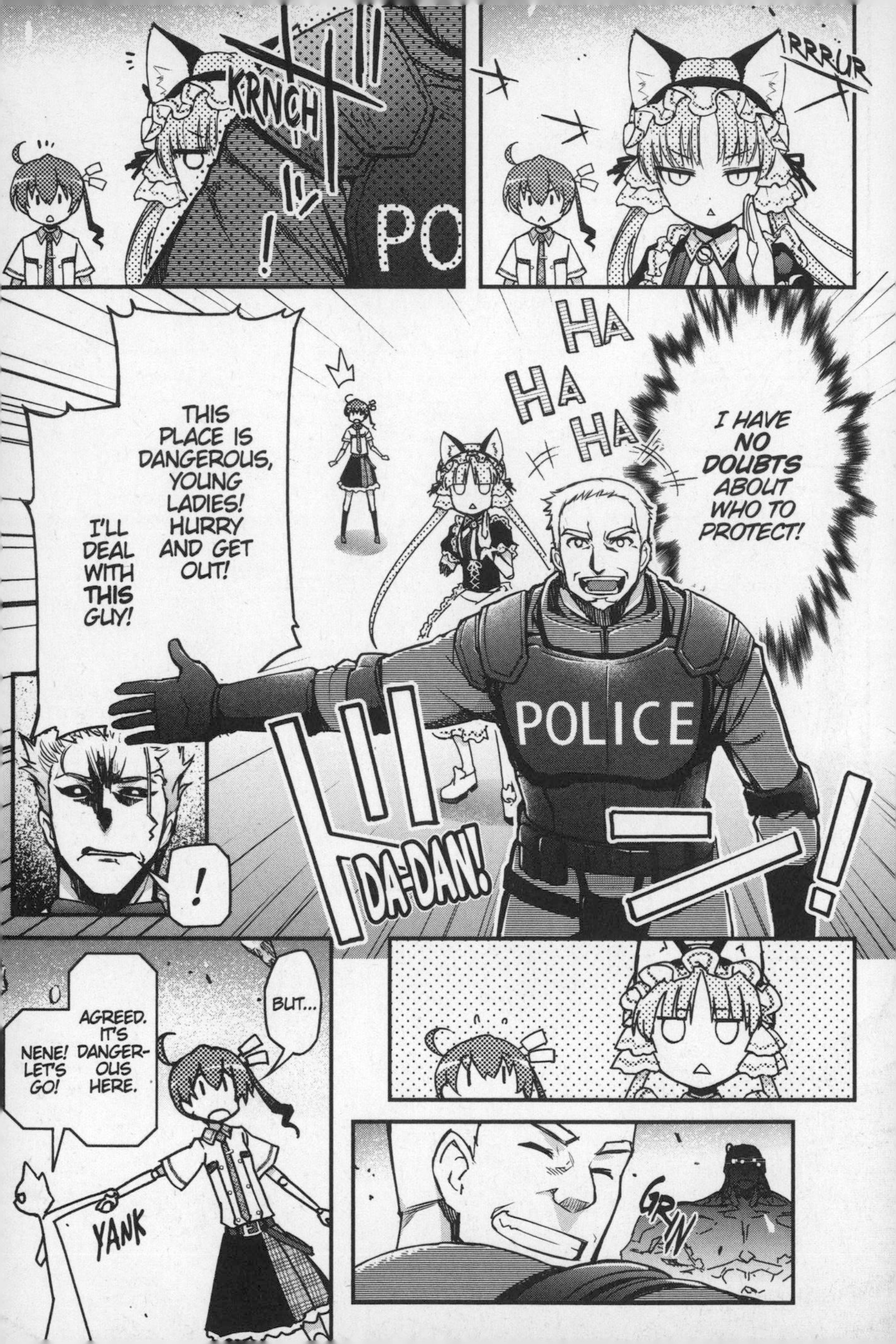
RRRRUR
KRNCH
PO
HA
HA
HA
I HAVE NO DOUBTS ABOUT WHO TO PROTECT!
THIS PLACE IS DANGEROUS, YOUNG LADIES! HURRY AND GET OUT!
I'LL DEAL WITH THIS GUY!
POLICE
DA-DAN!
!
GRYN
BUT...
AGREED. IT'S DANGER-OUS HERE.
NENE! LET'S GO!
YANK

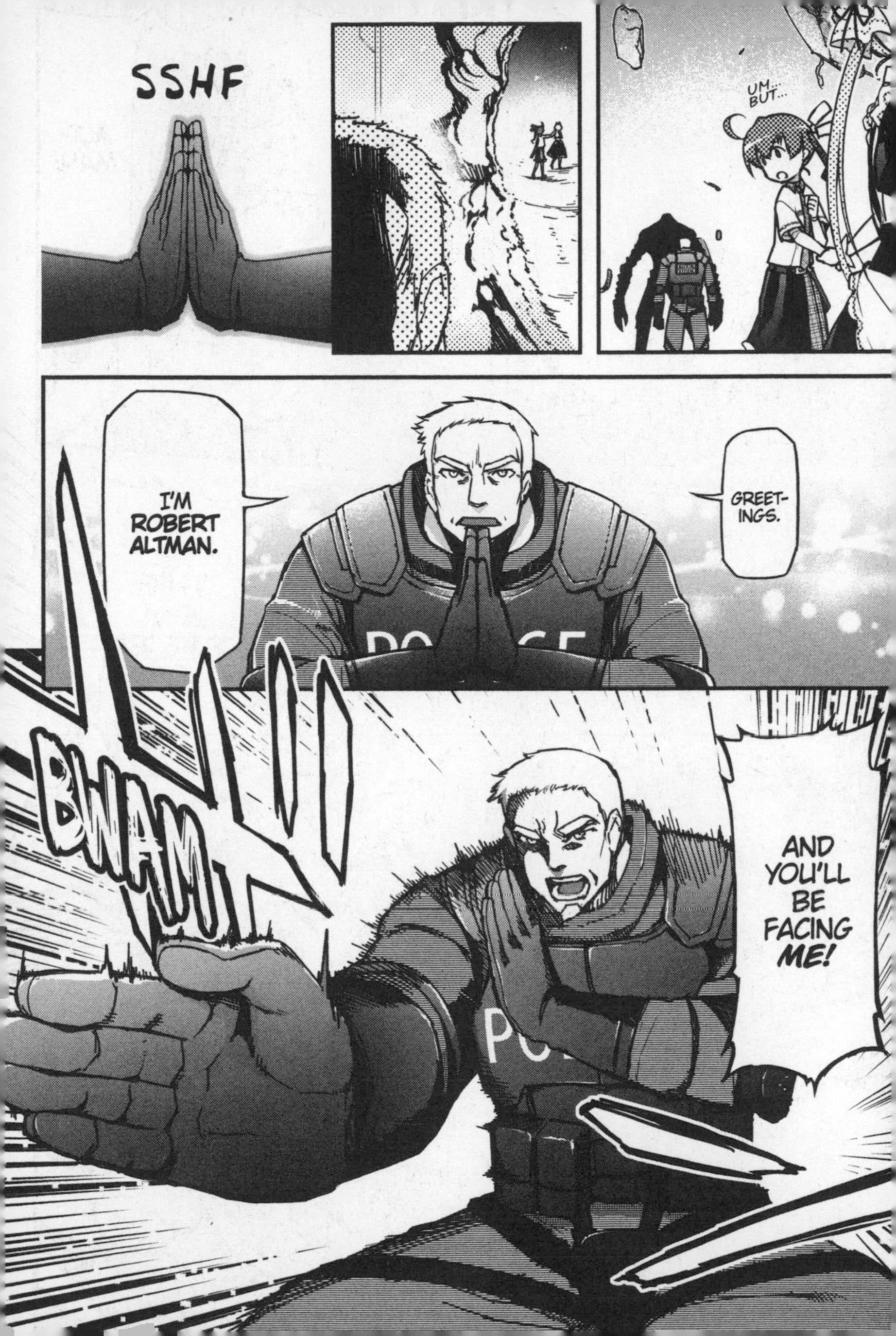

UM... BUT...
SSHF
GREET-INGS.
I'M ROBERT ALTMAN.
AND YOU'LL BE FACING ME!
BWAM

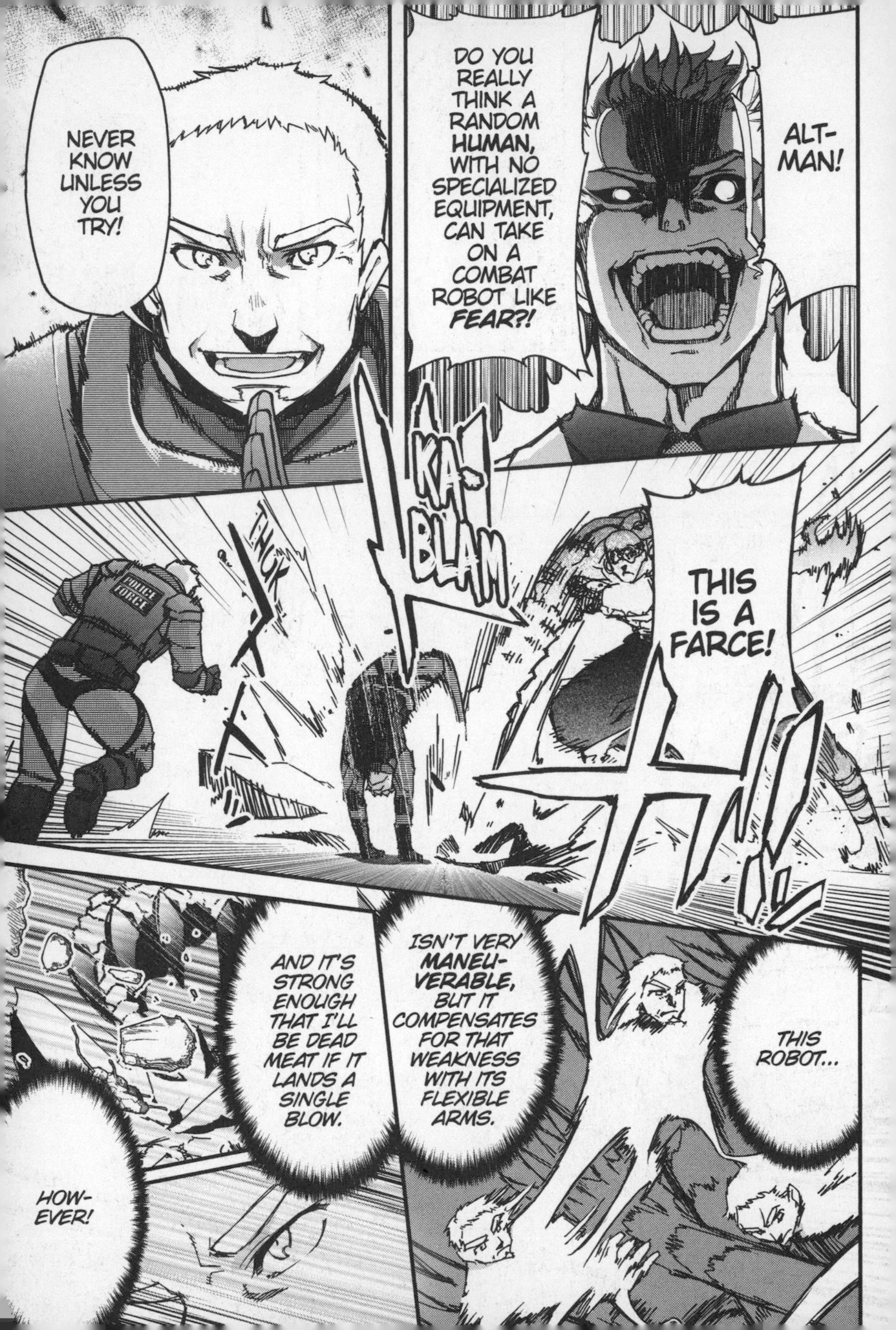
ALT-MAN!
DO YOU REALLY THINK A RANDOM HUMAN, WITH NO SPECIALIZED EQUIPMENT, CAN TAKE ON A COMBAT ROBOT LIKE FEAR?!
NEVER KNOW UNLESS YOU TRY!
THIS IS A FARCE!
KA-BLAM
THUK
POLICE FORCE
THIS ROBOT...
ISN'T VERY MANEU-VERABLE, BUT IT COMPENSATES FOR THAT WEAKNESS WITH ITS FLEXIBLE ARMS.
AND IT'S STRONG ENOUGH THAT I'LL BE DEAD MEAT IF IT LANDS A SINGLE BLOW.
HOW-EVER!

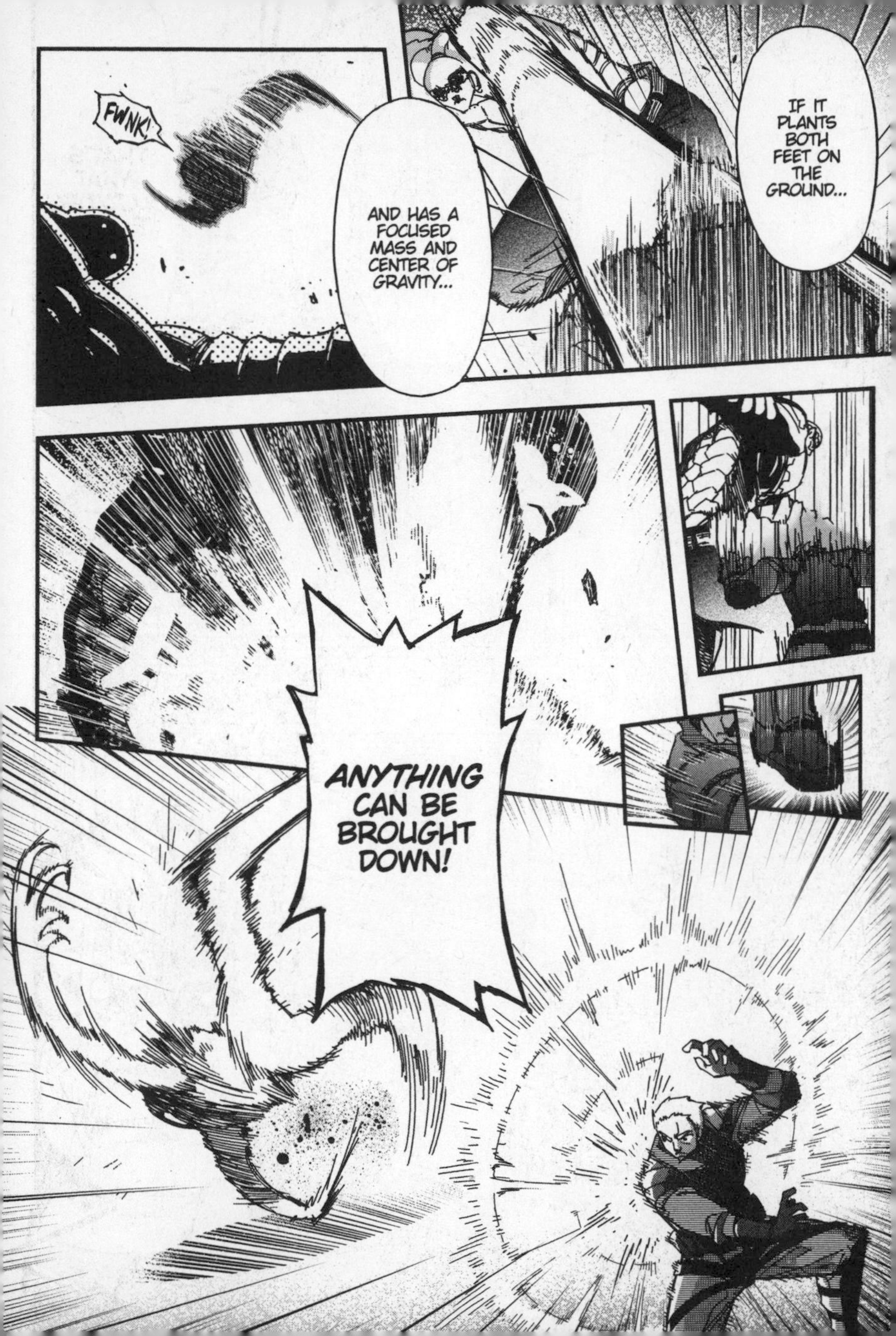
IF IT PLANTS BOTH FEET ON THE GROUND...
AND HAS A FOCUSED MASS AND CENTER OF GRAVITY...
FWNK!
ANYTHING CAN BE BROUGHT DOWN!

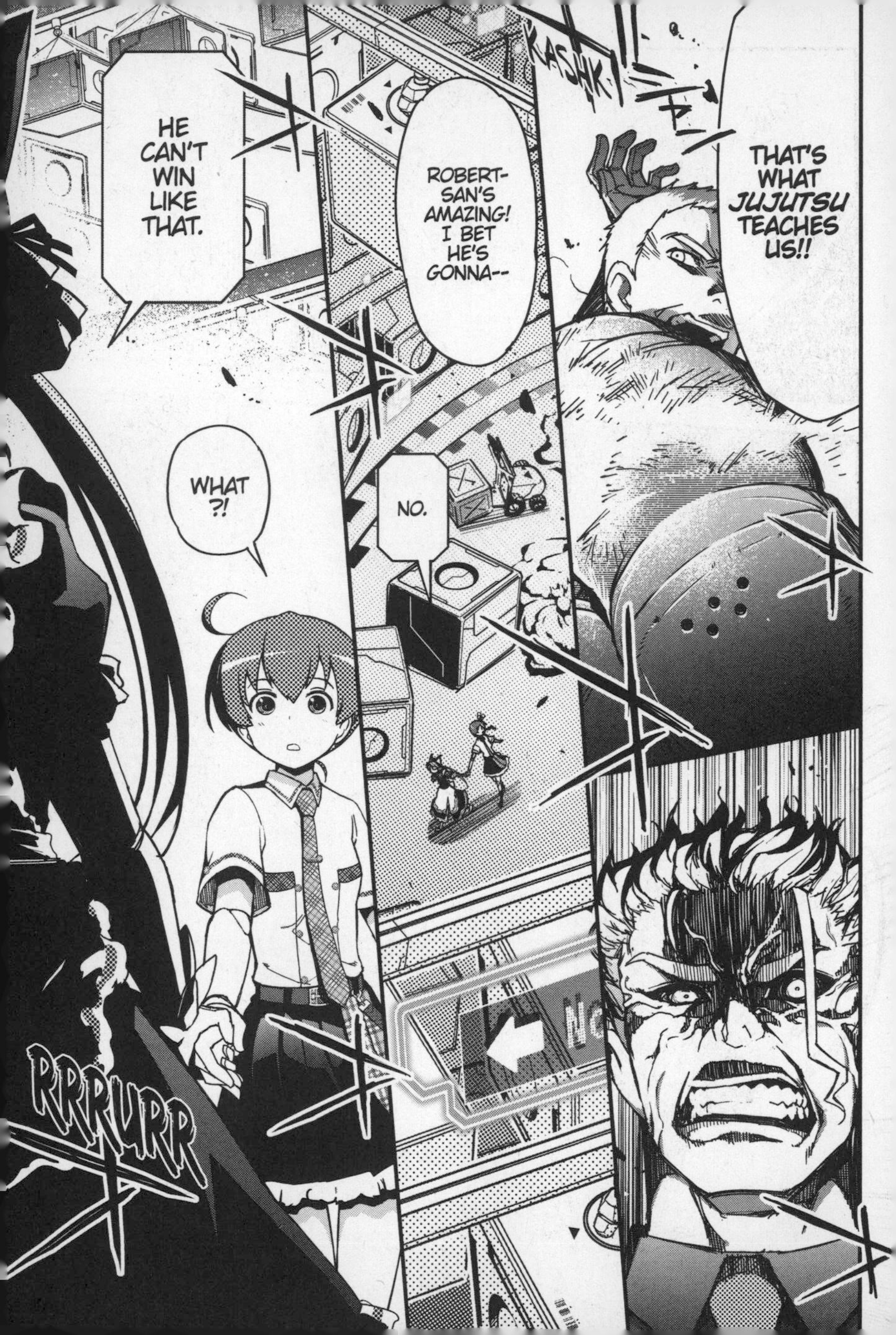
KASHK
THAT'S WHAT JUJUTSU TEACHES US!!
ROBERT-SAN'S AMAZING! I BET HE'S GONNA--
NO.
HE CAN'T WIN LIKE THAT.
WHAT ?!
RRRURR

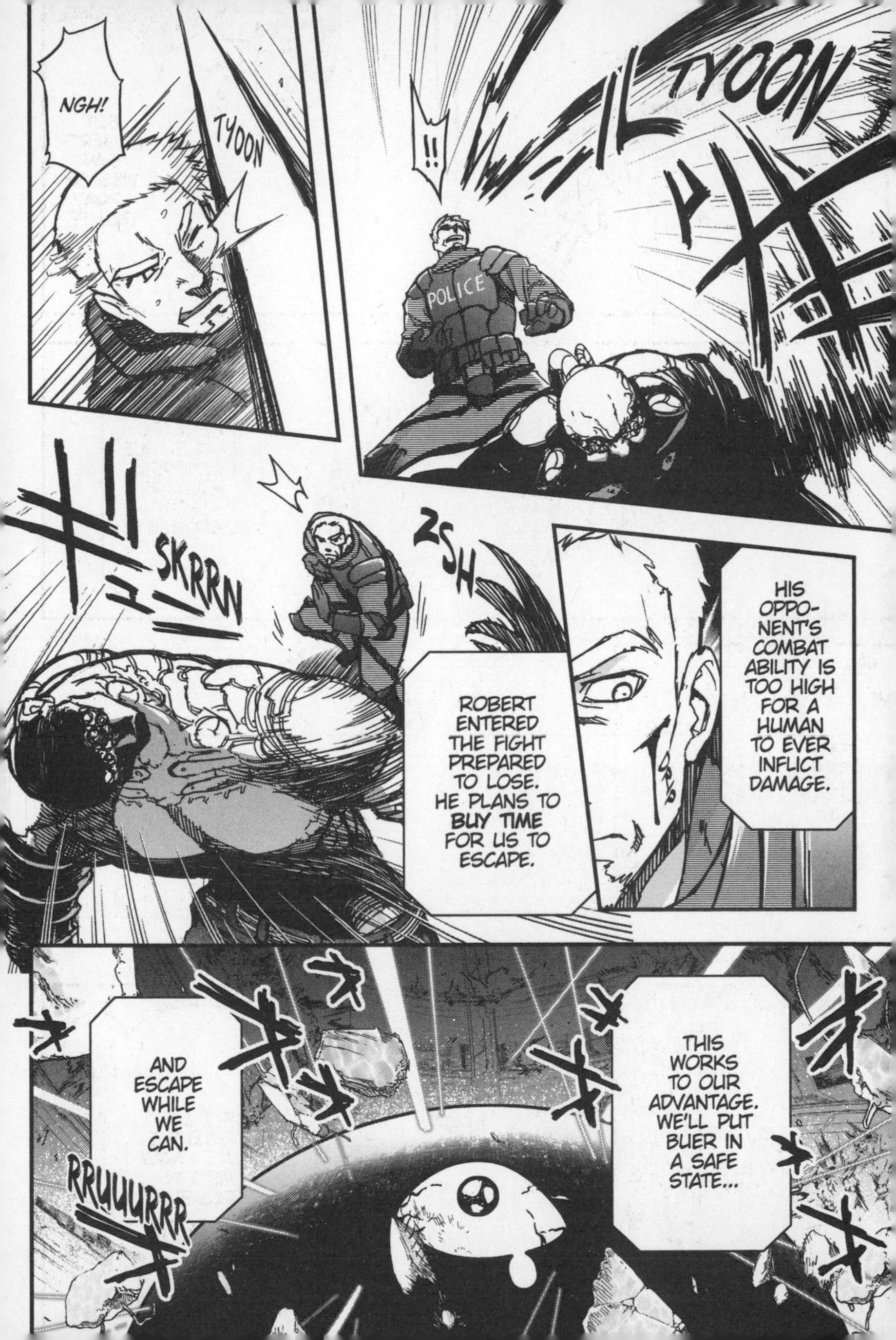
TYOON
!!
NGH!
TYOON
HIS OPPONENT'S COMBAT ABILITY IS TOO HIGH FOR A HUMAN TO EVER INFLICT DAMAGE.
DRIP
ZSH
SKRRN
ROBERT ENTERED THE FIGHT PREPARED TO LOSE. HE PLANS TO BUY TIME FOR US TO ESCAPE.
THIS WORKS TO OUR ADVANTAGE. WE'LL PUT BUER IN A SAFE STATE...
AND ESCAPE WHILE WE CAN.
RRUUURRR

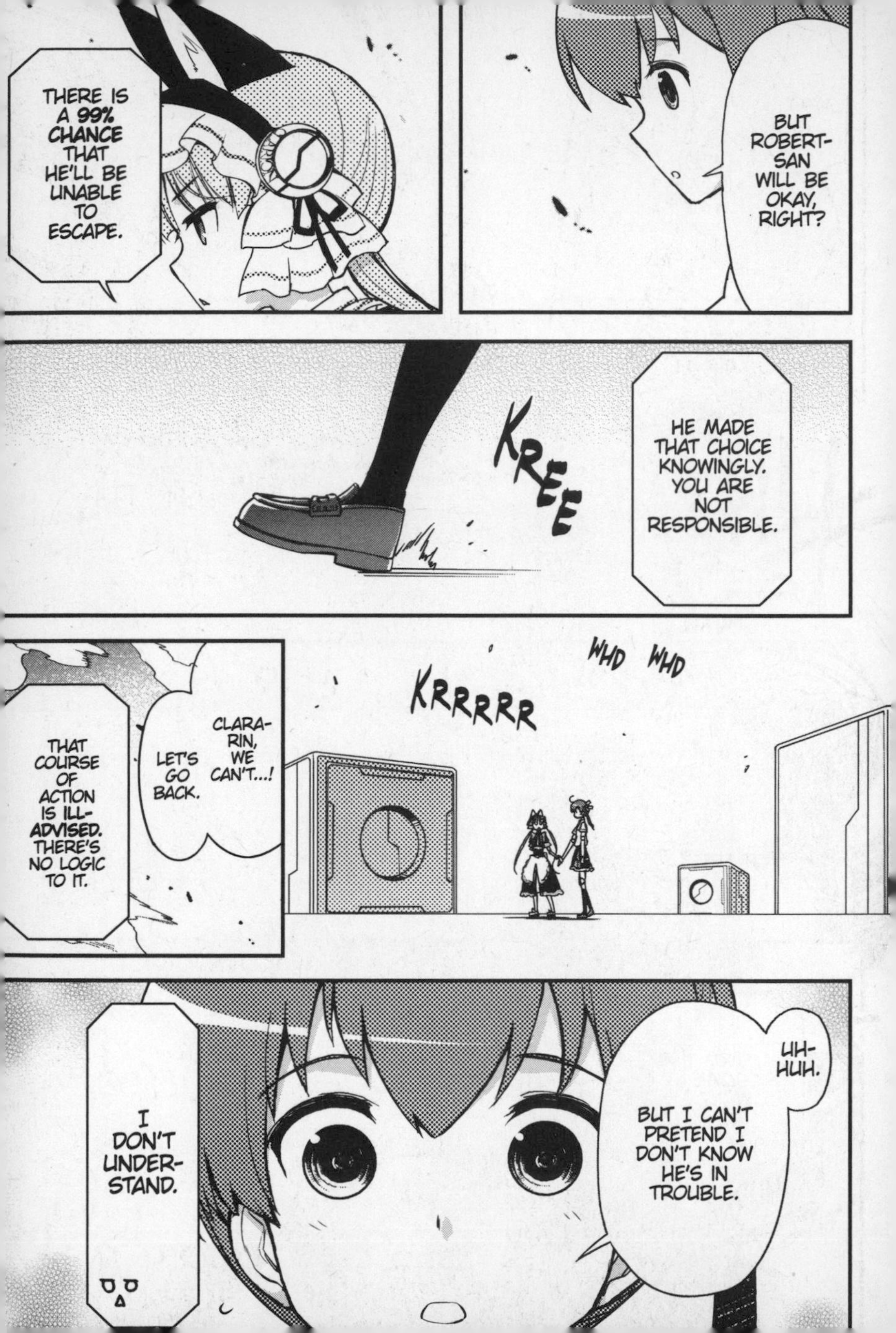
BUT ROBERT-SAN WILL BE OKAY, RIGHT?
THERE IS A 99% CHANCE THAT HE'LL BE UNABLE TO ESCAPE.
HE MADE THAT CHOICE KNOWINGLY. YOU ARE NOT RESPONSIBLE.
KREE
WHD WHD
KRRRRR
CLARA-RIN, WE CAN'T...!
LET'S GO BACK.
THAT COURSE OF ACTION IS ILL-ADVISED. THERE'S NO LOGIC TO IT.
UH-HUH.
BUT I CAN'T PRETEND I DON'T KNOW HE'S IN TROUBLE.
I DON'T UNDER-STAND.

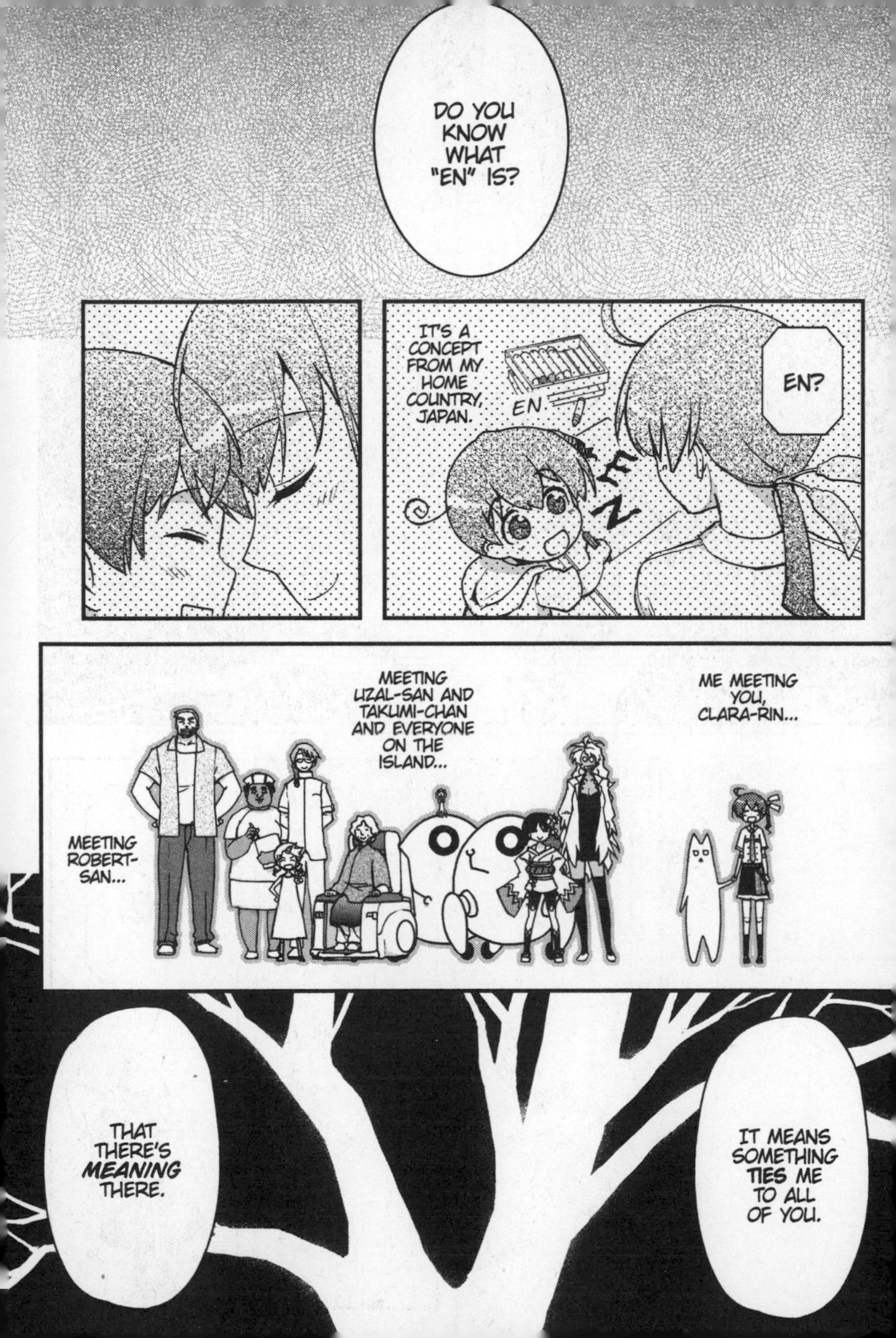

DO YOU KNOW WHAT "EN" IS?
EN?
IT'S A CONCEPT FROM MY HOME COUNTRY, JAPAN.
EN
EN
ME MEETING YOU, CLARA-RIN...
MEETING UZAL-SAN AND TAKUMI-CHAN AND EVERYONE ON THE ISLAND...
MEETING ROBERT-SAN...
IT MEANS SOMETHING TIES ME TO ALL OF YOU.
THAT THERE'S MEANING THERE.

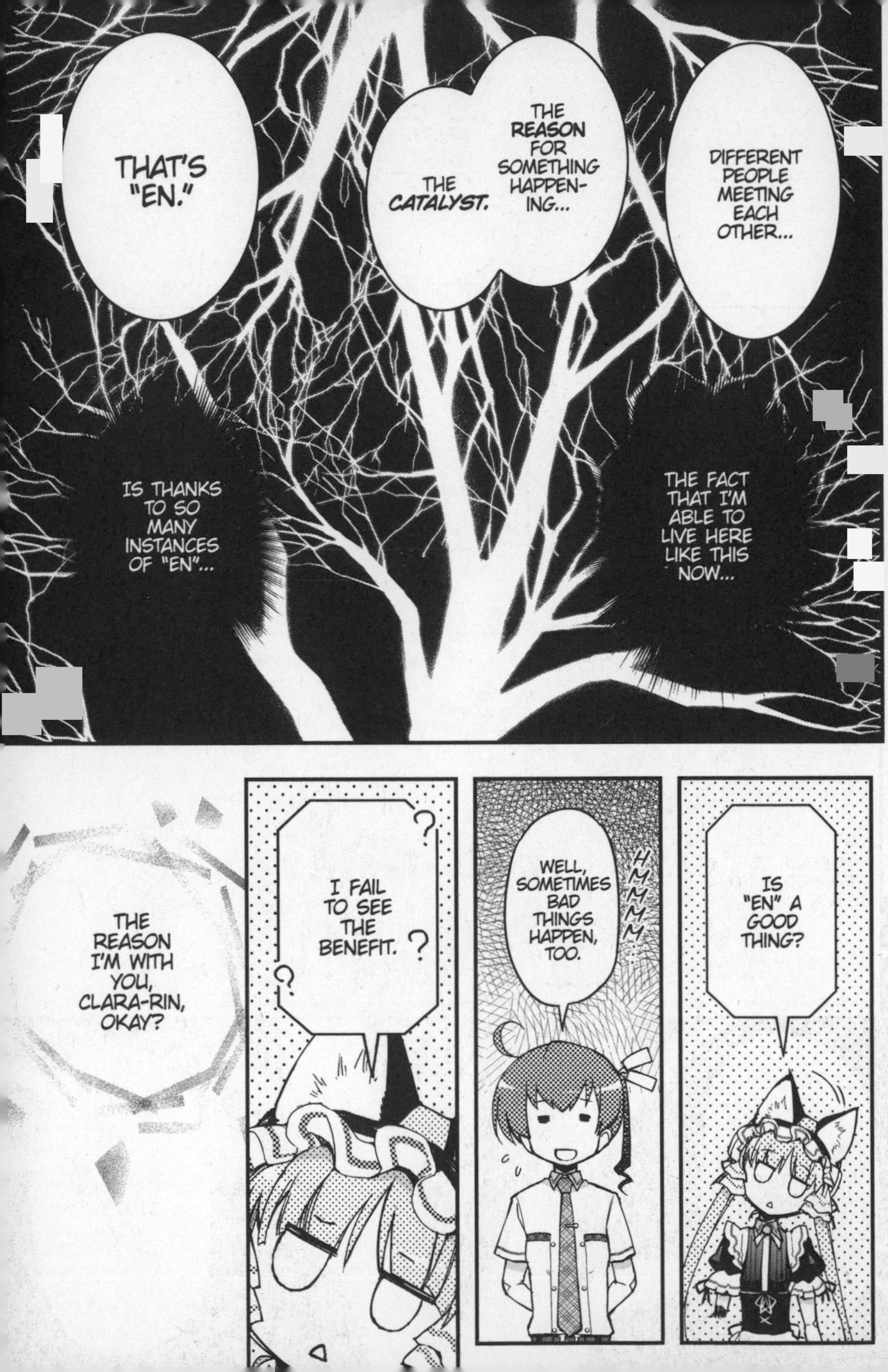
DIFFERENT PEOPLE MEETING EACH OTHER...
THE REASON FOR SOMETHING HAPPENING...
THE CATALYST.
THAT'S "EN."
THE FACT THAT I'M ABLE TO LIVE HERE LIKE THIS NOW...
IS THANKS TO SO MANY INSTANCES OF "EN"...
IS "EN" A GOOD THING?
HMMMM...
WELL, SOMETIMES BAD THINGS HAPPEN, TOO.
I FAIL TO SEE THE BENEFIT.
THE REASON I'M WITH YOU, CLARA-RIN, OKAY?

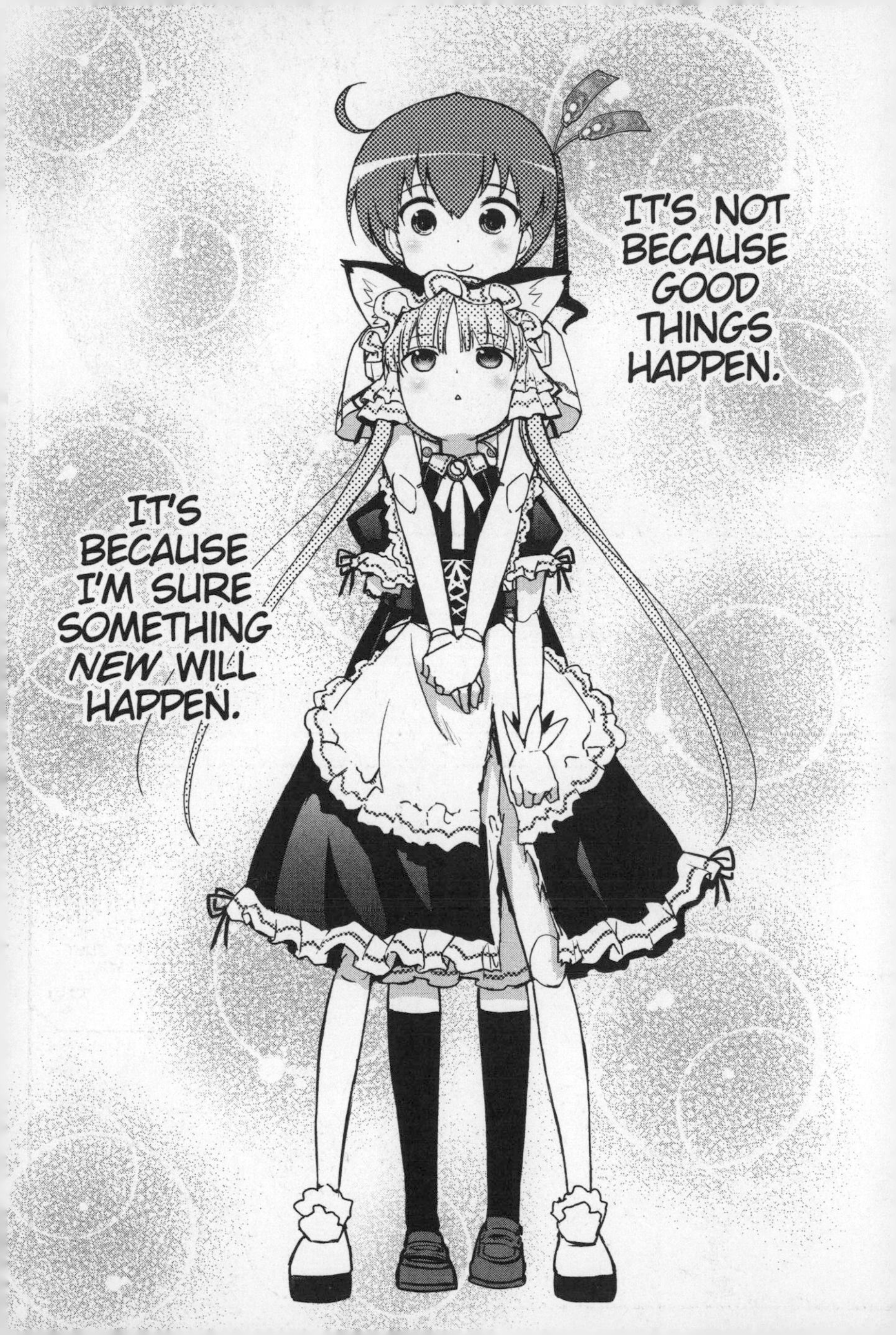
IT'S NOT BECAUSE GOOD THINGS HAPPEN.
IT'S BECAUSE I'M SURE SOMETHING *NEW* WILL HAPPEN.

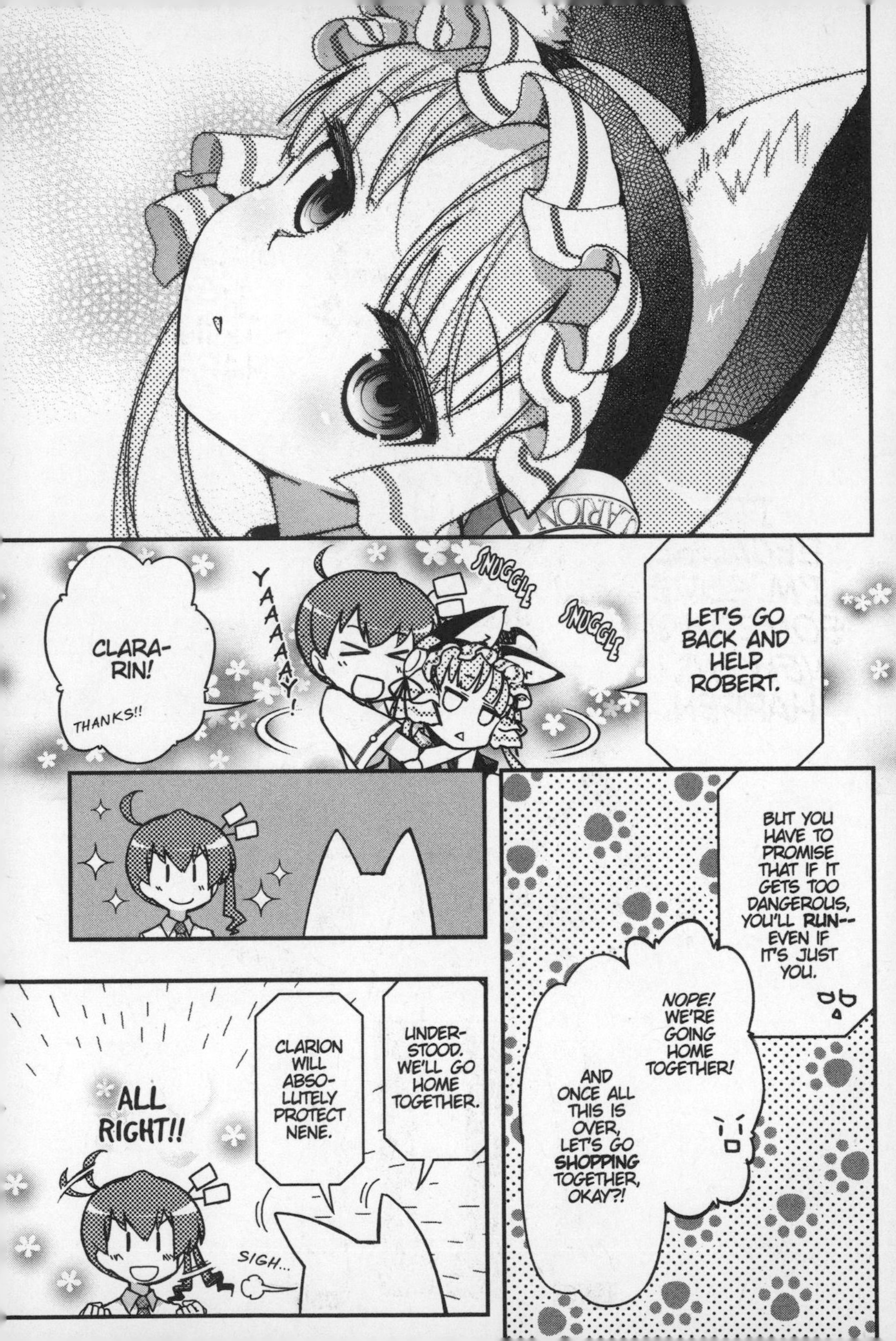
LET'S GO BACK AND HELP ROBERT.
SNUGGLE
SNUGGLE
YAAAAAY!
CLARA-RIN!
THANKS!!
BUT YOU HAVE TO PROMISE THAT IF IT GETS TOO DANGEROUS, YOU'LL RUN-- EVEN IF IT'S JUST YOU.
NOPE! WE'RE GOING HOME TOGETHER!
AND ONCE ALL THIS IS OVER, LET'S GO SHOPPING TOGETHER, OKAY?!
UNDER-STOOD. WE'LL GO HOME TOGETHER.
CLARION WILL ABSO-LUTELY PROTECT NENE.
ALL RIGHT!!
SIGH...

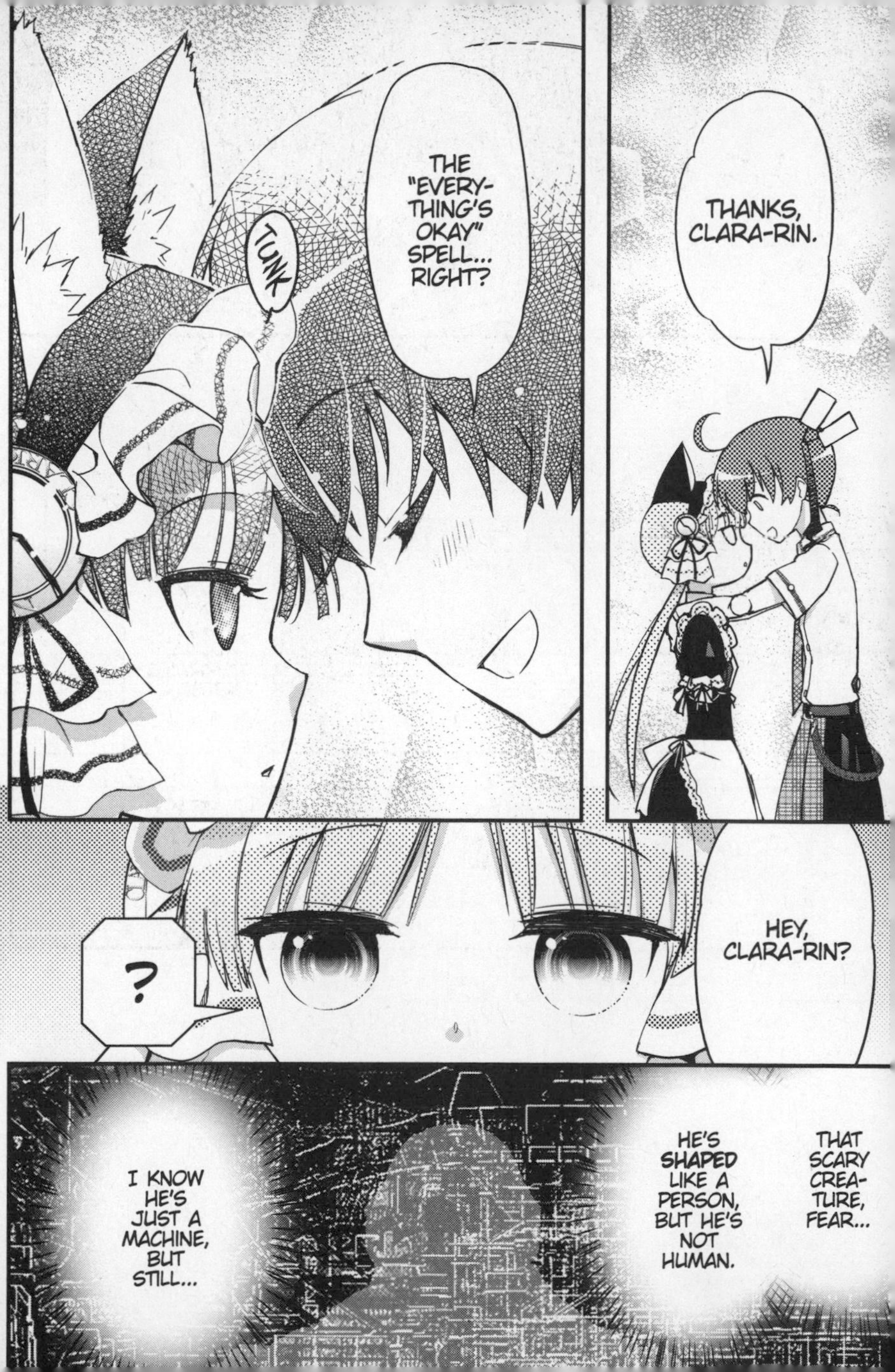
THANKS, CLARA-RIN.
THE "EVERY-THING'S OKAY" SPELL... RIGHT?
TUNK
HEY, CLARA-RIN?
?
THAT SCARY CREA-TURE, FEAR...
HE'S SHAPED LIKE A PERSON, BUT HE'S NOT HUMAN.
I KNOW HE'S JUST A MACHINE, BUT STILL...

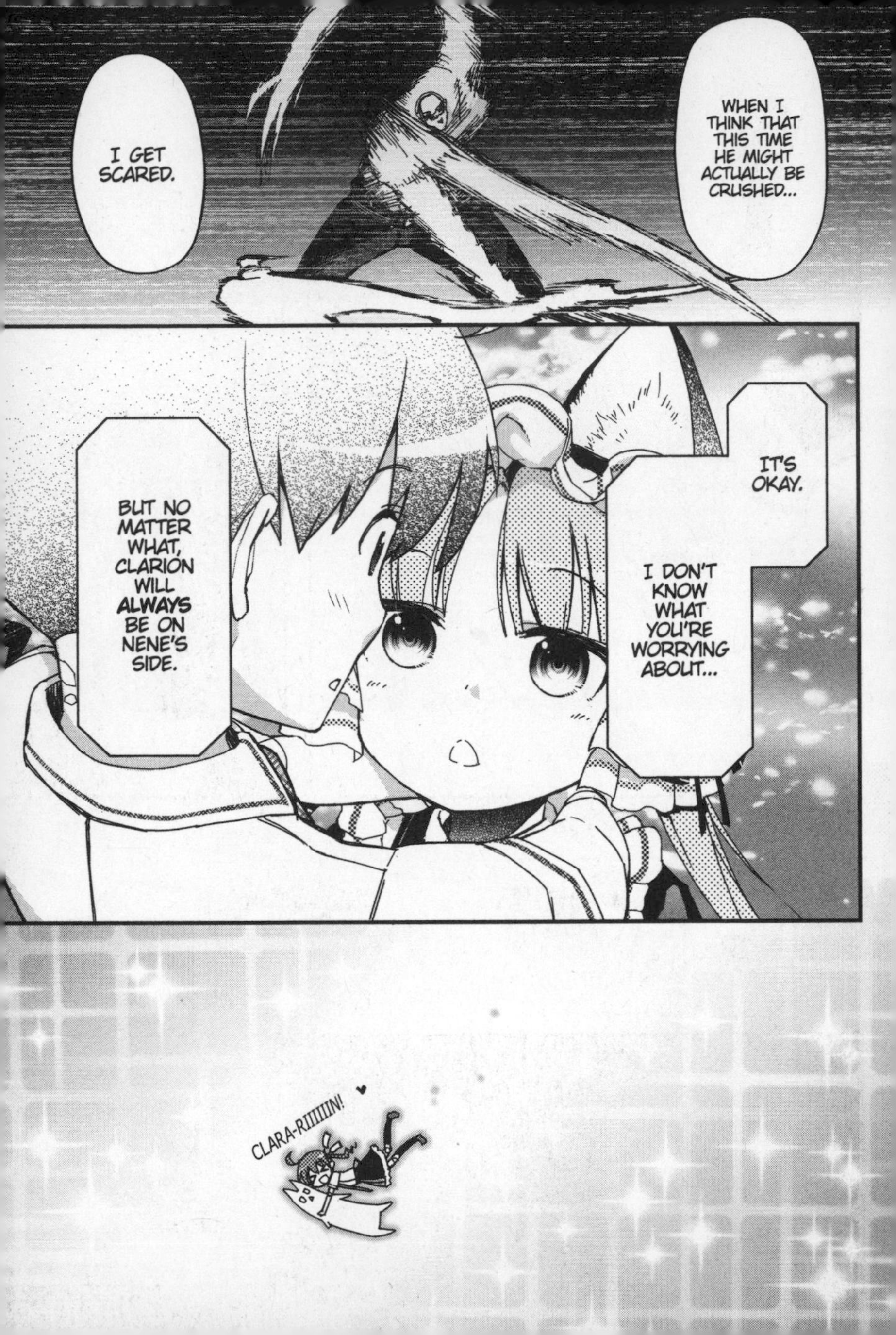
WHEN I THINK THAT THIS TIME HE MIGHT ACTUALLY BE CRUSHED...
I GET SCARED.
IT'S OKAY.
I DON'T KNOW WHAT YOU'RE WORRYING ABOUT...
BUT NO MATTER WHAT, CLARION WILL **ALWAYS** BE ON NENE'S SIDE.
CLARA-RIIIIIIN!

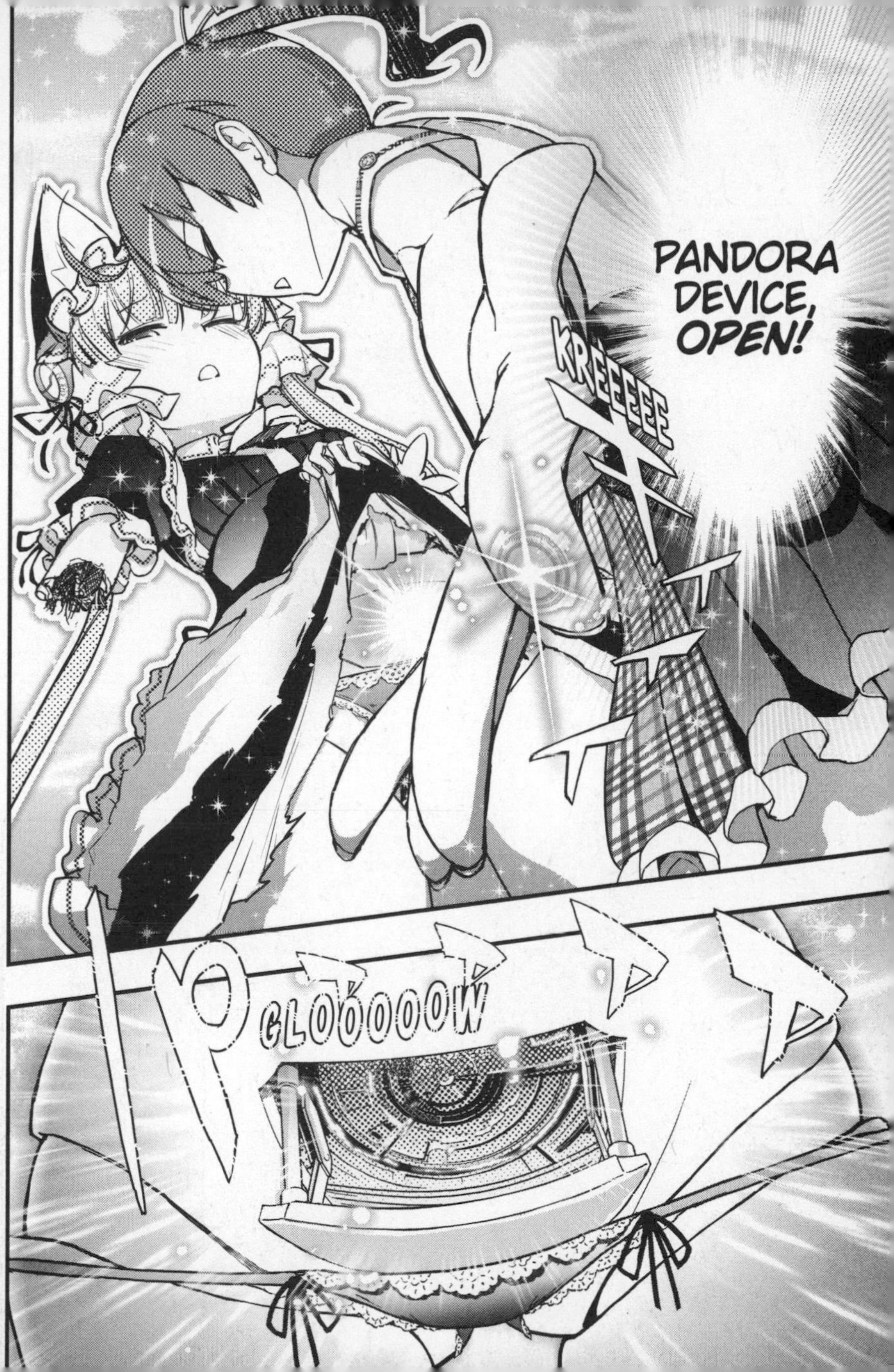
PANDORA DEVICE, OPEN!
KREEEEE
GLOOOOOW

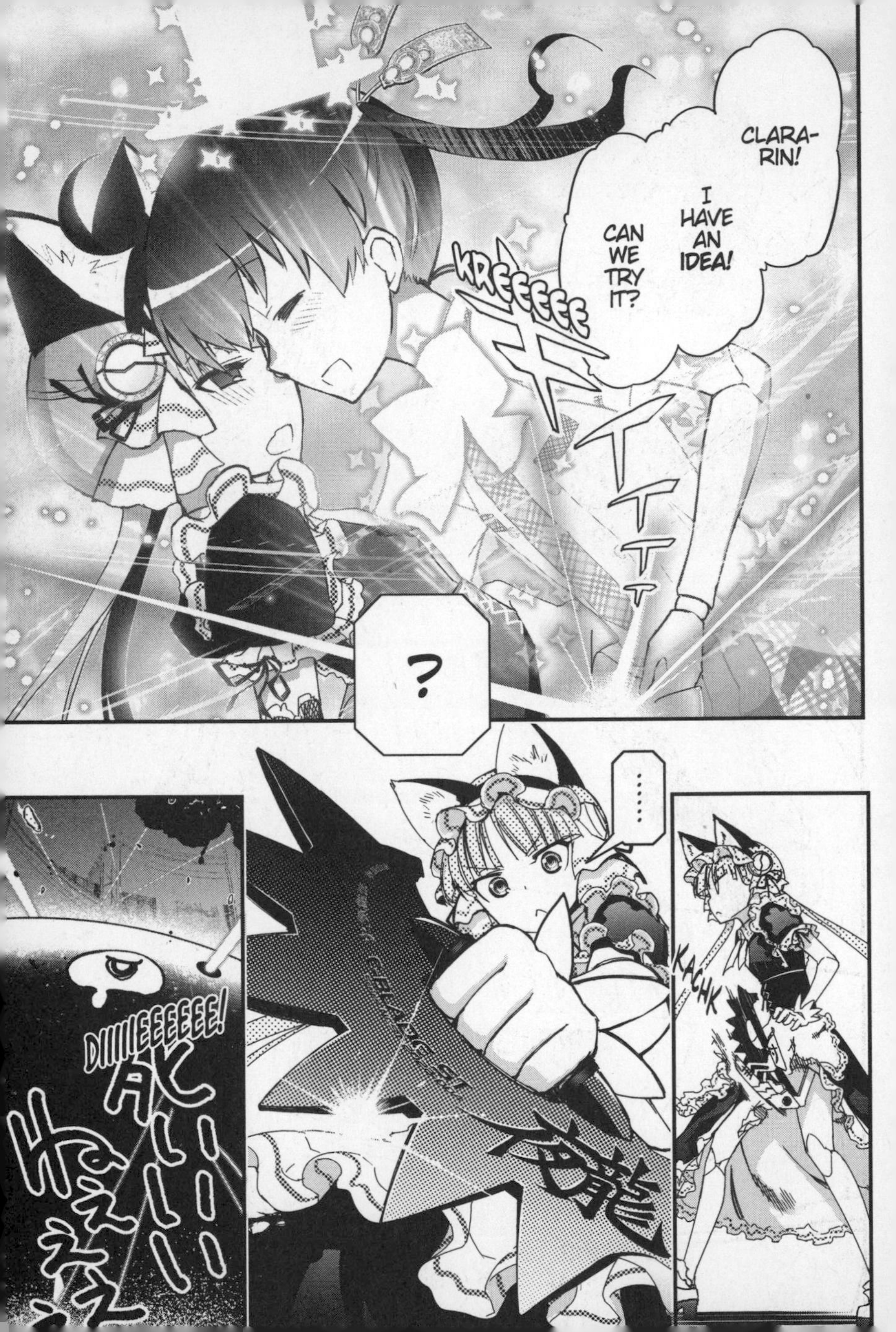
CLARA-RIN!
I HAVE AN IDEA!
CAN WE TRY IT?
KREEEEEE
?
KACHK
......
DIIIIEEEEEE!

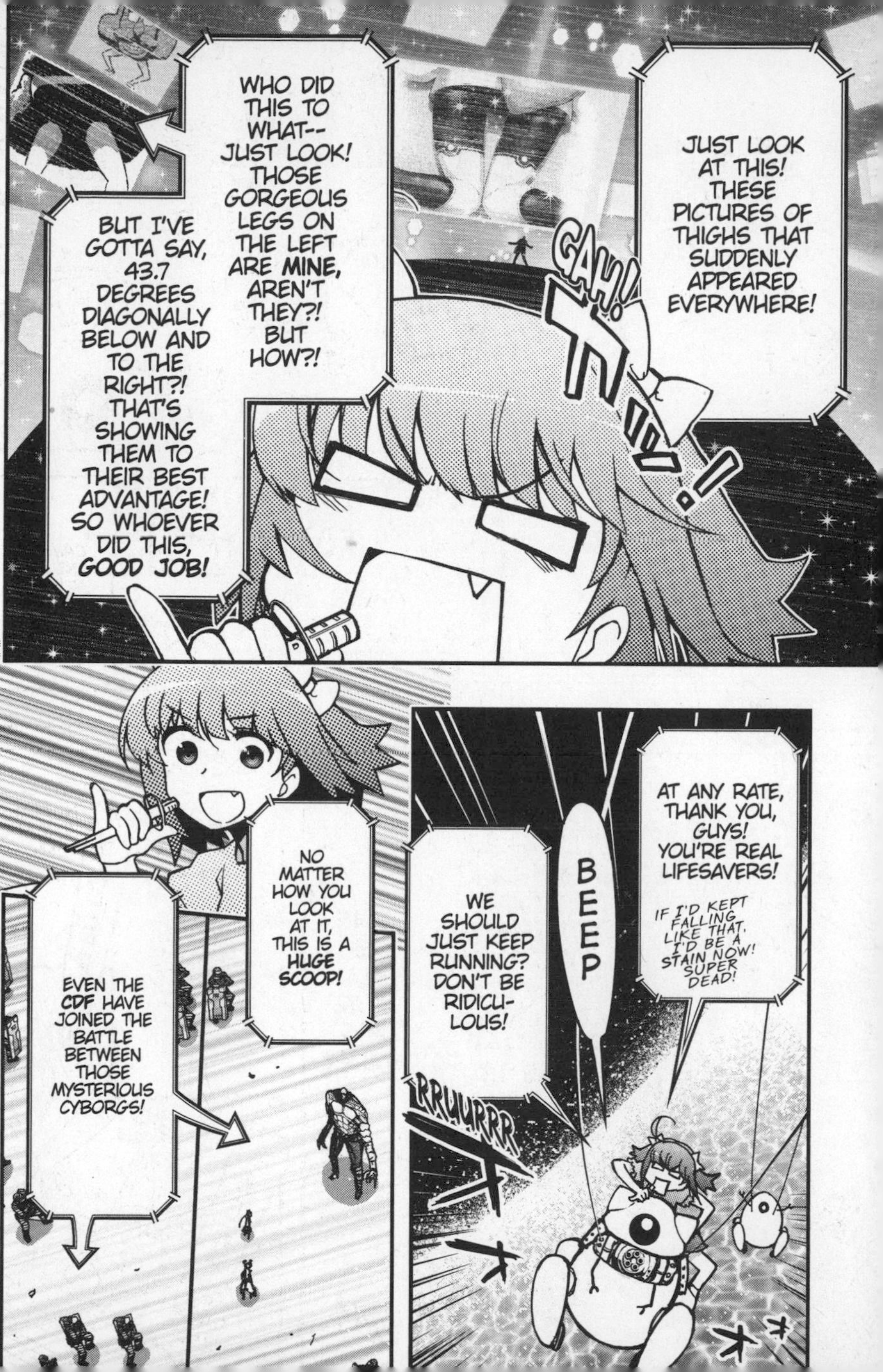
JUST LOOK AT THIS! THESE PICTURES OF THIGHS THAT SUDDENLY APPEARED EVERYWHERE!
GAH!!
WHO DID THIS TO WHAT-- JUST LOOK! THOSE GORGEOUS LEGS ON THE LEFT ARE MINE, AREN'T THEY?! BUT HOW?!
BUT I'VE GOTTA SAY, 43.7 DEGREES DIAGONALLY BELOW AND TO THE RIGHT?! THAT'S SHOWING THEM TO THEIR BEST ADVANTAGE! SO WHOEVER DID THIS, GOOD JOB!
AT ANY RATE, THANK YOU, GUYS! YOU'RE REAL LIFESAVERS!
IF I'D KEPT FALLING LIKE THAT, I'D BE A STAIN NOW! SUPER DEAD!
BEEP
WE SHOULD JUST KEEP RUNNING? DON'T BE RIDICULOUS!
RRUURRR
NO MATTER HOW YOU LOOK AT IT, THIS IS A HUGE SCOOP!
EVEN THE CDF HAVE JOINED THE BATTLE BETWEEN THOSE MYSTERIOUS CYBORGS!

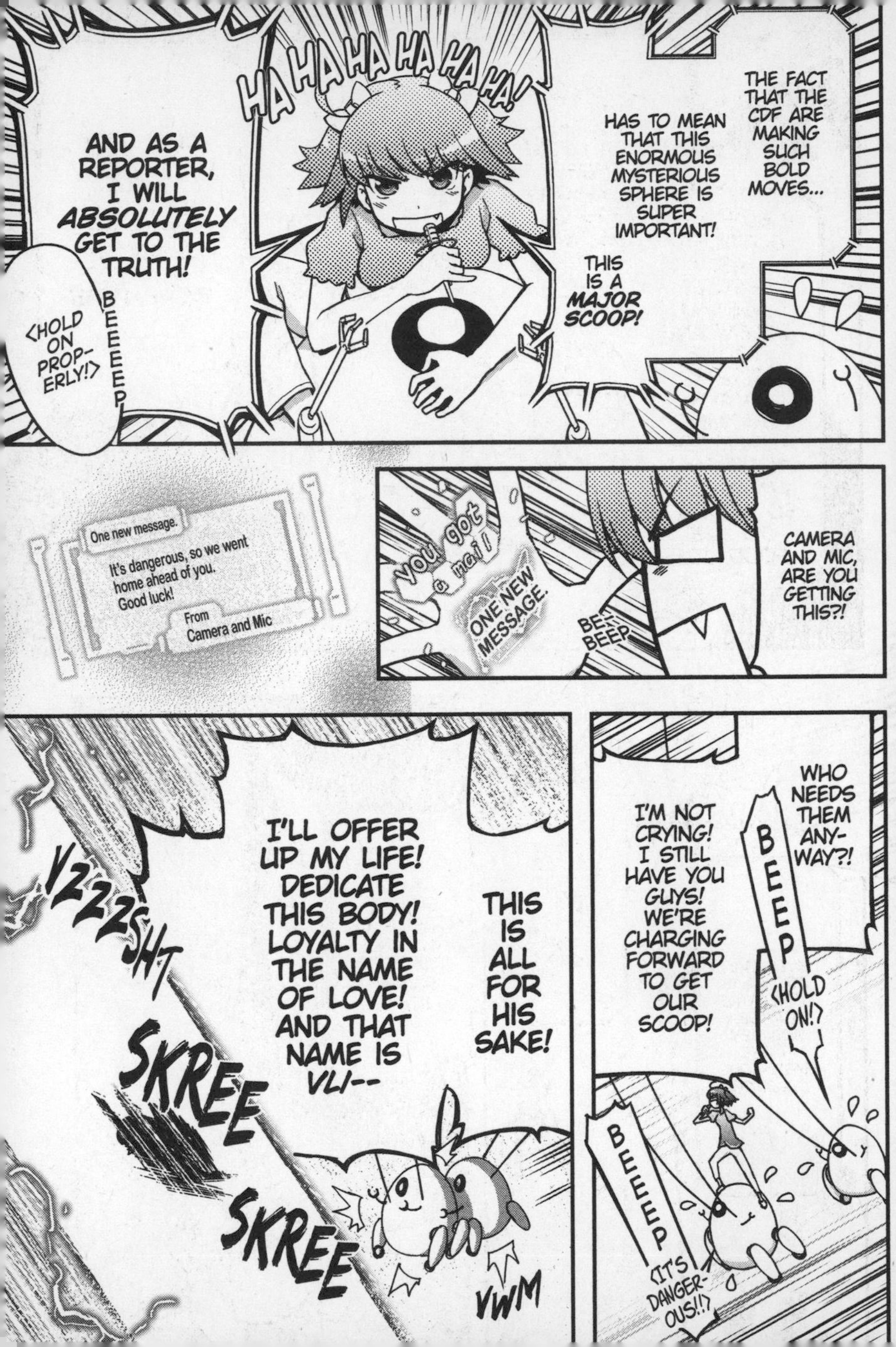
THE FACT THAT THE CDF ARE MAKING SUCH BOLD MOVES...
HAS TO MEAN THAT THIS ENORMOUS MYSTERIOUS SPHERE IS SUPER IMPORTANT!
HA HA HA HA HA HA HA!
THIS IS A MAJOR SCOOP!
AND AS A REPORTER, I WILL ABSOLUTELY GET TO THE TRUTH!
BEEEEEP
<HOLD ON PROPERLY!>
CAMERA AND MIC, ARE YOU GETTING THIS?!
you got a mail
ONE NEW MESSAGE.
BE-BEEP
One new message.
It's dangerous, so we went home ahead of you. Good luck!
From Camera and Mic
WHO NEEDS THEM ANYWAY?!
BEEP
I'M NOT CRYING! I STILL HAVE YOU GUYS! WE'RE CHARGING FORWARD TO GET OUR SCOOP!
<HOLD ON!>
BEEEEP
<IT'S DANGEROUS!!>
THIS IS ALL FOR HIS SAKE!
I'LL OFFER UP MY LIFE! DEDICATE THIS BODY! LOYALTY IN THE NAME OF LOVE! AND THAT NAME IS VLI--
VZZZSHT
SKREE
SKREE
VWM

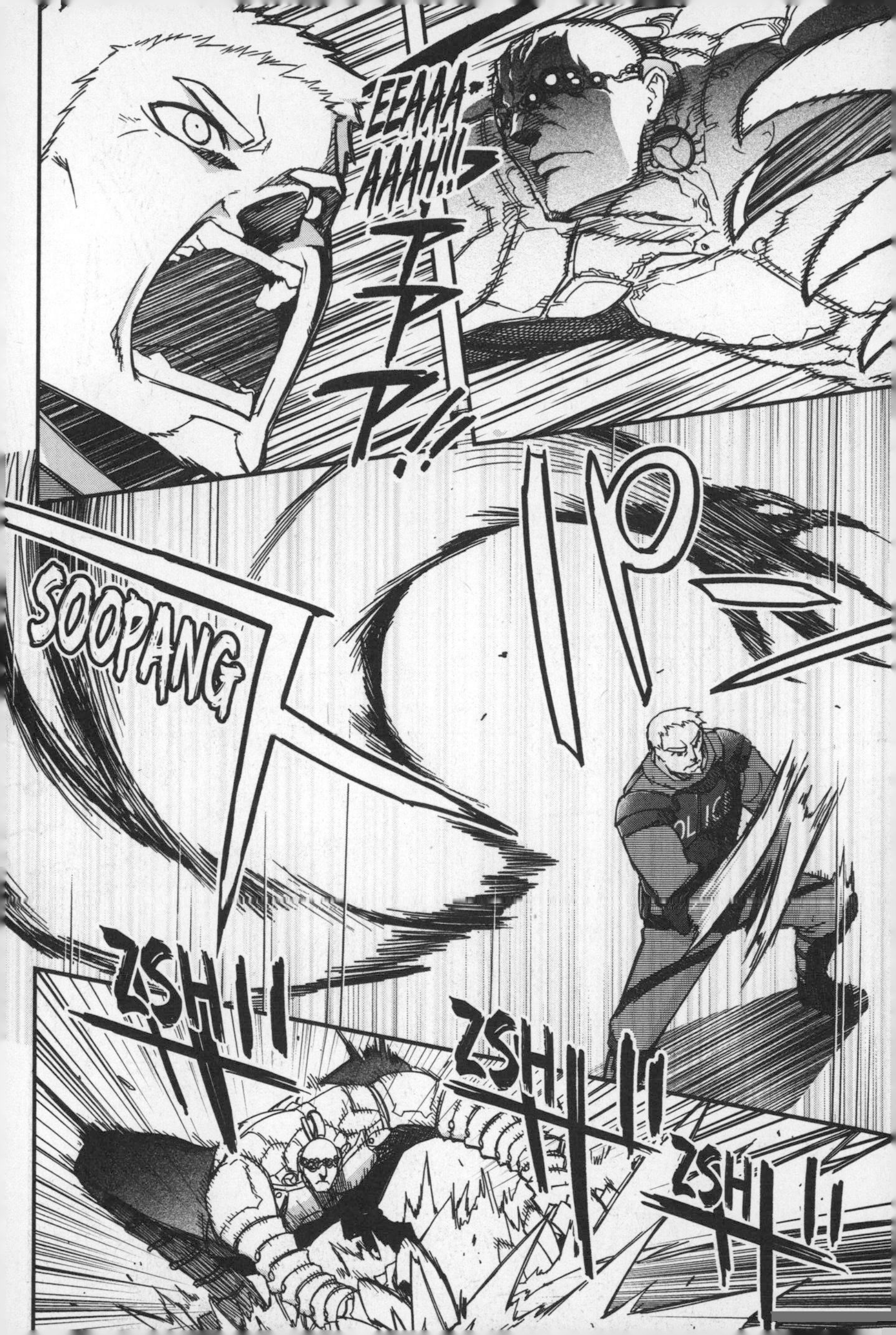
EEAAAAAAH!!
PPP!!
SOOPANG
ZSH!!
ZSH!!
ZSH!!

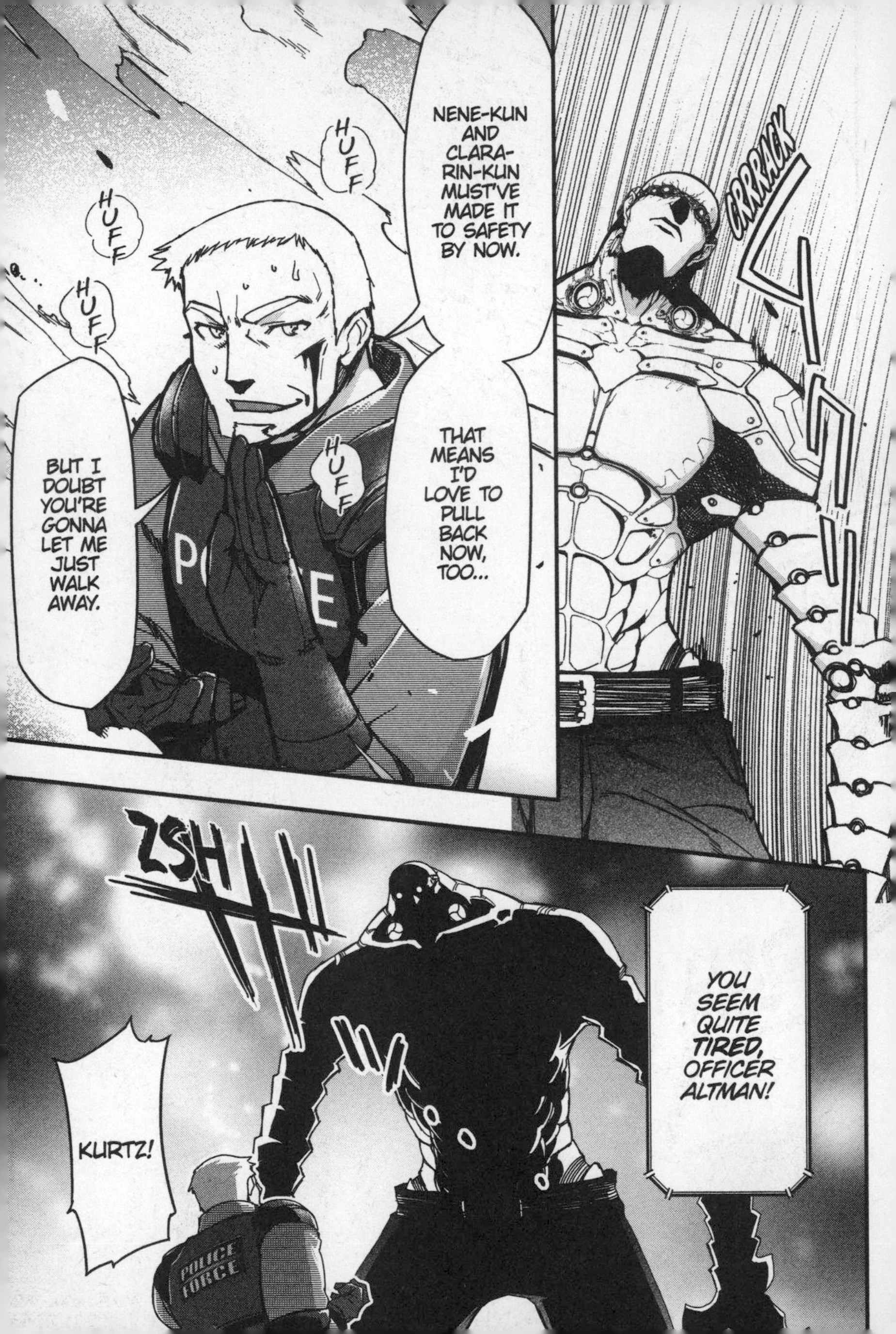
CRRRACK
NENE-KUN AND CLARA-RIN-KUN MUST'VE MADE IT TO SAFETY BY NOW.
HUFF
HUFF
HUFF
THAT MEANS I'D LOVE TO PULL BACK NOW, TOO...
HUFF
BUT I DOUBT YOU'RE GONNA LET ME JUST WALK AWAY.
YOU SEEM QUITE TIRED, OFFICER ALTMAN!
ZSH
KURTZ!
POLICE FORCE

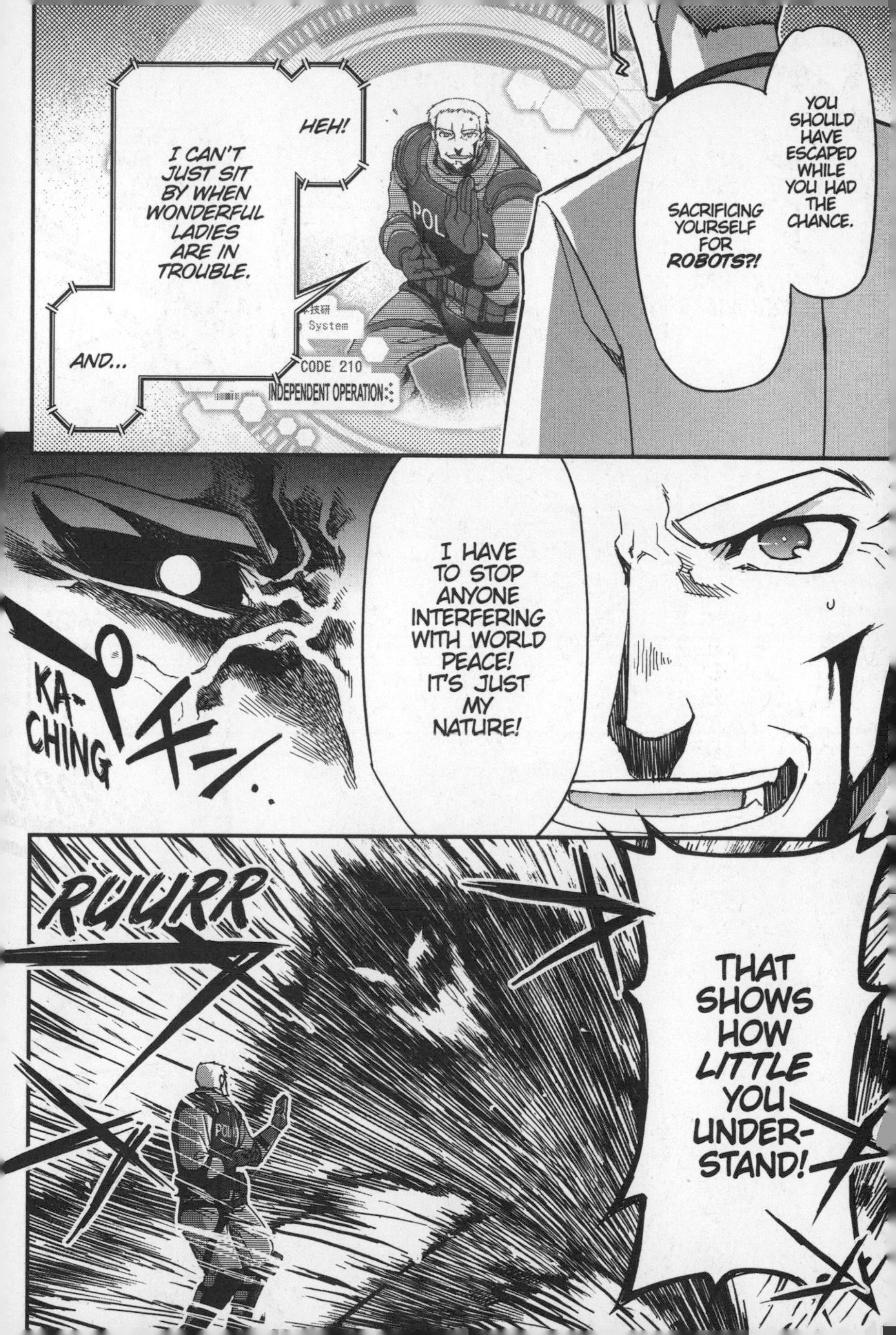
YOU SHOULD HAVE ESCAPED WHILE YOU HAD THE CHANCE.
SACRIFICING YOURSELF FOR *ROBOTS?!*
HEH!
I CAN'T JUST SIT BY WHEN WONDERFUL LADIES ARE IN TROUBLE.
AND...
System
CODE 210
INDEPENDENT OPERATION
I HAVE TO STOP ANYONE INTERFERING WITH WORLD PEACE! IT'S JUST MY NATURE!
KA-CHING
THAT SHOWS HOW *LITTLE* YOU UNDER-STAND!
RUURR

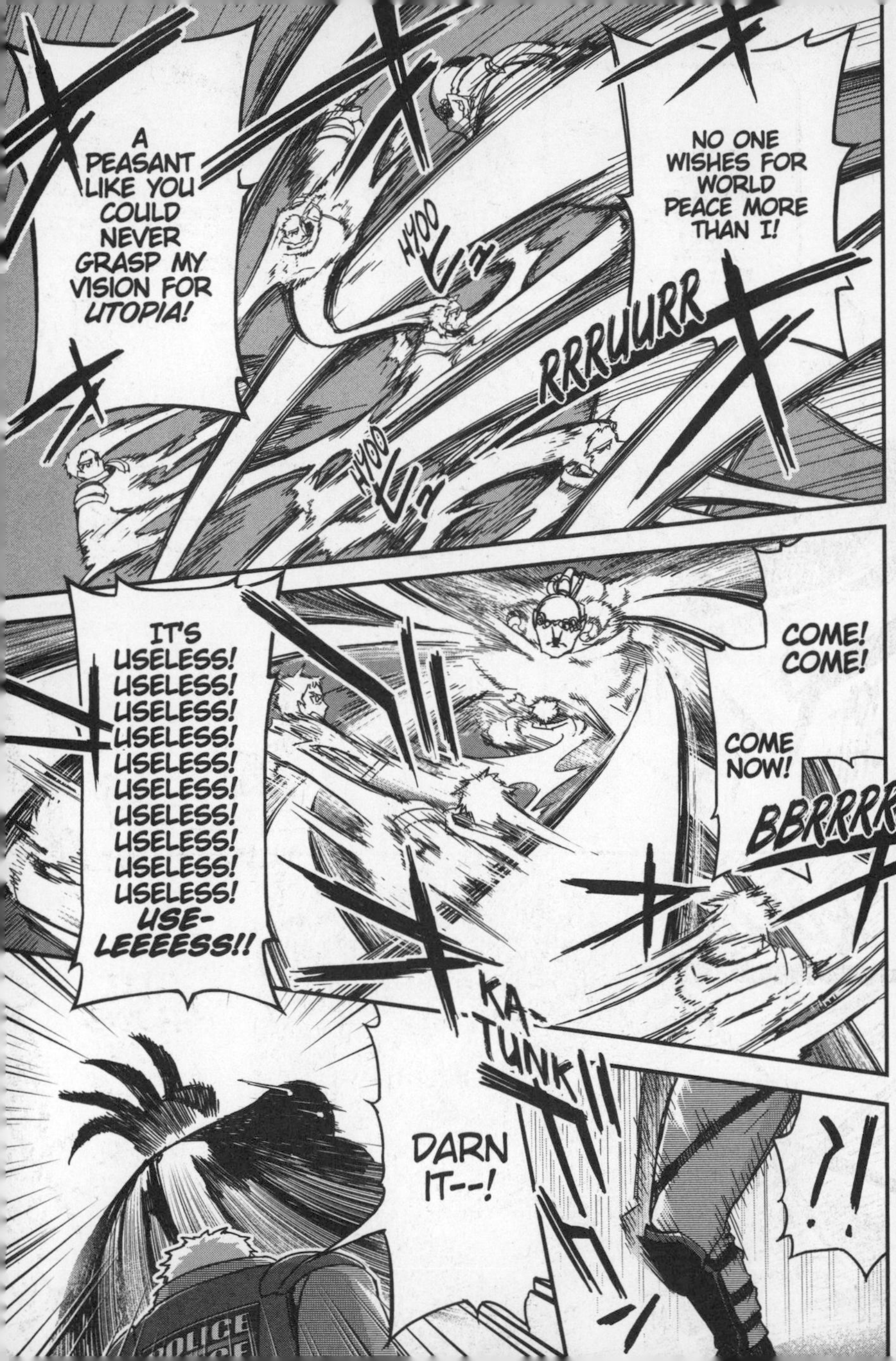
NO ONE WISHES FOR WORLD PEACE MORE THAN I!
A PEASANT LIKE YOU COULD NEVER GRASP MY VISION FOR UTOPIA!
HYOO
RRRUUURR
HYOO
COME! COME!
COME NOW!
BBRRRRR
IT'S USELESS! USELESS! USELESS! USELESS! USELESS! USELESS! USELESS! USELESS! USELESS! USELESS! USE-LEEEEESS!!
KA-TUNK
!?
DARN IT--!

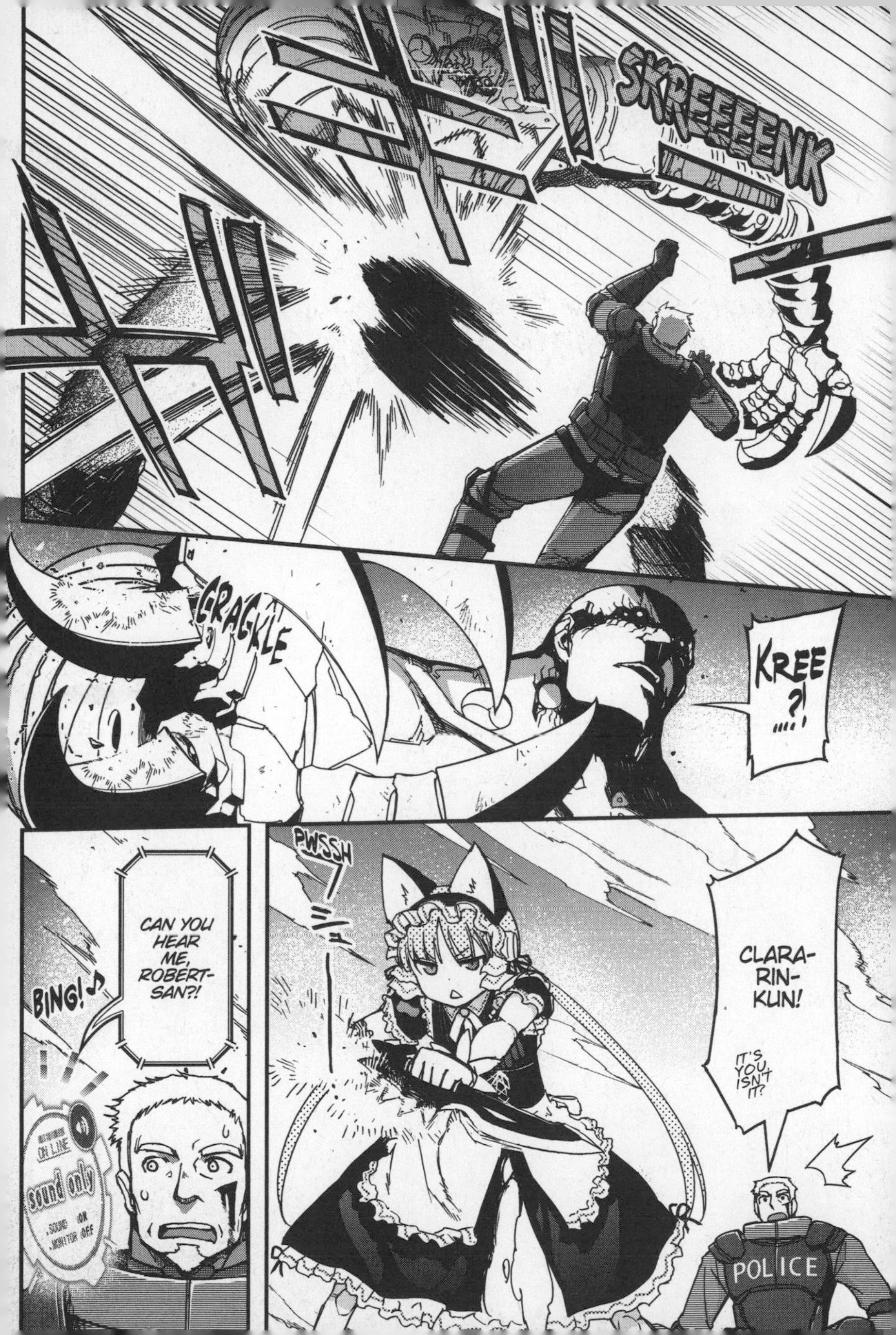
SKREEEEENK
KREE?! ....!
CRACKLE
CLARA-RIN-KUN!
IT'S YOU, ISN'T IT?
PWSSH
POLICE
CAN YOU HEAR ME, ROBERT-SAN?!
BING!♪
ON LINE
sound only
SOUND ON
MONITOR OFF

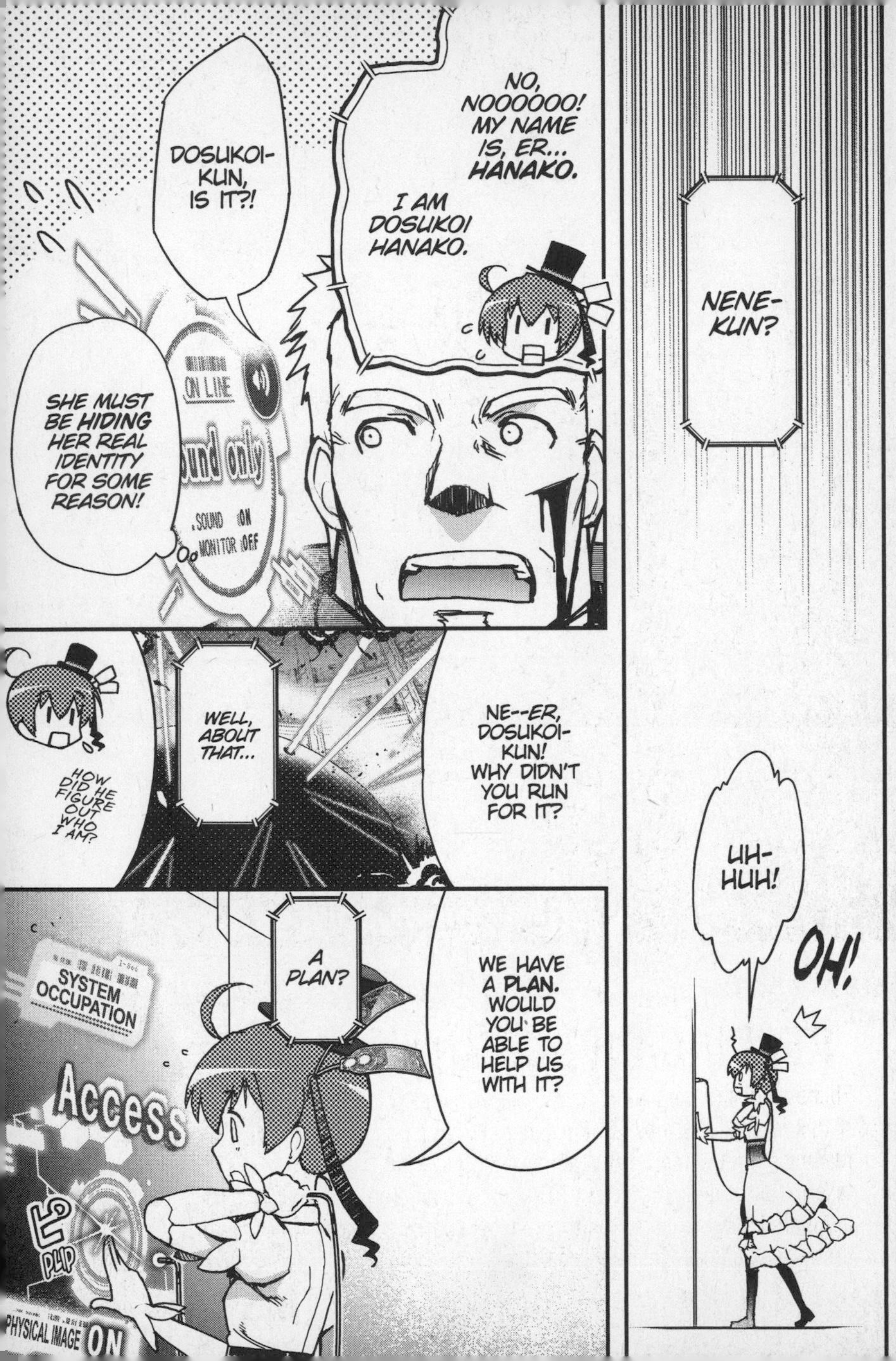
NENE-KUN?
UH-HUH!
OH!
NO, NOOOOOO! MY NAME IS, ER... HANAKO.
I AM DOSUKOI HANAKO.
DOSUKOI-KUN, IS IT?!
ON LINE
.SOUND ON
MONITOR OFF
SHE MUST BE HIDING HER REAL IDENTITY FOR SOME REASON!
NE--ER, DOSUKOI-KUN! WHY DIDN'T YOU RUN FOR IT?
WELL, ABOUT THAT...
HOW DID HE FIGURE OUT WHO I AM?
WE HAVE A PLAN. WOULD YOU BE ABLE TO HELP US WITH IT?
A PLAN?
SYSTEM OCCUPATION
Access
PLIP
PHYSICAL IMAGE ON

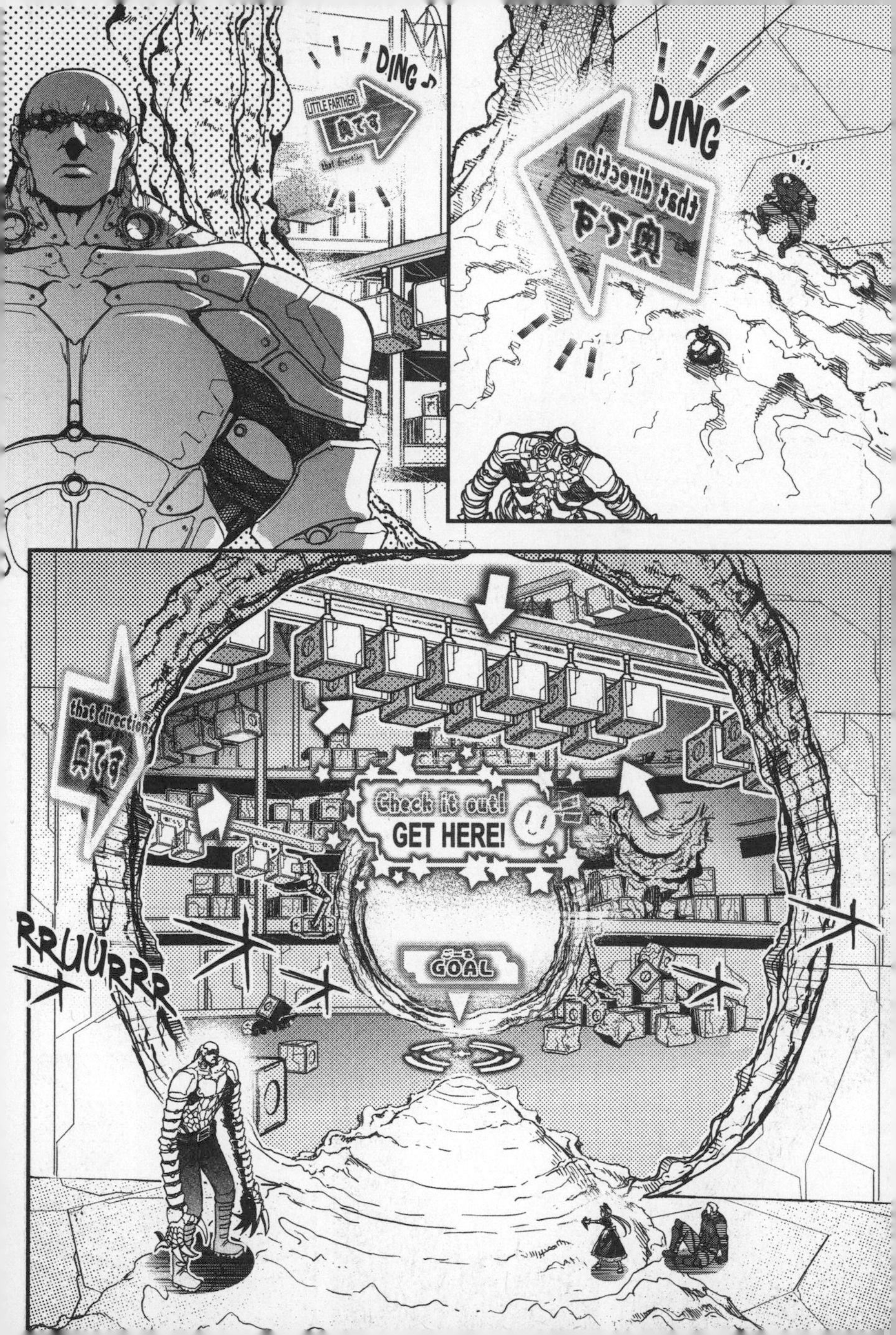
DING
that direction
奥です
DING ♪
LITTLE FARTHER
奥です
that direction
that direction
奥です
Check it out!
GET HERE!
ごーる
GOAL
RRUURRR

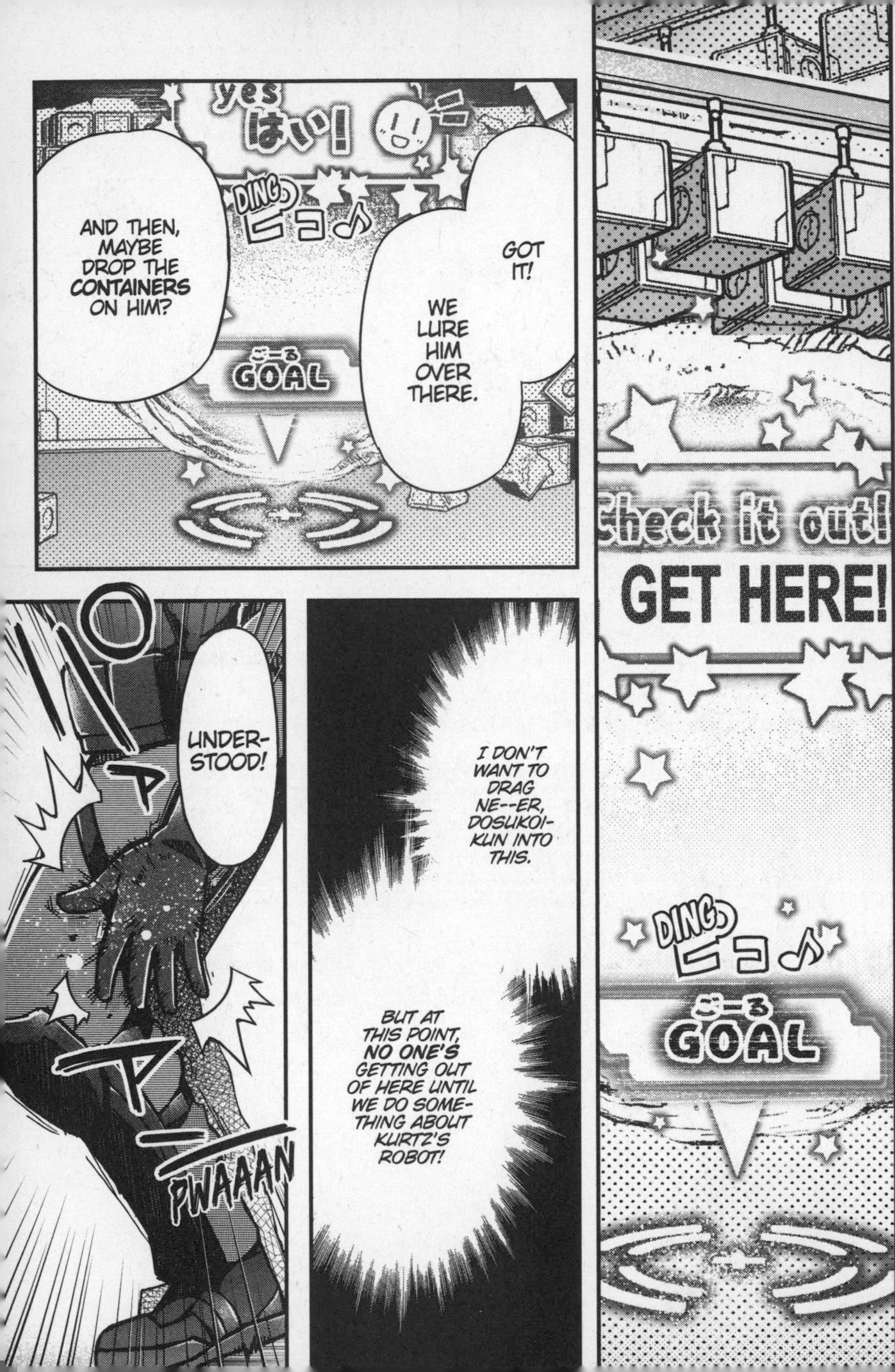
Check it out!
GET HERE!
DING ピコ♪
ごーる GOAL
yes はい!
DING ピコ♪
GOT IT!
WE LURE HIM OVER THERE.
AND THEN, MAYBE DROP THE CONTAINERS ON HIM?
ごーる GOAL
I DON'T WANT TO DRAG NE--ER, DOSUKOI-KUN INTO THIS.
BUT AT THIS POINT, NO ONE'S GETTING OUT OF HERE UNTIL WE DO SOMETHING ABOUT KURTZ'S ROBOT!
UNDER-STOOD!
PWAAAN

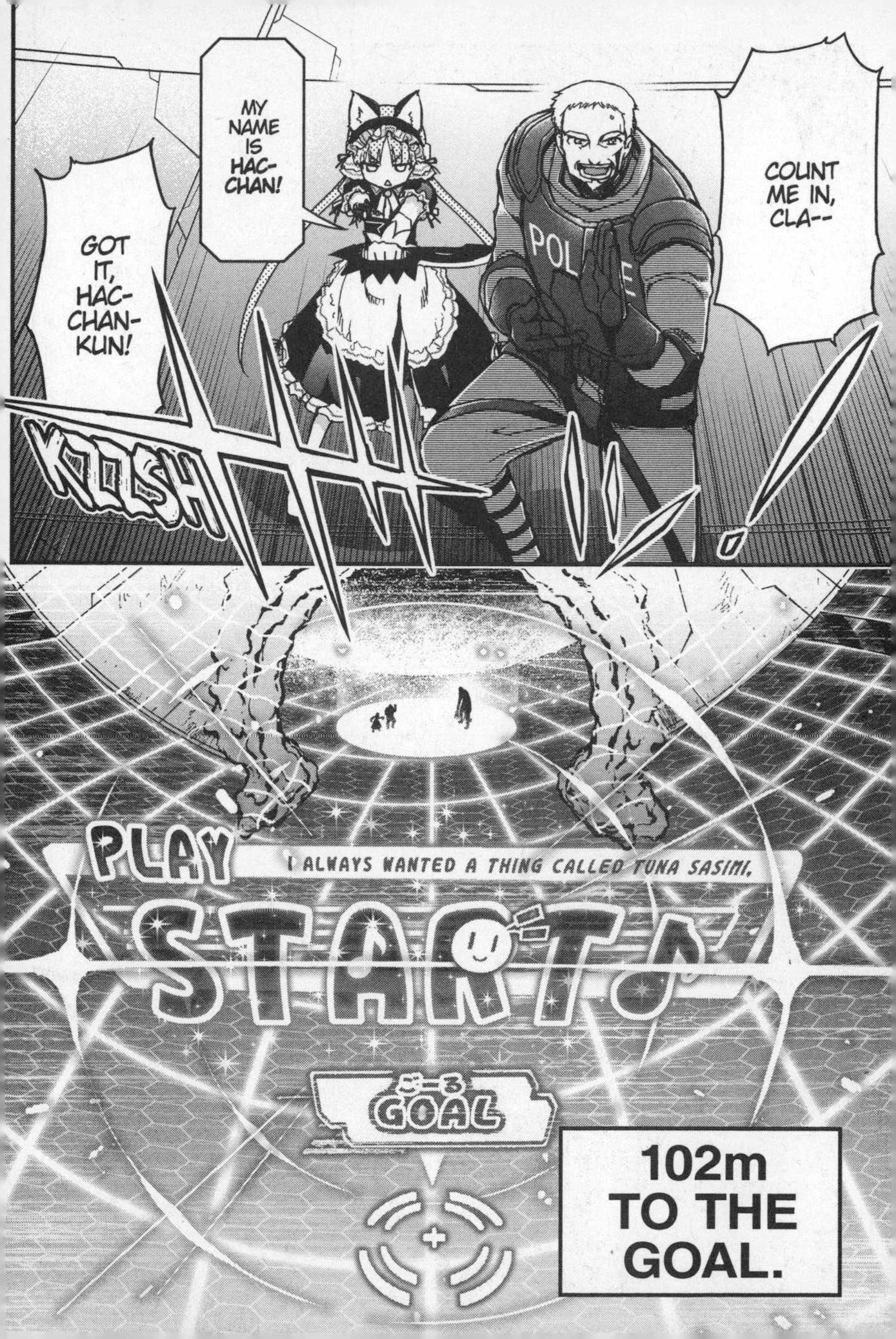
COUNT ME IN, CLA--
MY NAME IS HAC-CHAN!
GOT IT, HAC-CHAN-KUN!
POLICE
PLAY
I ALWAYS WANTED A THING CALLED TUNA SASIMI,
START
GOAL
102m TO THE GOAL.

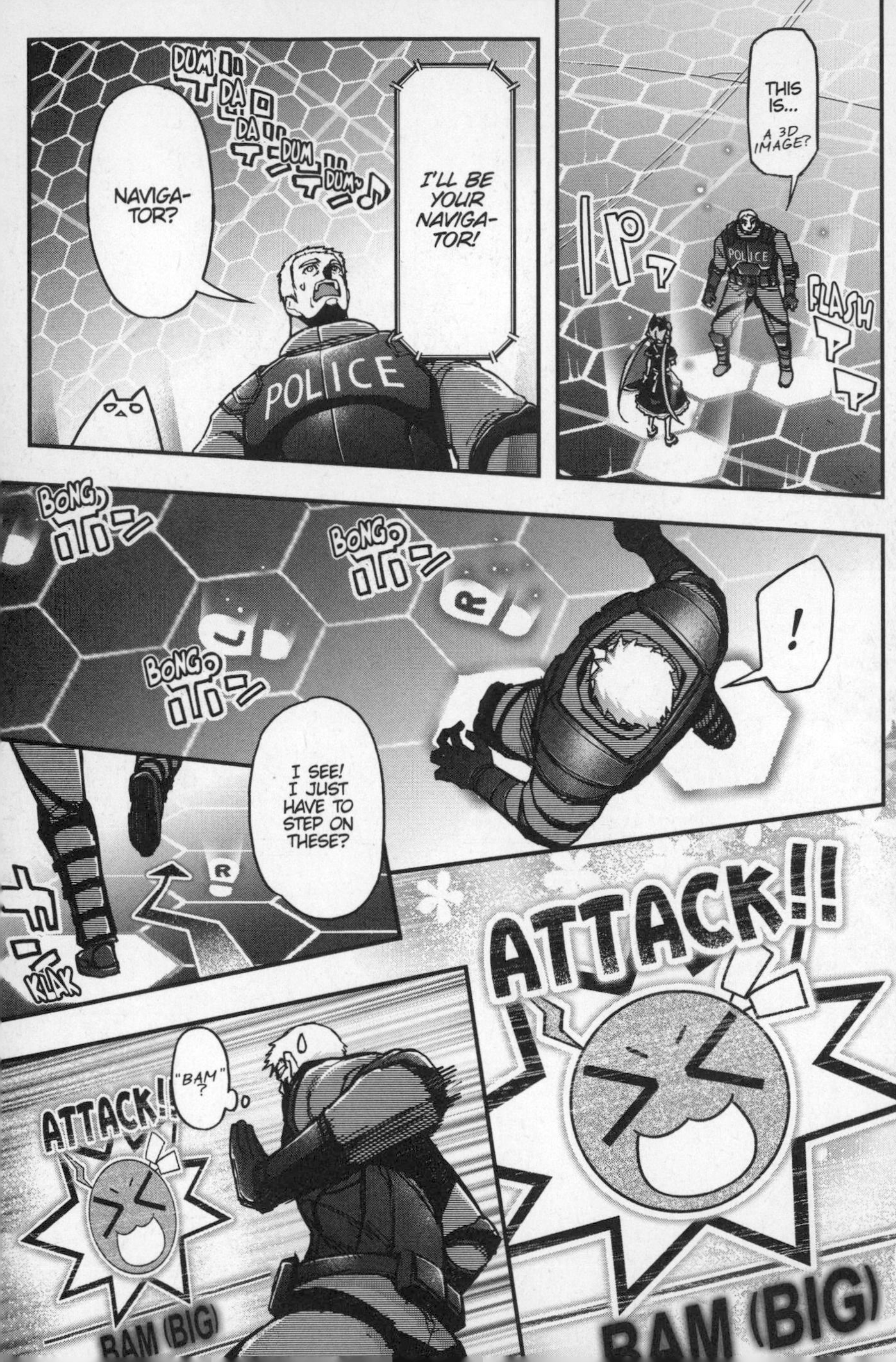
THIS IS... A 3D IMAGE?
FLASH
I'LL BE YOUR NAVIGATOR!
DUM DA DA DUM DUM
NAVIGATOR?
BONG
BONG
BONG
!
I SEE! I JUST HAVE TO STEP ON THESE?
KLAK
ATTACK!!
BAM (BIG)
"BAM"?
ATTACK!!
BAM (BIG)

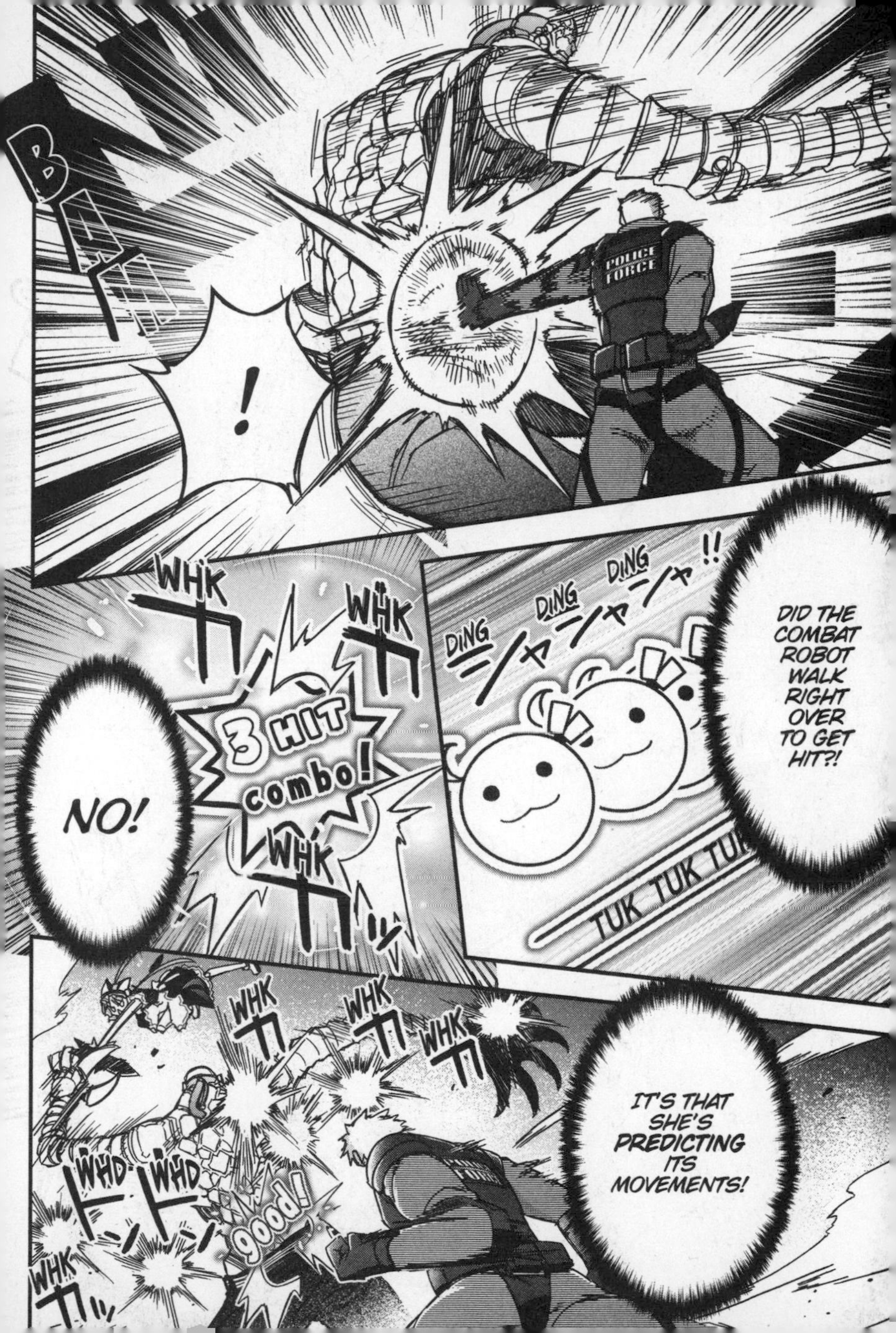
!
DID THE COMBAT ROBOT WALK RIGHT OVER TO GET HIT?!
DING DING DING
TUK TUK TUK
WHK
WHK
3 HIT combo!
WHK
NO!
IT'S THAT SHE'S PREDICTING ITS MOVEMENTS!
WHK WHK WHK
good!
WHD WHD
WHK

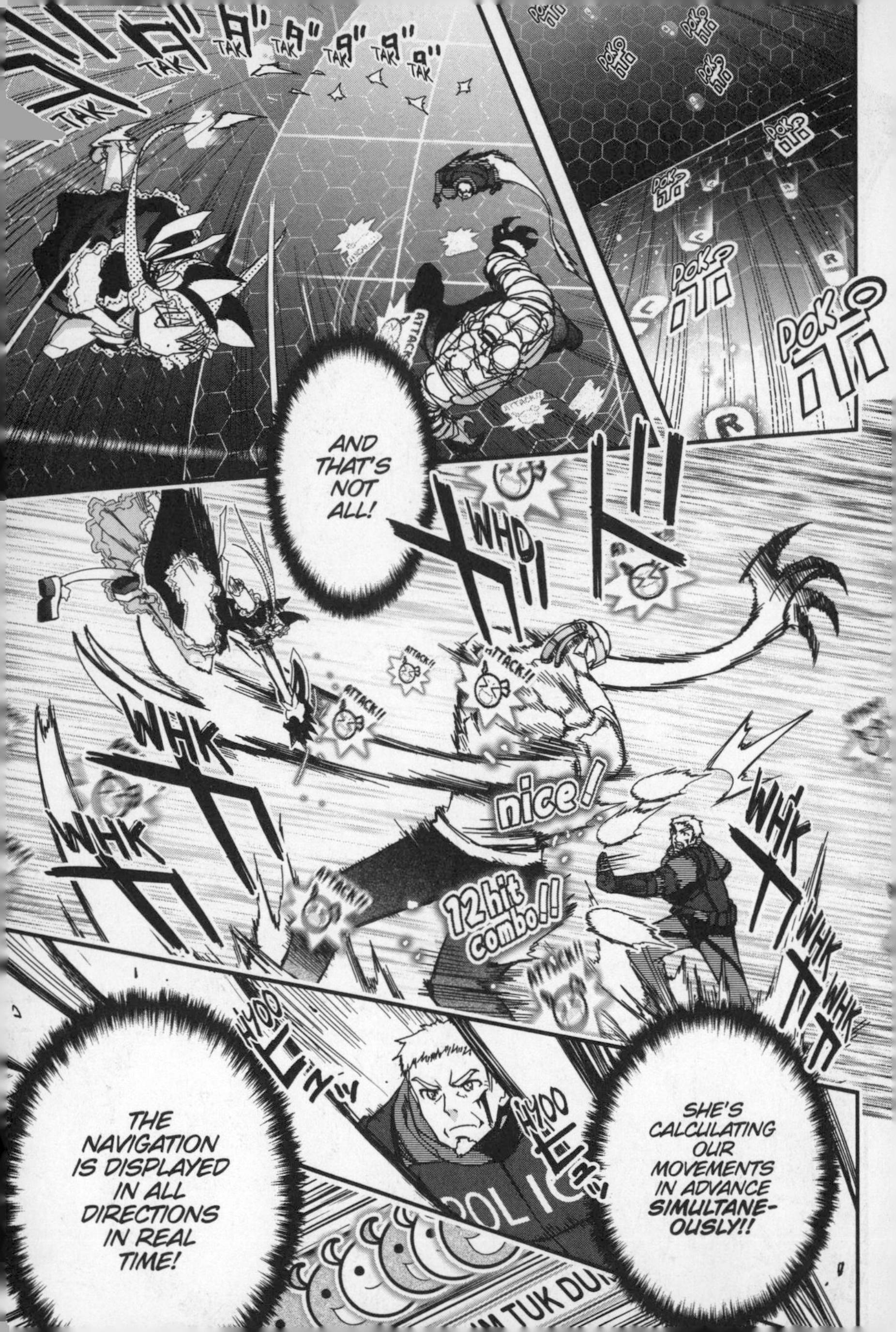
POK
POK
POK
POK
POK
POK
POK
TAK
TAK
TAK
TAK
TAK
TAK
TAK
ATTACK!!
AND THAT'S NOT ALL!
WHD
ATTACK!!
ATTACK!!
ATTACK!!
WHK
WHK
WHK
nice!
12 hit combo!!
WHK
WHK
WHK
ATTACK!!
HYOO
SHE'S CALCULATING OUR MOVEMENTS IN ADVANCE SIMULTANE-OUSLY!!
HYOO
THE NAVIGATION IS DISPLAYED IN ALL DIRECTIONS IN REAL TIME!
POLIC
IM TUK DU

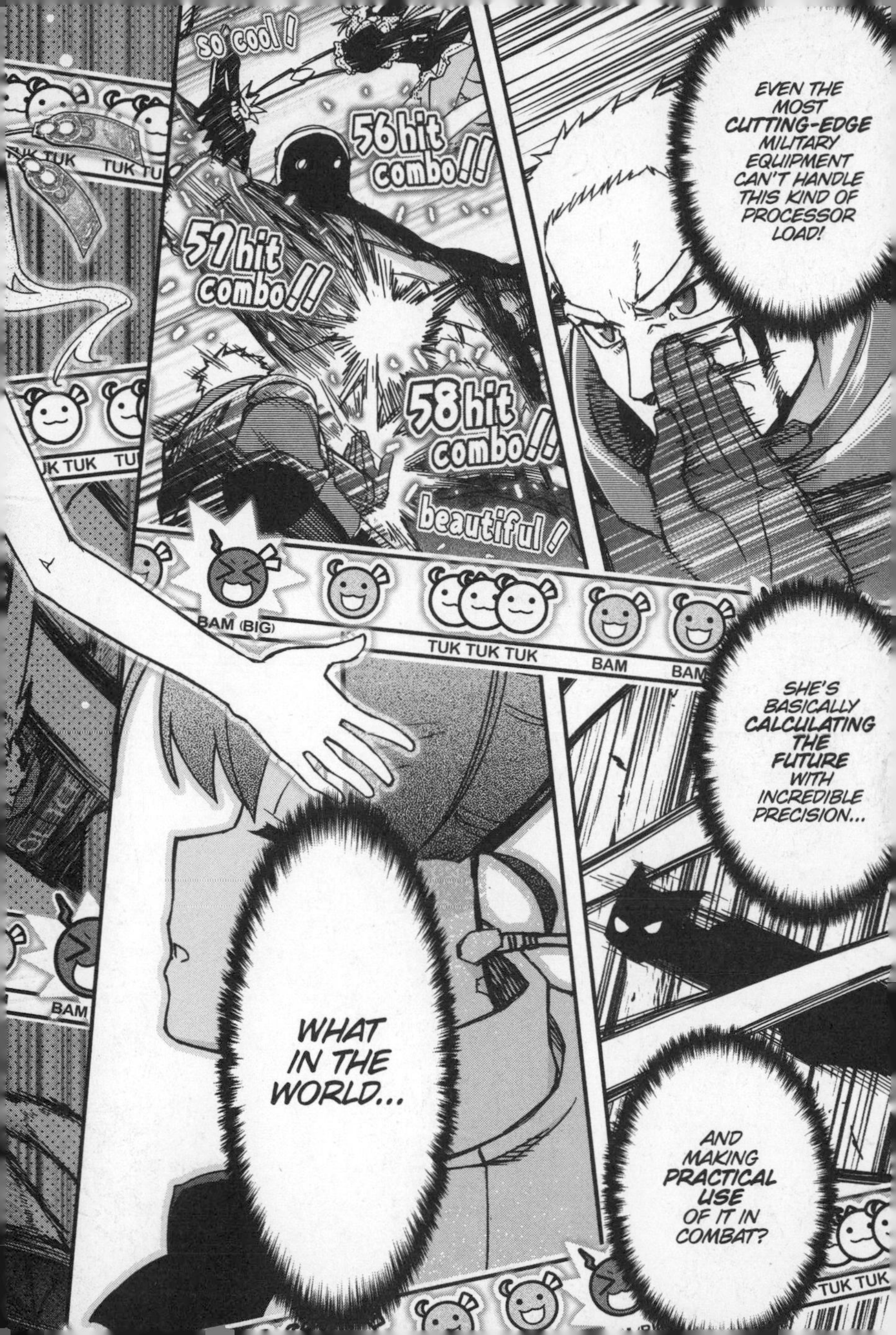
EVEN THE MOST CUTTING-EDGE MILITARY EQUIPMENT CAN'T HANDLE THIS KIND OF PROCESSOR LOAD!
so cool!
56 hit combo!!
57 hit combo!!
58 hit combo!!
beautiful!
TUK TUK
TUK TU
UK TUK
TU
SHE'S BASICALLY CALCULATING THE FUTURE WITH INCREDIBLE PRECISION...
AND MAKING PRACTICAL USE OF IT IN COMBAT?
BAM (BIG)
TUK TUK TUK
BAM
BAM
WHAT IN THE WORLD...
BAM
TUK TUK

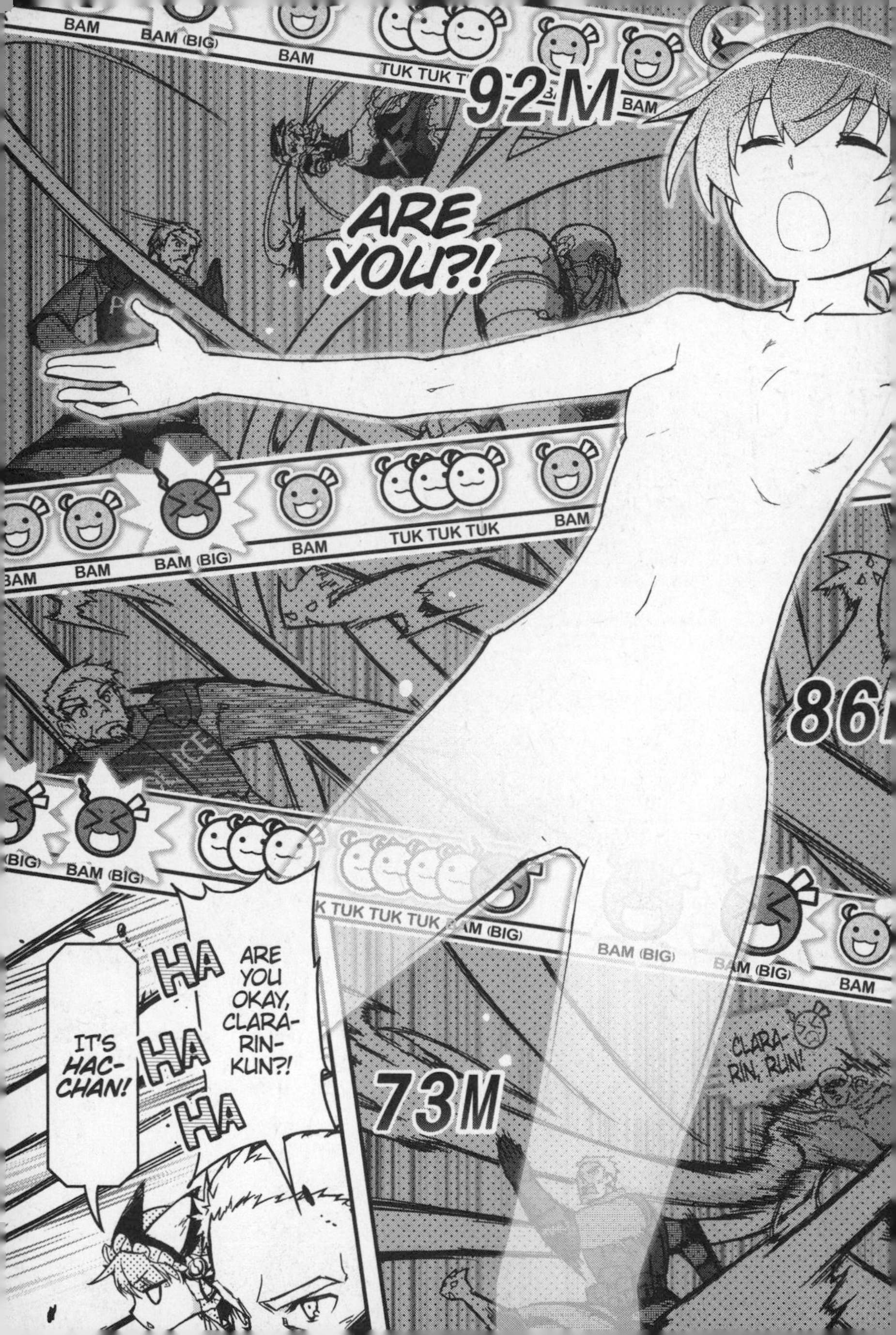
BAM BAM (BIG) BAM TUK TUK T BAM BAM
92M
ARE YOU?!
86M
BAM BAM BAM (BIG) BAM TUK TUK TUK BAM
(BIG) BAM (BIG) TUK TUK TUK BAM (BIG) BAM (BIG) BAM (BIG) BAM
CLARA-RIN, RUN!
73M
ARE YOU OKAY, CLARA-RIN-KUN?!
HA HA HA
IT'S HAC-CHAN!

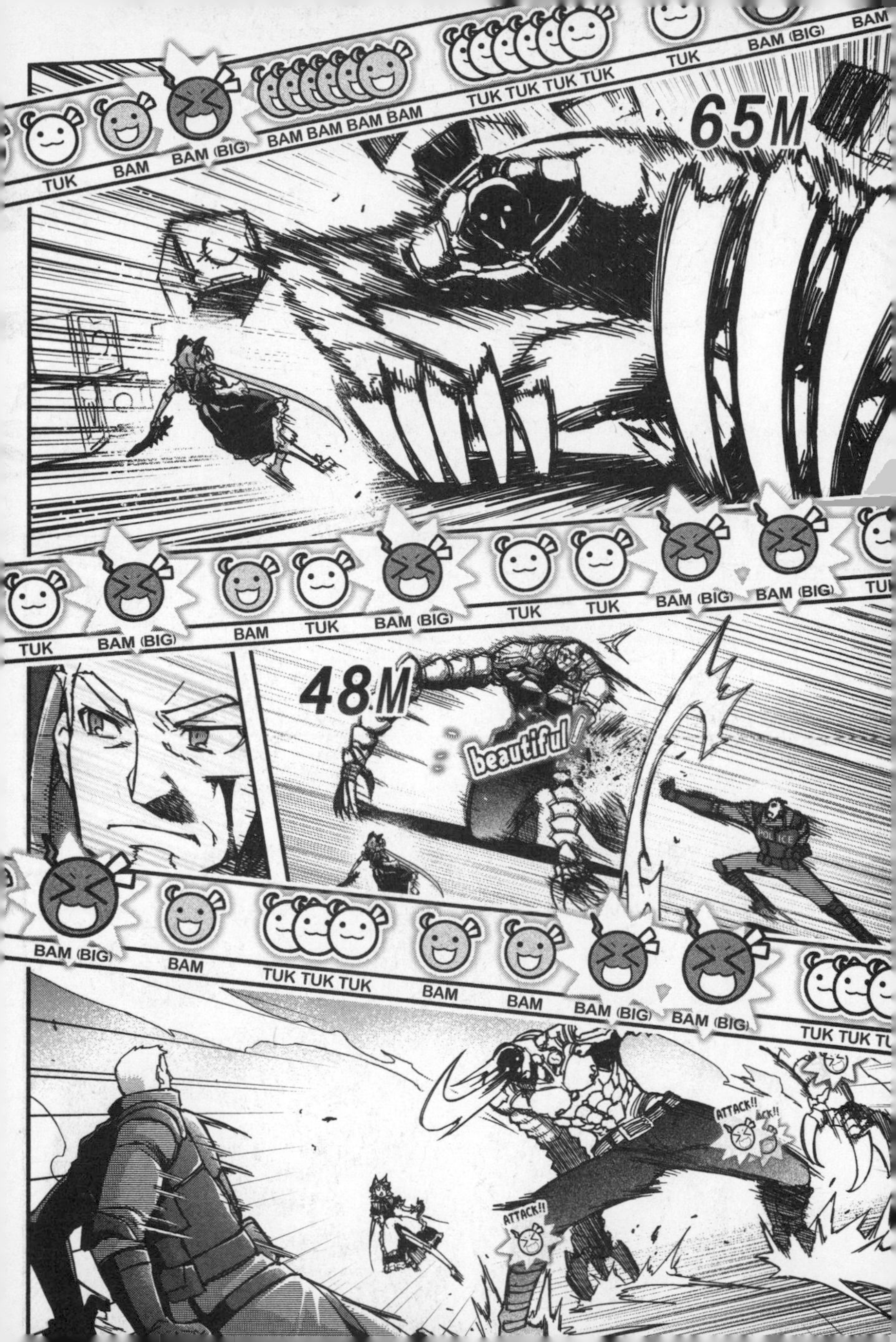
TUK BAM BAM (BIG) BAM BAM BAM BAM TUK TUK TUK TUK TUK BAM (BIG) BAM
65M
TUK BAM (BIG) BAM TUK BAM (BIG) TUK TUK BAM (BIG) BAM (BIG) TU
48M
beautiful!
BAM (BIG) BAM TUK TUK TUK BAM BAM BAM (BIG) BAM (BIG) TUK TUK TU
ATTACK!!
ACK!!
ATTACK!!

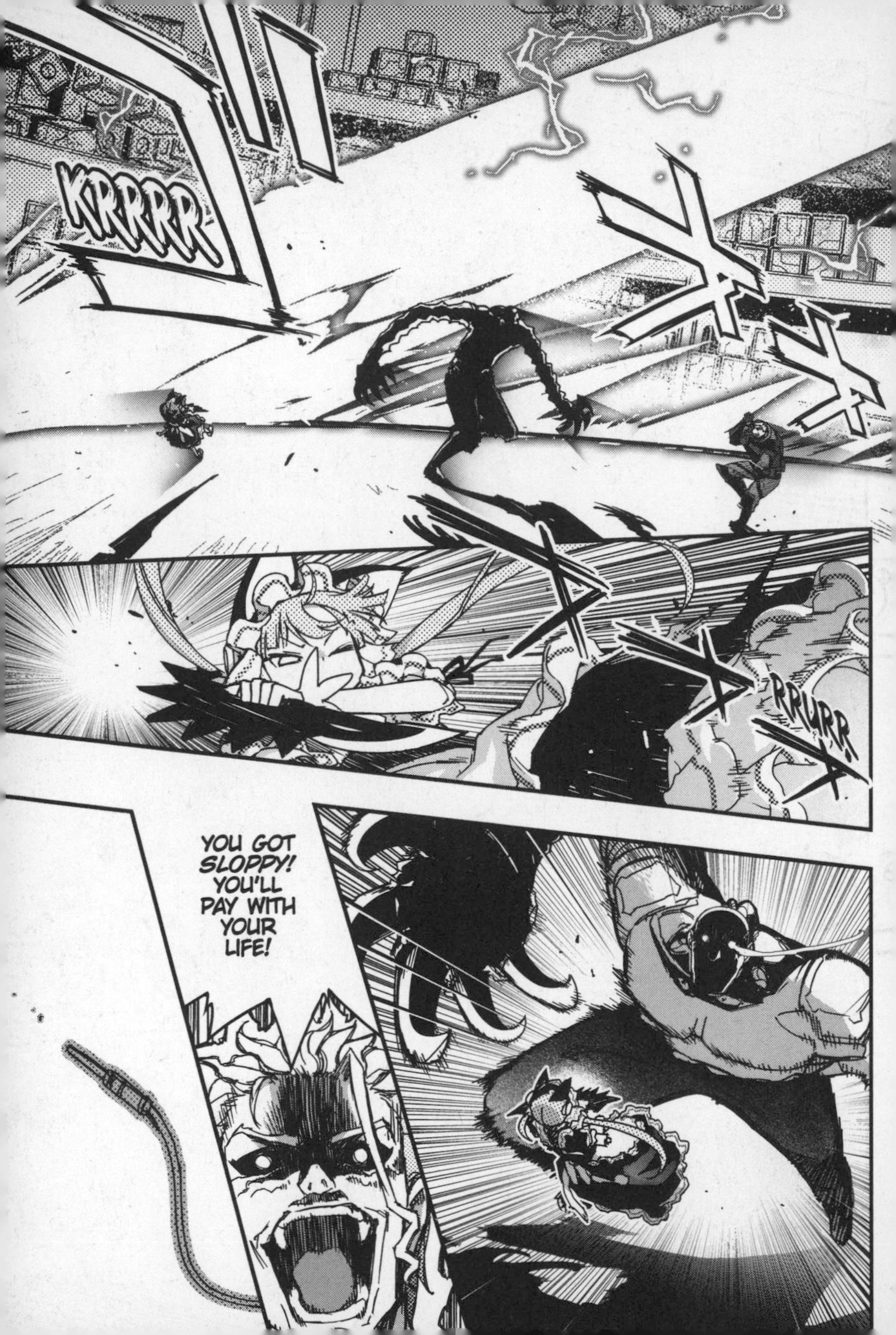
KRRRR
RRURR
YOU GOT SLOPPY! YOU'LL PAY WITH YOUR LIFE!

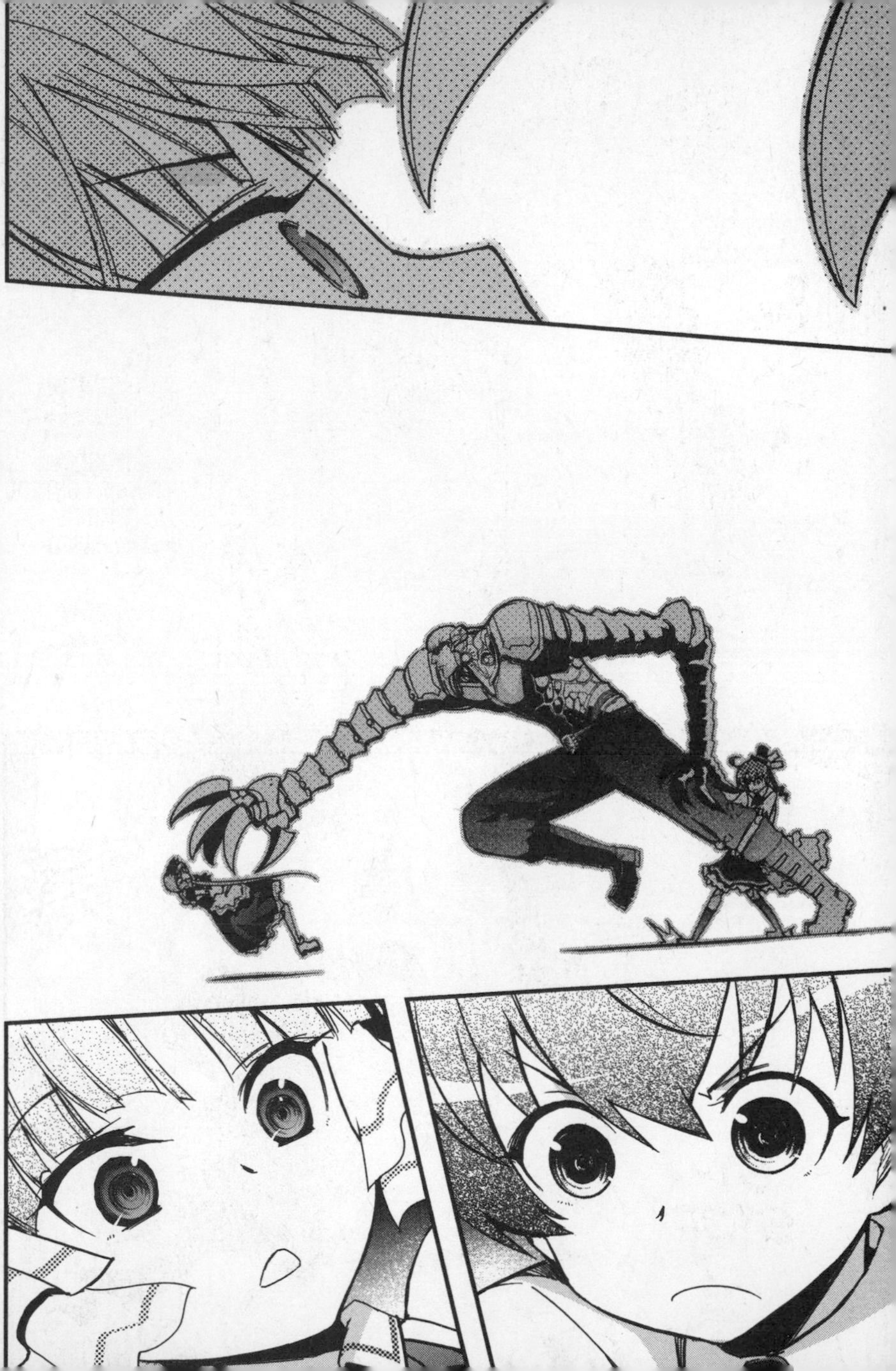

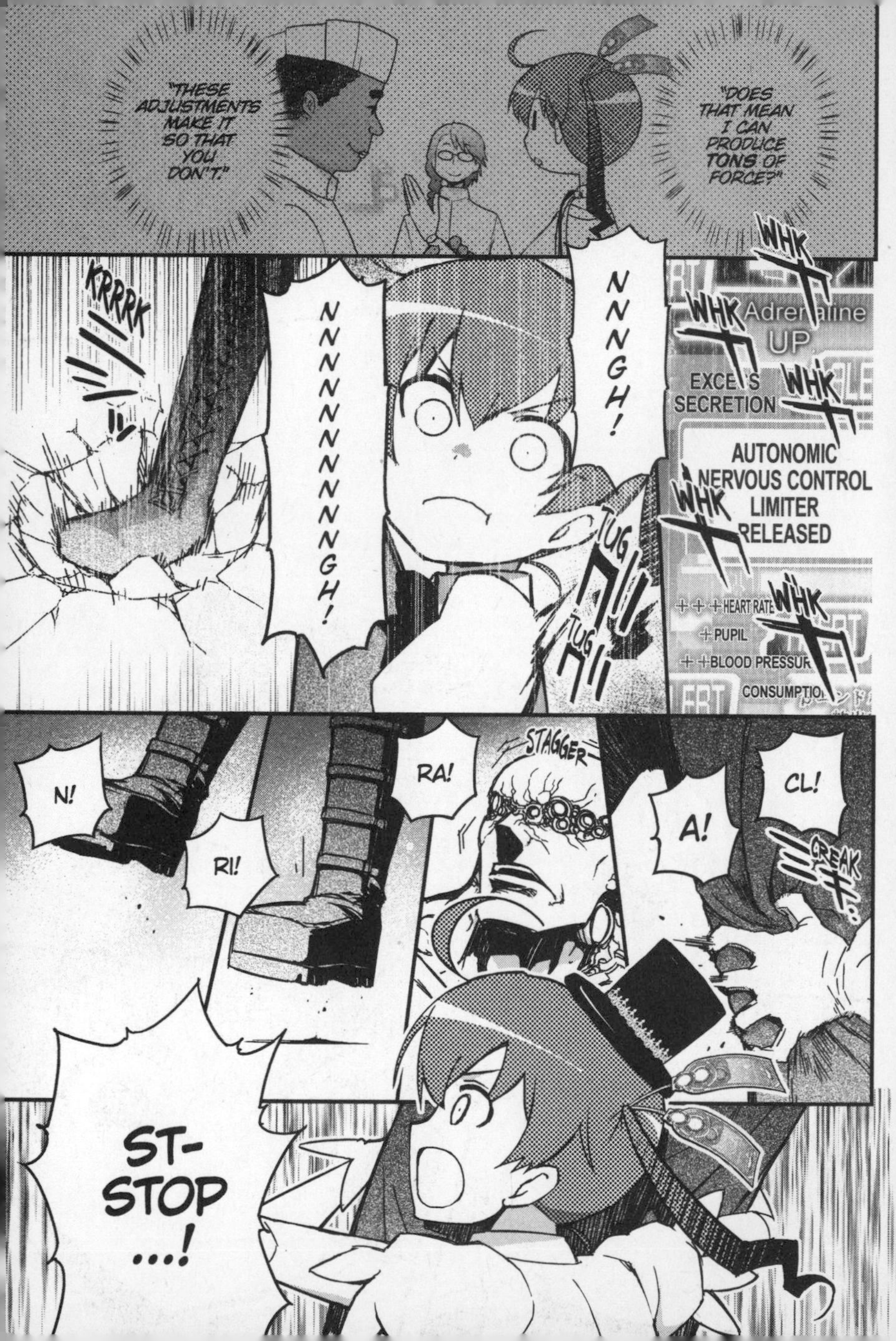
"DOES THAT MEAN I CAN PRODUCE TONS OF FORCE?"
"THESE ADJUSTMENTS MAKE IT SO THAT YOU DON'T."
WHK
WHK
Adrer aline UP
EXCE S SECRETION
WHK
AUTONOMIC NERVOUS CONTROL LIMITER RELEASED
WHK
WHK
+++HEART RATE
+PUPIL
++BLOOD PRESSUR
CONSUMPTIO
TUG
TUG
NNNGH!
NNNNNNNNNNNGH!
KRRRK
CL!
CREAK
A!
STAGGER
RA!
RI!
N!
ST-STOP...!

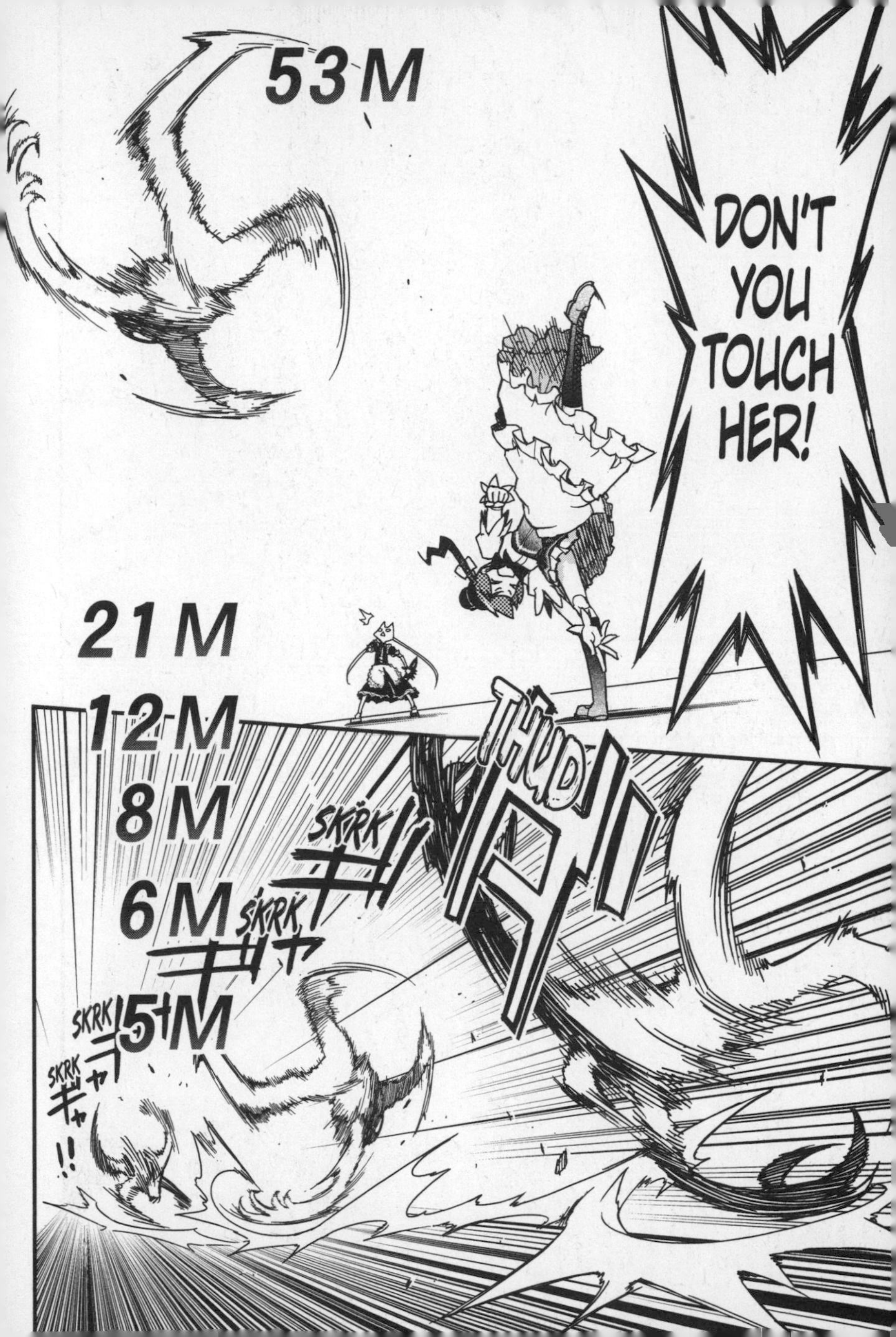
DON'T YOU TOUCH HER!
53 M
21 M
12 M
8 M
6 M
5 M
THUD
SKRK
SKRK
SKRK
SKRK

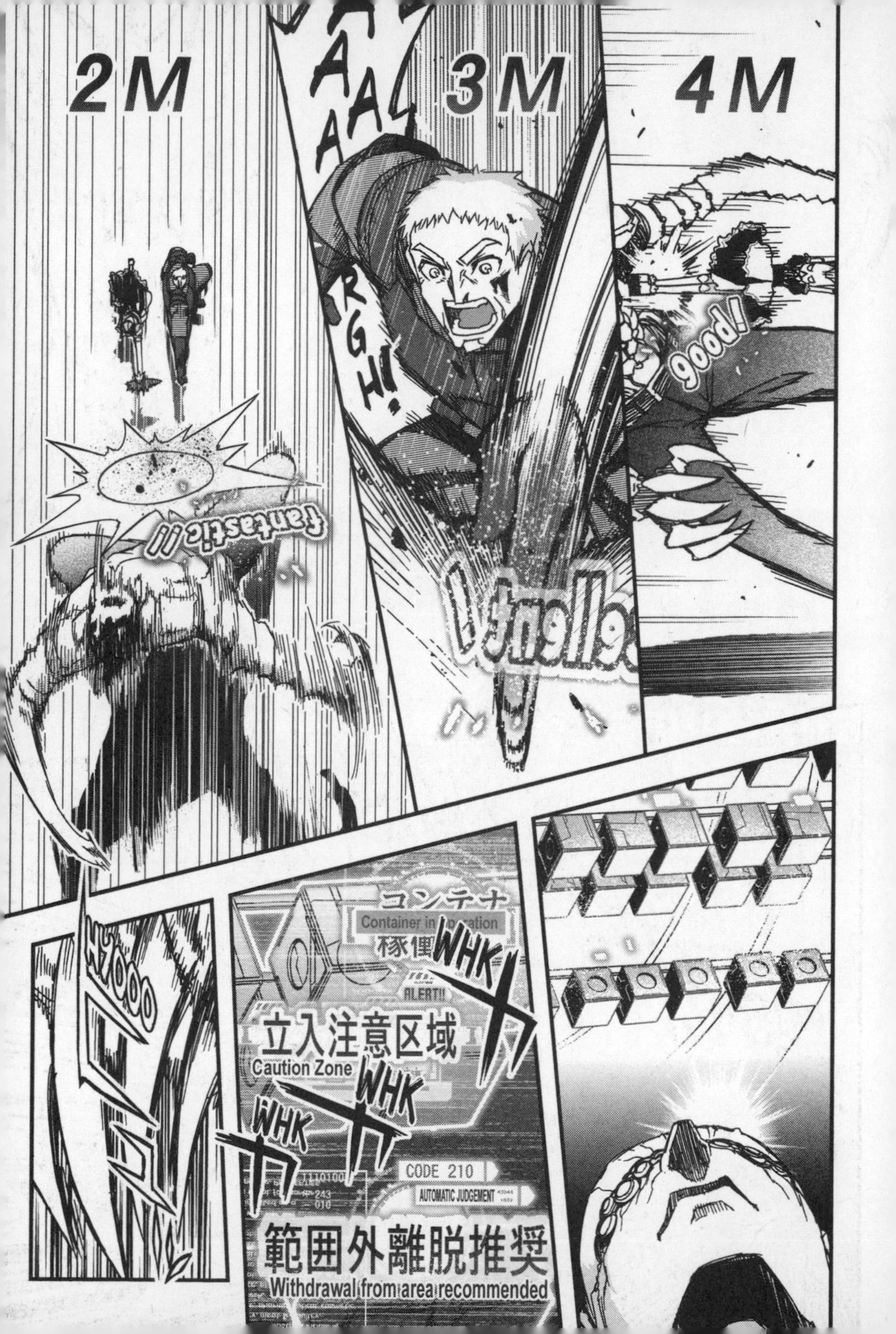
4M
good!
3M
AAAARGH!
ellent!
2M
fantastic!!
コンテナ
Container in operation
稼働
WHK
ALERT!!
立入注意区域
Caution Zone
WHK
WHK
CODE 210
AUTOMATIC JUDGEMENT
範囲外離脱推奨
Withdrawal from area recommended

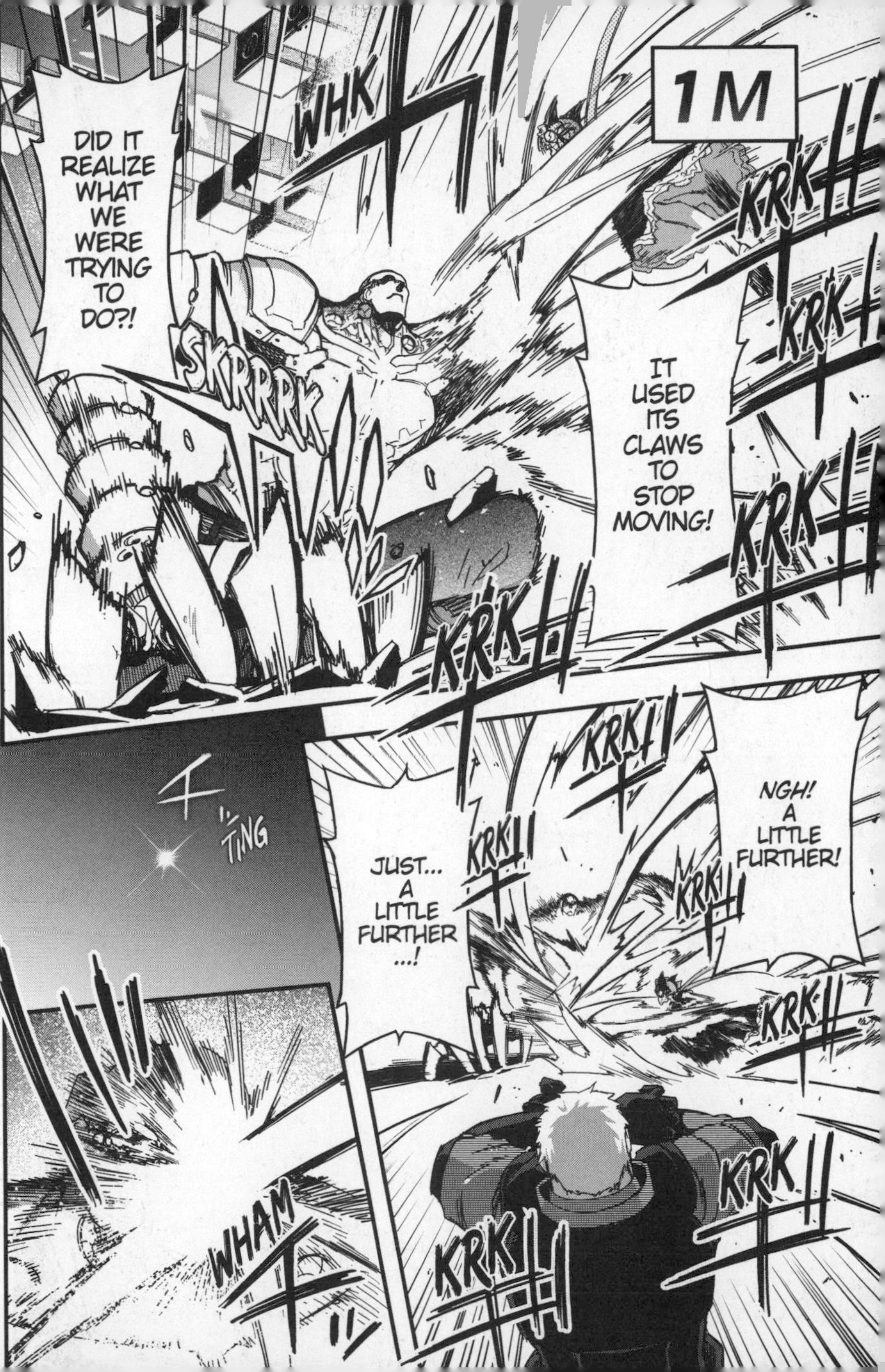
1M
KRK
KRK
IT USED ITS CLAWS TO STOP MOVING!
KRK
DID IT REALIZE WHAT WE WERE TRYING TO DO?!
WHK
SKRRRK
KRK
NGH! A LITTLE FURTHER!
KRK
KRK
JUST... A LITTLE FURTHER ...!
KRK
KRK
KRK
KRK
TING
WHAM

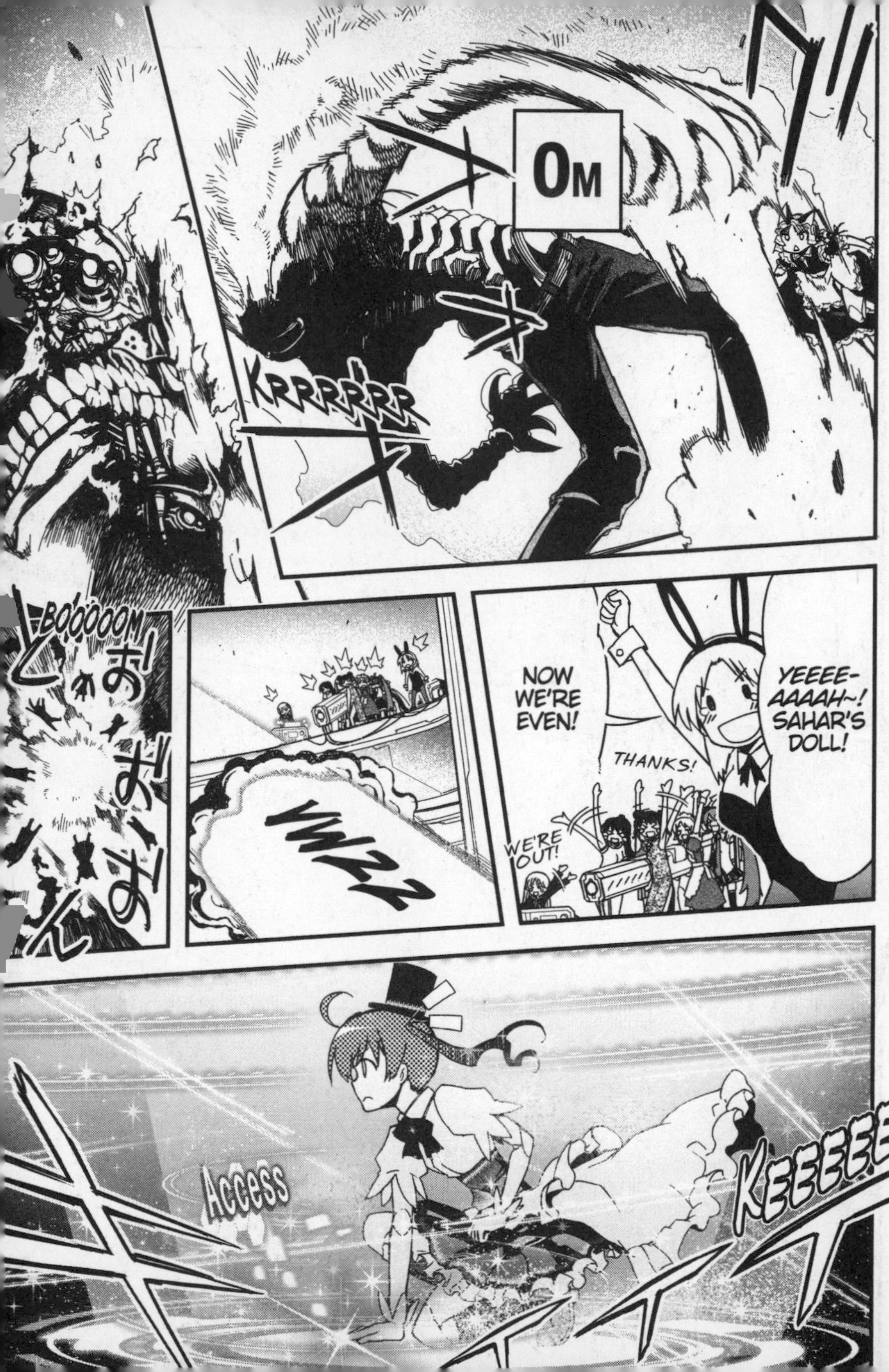
0M
KRRRRRRR
YEEEE-AAAAH~! SAHAR'S DOLL!
NOW WE'RE EVEN!
THANKS!
WE'RE OUT!
VWZZZ
BOOOOOM
どぉおおおん
KEEEEE
Access

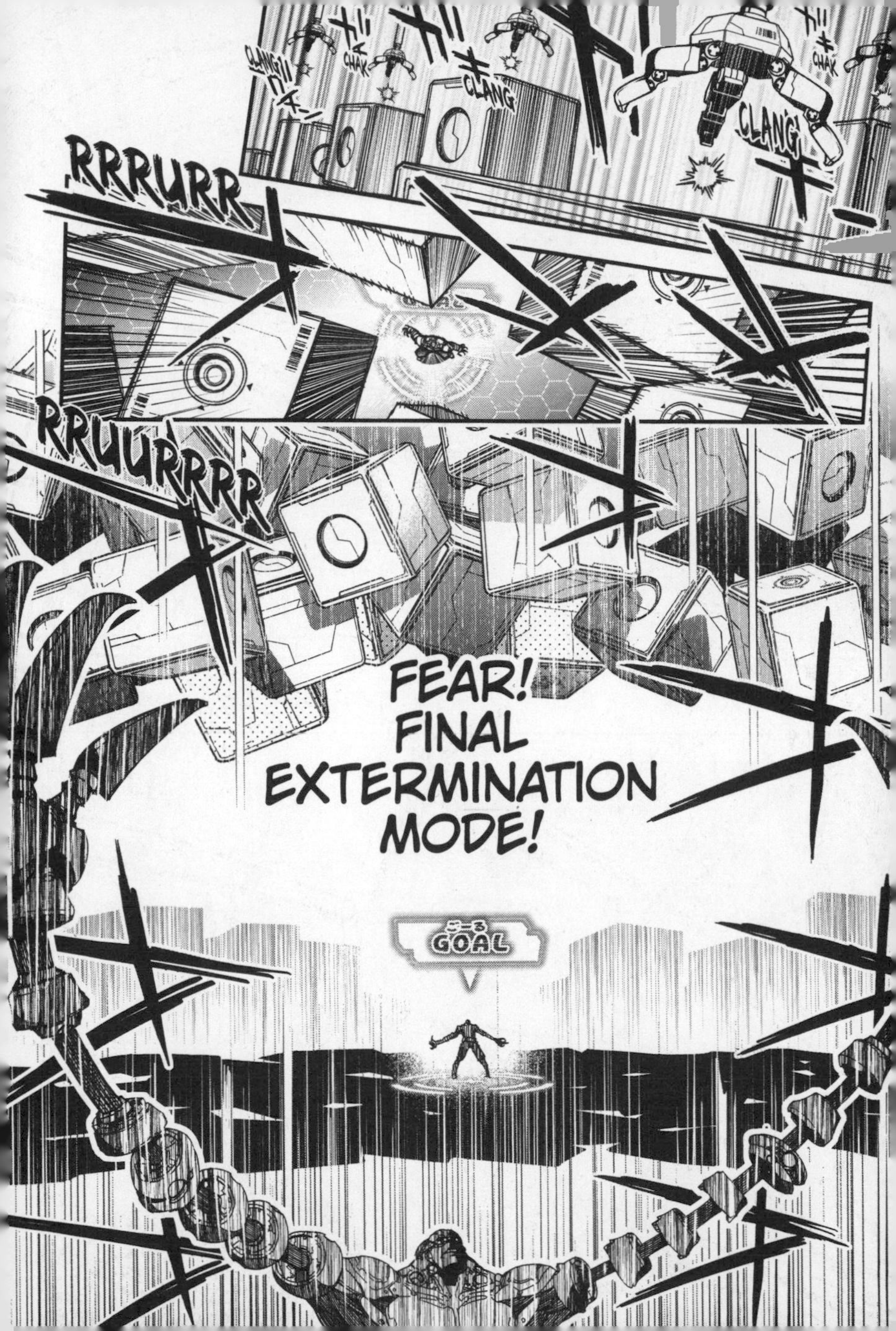
CHAK
CLANG!
CLANG
CHAK
CLANG!!
RRRURR
RRUURRRRR
FEAR! FINAL EXTERMINATION MODE!
GOAL

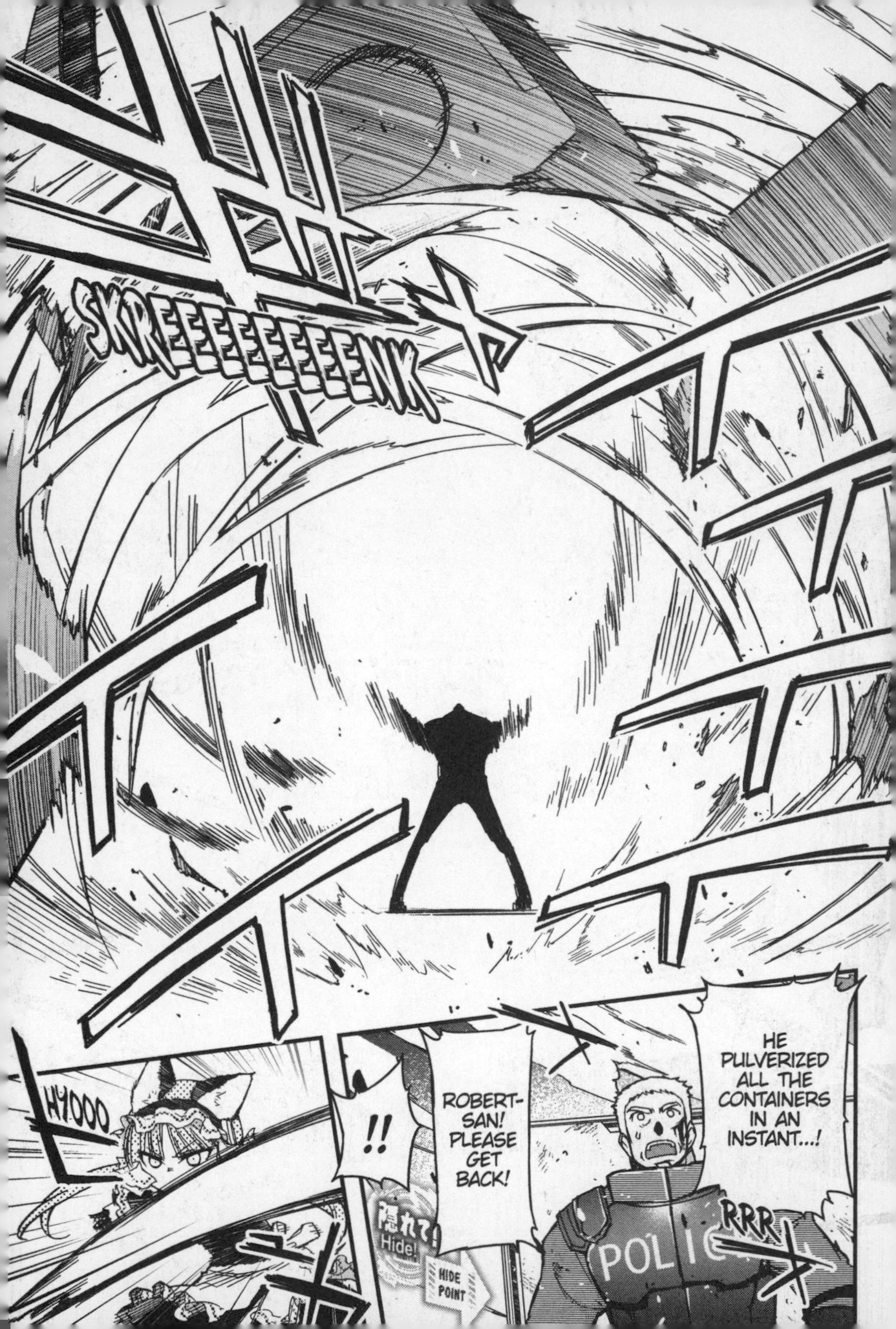
SKREEEEEEEEEENK
HE PULVERIZED ALL THE CONTAINERS IN AN INSTANT...!
RRR
POLIC
ROBERT-SAN! PLEASE GET BACK!
!!
隠れて!
Hide!
HIDE POINT
HYOOO

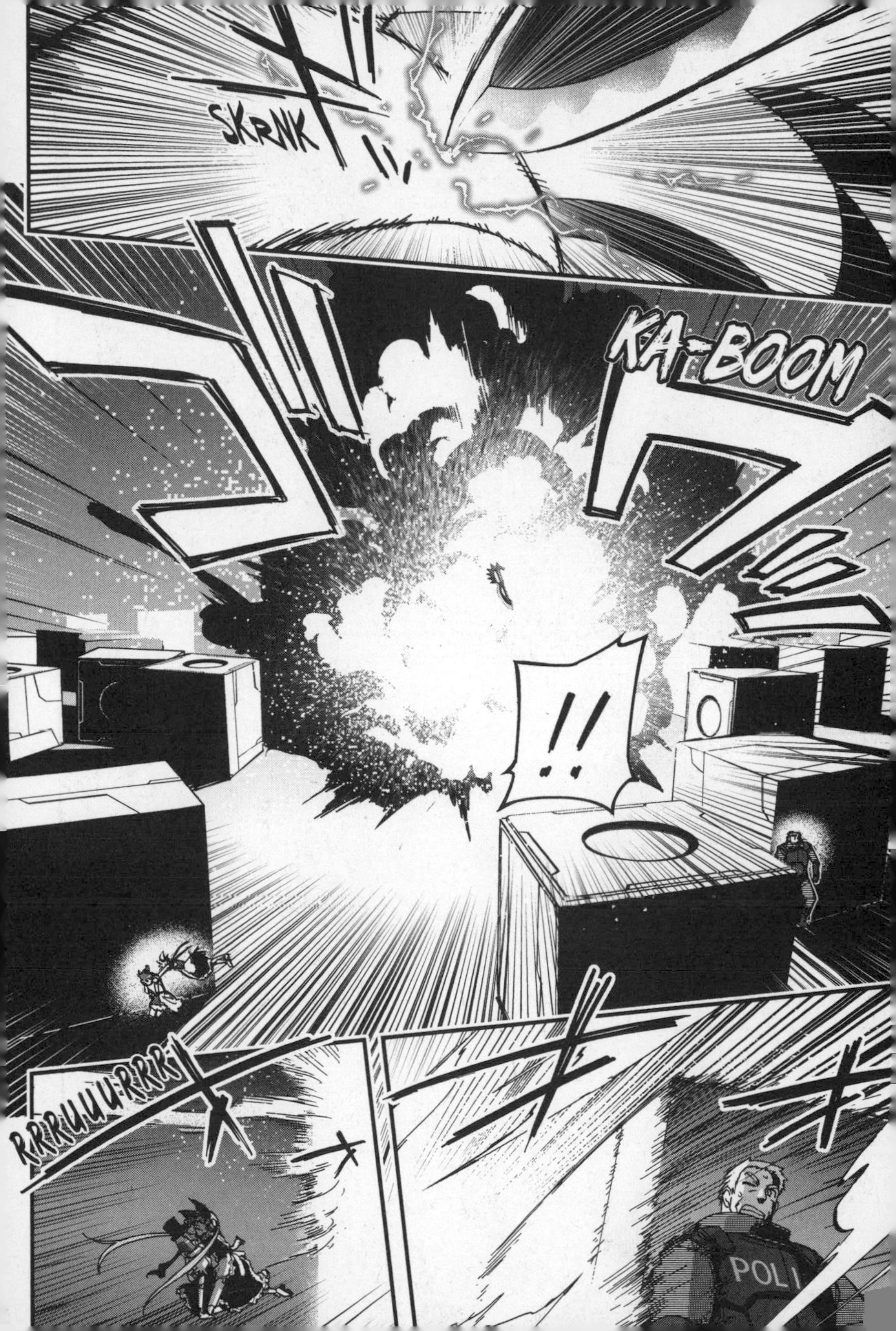
SKRNK
KA-BOOM
!!
POLI
RRRUUURRR

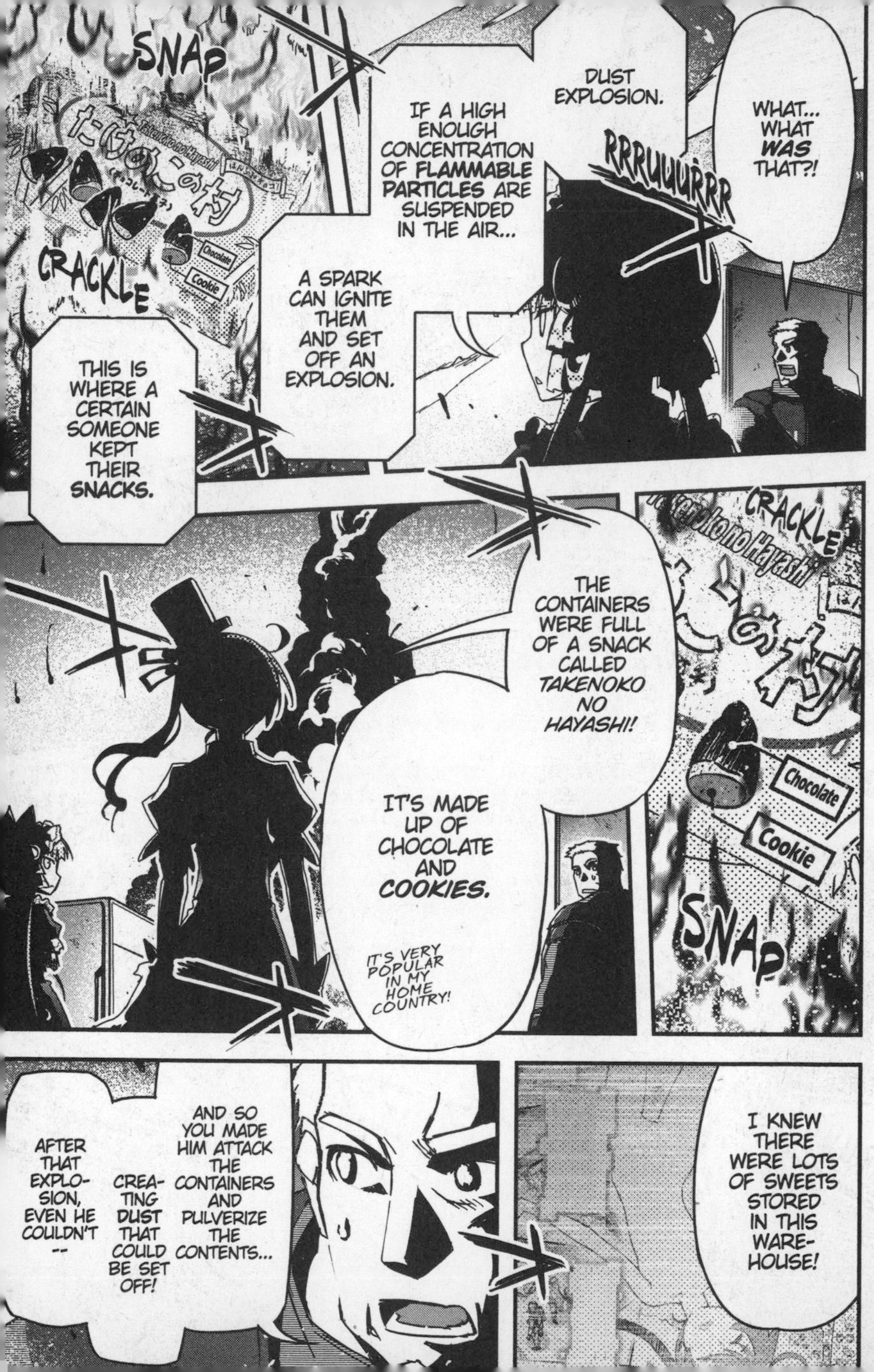
WHAT... WHAT **WAS** THAT?!
RRRUUURRR
DUST EXPLOSION.
IF A HIGH ENOUGH CONCENTRATION OF **FLAMMABLE PARTICLES** ARE SUSPENDED IN THE AIR...
A SPARK CAN IGNITE THEM AND SET OFF AN EXPLOSION.
SNAP
Chocolate
Cookie
CRACKLE
THIS IS WHERE A CERTAIN SOMEONE KEPT THEIR **SNACKS.**
CRACKLE
Chocolate
Cookie
SNAP
THE CONTAINERS WERE FULL OF A SNACK CALLED *TAKENOKO NO HAYASHI!*
IT'S MADE UP OF CHOCOLATE AND ***COOKIES.***
IT'S VERY POPULAR IN MY HOME COUNTRY!
I KNEW THERE WERE LOTS OF SWEETS STORED IN THIS WARE-HOUSE!
AND SO YOU MADE HIM ATTACK THE CONTAINERS AND PULVERIZE THE CONTENTS...
CREA-TING **DUST** THAT COULD BE SET OFF!
AFTER THAT EXPLO-SION, EVEN HE COULDN'T --

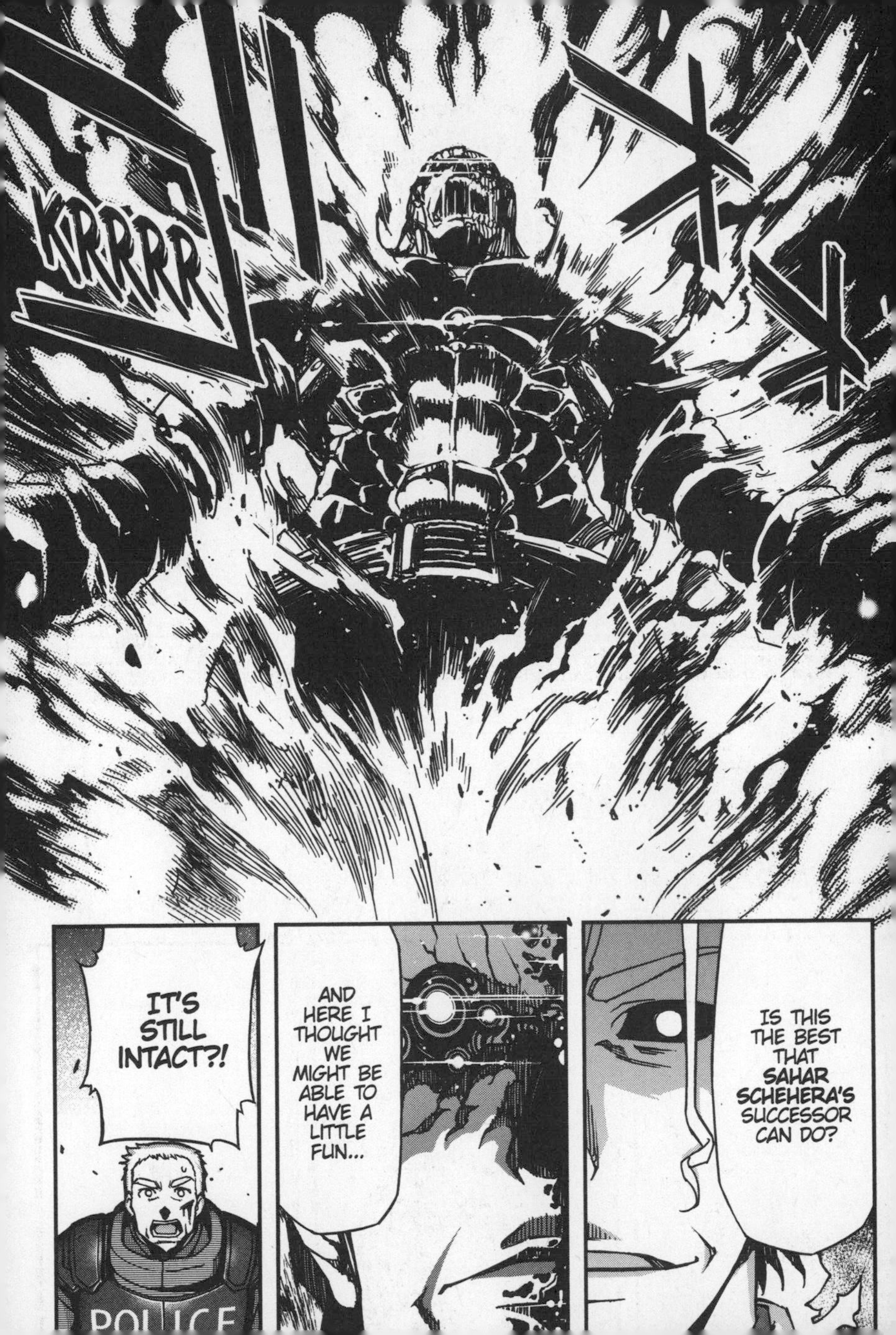
KRRRR
IS THIS THE BEST THAT SAHAR SCHEHERA'S SUCCESSOR CAN DO?
AND HERE I THOUGHT WE MIGHT BE ABLE TO HAVE A LITTLE FUN...
IT'S STILL INTACT?!
POLICE

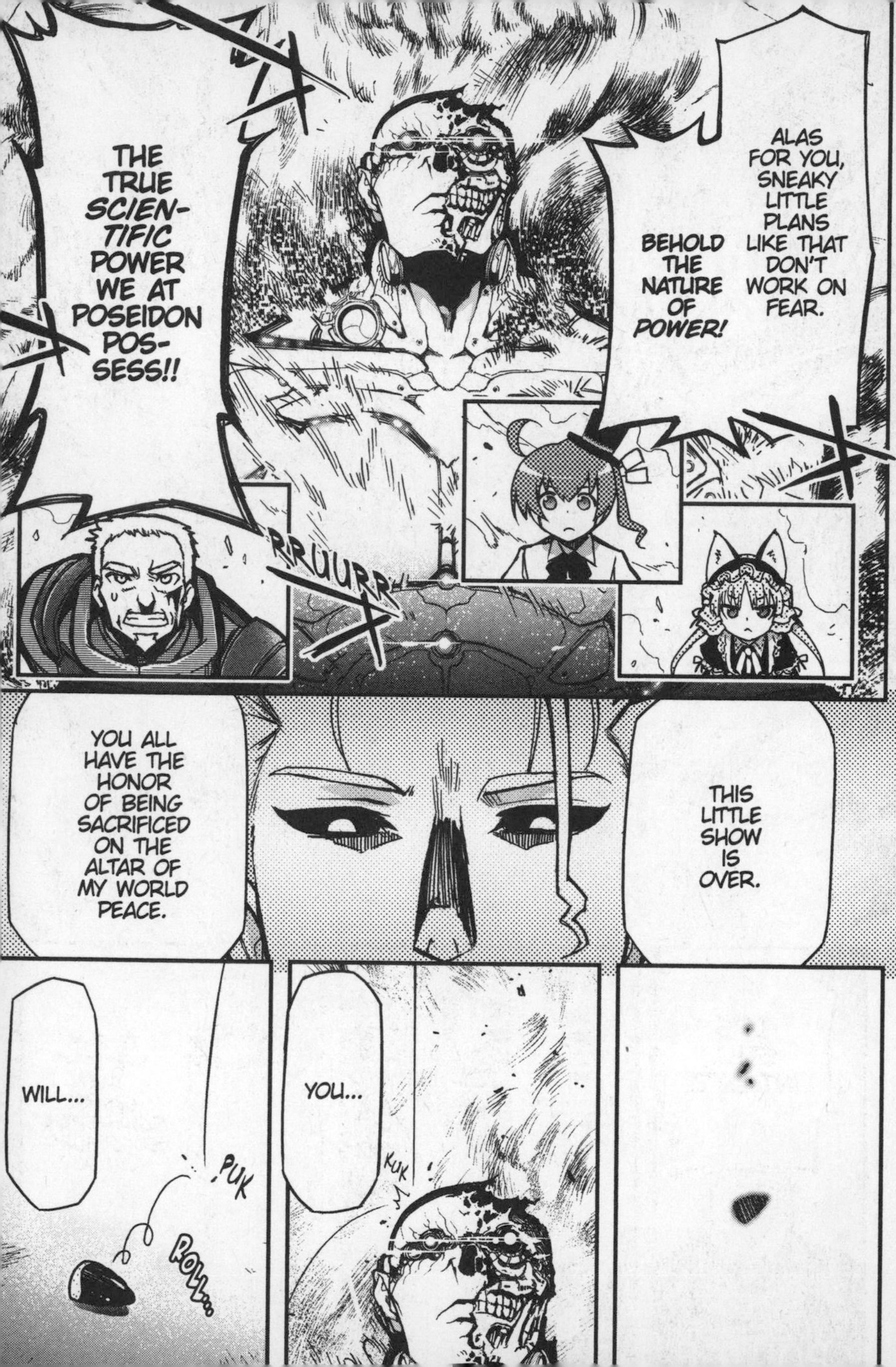
ALAS FOR YOU, SNEAKY LITTLE PLANS LIKE THAT DON'T WORK ON FEAR.
BEHOLD THE NATURE OF *POWER!*
THE TRUE *SCIENTIFIC* POWER WE AT POSEIDON POSSESS!!
RRUUURR
THIS LITTLE SHOW IS OVER.
YOU ALL HAVE THE HONOR OF BEING SACRIFICED ON THE ALTAR OF MY WORLD PEACE.
YOU...
KUK
WILL...
PUK
ROLL...

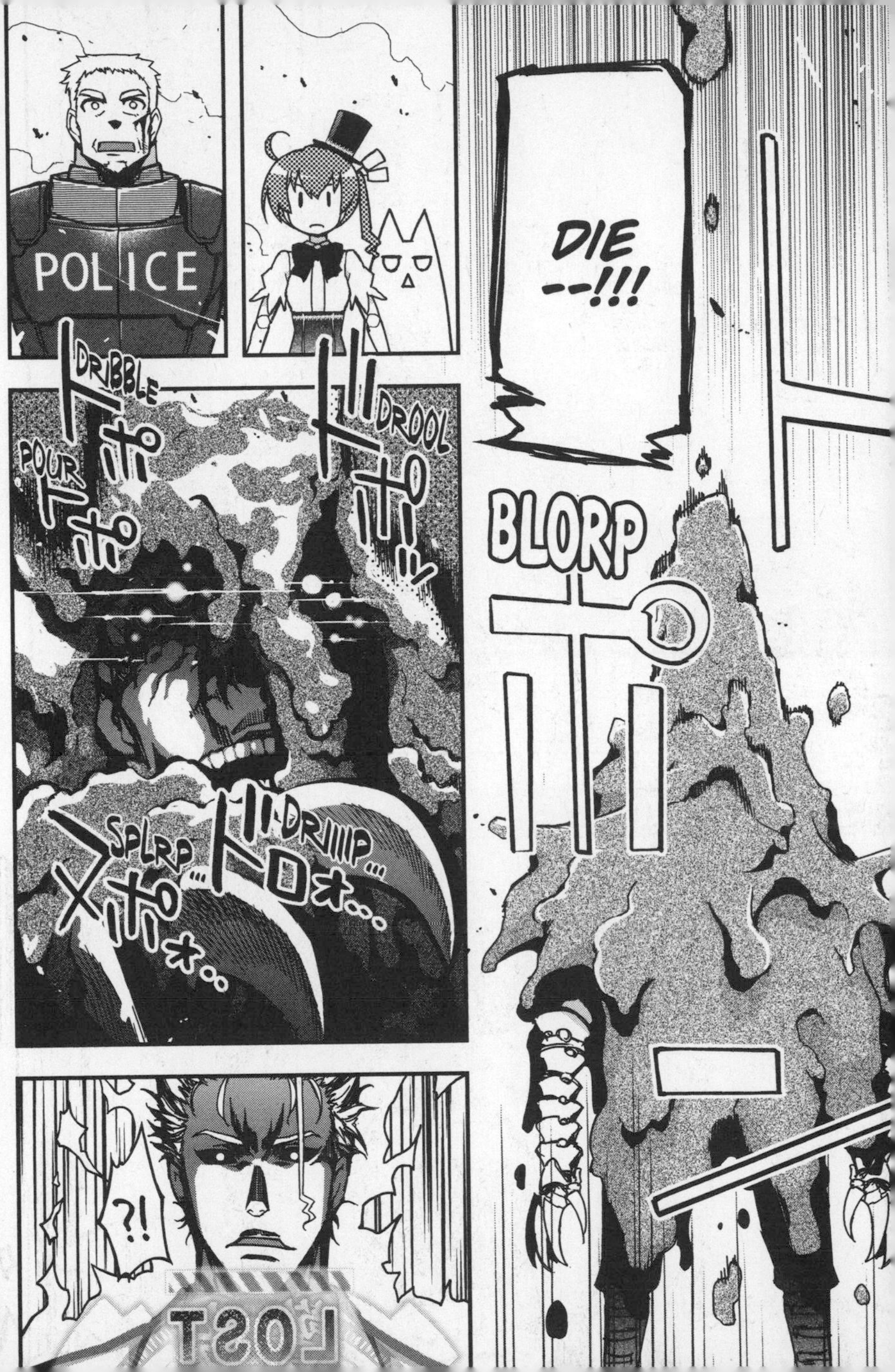
DIE --!!!
BLORP
POLICE
DROOL
DRIBBLE
POUR
DRIIIIP...
SPLRP
?!

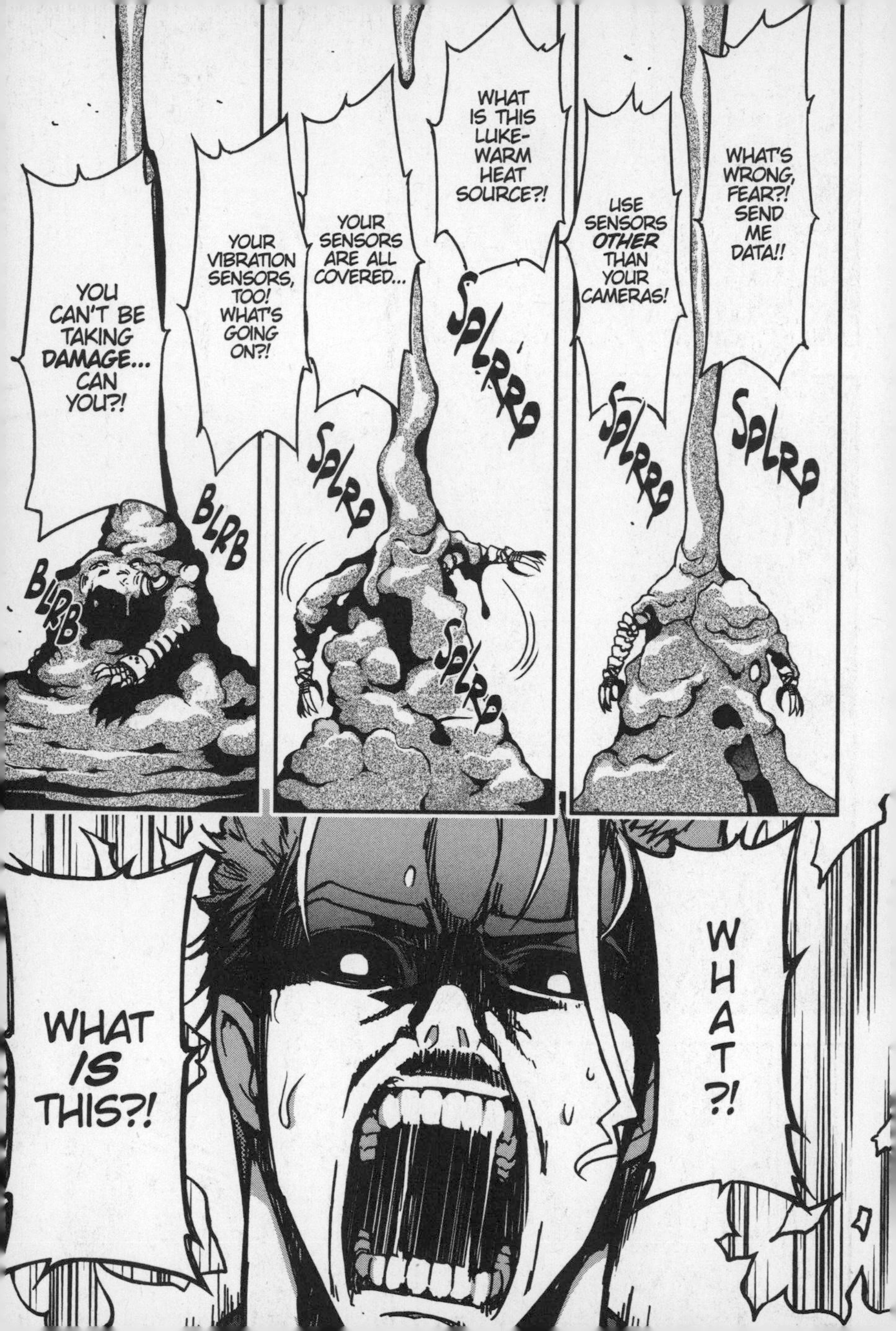
WHAT'S WRONG, FEAR?! SEND ME DATA!!
USE SENSORS OTHER THAN YOUR CAMERAS!
SPLRP
SPLRRP
WHAT IS THIS LUKE-WARM HEAT SOURCE?!
YOUR SENSORS ARE ALL COVERED...
SPLRRP
SPLRP
SPLRP
YOUR VIBRATION SENSORS, TOO! WHAT'S GOING ON?!
YOU CAN'T BE TAKING DAMAGE... CAN YOU?!
BLRB
BLRB
WHAT?!
WHAT IS THIS?!

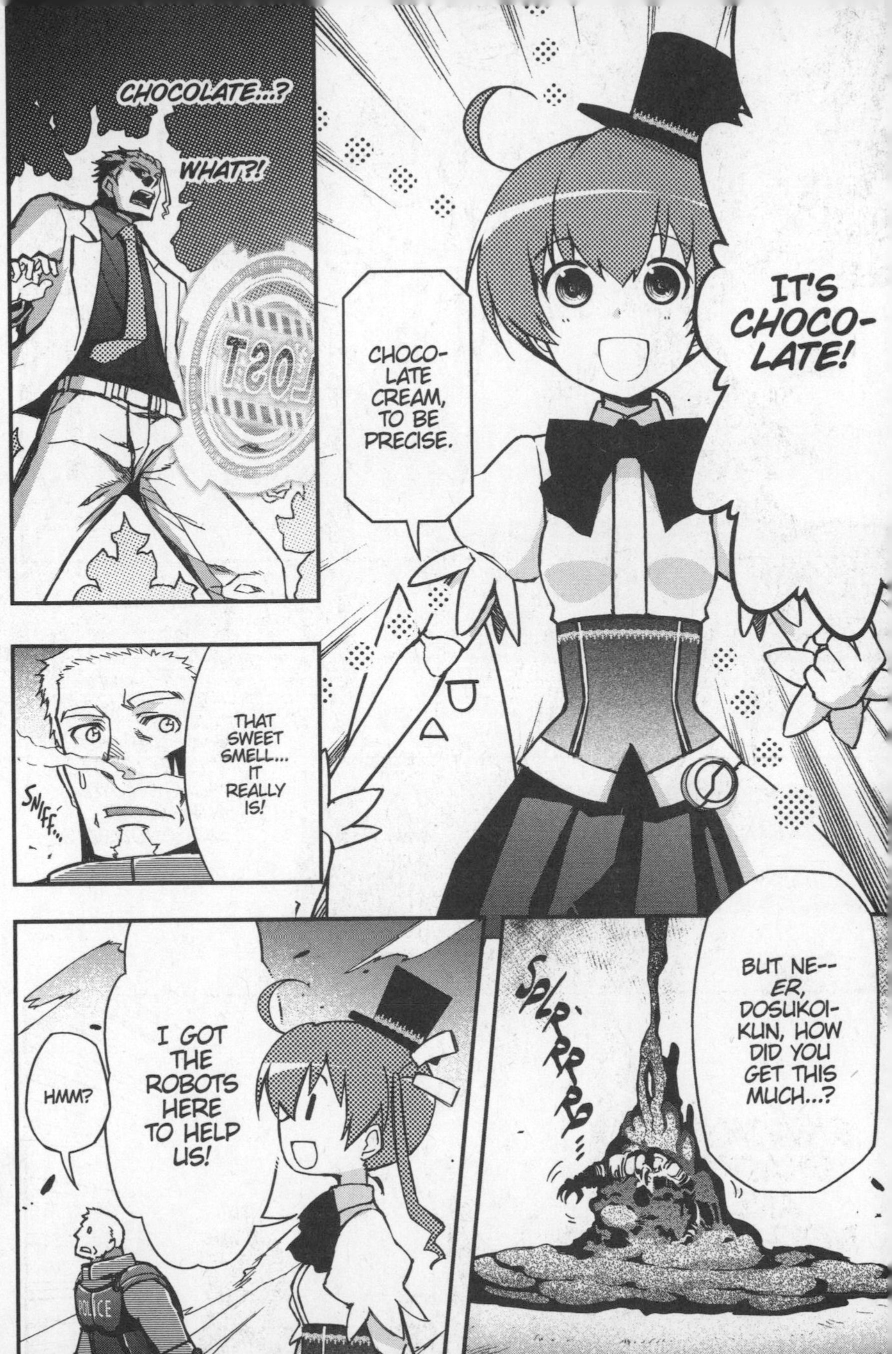
IT'S CHOCOLATE!
CHOCOLATE CREAM, TO BE PRECISE.
CHOCOLATE...?
WHAT?!
LOST
THAT SWEET SMELL... IT REALLY IS!
SNIFF...
BUT NE--ER, DOSUKOI-KUN, HOW DID YOU GET THIS MUCH...?
SPLRRRRG...
I GOT THE ROBOTS HERE TO HELP US!
HMM?
POLICE

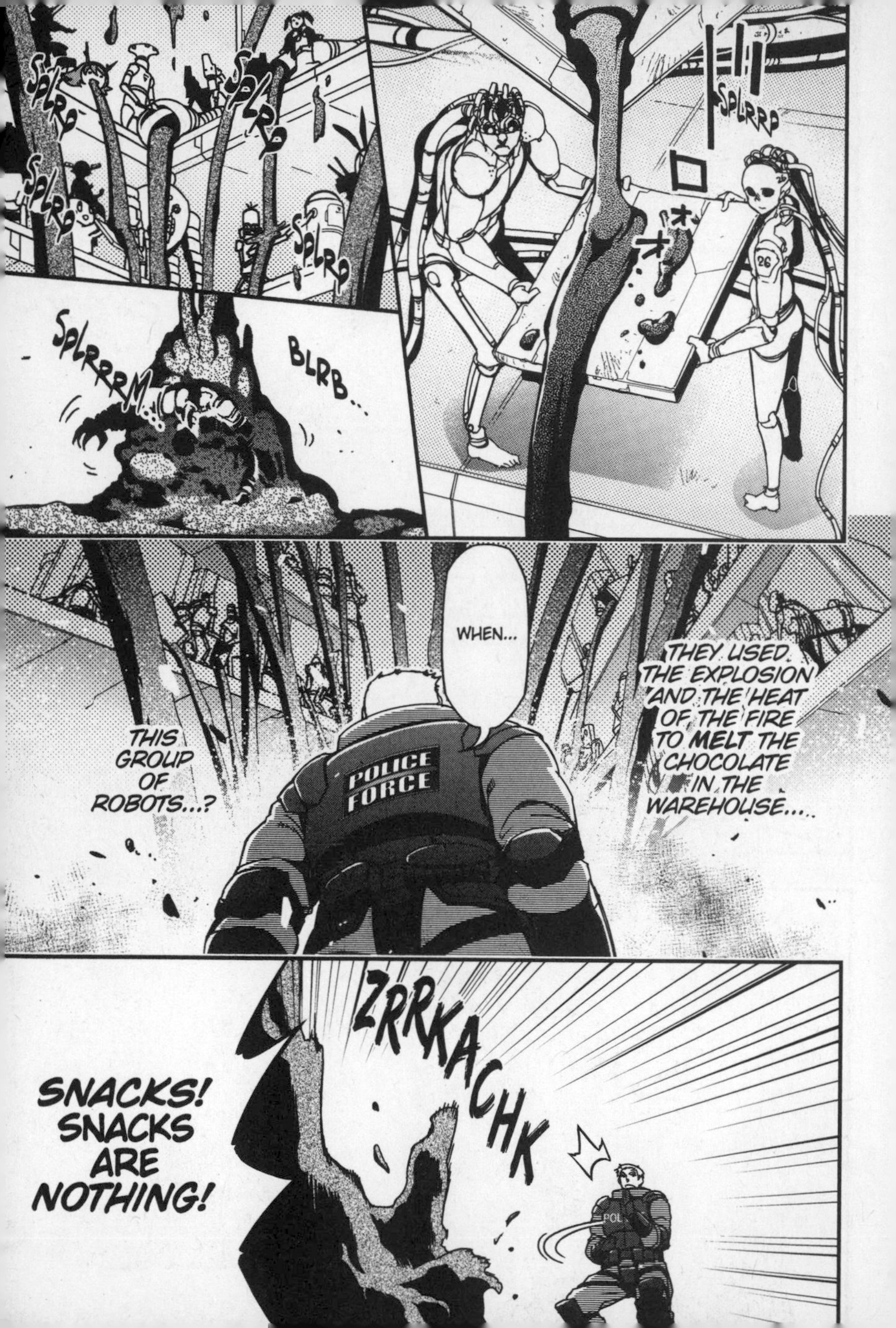
SPLRRP
SPLRP
SPLRP
SPLRP
SPLRP
SPLRRRM...
BLRB...
WHEN...
THEY USED THE EXPLOSION AND THE HEAT OF THE FIRE TO MELT THE CHOCOLATE IN THE WAREHOUSE....
THIS GROUP OF ROBOTS...?
POLICE FORCE
ZRRKACHK
SNACKS! SNACKS ARE NOTHING!

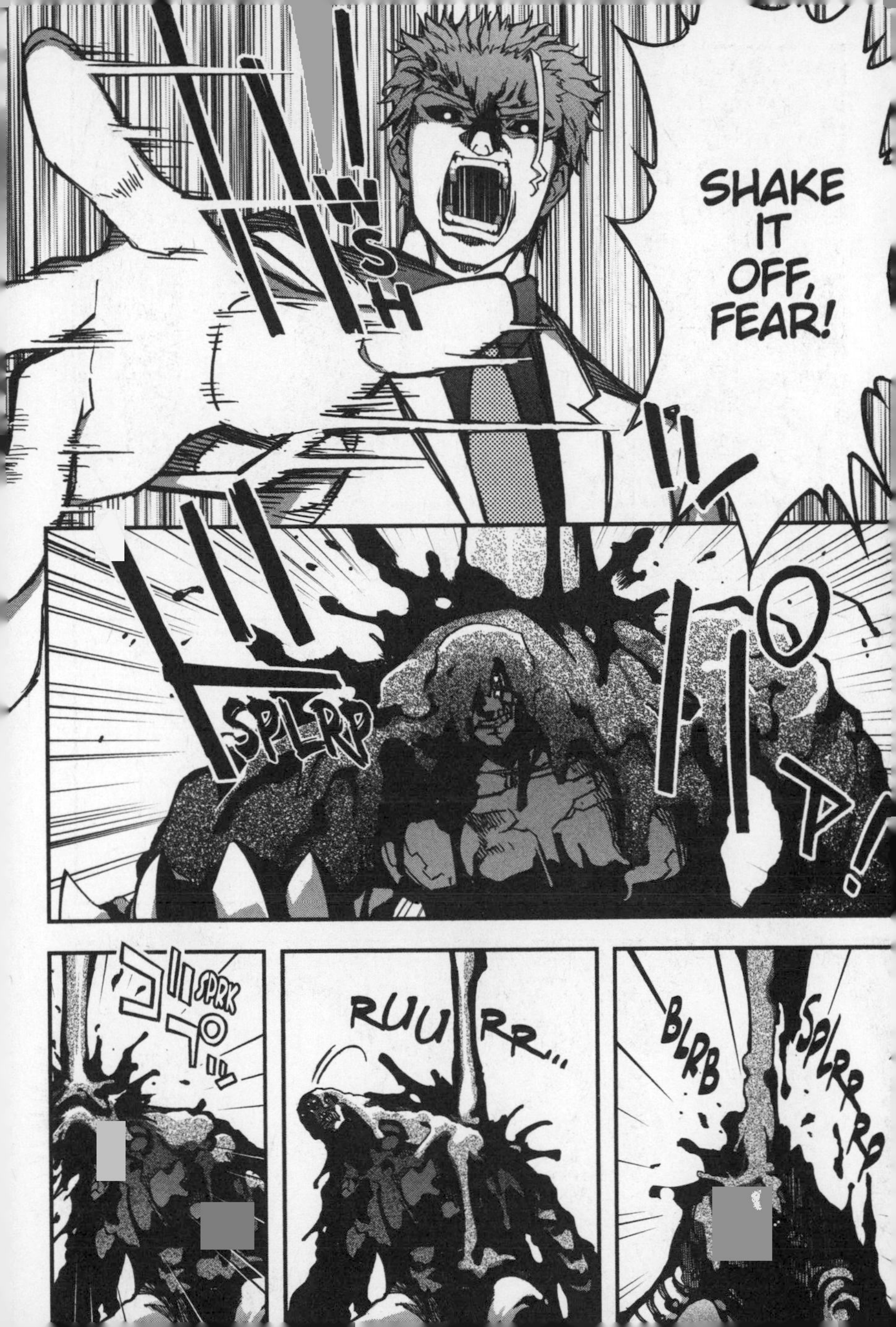
SHAKE IT OFF, FEAR!
WSH
SPLRP
SPLRRRR
BLRB
RUURR...
SPRK

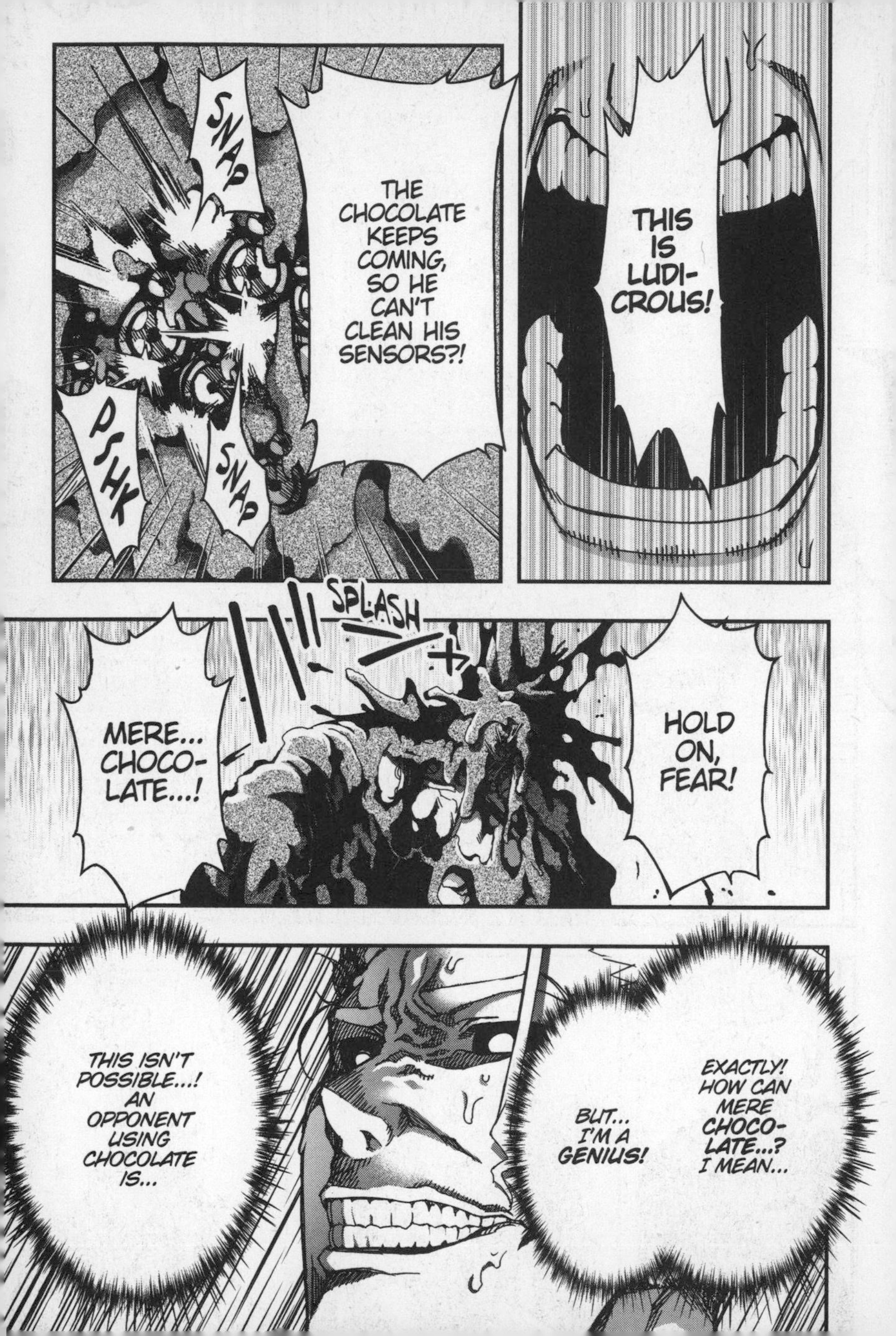
THIS IS LUDI-CROUS!
THE CHOCOLATE KEEPS COMING, SO HE CAN'T CLEAN HIS SENSORS?!
SNAP
SNAP
PSHK
SPLASH
HOLD ON, FEAR!
MERE... CHOCO-LATE...!
EXACTLY! HOW CAN MERE CHOCO-LATE...? I MEAN...
BUT... I'M A GENIUS!
THIS ISN'T POSSIBLE...! AN OPPONENT USING CHOCOLATE IS...

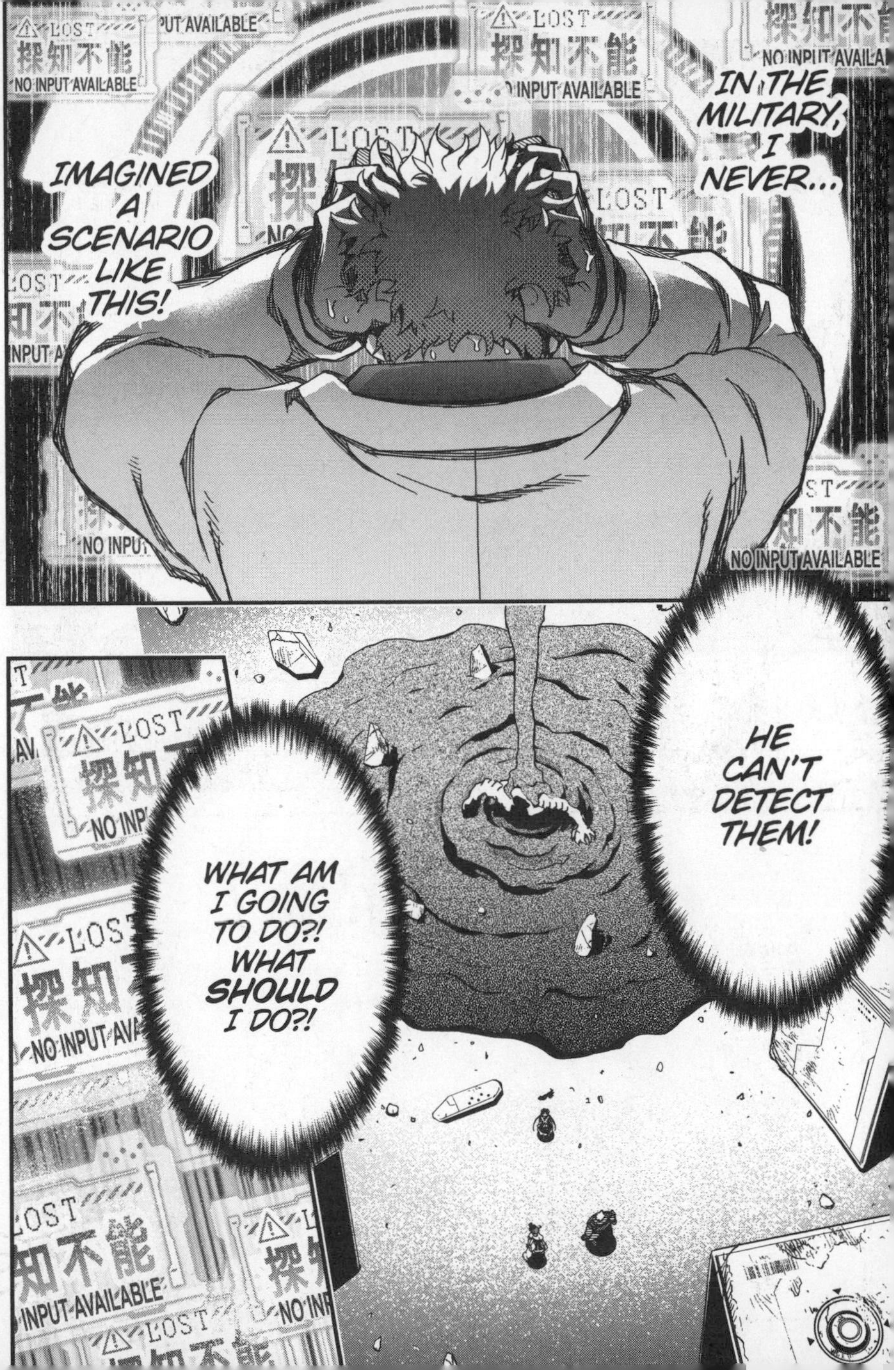
LOST
探知不能
NO INPUT AVAILABLE
IN THE MILITARY, I NEVER...
IMAGINED A SCENARIO LIKE THIS!
HE CAN'T DETECT THEM!
WHAT AM I GOING TO DO?! WHAT SHOULD I DO?!

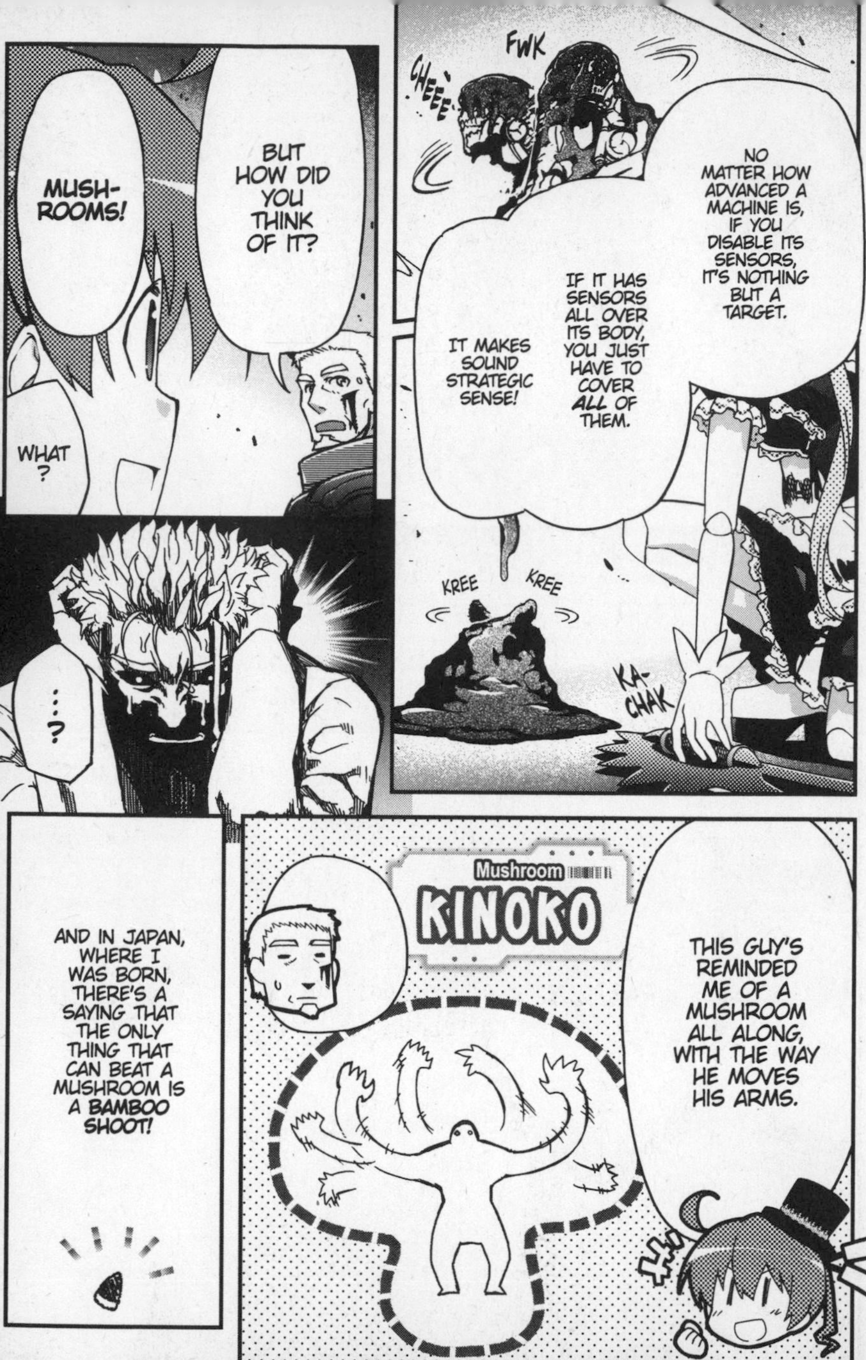
FWK
CHEEEE
NO MATTER HOW ADVANCED A MACHINE IS, IF YOU DISABLE ITS SENSORS, IT'S NOTHING BUT A TARGET.
IF IT HAS SENSORS ALL OVER ITS BODY, YOU JUST HAVE TO COVER ALL OF THEM.
IT MAKES SOUND STRATEGIC SENSE!
KREE KREE
KA-CHAK
BUT HOW DID YOU THINK OF IT?
MUSH-ROOMS!
WHAT?
...?
Mushroom
KINOKO
THIS GUY'S REMINDED ME OF A MUSHROOM ALL ALONG, WITH THE WAY HE MOVES HIS ARMS.
AND IN JAPAN, WHERE I WAS BORN, THERE'S A SAYING THAT THE ONLY THING THAT CAN BEAT A MUSHROOM IS A BAMBOO SHOOT!

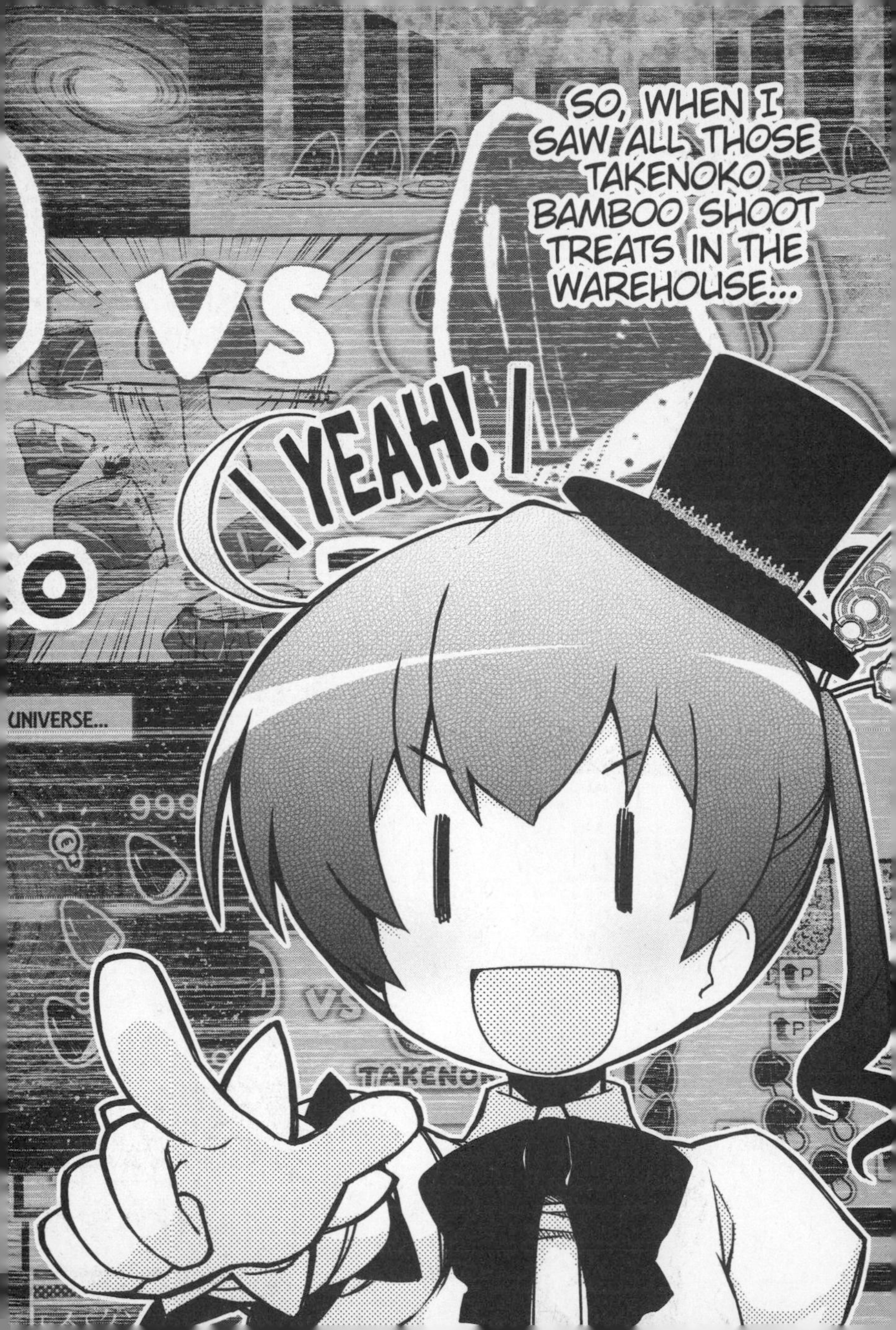
SO, WHEN I SAW ALL THOSE TAKENOKO BAMBOO SHOOT TREATS IN THE WAREHOUSE...
YEAH!
VS
UNIVERSE...
999
VS
TAKENO

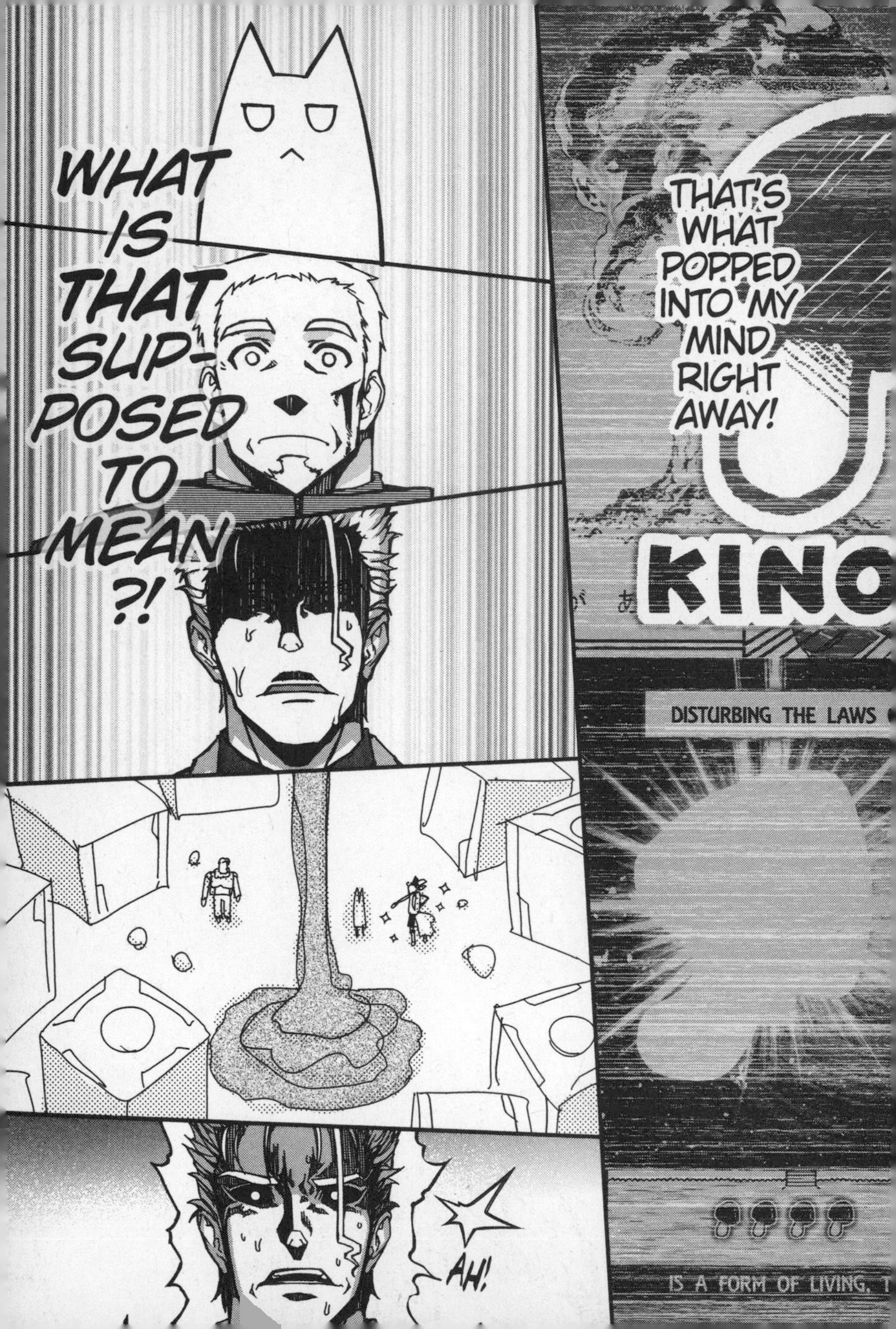
THAT'S WHAT POPPED INTO MY MIND RIGHT AWAY!
KINO
DISTURBING THE LAWS
IS A FORM OF LIVING, T
WHAT IS THAT SUP-POSED TO MEAN ?!
AH!

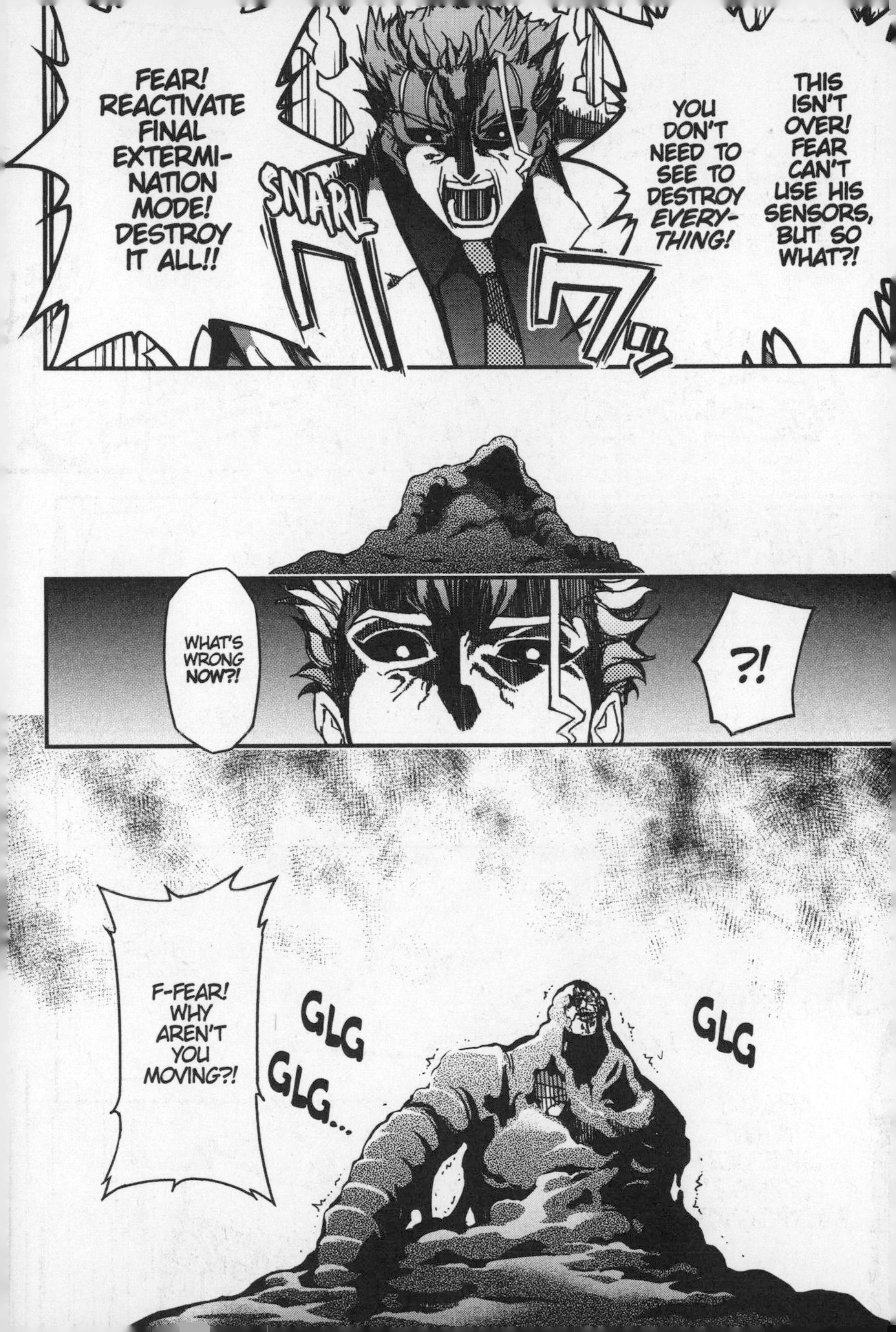
THIS ISN'T OVER! FEAR CAN'T USE HIS SENSORS, BUT SO WHAT?!
YOU DON'T NEED TO SEE TO DESTROY EVERY-THING!
SNARL
FEAR! REACTIVATE FINAL EXTERMI-NATION MODE! DESTROY IT ALL!!
?!
WHAT'S WRONG NOW?!
GLG
GLG
GLG...
F-FEAR! WHY AREN'T YOU MOVING?!

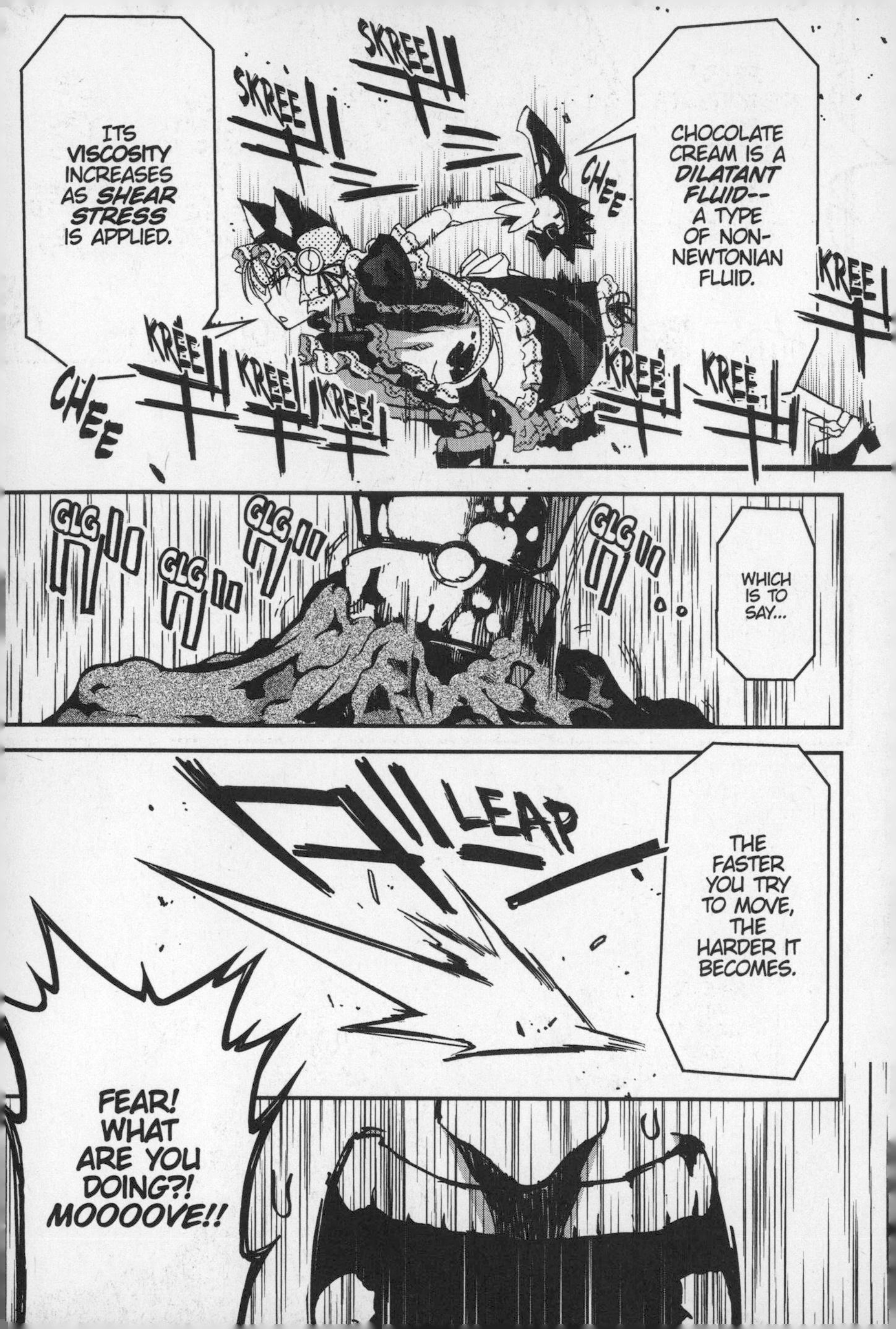

SKREE
SKREE
CHOCOLATE CREAM IS A *DILATANT FLUID*-- A TYPE OF NON-NEWTONIAN FLUID.
CHEE
KREE
ITS VISCOSITY INCREASES AS *SHEAR STRESS* IS APPLIED.
KREE
KREE
KREE
KREE
KREE
CHEE
WHICH IS TO SAY...
GLG
GLG
GLG
GLG
THE FASTER YOU TRY TO MOVE, THE HARDER IT BECOMES.
LEAP
FEAR! WHAT ARE YOU DOING?! *MOOOOVE!!*

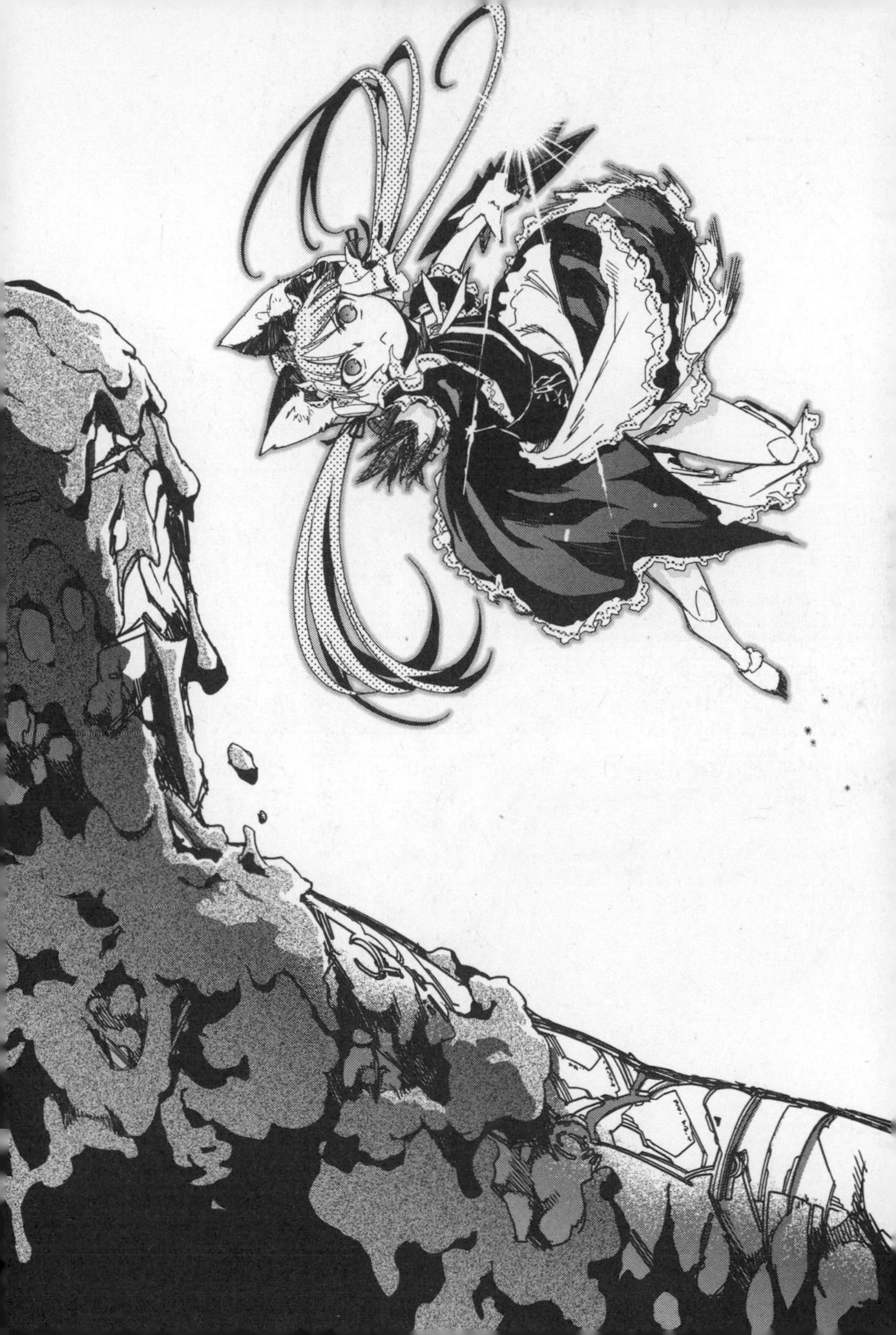

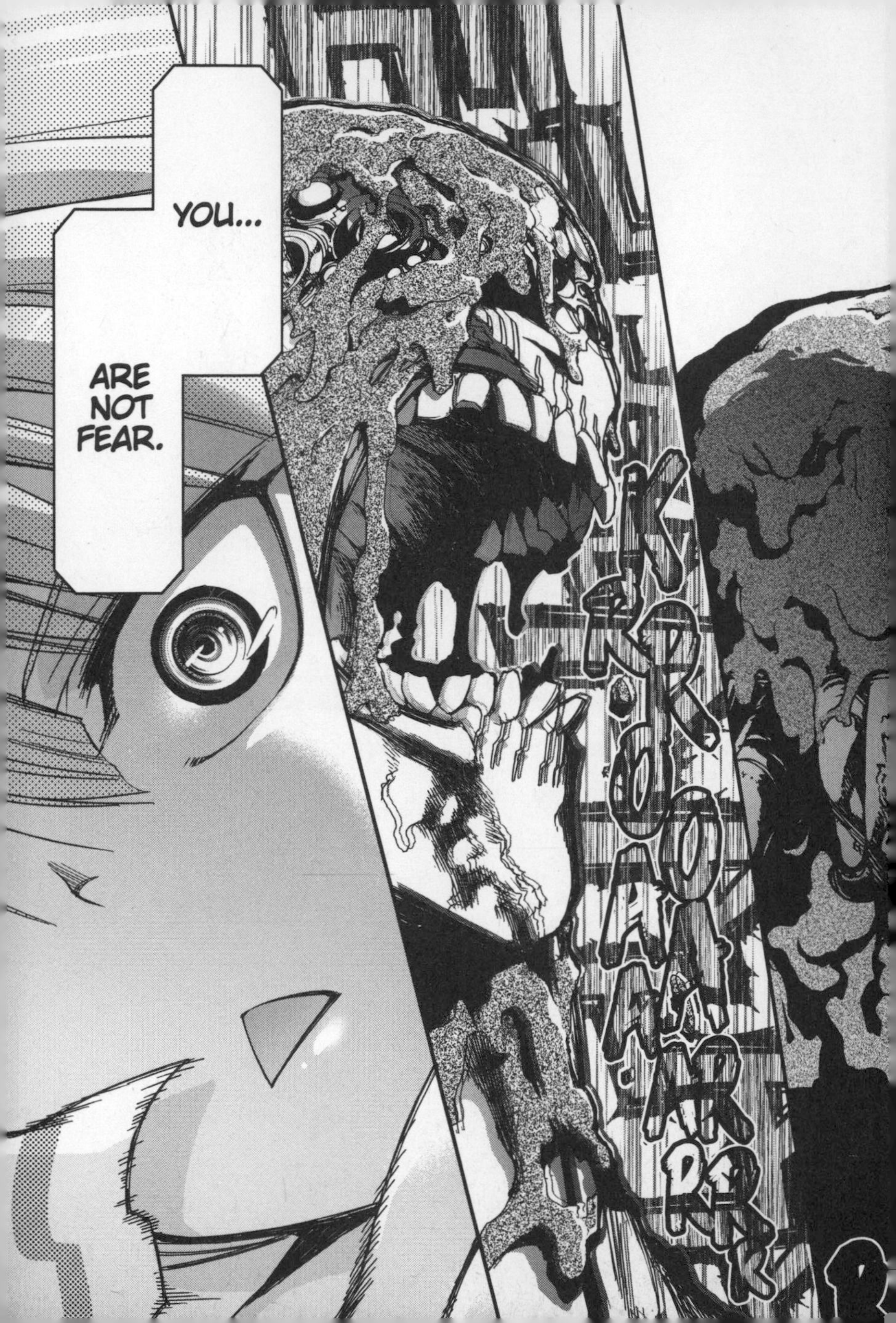
YOU...
ARE NOT FEAR.

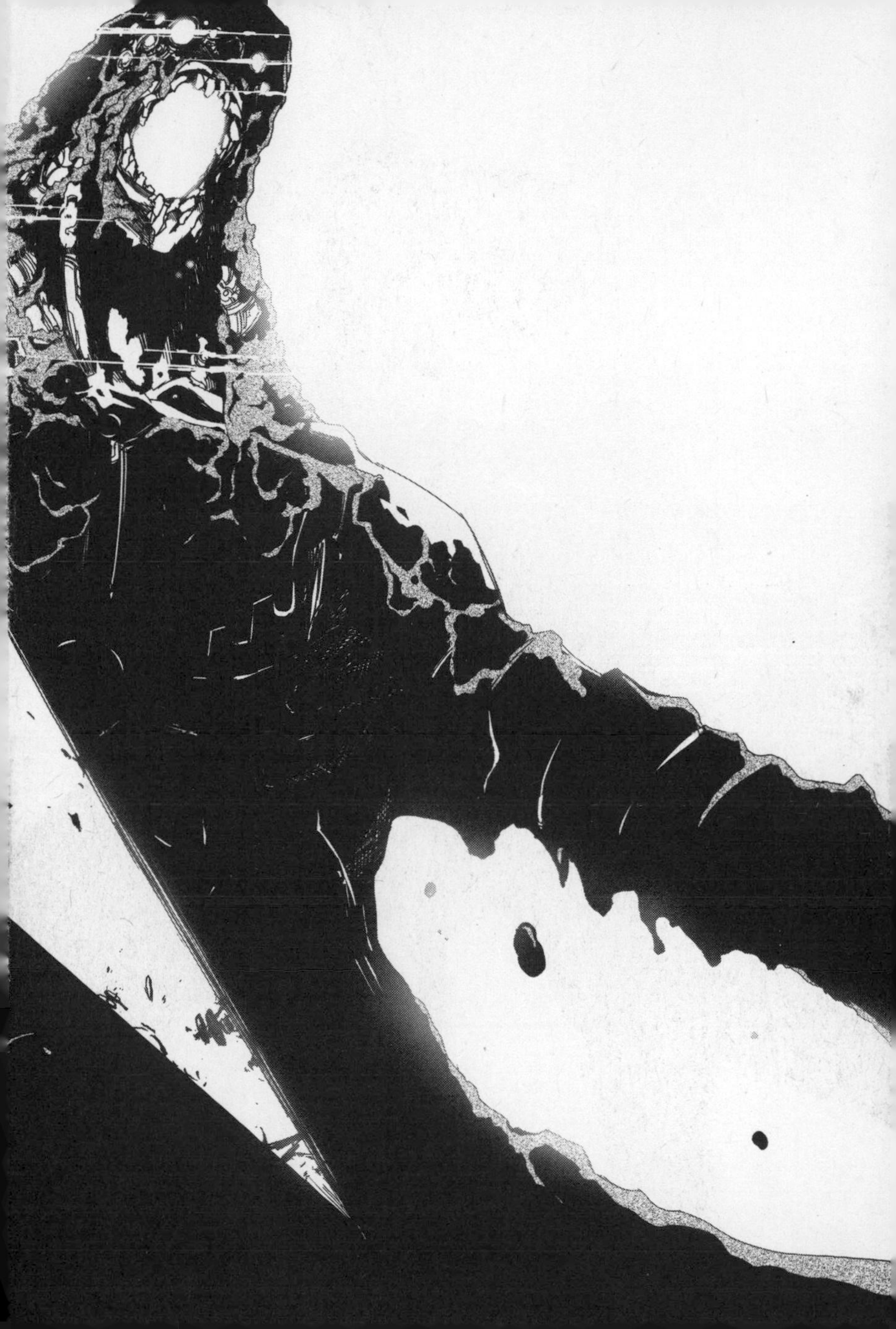

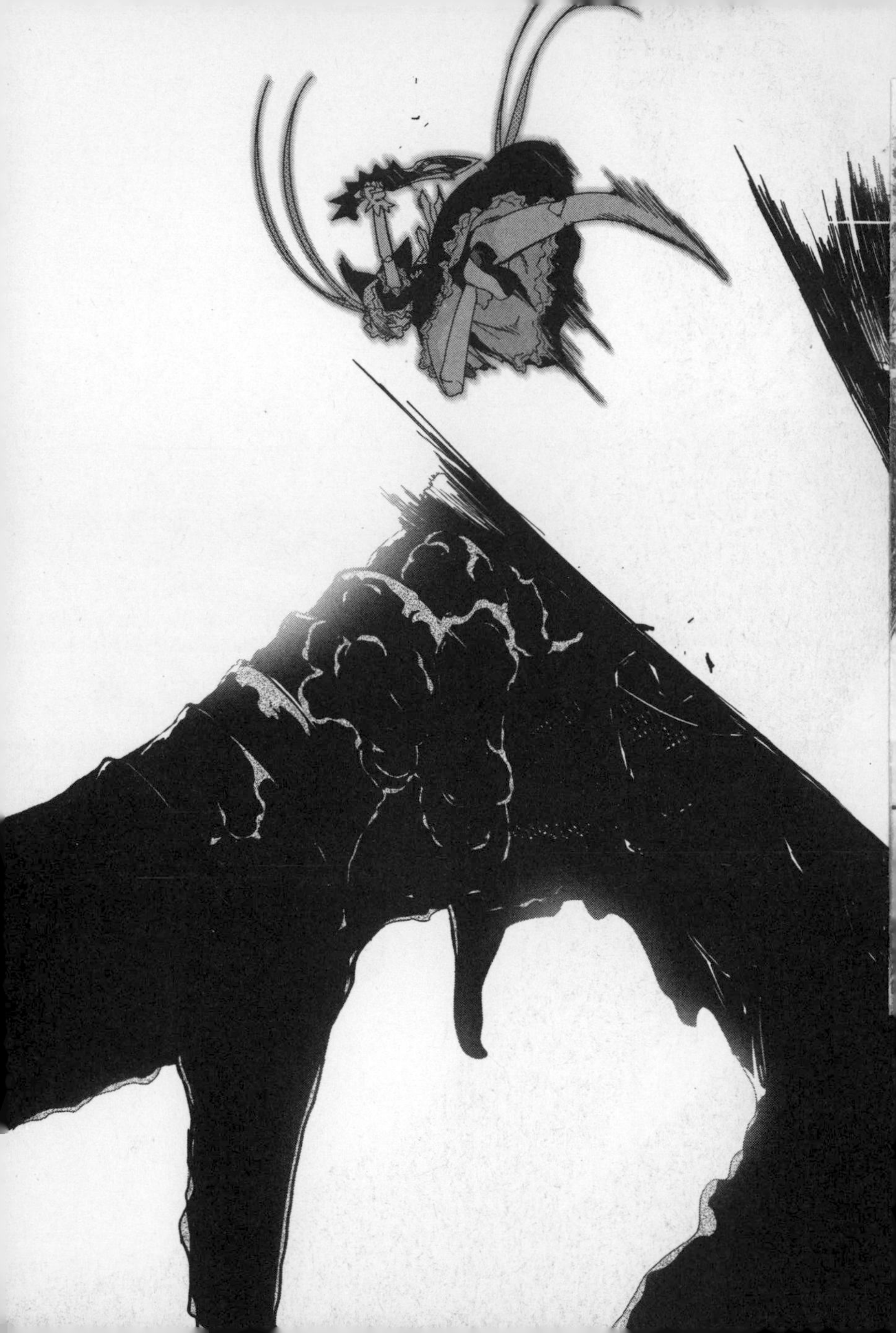

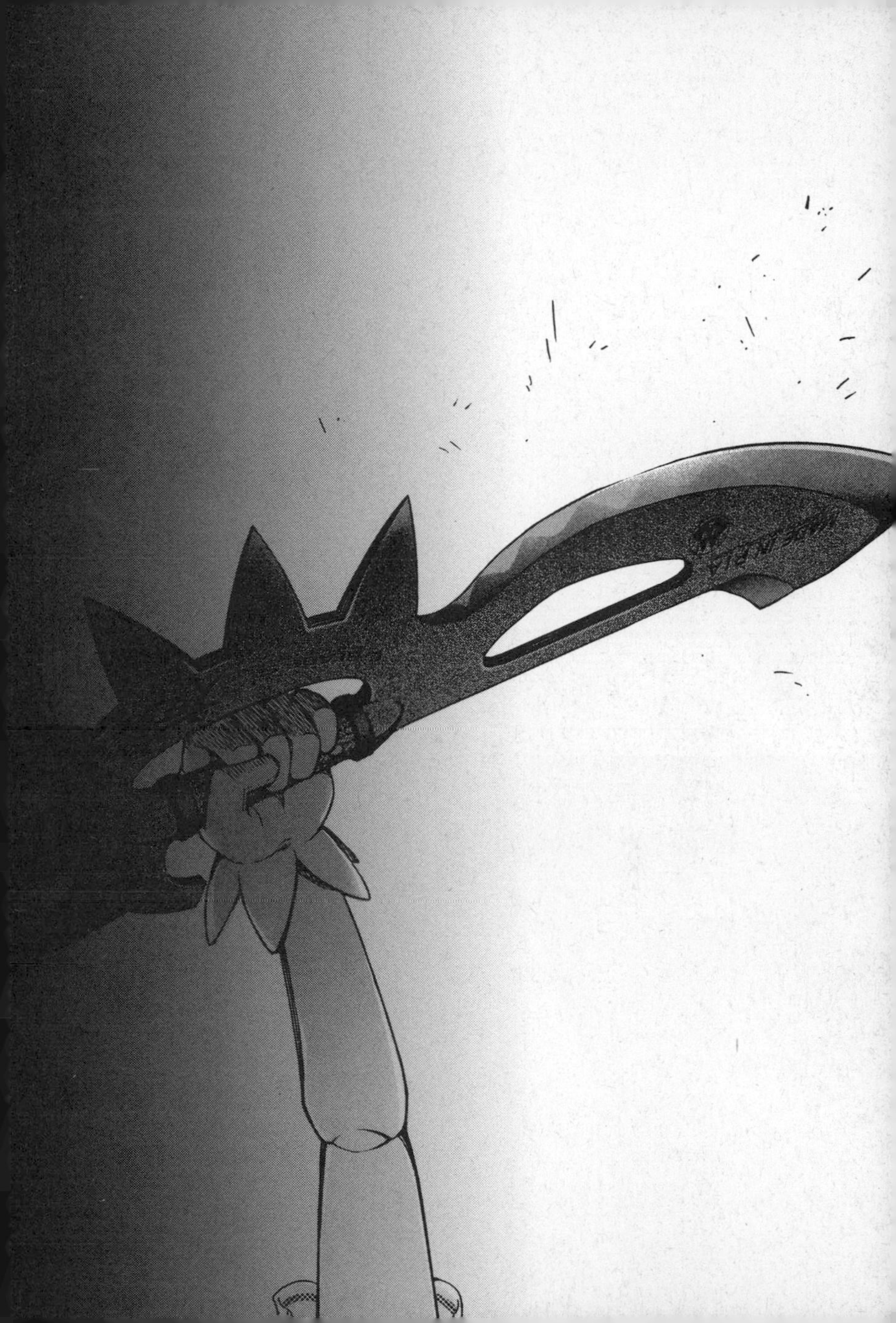

...TO BE CONTINUED

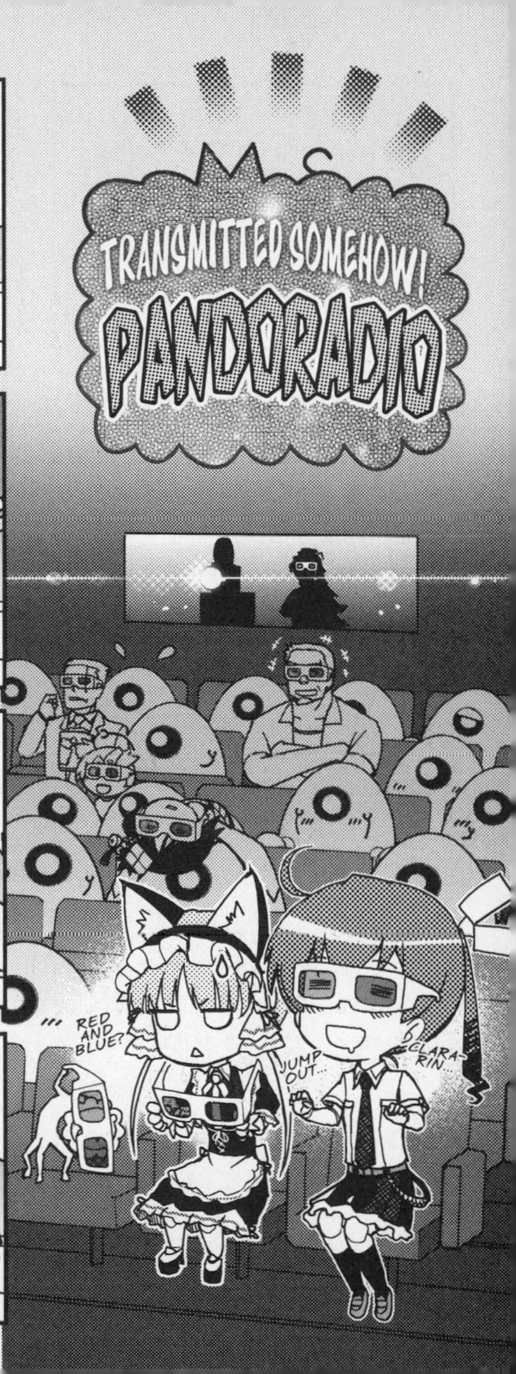
TRANSMITTED SOMEHOW!
PANDORADIO
CLARA-RIN...
JUMP OUT...
RED AND BLUE?

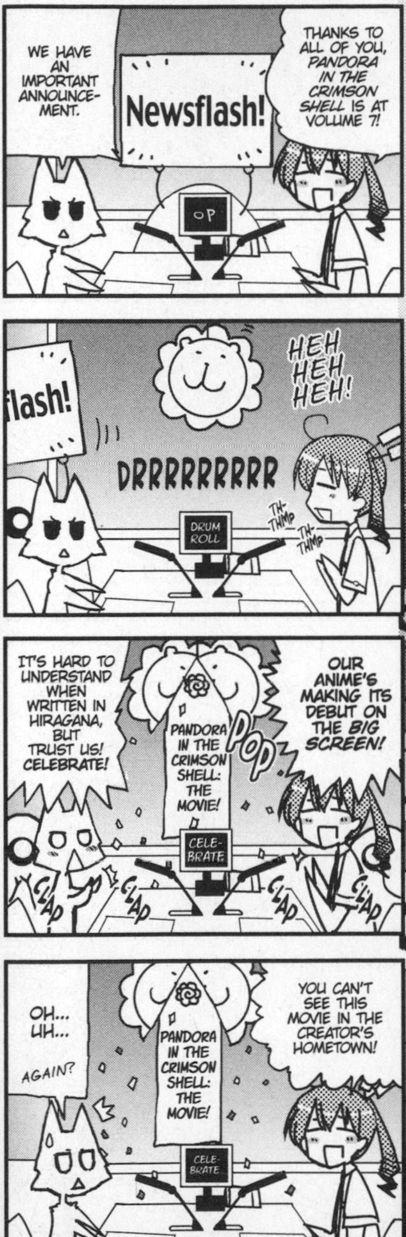
THANKS TO ALL OF YOU, PANDORA IN THE CRIMSON SHELL IS AT VOLUME 7!
Newsflash!
WE HAVE AN IMPORTANT ANNOUNCEMENT.
OP
HEH HEH HEH!
flash!
DRRRRRRRRR
TH-THMP TH-THMP
DRUM ROLL
OUR ANIME'S MAKING ITS DEBUT ON THE BIG SCREEN!
POP
PANDORA IN THE CRIMSON SHELL: THE MOVIE!
IT'S HARD TO UNDERSTAND WHEN WRITTEN IN HIRAGANA, BUT TRUST US! CELEBRATE!
CELEBRATE
CLAP
CLAP
CLAP
CLAP
YOU CAN'T SEE THIS MOVIE IN THE CREATOR'S HOMETOWN!
PANDORA IN THE CRIMSON SHELL: THE MOVIE!
OH... UH...
AGAIN?
CELEBRATE

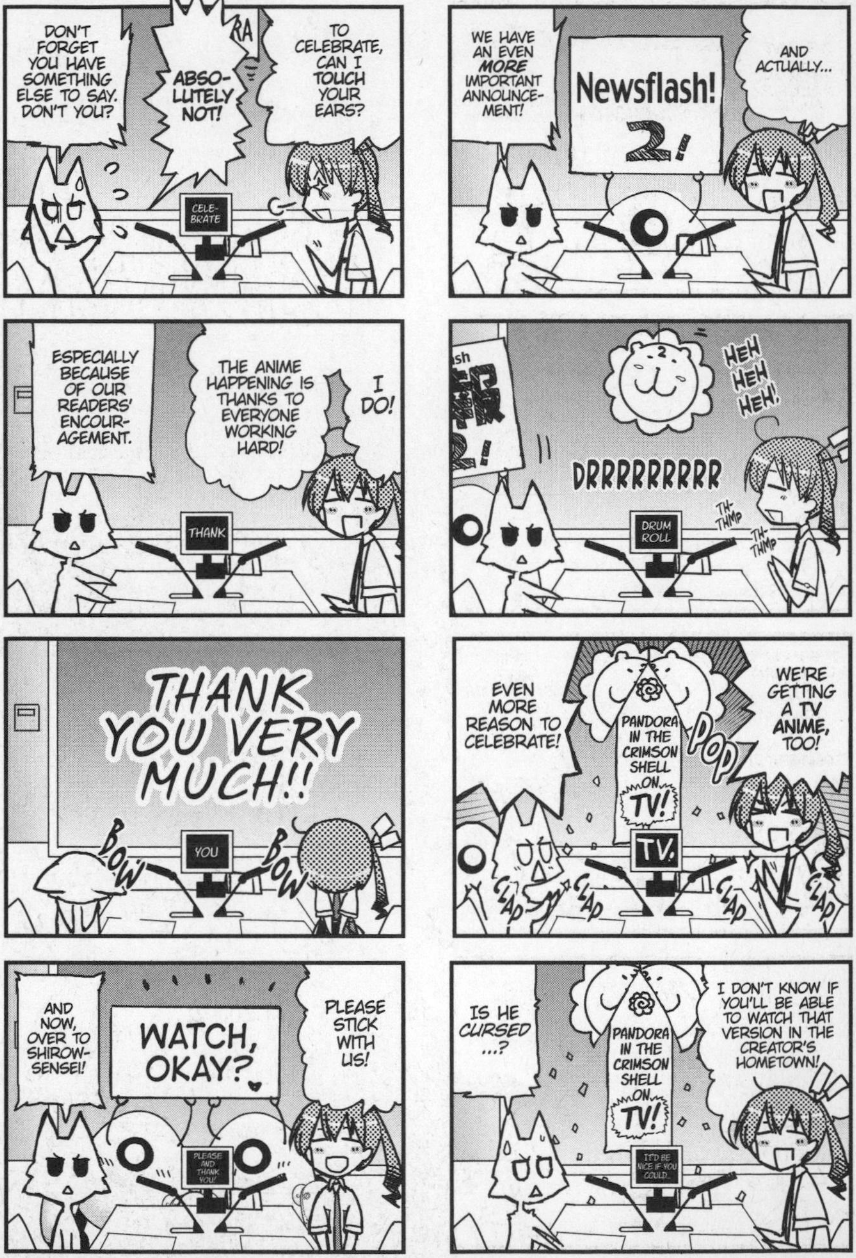
AND ACTUALLY...
WE HAVE AN EVEN MORE IMPORTANT ANNOUNCEMENT!
Newsflash! 2!
HEH HEH HEH!
DRRRRRRRRR
DRUM ROLL
TH-THMP
TH-THMP
WE'RE GETTING A TV ANIME, TOO!
POP
EVEN MORE REASON TO CELEBRATE!
PANDORA IN THE CRIMSON SHELL ON TV!
TV.
CLAP
CLAP
CLAP
CLAP
I DON'T KNOW IF YOU'LL BE ABLE TO WATCH THAT VERSION IN THE CREATOR'S HOMETOWN!
IS HE CURSED ...?
PANDORA IN THE CRIMSON SHELL ON TV!
IT'D BE NICE IF YOU COULD...
TO CELEBRATE, CAN I TOUCH YOUR EARS?
RA
ABSO-LUTELY NOT!
DON'T FORGET YOU HAVE SOMETHING ELSE TO SAY. DON'T YOU?
CELE-BRATE
I DO!
THE ANIME HAPPENING IS THANKS TO EVERYONE WORKING HARD!
ESPECIALLY BECAUSE OF OUR READERS' ENCOURAGEMENT.
THANK
THANK YOU VERY MUCH!!
BOW
BOW
YOU
PLEASE STICK WITH US!
WATCH, OKAY?
AND NOW, OVER TO SHIROW-SENSEI!
PLEASE AND THANK YOU!

ORIGINAL CHARACTER DESIGN SKETCHES

A sort-of apology.

I did these sketches on April 20, 2014, after I was asked to do so.

Enhanced Exoskeleton PLM-7

Since this was just a vague concept sketch, there aren't any detailed parts. Please tweak it however seems appropriate, given the pressure on the writer and the need for performance. I guess it feels kind of like a four-legged mini-Buer. I think it can use its arms and legs like a gorilla to move faster than it could on two legs.

This is the back.

The "head" part is a type of sensor. It constantly rotates at a fairly high speed to collect information from all around itself. It can't see at its feet.

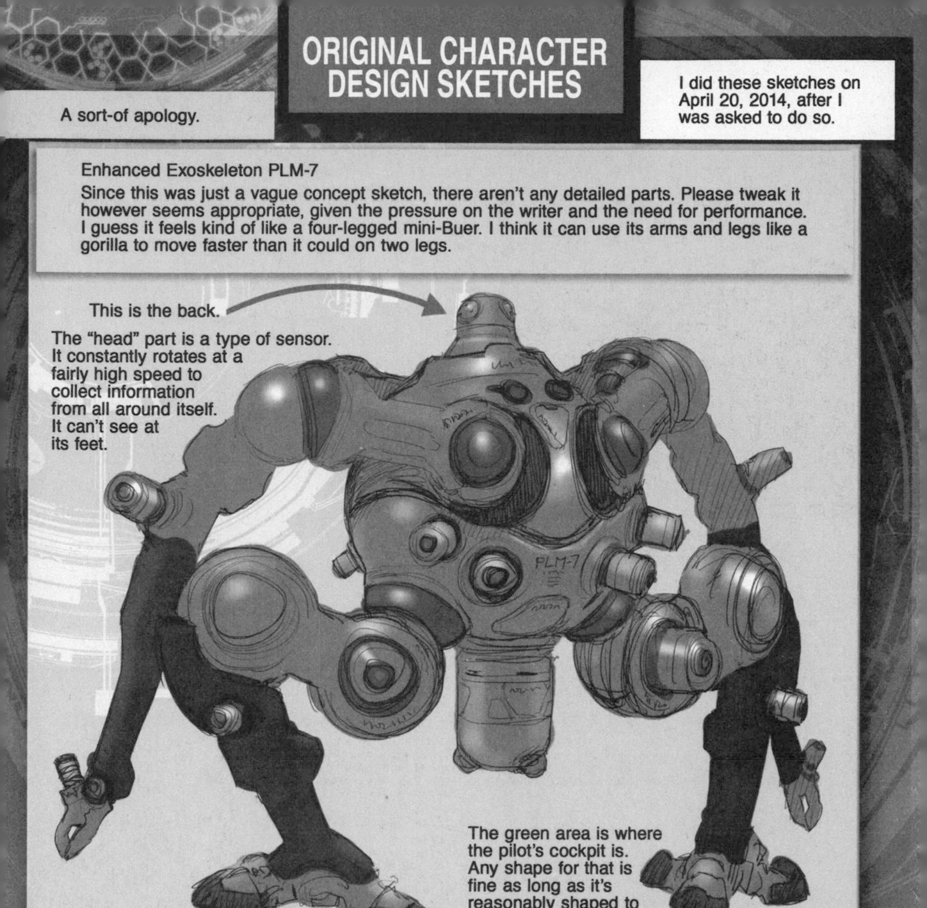
PLM-7

The green area is where the pilot's cockpit is. Any shape for that is fine as long as it's reasonably shaped to hold a person in there.

I considered a frame-only cockpit like the power loader in *Aliens*, to make it easy to show the character's face during combat, but given that it might be annoying to draw all the controls, I think it's better if it's covered in armor. But adapt it however you think best!

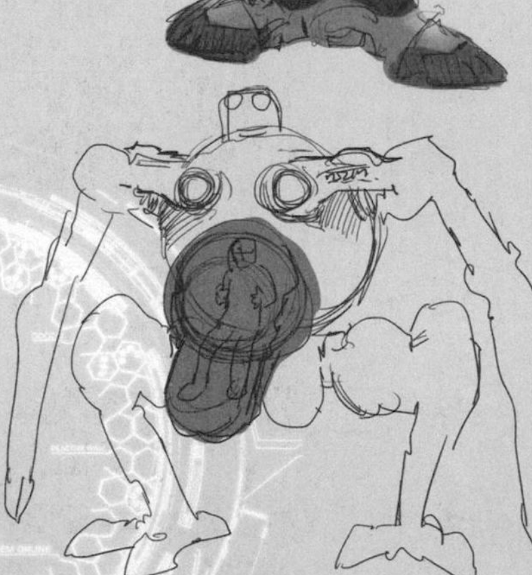

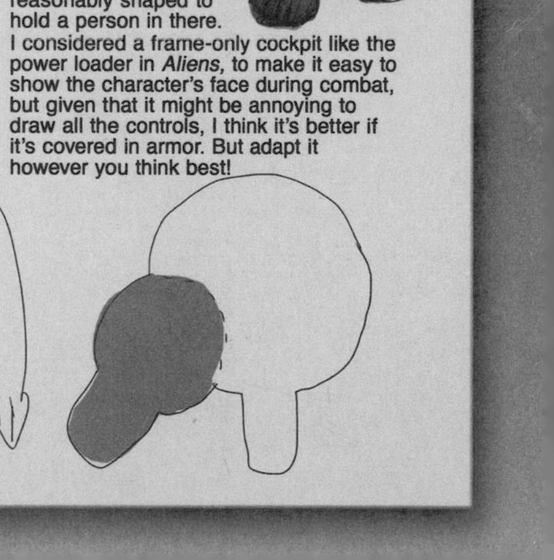

A logo I made for the 25th anniversary of *Ghost in the Shell.* I think the character silhouette was made by the designer.

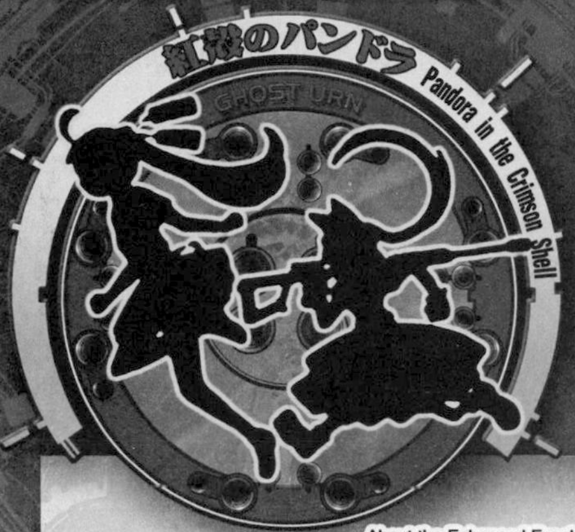
紅殻のパンドラ
Pandora in the Crimson Shell
GHOST URN

Enhanced Exoskeleton PLM-7
Sorry about the messy sketches. What about this as a concept? From the color of the series, I think that a mech--maybe like a sports car made up of sharper, cooler lines--would be appropriate, but if you have a better idea, then by all means, go ahead and use that!

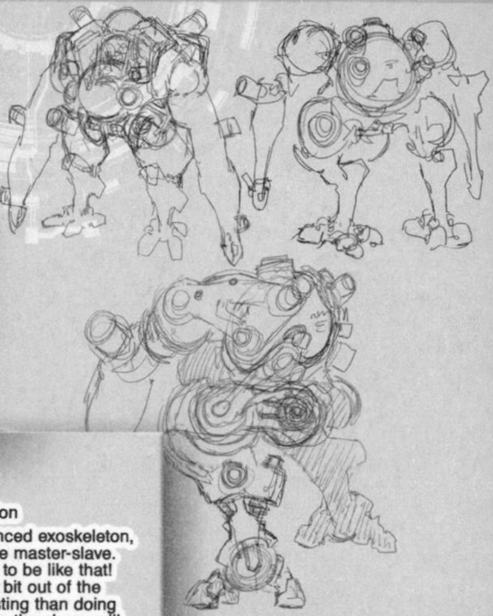

About the Enhanced Exoskeleton
In terms of operating the enhanced exoskeleton, I'd propose an internal arm-type master-slave. But it doesn't necessarily have to be like that! It's just that doing something a bit out of the ordinary would be more interesting than doing what's always been done. Since the shape will have the human neatly tucked away in the cockpit (since the internal arm doesn't show up outside), the scope of portrayal gets a little bigger.

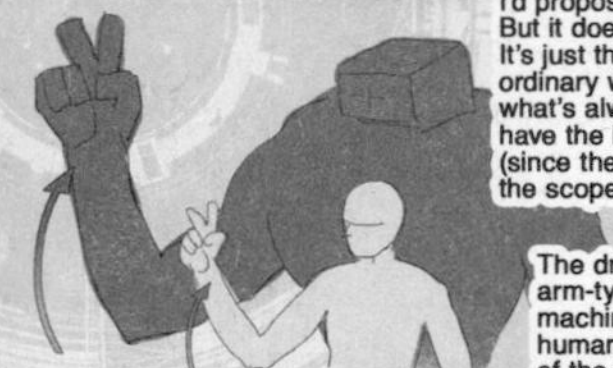

The drawing to the left is a normal external arm-type master-slave. The arm of the machine outside traces the movement of the human arm. (More precisely, the movement of the master arm. The human arm is inside.)

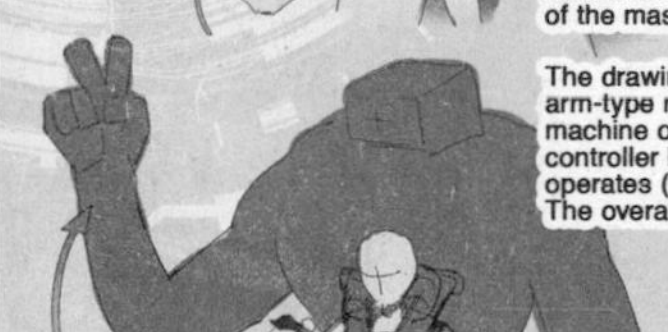

The drawing to the left is an internal arm-type master-slave. The arm of the machine outside traces the movement of a controller like a mini-arm the human operates (the part shown in red).
The overall idea is like the drawing below.

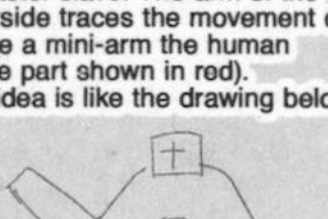

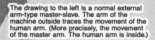

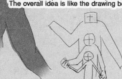

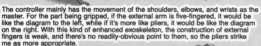

The controller mainly has the movement of the shoulders, elbows, and wrists as the master. For the part being gripped, if the external arm is five-fingered, it would be like the diagram to the left, while if it's more like pliers, it would be like the diagram on the right. With this kind of enhanced exoskeleton, the construction of external fingers is weak, and there's no readily-obvious point to them, so the pliers strike me as more appropriate.

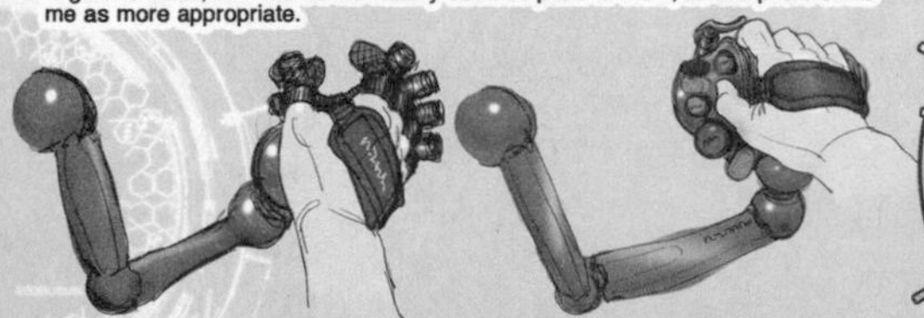

The biggest symbol of this enhanced exoskeleton may be how the upper arm is supported b a fulcrum that corresponds to the collarbone and shoulder bone.

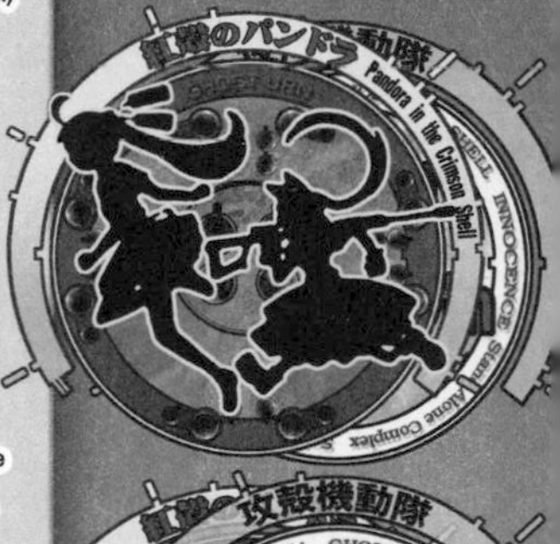
紅殻のパンドラ
Pandora in the Crimson Shell
INNOCENCE
Stand Alone Complex

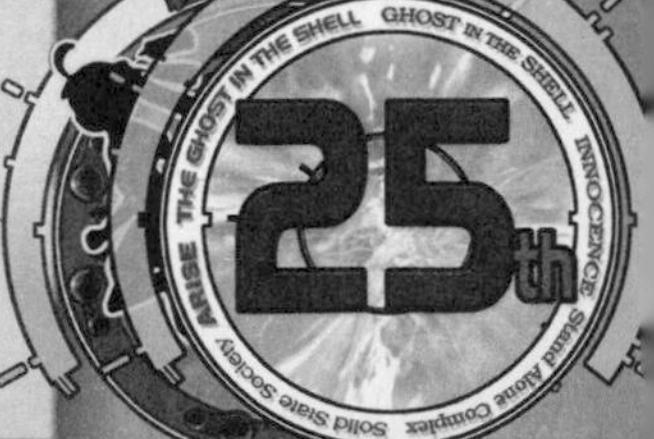
攻殻機動隊
GHOST IN THE SHELL
ARISE
THE GHOST IN THE SHELL
INNOCENCE
Stand Alone Complex
Solid State Society
25th

Greetings! (For the seventh time!)

My intention was to create a powered-suit design that would be a harmonious extension of the tech already used for Buer and the Gerukoma in the series, but that idea quickly collapsed, which probably inconvenienced everyone in the vicinity. (LOL) But I suppose it's dangerous, rather than a time for laughing.

People may say that a mobile exoskeleton like this is inherently something that appears in manga or anime and that there's no need for a mech that moves on two legs, but there's a demand for them appearing in fields like primary industry, logistics and freight handling, and caregiver assistance. Given how our society is aging and that we don't have enough people in the manual-labor fields, this is a natural result. I think that somewhere down the line, something smaller--maybe something that looks almost like clothing--will come about and be what really takes off, but in the early days, it's unsurprising that the tech would resemble what you see in anime or manga.

Personally, I don't think it's a great idea to outfit the elderly with exoskeletons like this or with prosthetic bodies. (Although, it's interesting if it's done in fiction!) We don't have to look back as far as *Roujin Z*; in recent years, there've been instances of the elderly driving the wrong way down the highway or losing control and crashing into convenience stores, and incidents like that are sure to keep happening.

For movement assistance and automatic collision avoidance, like Nene has in the story, you need more than power. You have to have the right software support. You have to limit the internal arm's range of movement to keep the external arm from crushing itself. For instance, if a pilot had an itch nose and instinctively tried to scratch it, the external arm would smash into and destroy sensors on the exoskeleton's head. And if there were workers around, there could be collateral damage, like if the arm started to fall and grabbed someone! There's a huge possibility of problems like that. (Bunny's girlfriend also sneezing...)

That said, there's no question that some elderly folks want to stay healthy and active forever. All you developers out there had better remember to include location beacons, remote status checks, and an automatic homing function for them.

January 25, 2015
Shirow Masamune